THE
Patterns of WAR
since the
Eighteenth Century

THE
Patterns of WAR
since the
Eighteenth Century

SECOND EDITION

Larry H. Addington

INDIANA UNIVERSITY PRESS

BLOOMINGTON AND INDIANAPOLIS

Manufactured in the United States of America

Library of Congress Cataloging-in-Publication Data
Addington, Larry H.
    The patterns of war since the eighteenth century / Larry H. Addington.—2nd ed.
      p. cm.
    Includes bibliographical references and index.
    ISBN 0-253-30132-7 (alk. paper).—ISBN 0-253-20860-2 (pbk. : alk. paper)
    1. Military history, Modern—18th century. 2. Military history, Modern—19th century. 3. Military history, Modern—20th century. 4. Military art and science—History—18th century. 5. Military art and science—History—19th century. Military art and science— History—20th century. I. Title.
U39.A33 1994
355′.009′03—dc20   93-21544

4 5 99 98 97

AGAIN, FOR
Amanda AND *Catherine*

CONTENTS

Illustrations

Maps

Diagrams

Preface to the Second Edition

One of the advantages of producing a revised edition is that the author has the benefit of the input of many readers of the original, whether the comments be laudatory or critical. Since the publication of the first edition in 1984, some commentators have pointed out factual errors, some have challenged my interpretations, and still others have suggested areas in which the book might usefully be expanded, contracted, or clarified. Whatever the source or intent of these comments, I have treated them all as worthy of examination and have tried to make the new edition an improvement over the old in their light. Although the contributors who took the trouble to write or talk to me about the first edition are too numerous to thank by name, I take the opportunity here to express my gratitude to them collectively.

In addition, in the new edition I have tried to include as much new data as practicable from the deluge of books that continues to pour from the presses on military history and related topics. And I have, of course, updated the bibliography. Still, my objective in this edition, as in the original, is to present in narrative form a synthesis of the many changes in war that have taken place from the late eighteenth century to the present; to suggest that these changes have fallen into patterns peculiar to each age, each age represented by a chapter in this book; and to demonstrate, as Theodore Ropp suggested three decades ago, that war is best studied as a process of change in its sociopolitical, technological, and organizational aspects. I have also tried to include as much knowledge about particular wars as space would permit.

Finally, since the Cold War has come to an end and the Soviet Union has dissolved, this edition has the advantage of having been revised at the close of an era and thus at the end of a particular set of patterns of war. But, for the historian, the end of one age means the beginning of another, and in the epilogue I speculate about the future of the patterns of war in the early post–Cold War period. Still, I hope that the search for patterns of peace will ultimately overshadow those for war, and that humankind may one day be spared the old scourge of armed conflict.

June 1993
Charleston, S.C.

Preface

I have attempted in this book to present, in a narrative form, a synthesis of the many changes in war that have taken place from the late eighteenth century to the present. The book is not intended to be a complete history of warfare or of wars in that crowded era, but I hope that I have suggested some themes and interpretations which will prove valuable to the student. In addition, I have tried to introduce as many useful facts as possible within a concise form. My underlying assumption in writing this book is that the history of warfare is best understood as a process of change in war's sociopolitical, technological, and organizational aspects. My information was mostly drawn from published sources, but a complete list of the works consulted would be too lengthy to include. I have therefore appended a list of selected sources which may be used as a recommended reading list for the student who wishes to delve further into any aspect of the subject. Finally, I acknowledge my debt to those scholars upon whose published work this book rests; without their labors no book of synthesis would be possible.

Perhaps my first debt of gratitude for help with this book is owed to Theodore Ropp, Professor Emeritus of History, Duke University, who taught me many years ago the importance of synthesizing history, and who kindly read and criticized much of the manuscript upon which this book is based. I also owe a great debt to Professor Gunther E. Rothenberg, Professor of History, Purdue University, who not only read most of the manuscript but who urged its publication on Indiana University Press. John S. Coussons, Professor and Chairman of the History Department, The Citadel, made every effort to secure for me reduced teaching duties so that I might find time to complete the project, and I owe him much for his splendid cooperation. The Citadel Development Foundation provided funds for the research and the writing of the book, and I express here my gratitude for that assistance. So many of my colleagues in the History Department at The Citadel have suggested themes and ideas for this book that I hesitate to mention any lest I do an injustice to others. However, John W. Gordon deserves to be named as one with whom it is always a pleasure to have intellectual exchanges. My wife, Amanda, reviewed the manuscript for style and errors of grammar and spelling, and, as always, provided the loving support and faith in the project that every author should be so fortunate to have from a spouse. My daughter, Catherine, typed and retyped much of the manuscript, and I am also grateful for her efforts to serve a perhaps too demanding father. And finally, I hope that Roger Bender, Professor Emeritus of Physics, The Citadel, will recognize through these pages that his encouragement to a younger colleague many years ago was not wasted.

March 1984
Charleston, SC

THE
Patterns of WAR
since the
Eighteenth Century

1

From Dynastic to National Warfare, 1775–1815

In the forty years between 1775 and 1815 there occurred a revolution in Western warfare that coincided with the coming of the American and French revolutions and the Age of Napoleon. This revolution swept away the traditional forms of dynastic warfare that had evolved in the European world during the previous three hundred years, and began an era of national warfare that persists in the late twentieth century. This study of the patterns of war since the late eighteenth century begins, therefore, with an examination of the process of change in armies between 1775 and 1815, a starting point that allows the setting of a benchmark from which all further changes in warfare may be measured. Although navies were less affected than armies by change in this period, they too will be examined in order to establish the background for understanding the tremendous impact of technological changes on navies over the course of the nineteenth century. Still, the central theme of this chapter is how warfare on land was transformed from conflicts between monarchs to great struggles between peoples—the essence of national warfare.

I. Dynastic Warfare

A. Armies.   Between the close of the Middle Ages and the last quarter of the eighteenth century, royal dynastic identification predominated over national identity in European armies. These armies had developed coeval with the rise of centralized monarchies in the Western world; originally, they were temporary combinations of feudal and mercenary forces assembled on the eve of war and were often composed of a variety of nationalities. As royal finances improved, the permanently assembled or standing army became the rule, but even then the early modern army was still multinational in composition. Dynastic armies reached the peak of their development in the first three-quarters of the eighteenth century, by the end of which time the great military states of the age were Bourbon France, Habsburg Austria, Hohenzollern Prussia, and Romanov Russia. Prussia and Russia were the most lately arrived: Prussia in the reign of Frederick II (the Great), with the outcomes of the War of the Austrian Succession (1740–48) and the Seven Years' War (1756–63), and Russia in the reign of Peter I (the Great) at the close of the Great Northern War (1700–21).

Except for Prussia, which never had more than about six million people in this period, the great military powers of Europe had populations varying from twenty to thirty million each. Prussia was something of a marvel. This relatively small German state counted so much in the European balance of power because it maintained a standing army equal to as much as 3 percent of its population, or, in proportion, three times as many as the other great military powers. In absolute numbers, the largest royal army in Europe before the Wars of the French Revolution was that of France under Louis XIV; it reached a peak strength of about 400,000 troops during the War of the Spanish Succession (1702–13). Only the army of Revolutionary France exceeded that figure in the eighteenth century and then not before 1794. At the other end of the military scale among the great powers of Europe was Britain. Though Britain's population in the home islands was about nine million on the eve of the American Revolution, the British royal army numbered only about 50,000 troops.

Royal dynastic armies were much alike in their social composition, except, to a degree, the British and Russian armies. In most European armies, the hereditary nobility held most of the commissioned officer positions, and the officer without noble patent might face arbitrary limits on his promotions and branch assignments. The officer corps of the British army was dominated by the country gentry, and, in addition, infantry and cavalry officers bought and sold their commissions from lieutenant through the rank of colonel. Few officers ever reached high rank without private means or a wealthy patron. When officers retired, the more impecunious among them had to live off the proceeds of the sale of their commissions. This so-called Purchase System was disappearing on the continent even before the French Revolution, but it survived in the British army until well past the middle of the nineteenth century. In contrast, Peter the Great commissioned so many foreign officers in the Russian army, and so many of them founded aristocratic military families, that as late as the eve of World War I the officer list of the Russian army was still studded with foreign, and especially German, names. In still another practice, the Hohenzollern monarchs of Prussia held the Junker nobility to commissioned service in the army as a compulsory duty as well as a noble privilege.

While commissioned officers of royal armies were drawn mostly from the upper classes of society, enlisted men came from the lowest orders. Serfs, landless peasants, the unemployed of the cities, vagabonds and drifters were either voluntarily recruited or impressed, some of them by that peculiar institution of eighteenth-century conscription, the press gang. Sergeants and corporals (i.e., the noncommissioned officers chosen from the ranks of the veteran soldiers) disciplined and trained the new recruits with close-order drill, the manual of arms, and physical punishments as necessary. The aim of such training was to make the private soldier into a "walking musket" who would perform his duties without question and with the mechanical precision bred of long practice. Desertion in peacetime was discouraged by housing troops in barracks and, in wartime, by close supervision of camps in the field.

Most soldiers in the royal armies of the eighteenth century served in the infantry, and the infantry battalion was the royal army's basic tactical unit, usually two battalions to a regiment. On the continent, a battalion had a typical strength of eight hundred officers and men, and was usually divided into six "companies of the line" and two specialist "flank companies," so called for their positions when the battalion was drawn up on parade. Infantry of the line normally fought in three close-packed ranks, their smoothbore, muzzle-loading flintlock muskets capable of being fired and reloaded at the rate of about two rounds per minute. Firing was done in volleys by platoon, each platoon being a section of a company. One flank company was usually composed of light infantry, soldiers trained to fight in extended order as skirmishers and sometimes armed with the rifle. The grenadier company, the other flank company, was drawn from the largest men in the battalion and was often used to lead charges with the bayonet, the infantry's principal shock weapon in the eighteenth century.

The rifled muskets (or rifles) with which some light infantry companies were equipped were distinguished by spiral grooves in the bore, giving the lead ball a spin that insured greater range and accuracy than the ball fired from the smoothbore musket. Whereas volleys fired by smoothbores had an effective range not exceeding a hundred yards, aimed rifle fire could be dangerous to twice that distance. But the rifled musket took about twice as long to load as a smoothbore musket because the ball had to be introduced at the muzzle and worked down the barrel against the resistance of the rifling, and it was about twice as expensive to make. Until the problems of rapid loading and the added costs of manufacture were solved in the mid-nineteenth century, the rifle remained a specialist's weapon.

In European armies of the late eighteenth century, two or more regiments of infantry composed a brigade, the latter being the largest standard unit found in armies before the Wars of the French Revolution. When deployed on the battlefield, the infantry battalions were supported by batteries of artillery (a battery was composed of two to six guns) and squadrons of cavalry (in size, each squadron was roughly equivalent to a small infantry battalion). A squadron was subdivided into "troops," each "troop" being the counterpart of an infantry company. When the infantry, cavalry, and artillery were combined with siege and supply trains for mobile warfare, the force was designated a field army. In the Seven Years' War, the last great conflict in the Western world before the American Revolution, the average size of a European field army was 47,000 men, and the largest field army slightly exceeded 100,000 men.

Unless it was the monarch himself, the commander-in-chief of a field army bore the rank of marshal, field marshal, colonel general, or lieutenant general, the practice varying from army to army. Whatever his rank, the commanding general was assisted in his staff work by an adjutant general and a quartermaster general, and in command of his forces by one or more major generals. A brigadier general commanded a brigade; a colonel commanded a regiment, a lieutenant colonel or a major commanded a battalion, a captain commanded a company, and a lieutenant, the lowest-ranking of the commissioned officers, commanded a platoon.

Since the uniforms of the eighteenth century were gaudy by today's standards, an army deployed on the battlefield presented a colorful spectacle. Cover and concealment played no significant role in combat for troops drawn up in large formations in which, as a practical matter, the infantry had to stand in order to load and fire their muskets. Artillery pieces were dragged into position before battle by draft animals driven by civilian teamsters who, once the guns were placed, retired with their animals to the safety of the wagon trains in the rear. Consequently, all guns, save those light enough to be wheeled by hand, had to remain stationary throughout the battle. When forming for battle, each infantry battalion approached at right angles the space in the army's line assigned to it, then wheeled to march across the space until it was occupied. By making a half-turn to left or right, it faced the enemy line, usually about 300–400 yards away. (See Diagram 1.) All this marching and wheeling about took time and required careful judgment on the part of the officers. The cavalry guarded the flanks of the deployed line of infantry and artillery, or remained in the rear until needed. Cavalry were rarely committed to battle except against other cavalry unless the enemy's infantry formations were in disorder. In order to repel the attack of cavalry, an infantry battalion usually formed a hollow "square" (actually a diamond-shaped formation), six ranks to a side and with two or more guns at the corners.

The biggest tactical problems facing infantry in the eighteenth century

DIAGRAM 1. Hypothetical Battalion forming from Column into Line of Battle. Each line represents a company of 90 men drawn up in three ranks. Each company has a frontage of 25 yards and a depth of 9 yards.

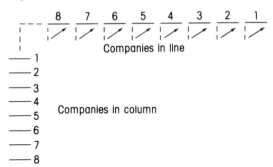

Once the companies were in line and allowing 3 yards between companies, the battalion frontage would be 221 yards, or more than two modern football fields laid end-to-end. Battalions with fewer men and tighter intervals might reduce the length of the line to about 150 yards. In some armies, No. 1 Company would be composed of grenadiers and No. 8 Company composed of light infantry.

were the time-consuming delay in forming into line before battle and the inflexibility of the line once formed. With each battalion having a frontage of 150–200 yards, an advancing line tended to weave and to develop gaps, and required frequent halts in order for the officers to redress its ranks. Until about the middle of the eighteenth century the common wisdom was that troops could not keep good order if they were marched faster than ninety paces per minute; when the Prussian infantry introduced the Quick Step (120 paces a minute) without jumbling up the ranks, they were judged the wonder of the age. Eventually, other armies mastered the Quick Step, today's standard marching cadence, but the Quick Step did not solve the basic problem of rapid and flexible tactical maneuver. The slow, parade ground–like movements of armies on the battlefield survived down to the eve of the Wars of the French Revolution.

The strategic movement of royal armies was as slow and deliberate as their tactical movements on the battlefield. In Europe, operations were mounted from large fortresses on the frontiers, i.e., fortified cities where supplies had been accumulated in magazines beforehand. Horse-drawn wagons hauled ammunition and food for the troops and fodder for the animals, but since hay and oats are especially bulky items and a horse eats at least twenty pounds of fodder per day, a supply train could not usually meet the needs of a field army further than seventy miles (or a five-day march) from its base. Food and fodder had to be replenished by staging supplies from the magazine in the rear or, more commonly, by drawing them from the local countryside. Relying on local resources necessitated long delays at intervals to enable contractors to make arrangements to buy and collect supplies, or, if in enemy territory, have the troops seize them by force. For logistical reasons, therefore, the mark of good generalship in the royal dynastic age was a careful regard for supply and the conservation of human and material resources.

One of the greatest practitioners of dynastic warfare was Frederick the Great, king of Prussia from 1740 to 1786. Even before Frederick reached the throne, his father, Frederick William II, was responsible for creating the fourth largest army in Europe when the Prussian population was thirteenth in size. Frederick William II made the Junker nobility serve as officers in the army and compelled large landowners to allow their serfs to undergo short-term military training so as to form a kind of trained reserve. His emphasis on rigorous drill and discipline resulted in an army especially strong in infantry of the line, his chief military legacy, but he recruited so many foreigners to keep up his army's strength that as many as a quarter of his soldiers were drawn from outside Prussia. His heir, Frederick II, discovered early in the War of the Austrian Succession that the Prussian army was deficient in both artillery and cavalry and that he must improve both branches as the war went along. Still, Frederick emerged from the war with the province of Silesia and enough resources to expand his army to 163,000 troops by 1756. He had also gained a practical fund of experience that served him well in the Seven Years' War, a conflict in which Prussia's very survival was at stake and in which the Prussian army, aided by generous financial subsidies from Britain and some assistance from foreign troops, managed to fend off invasions of the French, Russian, and Austrian armies.

In the late eighteenth century, Britain's royal army was small by continental European standards; in addition, it was scattered over an extensive overseas empire. After the English civil wars of the mid-seventeenth century and a military dictatorship under Oliver Cromwell, Parliament shared power over the army with the restored Stuart monarchy. Parliament remained suspicious of large standing armies, which might be converted into engines of internal tyranny, and it preferred to rely on the navy and the militia for defense of the home islands as much as possible. The Duke of Marlborough was one of Europe's most outstanding soldiers on the continent during the War of the Spanish Succession, but his army was more multinational than it was British. After the Hanoverian dynasty reached the British throne early in the eighteenth century, George II was the last British monarch to command an army in the field, narrowly winning the Battle of Dettingen in 1743 during the War of the Austrian Succession.

In the middle of the eighteenth century, the British East India Trading Company organized a private army to protect its holdings on the subcontinent of India from French and native rivals, and by the final decade of the century the company army numbered 150,000 troops, a larger force than the British royal army at the time. The company commissioned its own officers, promoting them on the basis of seniority through the rank of colonel, the highest rank held. The company army was divided among European regiments and native regiments officered by Europeans, the native soldiers being known as sepoys. The company army lasted down to the Great Mutiny of 1857, the subsequent abolition of the company, and the conversion of India to the status of a British crown colony.

In summary, the royal armies of the eighteenth century were dynastic rather than national institutions. Their social structures reflected the intense hierarchical nature of European society of the time; their weapons and equipment were merely improved versions of those used over the previous two centuries, and their organizations were essentially refinements of earlier managerial arrangements. Strategic and tactical thinking emphasized form and caution. When employed in war, the armies of the age were used to make good dynastic claims, seize border provinces, and secure overseas colonies. By their very nature, they were best suited to such limited objectives. While they also served as forces for internal security, the events of the American and French revolutions were to demonstrate that they were not always well suited for the suppression of mass revolt. Accordingly, when major social change stirred the European world toward the end of the eighteenth century, the resulting political and social upheavals began to sweep away the old military forms and to prepare the way for national warfare.

B. Navies. In the eighteenth century, navies, like armies, were chiefly instruments of monarchy; but, being a form of transportation as well, they were even more dominated by technological considerations. The long naval rivalries among Spain, France, Holland, and England had reached their climax in the Battle of Cap La Hogue in 1692 when an Anglo-Dutch combined fleet inflicted a decisive defeat on the French fleet. Thereafter, and throughout the remainder of the Age of Sail, Britain was unassailably the dominant naval power, often with a fleet the equal in size of the other European navies combined. Britain was able to maintain its naval advantage in part because of several unique advantages: (1) the insularity of the home islands allowed it to concentrate its resources on the navy rather than on the army; (2) slow technological obsolescence and long ship-life made it difficult for other powers to overcome Britain's numerical lead in warships; (3) its great seafaring population provided an abundance of experienced seamen who could efficiently man its fleets of war; and (4) its favorable geographical position off the western coast of Europe made it relatively easy for Britain's navy in time of war to blockade the ports of its most probable enemies or to intercept their fleets when they went to sea.

The dominant warship of the eighteenth century was the ship of-the-line-of-battle (shortened to ship-of-the-line or battleship), a vessel with at least three masts, two or three gun decks, and a minimum of sixty guns. A large ship-of-the-line might have three gun decks and 120 guns. A few even larger, more heavily armed ships-of-the-line were built. The "first rate," the most powerful of the type, carried a hundred guns or more, crews of eight hundred or more, and might displace 3,500 tons. More common was the "74 gunner," a vessel manned by about six hundred, displacing 2,000 tons. The largest ships-of-the-line were about two hundred feet in length, about fifty feet wide at maximum beam, and about forty feet (four stories) in height from keel to main deck.

The main types of vessels "below-the-line" were the three-masted frigate and the two-masted sloop-of-war. Until the 1790s, the typical frigate carried between 32 and 38 guns, had one gun deck, and was manned by about 350 men. Some American frigates built in the 1790s were designed to outfight anything they could not outrun, and might carry fifty guns or more. A sloop-of-war had no gun deck and carried about twenty guns on its weather deck. Frigates and sloops were used to scout for the battle fleet, hunt down enemy commerce raiders, support amphibious assaults, and carry out any other naval missions for which ships-of-the-line were unsuited or unnecessary.

The naval strategies practiced in the Age of Sail depended on the relative strengths of the opposing battle lines. The country with a decidedly superior battle fleet relative to the enemy preferred to wage Grand War, a strategy that called for seeking out the enemy's battle fleet and destroying it as soon as possible in order to have "command of the sea." If the enemy fleet would not leave port to risk battle, command of the sea was still achieved by blockading it in port. With command of the sea, a navy could blockade the enemy's commercial ports, drive its merchant ships from the sea, support raids and invasions of the enemy's coasts, and attack its overseas colonies. Clearly, only ships-of-the-line mattered much in Grand War, and, after 1692 Britain was free to follow that strategy against France, Spain, and Holland—its traditional naval rivals—throughout the remainder of the Age of Sail.

The next best naval strategies, used separately or in combination, were Fleet-in-Being and *guerre de course*. The objective of Fleet-in-Being was to conserve the weaker battle fleet until opportunities appeared for gaining temporary or local command of the sea for ulterior purposes, such as moving reinforcements to overseas colonies. *Guerre de course* (i.e., commerce raiding) did not require a battle fleet, for vessels below-the-line and even armed merchant ships could be sent to sea in order to raid the enemy's shipping lanes. Governments sometimes issued Letters of Marque to "privateers" in order that their crews might raid the enemy's commerce but, if captured, be protected from being treated as ordinary pirates. Still, in the Age of Sail, not even Britain was so dependent on the sea that a severing of its sea lanes would have destroyed its economy, much less starved it into surrender. Even when relatively successful, the usual effect of *guerre de course* was to drive up insurance rates and sometimes force enemy shipping to seek the protection of neutral flags.

When battle fleets fought in the eighteenth century, their tactics were as formal as those of contemporary armies on land. The stronger fleet normally formed line-ahead and sought the weather gauge, the position upwind of the enemy from which it was easier to close the range and press the attack. The weaker fleet, also formed in line-ahead, usually sought the lee or downwind position, from which it was easier to escape if matters turned out badly. During most of the eighteenth century, and while under the dominance of admirals known as the Formalists, the British fleet preferred to engage in a cautious formation known as the "conterminous line" (i.e., forming van-to-van, center-to-center, and rear-to-rear with the enemy line), so there was no danger of the enemy "crossing the T" (bringing his broadsides against the relatively weak bows of the sailing ships and raking them fore and aft.) But a minority of British admirals, known as Meléeists, were willing to leave the line and to take risks in order to break up the enemy's defensive formation. The Meléeists might resort to "Massing," "Doubling," or "Breaking" (see Diagram 2), each maneuver fraught with danger but, if successful, more likely than the conterminous line to achieve decisive victories. Before 1783, the official *Fighting Instructions* made it difficult for the bolder British admirals to signal for melée maneuvers even if they were willing to run risks, and not until revised and more flexible *Fighting Instructions* and an improved signaling system were introduced was the way paved for Horatio Nelson, the greatest admiral of the era, to win his three famous victories at the Nile (1798), Copenhagen (1801), and Cape Trafalgar (1805).

The largest naval gun carried in broadside batteries in a ship-of-the-line was the 32-pounder, so called for the weight of its solid shot. The gun and its wheeled truck together weighed about three tons and required nine men to work efficiently. The other types of typical muzzle loaders in use on ships-of-the-line in broadside were the 24-pounder and 18-pounder. Late in the period a ship-of-the-line might carry a few 64-pounder *carronades* on the weather deck. Solid shot (cannon balls) and *langrage* (small balls and chain) were favored for ship-to-ship action; exploding shell existed but was potentially as dangerous to friend as to foe because of

DIAGRAM 2. Fleet Tactics in the Age of Sail.

A. Fleet "A" forming a conterminous line with fleet "B."

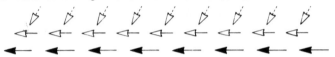

B. Fleet "A" massing on rear division of fleet "B."

C. Fleet "A" doubling on rear division of fleet "B."

D. Fleet "A" breaking the line of fleet "B."

E. Nelson's use of two columns at the Battle of Trafalgar.

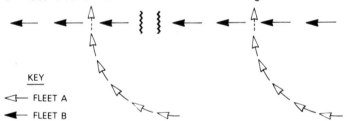

unreliable fusing. The danger of premature explosions was real enough that exploding shell was not used in a combat between fleets until the middle of the nineteenth century.

In the eighteenth century and into the nineteenth century, exploding shell was normally restricted to short-barreled mortars aboard bomb-ketches constructed for the bombardment of coast fortifications. The mortar threw its projectiles, known as "bombs," in a ballistic curve into the interior of a fort, the bombs intended to explode over the enemy gun crews without overhead cover and showering metal fragments down on their heads (hence the reference in "The Star-Spangled Banner" to the "bombs bursting in air" during the bombardment of Fort McHenry in the War of 1812). But even with the support of bomb-ketches, duels between wooden ships and masonry forts were unpredictable in outcome because guns ashore, enjoying stable platforms, were usually more accurate than guns and mortars on rolling decks, and because a fort's guns and crews were better protected than their counterparts on ships. But a large fleet might bring many more guns to bear than were found in a typical fort which, before the early nineteenth century, usually had only two tiers of guns, one in casemate (with overhead cover) and one *en barbette* (without overhead cover).

The naval officer corps of the eighteenth century were less dominated by the hereditary aristocracy than the officer corps in armies, perhaps because fewer nobles were interested in the demanding life at sea. In the British navy, officer candidates or midshipmen (so called from the area of the ship in which they were berthed) usually entered service in their early teens, and sometimes through the recommendation of a naval captain or admiral, or as a "King's Letter Boy." Most were from middle-class backgrounds, often with family connections with serving officers. After several years of learning ship-handling, navigation, and gunnery, the midshipman who could pass a formal examination was commissioned as a lieutenant. After he became a senior lieutenant, he might be given command of a sloop-of-war or other small craft and designated as a "lieutenant commanding" (the origin of the later ranks of lieutenant commander and commander). After being promoted to the rank of captain, he might command a frigate and eventually a ship-of-the-line. A commodore, the lowest ranking of the "flag officers," commanded a group of vessels below-the-line, a rear admiral commanded the trailing division of a battle line, the admiral and vice admiral commanded its van and center divisions, with the admiral, of course, commanding the whole force in addition.

Enlisted men in navies of the Age of Sail were ordinary mariners who either voluntarily signed on for a "hitch" or were pressed into service in time of war. Either way, the obligation was for service in a particular ship. The length of service varied according to circumstance and the convenience of the captain or of the government. At the conclusion of hostilities, the crews of excess ships were laid off wholesale and their vessels laid up "in ordinary," i.e., the fleet reserve. Recruits and able seamen were supervised and, when necessary, punished by the petty officers, the counterparts of sergeants and corporals in armies. Sailors slept in hammocks suspended from the overhead on the gun decks, and their diet consisted of unleavened bread (hardtack), salted beef, pork, and fish (known as junk). Their water was mixed with rum in a concoction known as grog (hence the term "groggy") in order to retard contamination and bacterial growth. Alcoholism was a chronic affliction of navies, and though officers enjoyed better food and accommodations than enlisted men, life at sea was hard for all hands.

II. The War of the American Revolution, 1775–83

Although the War of the American Revolution may be considered the first national war of modern times, the size of the conflict was small by the standards of previous European wars in the eighteenth century. No more than 35,000 Americans were under arms against the British at one time during the war (1776), no more than about 20,000 ever fought at one place (at New York in 1776 and at Saratoga in 1777), and no more than about 100,000 served under arms at any time during the war. The Continental Army, which approximated the regular army of the American forces, never had more than about 17,000 men at one time, and the great majority of Americans who bore arms during the Revolution did so as provincial troops or as state militia. In this period, about a fifth of the American population of 2.5 million were black, mostly slaves in the South, and about 5,000 African-Americans served with the Revolutionary forces. Of perhaps half a million white Loyalists in the colonies at the beginning of the war, 20,000 served with the British forces, but no more than 11,000 at a time and most of them in the southern colonies.

When clashes at Lexington and Concord between Massachusetts militia and British regulars ("Redcoats") ignited the war in April 1775, only about 8,500 British soldiers were stationed in North America. Within a few days, some 16,000 New England militia and provincial troops massed on the landside of Boston and imposed a siege on its fewer than 4,000 British defenders. The small British garrisons elsewhere in the colonies were sent to reinforce the garrison in Boston or were withdrawn to Canada. The Continental Congress, meeting in Philadelphia, "adopted" the forces around Boston in June, the so-called Eight Months Army, which was to serve until a more formal "Continental Army" could be formed. The Congress also commissioned George Washington of Virginia as a lieutenant general and made him the American commander-in-chief. In the meantime, the garrison at Boston under General Thomas Gage, the British commander-in-chief for North America, had been increased to 6,500 troops, and in mid-June Gage tested the American siege lines in the Battle of Bunker Hill (actually Breed's Hill) with an attack by 2,500 troops. The

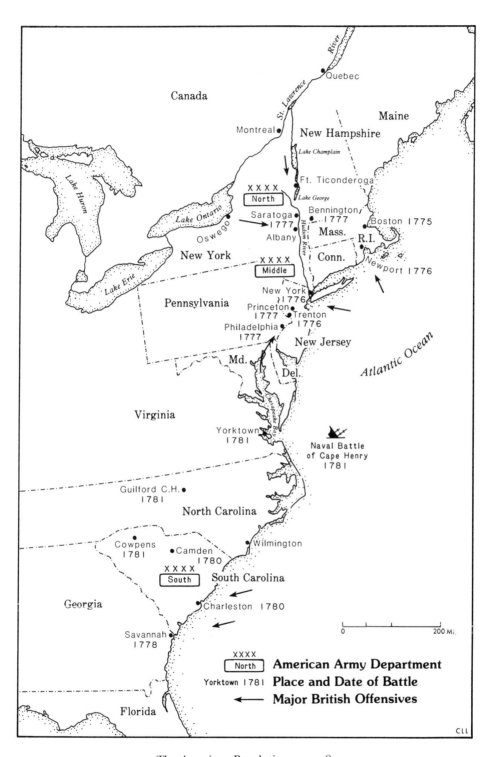

The American Revolution, 1775–81

Americans repelled the British frontal assaults twice before losing the position, and they inflicted over a thousand casualties on the British regulars. Although the battle ended as a defeat for the Americans (the British finally seized both Breed's Hill and Bunker Hill above it), it demonstrated that even militia could be formidable on defense and behind cover, and that small British garrisons could not afford to seize many hills at such a price. Gage did not order another attack on the American lines before handing over his command to General Sir William Howe in October 1775.

Washington arrived at Boston in early July 1775, too late to participate in the Battle of Bunker Hill, and from his assumption of command worked mightily to improve his army's condition. The Continental Army came into official existence on January 1, 1776, with about 9,500 troops at Boston and a few hundred elsewhere, the men having agreed to serve for one year. But most of the militia and provincial troops serving at Boston promptly went home at the beginning of the new year, and Washington had to recall some of them in order to raise his army's strength to 14,000 men. For their part, the British successfully defended Canada from invasion by small American forces led by Richard Montgomery and Benedict Arnold during the winter of 1775–76. Still, they abandoned Boston, the last British foothold in the original thirteen American colonies, in March 1776, as Howe shifted his headquarters temporarily to Halifax, Nova Scotia. He planned that after enough British reinforcements had arrived, he would suppress the rebellion by starting afresh.

When the Continental Congress commissioned Washington in June 1775, it appointed thirteen general officers to serve under him. Of the original thirteen, only three had previously held commissions in the British army, and none of them in a rank higher than lieutenant colonel. But several of the new generals, like Washington himself, had seen service as provincial officers in the French and Indian War and were not completely devoid of military experience, and, as the war proceeded, Congress commissioned a number of foreign officers to help Washington meet his pressing need for qualified commanders. Among the best of them were the Marquis de Lafayette (a captain on leave from the French army), Johann de Kalb (a former major in the French army), and Friedrich von Steuben (a former major in the Prussian army of Frederick the Great).

Between April 1775 and the summer of 1776, Britain almost doubled the size of its pre-war army by mobilizing 95,000 troops, 30,000 of them German mercenaries. (The Americans dubbed all German troops in British pay "Hessians" because over half of them were from the German state of Hesse-Cassell.) In 1776 Britain devoted 50,000 troops to garrisoning Canada and suppressing the revolt in North America, and never had as many troops there again for the rest of the war. The Americans also had serious problems in mobilizing manpower, and even greater problems with supply. Their supply problems might have proved unsolvable had not royal France provided them aid, the Bourbon monarchy of Louis XVI arranging to smuggle $8 million worth of arms and equipment to the colonies even before France became a formal ally in February 1778. About 90 percent of all the gunpowder used by the Americans during the war came from French sources. In 1775 the Americans found three hundred British cannon stored at Fort Ticonderoga, and some ammunition was procured when an armed merchant ship, commissioned by Washington while his army was laying siege to Boston, captured a British vessel loaded with powder and ball. The Americans attempted domestic manufactures of arms, ammunition, and equipment, but this production never became as important as foreign aid and captures in fueling the American war effort.

In the fall of 1775, Congress founded a Continental Navy and Marine Corps, but by July 1776—the month of the Declaration of Independence and the formal birth of the United States of America—the aggregate of the Continental and state navies came to only twenty-seven converted merchantmen with an average of twenty guns each. Such a force could wage *guerre de course,* but could never vie with the royal navy for command of the sea. Even in the war against British commerce, the several hundred privateers sailing under Letters of Marque over the course of the war captured twice as many British merchantmen as the Continental and state navies put together. Congress tried to expand the Continental Navy by approving the building of five ships-of-the-line and eighteen frigates, but only one ship-of-the-line—the 74-gun *America*—was ever finished, and then only near the end of the war; it was given to France in partial payment of the American war debt. Only six American-built frigates ever got to sea, and only one of those survived the war. France converted a few merchantmen to American raiders, the most famous being John Paul Jones's *Bon Homme Richard,* but at the end of the war the surviving ships of the Continental Navy consisted of a frigate built in America and another donated by France.

In contrast to the relatively puny American naval effort, Britain commissioned 120 ships-of-the-line and 222 frigates and sloops-of-war, the whole manned by 100,000 sailors and marines. In consequence, the only real challenge to Britain at sea came with the French intervention in 1778 with eighty ships-of-the-line, the Spanish intervention in 1779 with sixty ships-of-the-line, and the Dutch intervention in 1780 with twenty ships-of-the-line. Britain's navy was spread thinly after the war reached Europe, the Mediterranean, and the Caribbean. It was strained even further when a native revolt led by Prince Hyder Ali broke out in India in 1782. The British navy did well to prevent any superior hostile naval combination at the Channel and to relieve Gibraltar after the longest siege in the history of the "Rock" (1779–81). But it was a local failure of British sea power off the coast of Virginia in 1781 that was largely responsible for the British defeat at Yorktown, the deciding event for the war in North America, although that defeat was inflicted by an allied coalition and occurred against the background of a global conflict.

American battlefield tactics in the Revolution were not as un-European as is widely supposed. The Continentals usually fought in linear, close-order formations, though as a rule in two ranks rather than in three. Militia, like all irregular troops, fought best in extended order or from behind natural or man-made cover, as, for example, the breastworks at Breed's Hill outside Boston in 1775. Some backwoodsmen were excellent skirmishers, especially when armed with the "Kentucky" (actually the "Pennsylvania") rifle, but militia caught in the open were no match for charging Redcoats. On more occasions than the Americans cared to remember, the flight of militia brought on near-disasters for the rest of the army. Still, militia provided the "flesh" to the "skeleton" of the Continental Army, and even on the formal battlefield they often fought well if the local American commander understood their strengths and weaknesses and laid his plans accordingly.

The key in part to American battlefield success was in choosing the right tactics for combining Continentals, provincial troops, and militia. Washington's surprise attacks on the Hessian outpost at Trenton, N.J., in December 1776, and on a British column leaving Princeton in January 1777, are examples of imaginative leadership in this regard. On the other hand, Horatio Gates's deployment of unsupported militia in open terrain at Camden, S.C., in August 1780 contributed to the rout of the whole American Army of the Southern Department. A more inspired Daniel Morgan used militia as skirmishers to screen his line of Continentals at the Battle of Cowpens in January 1781, and his tactics contributed to the annihilation of the British (Tory) Legion. Using similar tactics at the Battle of Guilford Courthouse, N.C., in March 1781, Nathanael Greene's army inflicted almost fatal losses on a British army under Charles, Lord Cornwallis, though the British were left in command of the field. In general, the Americans did better when fighting behind cover, against small enemy units, and where they were not required to perform complicated maneuvers.

The British army had experienced much fighting in forested terrain in North America during the French and Indian War (1754–63), and it is a myth that they were unaware of North American conditions at the beginning of the American Revolution. Understandably, they preferred to remain within supporting range of water lines-of-communication in thinly populated areas with few roads and little forage. When they failed to do so, they sometimes got into great difficulty. The classic example is General

John Burgoyne's invasion of New York from Canada in 1777 with 8,500 troops and Indian allies. His army's movement by water down Lake Champlain and Lake George went smoothly enough, the British capturing Fort Ticonderoga on the way, but the expedition ran into trouble after it left Lake George and plunged into the largely trackless country of upper New York. Loyalists and Indians trying to link up with his army by way of the Mohawk Valley were defeated by American militia, and a Hessian foraging force sent out by Burgoyne was defeated by other militia at Bennington, Vt. Burgoyne's army finally floundered to the upper Hudson River in mid-September, only to find its way to Albany blocked at Bemis Heights by 9,500 entrenched troops of General Horatio Gates's Army of the Northern Department. Some of Gates's troops under Benedict Arnold defeated British attempts to bypass this position in the two successive battles at Freeman's Farm, and, in early October, Burgoyne ordered a retreat to Lake George. But the British withdrawal came too late. The remains of Burgoyne's army—5,800 men—were finally encircled by four times their numbers on Saratoga Heights, some twenty miles north of Bemis Heights, and compelled to lay down their arms on October 17. Saratoga turned out to be the largest unassisted American victory of the war.

The British did much better against the Americans in coastal areas compared to their performance in the back country, in part because all the major American population centers, such as they were, were adjacent to navigable water. With the exception of Boston, the British regained control of all of them at one time or another during the war. In 1776, Howe's army captured New York and Newport, R.I., towns which—like Boston— had populations of about 20,000 each. By approaching Philadelphia from the head of Chesapeake Bay, Howe's army captured the American capital (with 40,000 people, the largest city in the American colonies) in September 1777, after defeating the American army at the Battle of Brandywine Creek. The British also captured Wilmington, N.C., and Savannah, Ga., but their biggest victory of the war came at Charleston, S.C., in May 1780. With 12,000 people, Charleston (then called Charlestowne) was the major port and largest city in the southern colonies. General Sir Henry Clinton, who had succeeded Howe as the British North American commander-in-chief in 1778, used an army of 10,000 troops and a large fleet in skillful maneuvers to trap the entire Army of the Southern Department and most of the remaining ships of the Continental Navy. When the ships were scuttled and General Benjamin Lincoln surrendered his 5,500 troops to Clinton, it seemed for a time that the defeat at Charleston would bring down the whole American war effort in the southern colonies.

But in order to find enough forces for his campaign against Georgia and the Carolinas, Clinton had earlier weakened his position in the northern colonies. In July 1780 a small French fleet arrived from Europe to seize undefended Narragansett Bay and to land a French army of 4,500 troops under General Comte de Rochambeau at Newport, R.I. While still in Charleston, Clinton had learned that a French force was on its way to some undisclosed destination in the northern colonies, and he and much of his army at Charleston moved by sea to New York City in June in order to prevent a French linkup with Washington's Army of the Middle Department, then camped around West Point on the Hudson. Cornwallis, left in charge in the southern colonies, subsequently launched an offensive into the hinterland of the Carolinas with an army short on manpower and harassed by partisans. The defeats of British and Loyalist detachments at Kings Mountain (October 1780) and Cowpens (January 1781) in South Carolina, followed by heavy British casualties at the Battle of Guilford Courthouse (March 1781) in North Carolina, caused Cornwallis to abandon the interior of the Carolinas and finally to rebase his forces in coastal Virginia near Chesapeake Bay. By August 1781 Nathanael Greene's new Army of the Southern Department had restricted British control south of Virginia to areas around the ports of Wilmington, N.C., Charleston, and Savannah.

The war had reached a stalemate by the late summer of 1781. The British had failed to regain control of the interior of the American colonies, but the Americans had been unable to drive them from key areas along the coasts. The deadlock was broken by the French admiral Comte de Grasse when he came north from the Caribbean with twenty-eight French ships-of-the-line and 3,300 troops for an attack on Cornwallis's army near Yorktown. Alerted to de Grasse's plans, Washington and Rochambeau, who had earlier united their forces on the Hudson, started for Virginia in mid-August. Clinton, still in New York City with 14,000 troops, remained ignorant of the fact that the main Franco-American forces were no longer in his front. While Washington's and Rochambeau's combined army was still on its way to Virginia, de Grasse's fleet entered Chesapeake Bay in late August, then sortied into the Atlantic to defeat a British fleet of nineteen ships-of-the-line under Admiral Sir Samuel Graves in the Battle of Cape Henry (or the Battle of Virginia Capes) on September 5. When de Grasse's fleet returned to Chesapeake Bay, it found that the French fleet based at Newport had arrived, bearing the allied siege train. When Washington's and Rochambeau's land forces completed their concentration around the landside of Cornwallis's fortified position at Yorktown on September 30, Washington found himself the commander-in-chief of the largest allied force in North America during the war: 38 French ships-of-the-line, 15,000 French sailors and marines, 7,800 French troops, and 9,000 American troops. After Cornwallis had lost 2,000 troops during a siege of nearly three weeks and the allied forces threatened to overrun his earthworks, he despaired of relief and surrendered his remaining 6,500 men to Washington on October 19, 1781.

After the defeat at Yorktown, the British abandoned their attempts to reconquer the original thirteen colonies in North America, and by the end of 1782 they had withdrawn their garrisons from all the American ports save New York. In January 1783 they signed the preliminary Peace of Paris, ending the war everywhere except in India. New York, the first city Washington had lost in the war, was reoccupied by his army after the peace treaty was ratified. Fighting associated with the American Revolution continued in India until the summer of 1784, when the British finally put down Hyder Ali's revolt.

The toll for American independence was relatively high. Of the approximately 100,000 men who had borne arms, 35,000 were casualties, and 25,000 of those had lost their lives. Over 8,000 of the dead had died while prisoners of war. The British and their Loyalist supporters in North America may have suffered 20,000 casualties, perhaps 10,000 of them fatalities. Most significant for the patterns of war, however, is the fact that a national army, however small and much assisted by European powers, had waged a successful war against a royal army and the world's largest overseas empire.

III. The French Revolution and Napoleon, 1789–1815

If the War of the American Revolution may be said to have given birth to national warfare on a limited scale, then the Wars of the French Revolution and Napoleon may be said to have brought about national warfare on a massive scale. The Revolution of 1789 took place in a nation of 25 million, or ten times the size of the American population in 1775, and second only to the Russian in size in Europe. When royal powers attempted counterrevolution in 1792, France was able to go far beyond anything attempted militarily by the United States in waging the war for American independence. The adoption of the *levée en masse* in 1793 and a centrally directed and powerful war economy produced the first mass national army in modern history. When that army became a tool of French expansion under Napoleon Bonaparte, it was for a time almost irresistible. Indeed, the traditional dynasties were forced to remodel their royal armies in a more national direction in order to survive. The old forms of war never fully recovered from the events between 1792 and 1815. As the military philosopher Carl von Clausewitz observed, it was as if war itself had been lecturing.

A. *Ideas Borrowed from the Old Royal Army before 1789.*   The power of the French Revolutionary army was not alone due to its numbers and the popular enthusiasm released by the upheaval of 1789. That power was

DIAGRAM 3. Guibert's Proposed Battalion Column-of-Divisions on a One-Company Front. (Each company is assumed to have 90 men in three ranks with a breadth of 25 yards and a depth of 9 yards. Diagram not to scale.)

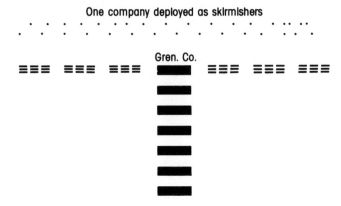

also due to the intelligent application of ideas borrowed from innovators in the old royal army who could never apply them with the same force before the Revolution. In summary form, these ideas called for: (1) infantry tactics based on the column for rapid maneuver and deployment; (2) the exploitation of improved artillery for quick concentrations against a hostile line; and (3) the organization of the armies into "army divisions" for greater strategic flexibility, surprise, and ease of foraging.

The improved infantry tactics were based on the Comte de Guibert's proposals for a "column-of-divisions," the companies of an infantry battalion drawn up one behind the next with short intervals or "divisions" between them, in order to move rapidly toward the enemy line behind a screen of skirmishers and then either to close with the bayonet while remaining in column, or deploy quickly into a firing line by having the first company stand fast and the others quickly form on its right and left. (See Diagram 3.)

The generals of the French Revolution applied many variations of the column-of-divisions. In order to speed up the transition from column into line on the battlefield, they deployed the battalion column on a two-company front and thus reduced its depth. (See Diagram 4.) During the Napoleonic Wars (1803–15), they experimented with forming regiments, brigades, and even a whole army division into columns-of-divisions. The trend had gone too far when, at Waterloo, one French division was formed into a column two hundred files wide and twenty-six ranks deep. This unwieldy phalanx of 5,200 infantrymen was shot to pieces before it could

DIAGRAM 4. French Battalion of Column-of-Divisions on a Two-Company Front. Proportions are the same as in Diagram 3. Diagram not drawn to scale.

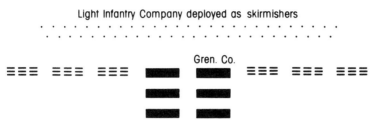

Light Infantry Company deployed as skirmishers

Gren. Co.

either close with the bayonet or deploy into line for firing. Still, when used on the level of the battalion, the column-of-divisions greatly improved the French infantry's speed and flexibility on the battlefield, and the French system was eventually copied in nearly all armies but the British.

General Jean de Gribeauval, the inspector-general of French artillery before the Revolution, greatly improved the technical qualities of field guns by 1789. The French 12-pounder gun and its carriage were so reduced in weight that two pairs of horses could pull the piece at a trot. Accordingly, the firepower of such guns was less hobbled by a lack of mobility than older cannon. Baron du Teil, head of the Artillery School of Practice at Auxonne, and his brother and fellow artillerist the Chevalier du Teil, were among the first European officers to stress tactical speed and mobility with the improved field guns. The young French artillery officers at Auxonne just before 1789, among them Napoleon Bonaparte, were taught to think in terms of a rapid concentration of guns to blast gaps in the enemy's line, which could then be penetrated by French infantry or cavalry. Later, General Bonaparte's preference for massed artillery in battle—often using canister at five hundred yards or less—reflected his training as well as his experience. Bonaparte made his own contribution to the French artillery when in 1800 he replaced civilian teamsters with soldiers. The mobility of his artillery on the battlefield became as legendary as its firepower.

Another idea drawn from the old army was that of dividing field armies into self-contained "army divisions" which, for a limited time, could both march and fight independently. The idea probably originated about the middle of the eighteenth century with Colonel Pierre de Bourcet. Marshal de Broglie experimented with army divisions in the Seven Years' War, but the idea was not really a practical one until many more and better parallel highways were constructed in parts of Europe before 1789. The "macadamized" highway—a sand base with crushed rock surface, crowned so that water was drawn to ditches on either side—became the first "all-weather" highway design in modern times and one that stood up well to the pounding of boots and the wheels of guns and wagons. Then, when the French Revolution produced the mass army, it became at one time natural, necessary, and possible to divide field forces into army divisions to exploit such a system of highways. The divisions, advancing in a fanlike spread over parallel roads, could forage over a much larger area than a concentrated force, hence could move with fewer delays, and also could be maneuvered to concentrate against an enemy force from several directions at once.

The French army division—often numbering 10,000 men and being essentially a miniature field army—permitted a strategic flexibility previously unknown. When too many divisions produced a problem of span-of-control for the army commander, Bonaparte solved it in 1800 by inventing the army corps, two to four divisions coordinated by an army corps commander who became the link between the commander-in-chief of the field army and his division commanders. The army corps system worked so well that in 1805 Bonaparte (by then the Emperor Napoleon) transferred all cavalry and part of the artillery in every corps to the corps reserve under the direct control of the corps commander. The French army corps, varying from 20,000 to 40,000 men, then became Napoleon's principal element of strategic maneuver. Much of his reputation rests on his uncanny ability to use numerous corps and divisions during the approach march in ways that confused the enemy, and then to unite his forces in a kind of net with which he crushed the enemy army. It hardly goes too far to say that, through his use of army divisions and army corps, Napoleon revolutionized the whole technique of strategic movement. (See Diagram 5.)

B. *The Wars of the French Revolution and the Rise of Napoleon Bonaparte, 1789–1802.* The national revolt in France in 1789 resulted in the transfer of many royal powers to an elected National Assembly, the abolition of the last vestiges of feudalism, and the formation of a citizen-soldier militia called the National Guard. After Louis XVI tried unsuccessfully to leave France in 1791, the National Assembly required a new oath of allegiance to the French nation from every French military and naval officer. Those who refused to take the new oath were discharged and replaced by supporters of the Revolution. When Prussia and Austria threatened France with the invasion of an expeditionary force of 100,000 troops under the Prussian Duke of Brunswick in the spring of 1792, the National Assembly declared a state of war and strengthened the regular army by adding *demi-brigades,* regiments of volunteer citizen-soldiers serving under their own officers. Under General Charles Dumouriez,

DIAGRAM 5. Napoleonic Strategy.

A. Approach Phase. Divisions or corps are deployed on a wide front to locate main enemy force.

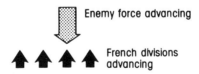

B. Concentration Phase. Some divisions make contact and attack in order to force the enemy to deploy his forces. Other divisions "march to the sound of the guns" to reinforce divisions already engaged or to turn the enemy's flank.

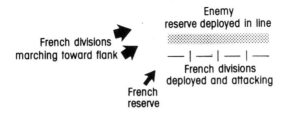

C. Deployment of the Reserve. Here deployed opposite the junction between the enemy's front and his refused flank. Artillery concentration to prepare for a breakthrough.

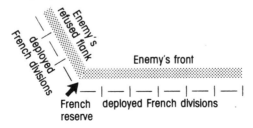

D. Breakthrough and Exploitation. The enemy's line is severed and cavalry sweep into the rear of his regiments. As his forces disintegrate, vigorous pursuit is carried out to prevent a rally and to inflict maximum casualties.

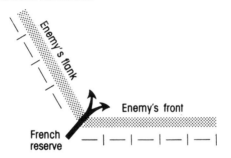

50,000 troops of this regular-volunteer combination turned back 35,000 of Brunswick's troops forty miles east of Paris in September at the Battle of Valmy, the first major battle of the Wars of the French Revolution, and subsequently Brunswick withdrew his expedition from France. The National Convention, which had replaced the National Assembly, declared France a republic and ordered its armies to carry the war into the Austrian Netherlands (Belgium) and German Rhineland. In January 1793 the Convention sent Louis XVI to the guillotine.

The execution of the king inflamed much of royal Europe against the Revolution. In the spring of 1793, Britain, the Dutch Netherlands, Spain, Prussia, Austria, and lesser powers formed the First Coalition and sent 400,000 troops into the field against France. When the Allied forces expelled the French armies from Belgium and the Rhineland, Dumouriez and the Marquis de Lafayette, a hero of the American Revolution and the first commander of the National Guard, deserted to the Allied side. In order to save the Revolution, the National Convention took drastic measures. It conferred extraordinary powers on a Committee of Public Safety headed by Maximilien de Robespierre, and sent deputies-on-mission to all army headquarters to insure the loyalty of the generals and to supervise the political indoctrination of the troops. But for the patterns of war, the Committee's most important measure was to proclaim a *levée en masse* in August 1793. This action made all able-bodied French males of military age liable to conscription. In addition, its measures of "war socialism" placed all of the economic resources of France, including its civilian labor, at the disposal of the government for waging war. No such total mobilization for war had been seen before in modern times.

By December 1794 a million Frenchmen were under arms and Paris had become the largest arms-producing center in the world. The "Organizer of Victory" was Lazare Carnot, a former captain of engineers in the old royal army, who, as a revolutionary general, both advised the Committee of Public Safety and, after Robespierre's fall from power in the summer of 1794, served as Minister of War under the Directory. Carnot organized a prototype of a modern "general staff" with which he provided centralized direction to the French armies in the field, at one time numbering as many as fourteen, one of which was devoted to suppressing a peasant revolt in the Vendée. Never before had one government commanded so much power. Never before had the revolutionary idea so kindled fires in the minds of men.

The revitalized French armies carried the war again into Belgium, overran the Dutch Netherlands, and occupied the Rhineland. In 1794 Prussia made a separate peace with France and Spain changed sides. By 1796 only Britain and Austria among the major powers of Europe remained at war with France.

In the midst of these events, Napoleon Bonaparte rose to prominence. Promoted rapidly from captain to brigadier general in 1793 for his service at the siege of British-occupied Toulon (at the time he was twenty-four years old), he served with the garrison at Paris, helped to suppress a royalist-inspired revolt against the Directory in 1795, and in the spring of 1796 was appointed by Carnot to command the French Army of Italy on the Italian Riviera. Bonaparte's first major command turned out to be 40,000 outnumbered, ragged, and hungry troops, yet he managed to lead this unpromising force to victory over the Austrian and Piedmontese armies in northern Italy. With a larger army in 1797, he advanced to a point within eighty miles of Vienna and then dictated terms of peace to the envoys of the Habsburg emperor. By the time Bonaparte returned to Paris, he was the most popular as well as one of the youngest of the French generals.

When the Directory had no better ideas for bringing Britain to terms, it approved Bonaparte's plan to lead an army to Egypt, establish a base there, and then march to British India by way of the Levant, Persia (Iran), and Afghanistan, essentially the same route taken over twenty-one hundred years earlier by the army of Alexander the Great. Bonaparte and 25,000 troops sailed from Toulon in May 1798, evaded the British fleet, occupied Malta on the way to Egypt, and landed at Alexandria in July. Bonaparte's Army of the East then marched up the Nile, defeated an Egyptian army at Omm-Dinar (the "Battle of the Pyramids"), and occupied Cairo. In August, a detachment of the British Mediterranean fleet under Admiral Horatio Nelson found most of the French fleet anchored at Aboukir Bay, a dozen miles from Alexandria, and in an all-night battle destroyed or captured most of the French force. But Bonaparte, undeterred by the fact that his sea communications to France had been severed, led 13,000 French troops into Turkish Palestine in February 1799, and defeated all opposition until his way was blocked by the seacoast fortress city of Acre, near Beirut. When his army could not take the fortress by assault from its Anglo-Turkish defenders, or starve its garrison into surrender, Bonaparte was forced to lead his army, greatly reduced in size by battle and disease, back to Egypt. The French beat off a British landing at Aboukir Bay in July, but Bonaparte realized that it was only a matter of time until the enemy mounted overwhelming forces against his trapped army.

Bonaparte's solution was to take a few chosen officers and, in a flotilla of two frigates, leave Alexandria for France in August 1799. The Army of the East was left to fend for itself. (In 1801 it was finally compelled to surrender to the British.) By the time Bonaparte's vessels reached the southern coast of France in October 1799, war had commenced between France and the Second Coalition, consisting of Britain, Austria, and Rus-

Admiral Horatio Nelson

SOURCE: Geoffrey Bennett, *Nelson the Commander* (New York: Charles Scribner's Sons, 1972).

sia. Meanwhile, Carnot had fled to Switzerland after an unsuccessful coup against the Directory. The Directors were involved in plots against each other, and, soon after his arrival in Paris, Bonaparte threw in his lot with one of the factions and wound up as its leader. In the coup of November 1799, he toppled the Directory and brought the Consulate to power.

As First Consul, Bonaparte became general-in-chief of the French armies, personally commanding one of them in a campaign in northern Italy against the Austrians, and narrowly winning the Battle of Marengo in June 1800. After the French armies in Germany inflicted more defeats on the Austrians, Bonaparte dictated terms of peace to the Habsburg emperor in 1801. But Bonaparte's scheme for forming a League of Armed Neutrality among the Baltic states in order to deprive Britain of vital trade came to a bad end in 1801 when Nelson's fleet destroyed the Danish fleet at the Battle of Copenhagen. The Peace of Amiens in March 1802 between Britain and France officially closed the Wars of the French Revolution. But the peace proved fragile. In May 1803 war between France and Britain broke out again. In 1804 Bonaparte crowned himself Napoleon I, Emperor of the French, transformed the French republic into the French Empire, and prepared his Imperial Army for new conquests.

     C. Napoleon and the Imperial Army at Zenith, 1804–7.   Napoleon retained the Directory's law of 1798 which allowed resort to the *levée en masse* when French soil was threatened but otherwise provided men to the army through volunteering and choosing by lot. Under Napoleon's system of lottery conscription, men with "bad numbers" faced up to seven years of compulsory military service, but the system was softened by excusing married men and allowing single men to provide substitutes. In 1804 Napoleon revived the rank of marshal and established patents of nobility for service to the empire. In addition, the Imperial Guard, also founded in 1804, was composed of soldiers who had distinguished themselves in earlier campaigns, and to this "Old Guard" Napoleon later added the "Middle Guard" and the "Young Guard." By 1815 at least 100,000 soldiers had served in various guard units which together were considered a *corps d'élite.*

At the beginning of the Napoleonic Wars (1803–15), the French army had about 750,000 troops and was predominantly a national force. The Grande Armée (Main Army) of 1805–7 gave Napoleon victories over Austria, Prussia, and Russia, making him master of most of Europe, from the English Channel to the Russian frontier. But rising casualties and the need to find new sources of manpower led Napoleon to expand membership in his forces to include foreigners. No fewer than a quarter of the million men who entered the French army between 1800 and 1812 were born outside the 1792 frontiers of France, and included Belgians, Germans,

Italians, and Poles. While many of these foreign troops served well, their presence tended to dilute the national quality of Napoleon's army when other armies were trying to increase national homogeneity. By 1812 only the rewards of conquest united all of Napoleon's soldiers, and the original values of the French Revolution were increasingly subordinated to the objectives of French domination over Europe and a reward system that rested at heart on military aggression.

When war broke out between France and Britain in May 1803, Napoleon tried to limit the conflict by scheming for an early invasion of England before other powers could intervene on the side of Britain. Napoleon induced Spain to enter the war on the French side in December 1804, and in March 1805 a Franco-Spanish Combined Fleet under French admiral Pierre Villeneuve left the Mediterranean for the West Indies in hopes of drawing the British Channel fleet to that quarter long enough for a French Army of England—200,000 of Napoleon's best troops camped at Boulogne—to invade England. But Nelson's fleet in the Mediterranean, not the Channel fleet, followed Villeneuve's fleet to the West Indies and then relentlessly tracked it back across the Atlantic late in the summer of 1805. In August, Napoleon scrapped his plans for an invasion of England when he learned that Austria and Russia had signed an alliance with Britain and that Allied armies were on the march across central Europe. After Villeneuve's fleet put in at Cadiz, it made a dash for the Straits of Gibraltar, but, upon sighting Nelson's fleet in pursuit, it tried in vain to return to Cadiz. Nelson's fleet caught up with the Combined Fleet off Cape Trafalgar on October 21, and, in a brilliant melée action, thoroughly demolished it. The action was only marred for the British by Nelson's death in his hour of victory. Napoleon's naval power never fully recovered from the defeat at Trafalgar.

The French Army of England, rechristened the Grande Armée in August 1805, was the finest field force that Napoleon ever led. All of its marshals and generals were experienced campaigners, yet had lost none of their vigor, and the troops were either veterans or well-trained recruits. The phenomenal speed of the army's march from the Channel to the Rhine wrecked Allied plans for concentrating on the French frontiers before Napoleon could parry their blow, and in late September the Grande Armée swept into southern Germany on a front of seventy miles. Marshal Karl Mack's Austrian army was encircled, and the last of his troops compelled to surrender at Ulm on October 20, the day before Nelson's victory at Trafalgar. Napoleon left detachments to hold southern Germany and to sever Allied communications with northern Italy, and then marched with the rest of his army down the Danube to capture Vienna. After occupying the Habsburg capital, Napoleon's army invaded the province of Bohemia (now in the Czech republic) in order to engage an Austro-Russian army at Austerlitz. Though the Allied army slightly outnumbered Napoleon's army (85,000 Allied troops to 72,000 French troops), the French won a smashing victory on December 2. In the wake of the Battle of Austerlitz, Emperor Francis of Austria made peace with Napoleon and the Russian army retired to its own territory in order to recover from its defeat.

During the winter of 1805–6 the Grande Armée camped in southern Germany while warily watching Prussia, which had remained neutral during the campaigns of 1805. In the late summer of 1806 King Frederick William III finally summoned up his courage and declared war. But, as the old-style Prussian army marched ponderously toward the French line-of-communication to the Rhine, the Grande Armée swept north to sever the Prussian army's communications with Berlin and to bring it to battle on October 14 while divided at Jena and Auerstädt. Even though Napoleon was present at Jena with a majority of his forces, Marshal Louis Nicolas Davout, with outnumbered forces, won an impressive victory at Auerstädt. Among the Prussians mortally wounded at Jena-Auerstädt was the Duke of Brunswick. The French pursued the remnants of the Prussian forces, in the process overrunning most of Prussia and forcing Frederick William III to flee from Berlin to the protection of Tsar Alexander I.

The Russian army tried to defend East Prussia on a snow-covered battlefield at Prussian Eylau in February 1807, and even fought the French to a draw. Napoleon then withdrew his army to a winter camp in Poland and awaited better weather. In June, he had his revenge for Eylau at the Battle of Friedland when he cornered and severely mauled the Russian army under General Levin Bennigsen before it made good its retreat into Russian territory. After Friedland, Alexander I was willing to make peace, and, on July 7, the Tsar agreed to Napoleon's terms under the Peace of Tilsit, one that confirmed the French emperor's control of most of Europe west of the Russian frontier and reduced once-mighty Prussia to the status of a French vassal state.

D. The Decline of French Fortunes in the West and the Anglo-American War of 1812. Despite Napoleon's victories in Europe to July 1807, he was still left with the problem of how to bring Britain to terms. An invasion of the British Isles was out of the question after Trafalgar, and another expedition to Egypt seemed impractical. But as early as the French occupation of Berlin in December 1806 Napoleon believed that he had the answer. The issuance of the Berlin Decree inaugurated the so-called Continental System, a European-wide boycott of trade with Britain. Though the boycott worked some hardship on continental Europe, Napoleon calculated that most trade with Britain had been in luxury items and that continental substitutes, such as sugar beets for cane sugar, would

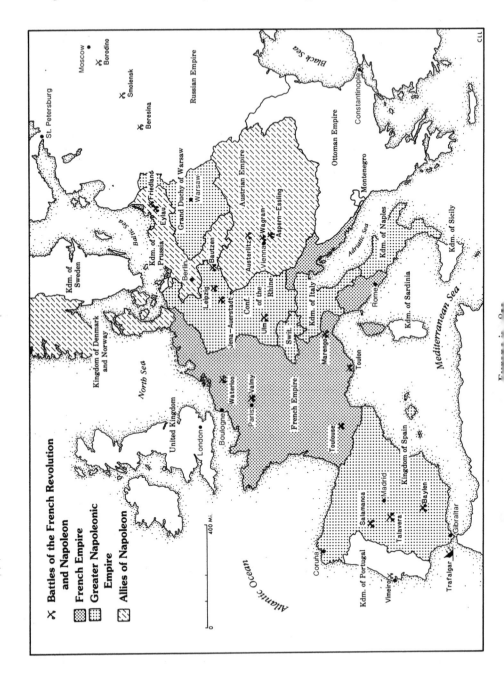

meet the need. Where necessary, exceptions to the boycott could be permitted. With Tsarist Russia committed to cooperate, Napoleon believed that such stress would be placed on the pocketbooks of Britain's "nation of shopkeepers" that they would pressure their government to make peace and leave him a free hand on the continent.

But in order for the Continental System to be effective, it had to have no big holes in its dike, and Portugal, a long-time trading partner with Britain, was still beyond Napoleon's grasp. In addition, British goods landed in Portugal were sometimes smuggled into Spain and even into France itself. In the fall of 1807 Napoleon pressured King Charles IV of Spain to allow a French army under General Jean Andoche Junot to pass through his country on the way to Portugal. Junot's army had no difficulty in defeating the royal Portuguese army or occupying the capital at Lisbon, and the Portuguese royal family fled into exile in Brazil. Under the pretense of maintaining Junot's lines of communication across Spain and aiding the Spanish authorities in stopping the smuggling of illicit goods, Napoleon poured 200,000 troops into the country in the spring of 1808. Charles IV and his heir, Ferdinand, were summoned to Bayonne where they were forced to abdicate the Spanish throne in favor of Napoleon's brother Joseph. Napoleon presented the Spanish people with a *fait accompli* and expected their subservience.

But Napoleon's treacherous removal of the Spanish royal family outraged most Spaniards, and a major revolt against the occupying French forces commenced in Madrid on May 4, 1808. As the revolt spread across Spain, French troops found themselves under attack by both regular Spanish troops and civilians. In July, an entire French army corps was trapped at Bailen and compelled to surrender. After Joseph had withdrawn French forces to northern Spain, Napoleon was forced to lead 200,000 additional troops into Spain in order to come to his assistance. In November 1808 Napoleon decisively defeated the regular Spanish army at the river Ebro, and, after reseating Joseph on the throne at Madrid in December, returned to Paris. He believed that the French forces he had left in Spain had matters well in hand, but a Spanish junta and remnants of the Spanish army, supplied by the British, held out in the port of Cadiz, and peasants in the mountainous interior of Spain continued to wage *guerrilla* ("little war") against the French invaders. Spain had been conquered but not subdued.

While these events were unfolding, Britain sent two armies to assist Spain and Portugal, respectively. The army sent to Spain under General Sir John Moore was caught up in the Spanish army's defeat at the Ebro in November 1808, but, after a grueling march over the mountains, it reached the safety of Corunna and was evacuated by the British fleet in January 1809. Moore, however, was killed. Another British army of 25,000

Duke of Wellington
Source: David Howarth, *Waterloo: Day of Battle* (New York:
Atheneum, 1968).

troops commanded by General Arthur Wellesley was more successful. After it landed in Portugal, it defeated Junot's army at the Battle of Vimeiro and subsequently occupied Lisbon. In 1809 Wellesley's army drove the French from the rest of Portugal and even made a sortie into Spain, where it defeated a French army under marshals Jean-Baptiste Jourdan and Claude Victor-Perrin at the Battle of Talavera. Even though numerically superior French forces finally forced Wellesley to withdraw his army from Spain to Portugal, he was rewarded for his performance against the French with the title of Viscount Wellington of Talavera. Eventually raised to the Duke of Wellington in 1814, he proved to be the ablest of the British commanders in the field.

Alhough the Duke of Wellington never had more than 60,000 troops at a time during his six years in the Iberian peninsula, including Portuguese soldiers under British officers, he did well there in part because his earlier service in India had accustomed him to the command of a multinational army in difficult country. When Marshal André Masséna's 110,000 troops invaded Portugal in 1810, Wellington's smaller army slowly gave ground before its advance, inflicted a bloody repulse on the French when they attacked at Busaco, and then retired to the safety of the Lines of Torres Vedras, earthworks built across the Lisbon peninsula that could not be outflanked or be taken by frontal assault. Masséna had not even known that the lines existed. After an unsuccessful siege, in which the besiegers suffered more than the besieged, Masséna was finally forced to return his starving army to Spain in 1811. The French had suffered 40,000 casualties in the campaign and accomplished nothing; Wellington had lost only 4,000 soldiers and had maintained his position in Portugal. The other French marshals sent against Wellington were to be as baffled as their predecessors by Wellington's tactics and strategy.

Wellington's favorite tactic was to cause his army to occupy high ground that could not be easily outflanked, deploy skirmishers on its slopes facing the enemy, and form his main line of infantry in two ranks behind the protection of a crest. His skirmishers included the green-uniformed sharpshooters of the Rifle Corps (created earlier by Sir John Moore), who served to fend off French skirmishers trying to bring the main British line under fire. The crest protected the main British line from direct fire by the French artillery. When the French infantry columns, ineffectually supported by skirmishers and artillery, tried to rush the crest, they were shattered by the massed fire of the British line before the French could either close with the bayonet or deploy into line.

But Wellington was also capable of seizing the tactical offensive. In another of his invasions of Spain in 1812, and after he had positioned his army near Salamanca, he detected a French army under Marshal Auguste de Marmont attempting to turn his army's flank. Judging that the French were careless about their security, Wellington launched an unexpected counterattack that sent the enemy flying. Supposedly he defeated 40,000 Frenchmen in forty minutes.

Despite Wellington's skill as a general and the attrition that both his operations and those of the Spanish guerrillas inflicted on the French, Napoleon did not completely lose his grip on Spain until after his disastrous invasion of Russia in 1812. In his effort in 1813 to build a new army to hold his possessions in Germany, Napoleon ordered Joseph to send him reinforcements from the French army in Spain. Once these troops were gone, Wellington was quick to take advantage of the weakened enemy by carrying out a brilliant strategic march across northern Spain. He finally routed the last major French resistance on Spanish soil when he defeated a French army under Marshal Jourdan at the Battle of Vitoria in June 1813. That fall Wellington's forces crossed the Pyrenees into southern France, and in April 1814 they defeated a French army under Marshal Jean Soult at Toulouse. Wellington was on the point of launching a drive deeper into France when he received news of Napoleon's abdication. The Peninsular War cost the French 400,000 men over the course of six years, or nearly as many troops as they lost in Russia in six months in 1812. Thus, the "Spanish Ulcer" ultimately did about as much damage to the French Imperial Army as the gaping Russian wound.

The Anglo-American War of 1812 was a sideshow of the Napoleonic Wars. Only 5,000 British regulars were in Canada when the United States of America—provoked by British interference with American trade and supposed incitement of the Indians against American frontier populations—declared war in June 1812. But the U.S. regular army numbered only 7,000 troops, and a botched American mobilization and incompetently led forces saved Canada from invasion until British reinforcements began to arrive. Jacob Brown and Winfield Scott were among the few capable American generals who emerged as the war went along, but even Brown's and Scott's invasion of Canada in 1814 was turned back. Meanwhile, the British navy carried out raids along the American coastline and gradually hunted down or blockaded the American warships and privateers attempting to wage war on Britain's commerce. The worst American defeat in the war came at Bladensburg, Md., in August 1814, when a force of about 2,000 British troops, landed from Chesapeake Bay, routed 5,000 American regulars and militia attempting to defend the new capital at Washington, D.C. The British occupied Washington and then burned the capital before returning to their ships. A more credible American showing occurred in September 1814, when the stubborn American defense of Fort McHenry blocked the British attack on Baltimore and inspired Francis Scott Key to write the "The Star-Spangled Banner," a poem that would provide the words for the future American national anthem. In the same month that the abortive British attack on Baltimore occurred, an American flotilla and army turned back a British drive from Canada by way of Lake Champlain at the Battle of Plattsburg, N.Y. General Andrew Jackson's celebrated repulse of the British attack on New Orleans in January 1815, came after the signing of the Peace of Ghent but before the news had crossed the Atlantic.

Among the 104,000 Americans who served during the War of 1812, some 7,000 died in the line of duty, far fewer than died in the American Revolution. Moreover, though the American population of 1812 came to 7.7 million, or about three times that of 1775, hardly more men were mobilized at one time—36,000—than at any time during the American Revolution. New England's threat to secede from the Union in order to make a separate peace with Britain was never carried out, but it was an indication that the cause of nationalism was far from perfected in the United States. The relatively poor American showing in the War of 1812 did prod Congress to reform the administration of the army and to approve the building of an improved system of seacoast defenses, but down to the eve of the outbreak of the American Civil War in 1861 the system of coastal defenses remained incomplete. Nor before the Civil War were the U.S. army and navy very impressive by European standards.

The British army in the Napoleonic period may be described as semi-national in character. Parliament never adopted the equivalent of the French *levée en masse* or other continental European army reforms, but by various inducements it encouraged militia to volunteer in relatively large numbers for overseas service with the regular army. At the army's peak strength in 1813, it had 220,000 men, a respectable number for a country with a home population of 11 million and which had also furnished the navy with 330,000 sailors and marines.

E. The Decline of Napoleon's Fortunes in the East, the First Abdication, and the Return of the Hundred Days, 1808–15.   In the wake of Austria's defeat in 1805, the Habsburg monarchy made efforts toward creating a more national army, although the polyglot nature of the empire made the task difficult. Still, in the spring of 1809, a semi-national army of 300,000 Austrian troops took the field in hopes of exploiting the French preoccupation with Spain and Portugal. Commanded by the Archduke Charles, the Austrian troops fought Napoleon's Army of Germany to a bloody draw at Aspern-Essling in May, a battle in which Jean Lannes was to be the first French marshal to die in action. Napoleon finally defeated the Austrians decisively at the Battle of Wagram in July, but only by accepting very heavy casualties. Significantly, his terms of peace not only stripped Austria of territory and population, but forbade an Austrian army larger than 150,000 troops.

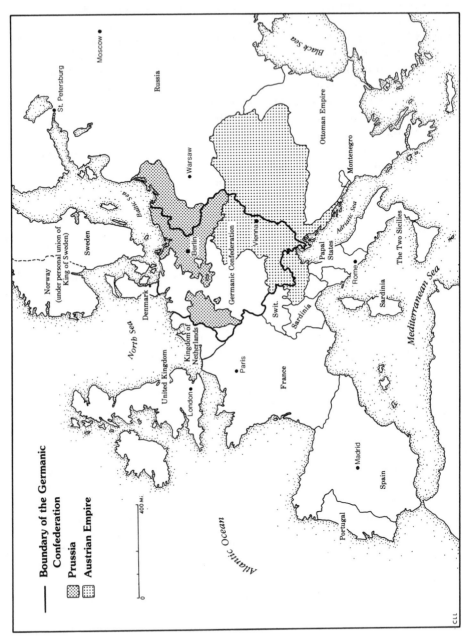

Europe in 1815

General Gerhard von Scharnhorst

SOURCE: Walter Goerlitz, *History of the German General Staff, 1657–1945*, trans. Brian Battershaw (New York and London: Praeger, 1953).

In the wake of its defeat in 1806, Prussia carried out more sweeping social and military reforms than Austria. Frederick William III was not enthusiastic about abandoning royal prerogatives and the military privileges of the Junkers, but serfdom was partially abolished and the middle class was given a greater voice in government. General Gerhard Johann David von Scharnhorst, one of the few Prussian generals before 1806 who favored reforms, was made president of the Military Reform Commission. The commission cashiered numerous incompetent or overage generals and sponsored the legislation through which Frederick William offered commissions to the sons of the middle class on a more equal footing with the Junkers. In order to get around the limit of 42,000 troops placed on the Prussian army by Napoleon, the Prussians devised a system for the army's short-term training of civilian volunteers who were then sent into the army's reserve. The reserve had about 20,000 men by 1812. Napoleon suppressed Scharnhorst's plan for a Landwehr (national militia), but after Prussia broke with Napoleon in 1813 and launched its "War of Liberation," the Landwehr was organized to supplement the army and its reserve. Finally, the reforms included the founding in 1810 of a military institution for the higher study of war, a forerunner of the later Kriegsakademie (War College). Officers chosen to attend were prepared systematically to carry out the duties of high command and staff work. In 1812 Napoleon insisted on including a sizable part of the Prussian army in his forces that invaded Russia, and many reform-minded Prussian officers either resigned, retired, or offered their services to armies opposed to Napoleon. In 1813, after Napoleon's defeat in Russia, many of the same officers returned to Prussia's service and helped to lead its army to victory over Napoleon.

Though his involvement in Spain and Portugal had presented serious problems for Napoleon, his decision to invade Russia in 1812 proved fatal to his cause. However, his decision reflected the fact that he could not afford to allow Alexander I's break with the Continental System in 1811 to go unpunished, and he saw no other way to maintain his aura of military invincibility in the eyes of the rest of Europe. Hence, in the spring of 1812, he assembled a new Grande Armée of 600,000 troops in East Prussia and the Duchy of Warsaw (French-occupied Poland), more than twice as many soldiers as the Tsar had in European Russia. Napoleon's plan was to launch a surprise invasion of the Russian frontier, destroy most of the Tsar's forces while close to French bases, then follow the remnants of the Russian army either to St. Petersburg or to Moscow, and at either place dictate terms of peace to a penitent Tsar.

Napoleon's strategy began to go wrong almost from the moment that the Grande Armée began crossing the Russian frontier on June 22, 1812. There was no strategic surprise; the Tsar had been expecting an attack for weeks. Still worse for Napoleon, the Russian army, about 250,000 strong, avoided a general engagement and made a fighting retreat, drawing the French toward Moscow and through some of the worst agricultural land in western Russia. Insofar as possible, the Russians destroyed or removed food and fodder supplies as they retreated, and Napoleon's system for supplying his army from bases at the frontier broke down in the face of great distances and poor roads. Troops in the lead of his columns consumed what food and forage remained on the line of advance, leaving little for those who followed. By the time the Grande Armée had reached Smolensk in August, it had already lost 100,000 men to the effects of fighting, hunger, thirst, typhus and heat. Napoleon canceled plans to bring reinforcements into Russia because the country could not sustain them. Still, he was given a chance to fight a decisive battle when on September 7, at the insistence of the Tsar, old Marshal Mikhail Kutusov ordered the Russian army to make a stand at the village of Borodino, seventy miles west of Moscow. The battle that followed was sanguinary—40,000 Russian and 30,000 French casualties—but proved indecisive when Napoleon hesitated to commit the Imperial Guard at the critical moment. The Russian army resumed its retreat and again Napoleon had no choice but to follow.

By the time Napoleon reached Moscow a week after Borodino, about 250,000 troops were still with him, but the city was deserted. Its population of a half million had joined the Russian army in a migration further east. Worse, fires broke out in the largely wooden city, and within a few days the Grande Armée occupied a burned-out shell, devoid of food and shelter against the approach of winter. Napoleon waited in the Kremlin in the vain hope that Alexander would negotiate with him, then on October 19 ordered the Grande Armée to begin a withdrawal toward Poland. But Kutusov adroitly maneuvered the Russian army to block the line of retreat toward Warsaw, and forced the Grande Armée to retrace its steps over the plundered route to East Prussia. By late November, when it crossed the Beresina River, attacks by the Russian army and guerrillas, and the effects of hunger and cold, had combined to reduce its strength to 50,000 men. In early December, Napoleon turned over command of the survivors to Marshal Joachim Murat and rushed on to Paris to prepare public opinion for news of the disaster and to mobilize new forces. About 30,000 of Napoleon's troops finally escaped to the relative safety of East Prussia. Excluding those who reached Prussia, of the approximately 500,000 troops who entered Russia, 250,000 had died, 100,000 had been taken prisoner, and the balance had deserted.

In the wake of Napoleon's disastrous campaign in 1812, Russia, Sweden, Prussia, and Britain, among other powers, formed the Fourth Coalition against France. Upon Prussia's mobilization in March 1813, Frederick William III entrusted command of the Prussian army to old Marshal Gebhard von Blücher, who, in turn, appointed Scharnhorst as his chief-of-staff. August von Gneisenau, a disciple of Scharnhorst, served as chief of operations until Scharnhorst's mortal wound at the Battle of Lützen in May, then took Scharnhorst's place as Blücher's chief-of-staff. Many other officers who served in key positions in the Prussian army of 1813–15 were also products of advanced military schooling. Moreover, after Prussia adopted general conscription, its army swelled to 300,000 troops. Meanwhile, a Swedish army under Crown Prince Bernadotte, formerly one of Napoleon's marshals, entered the field on the side of the Allies. After Kutusov's health broke in April 1813, command of the Russian army passed to Prince Ludwig Wittgenstein.

Allied delays in the spring of 1813 allowed Napoleon time in which to form 250,000 troops into a new Army of the Elbe, and, in May, to launch an offensive to recover eastern Germany. In rapid succession he inflicted sharp defeats on the Allied forces at the battles of Lützen and Bautzen, and in June the eastern Allies agreed to an armistice while Austria tried to mediate a peace. Negotiations dragged on through the summer, and Napoleon used the time to increase the strength of the Army of the Elbe to 440,000 troops. But the Allies used the lull to even greater advantage. They convinced Emperor Francis I to commit the Austrian empire to the Fourth Coalition if negotiations failed. As a result, when the armistice ended in August, the strength of Allied forces in the east swelled to 500,000 men. The Allies organized their troops into three international armies, commanded respectively by Bernadotte, Blücher, and the Austrian Prince Felix von Schwarzenberg. None of the Allied commanders were Napoleon's equal as a military commander, but all of them were about as good as his marshals.

The war resumed on the eastern front, but Napoleon was frustrated in his attempt to achieve a quick victory at Dresden in August. The fighting continued indecisively in eastern Germany until mid-October, when, in a four-day battle at Leipzig (October 16–19), the fate of Germany was sealed. In this "Battle of the Nations," involving 195,000 French troops against 257,000 Allied troops (more troops than in any other battle of the Napoleonic Wars), Napoleon came close to victory. But mistakes of his subordinates nearly caused his army to be encircled, and only through a hasty retreat was Napoleon able to save most of his command. Even so, he lost 68,000 troops to an Allied loss of 57,000. With the defeat at Leipzig, any chance of stopping Napoleon's enemies east of the Rhine had vanished, and by December 1813, when the last of Napoleon's forces had retreated behind that barrier, the Army of the Elbe was down to 100,000 men.

Napoleon tried to arrange a new armistice in order to buy time in which to mobilize more troops, but the Allies were not to be deceived a second time. About 450,000 Allied soldiers crossed the Rhine into the Low Countries and France in January 1814. With inferior numbers but through a series of dazzling maneuvers, Napoleon fended his enemies away from Paris for a time. But even his wizardry had its limits. The Allies finally entered Paris at the end of March, and Napoleon's army, by then down to 60,000 men, was driven back on Napoleon's new capital at Fontainebleu, sixty miles south of Paris. It was only a matter of time before it would be crushed between the converging armies of the eastern Allies and Wellington's army advancing through southern France. Accordingly, in mid-April, Napoleon accepted Allied peace terms in the Treaty of Fontainebleau. He exchanged the throne of France for an island kingdom on Elba and a French pension for life. The Allies placed Louis XVIII on the French throne, and on April 28 Louis signed the First Peace of Paris which returned France to its frontiers of 1792. The division of Napoleon's empire outside France was to be decided at an all-European congress at Vienna to open in September 1814.

Napoleon made a final effort to restore his fortunes at the beginning of March 1815, when he and a few supporters landed on the southern coast of France and appealed to the French people and soldiers to rally to him. As Napoleon advanced toward Paris, Marshal Michel Ney, who had earlier transferred loyalties from Napoleon to Louis XVIII, led a body of troops to intercept Napoleon's party, but both Ney and his troops were won over by Napoleon's oratory. As Napoleon's forces continued to advance on Paris and more French troops went over to his cause, Louis XVIII and the royal family fled France. After reaching a welcoming Paris, Napoleon commenced the Reign of the Hundred Days (March 20–June 22).

The Congress of Vienna had nearly finished its work when, on March 25, the Fourth Coalition (save Sweden) reformed its ranks and declared war on Napoleon. Wellington and Blücher began assembling separate armies in Belgium (then part of the Dutch Netherlands), preparatory to joining ranks and marching on Paris. But Napoleon moved more quickly than his adversaries. Having formed 124,000 veteran troops into an Army of the North, Napoleon crossed the frontier on June 15 and the next day defeated Blücher's army at the Battle of Ligny. The same day a detached French force under Ney blocked Wellington's way from Brussels at Quatre-Bras. But Napoleon then made a mistake by waiting until June 17 to send Marshal Emmanuel de Grouchy's 30,000 troops after the retreating Prussians. Ney made another error by allowing Wellington's army at Quatre-Bras to fall back toward Brussels. On that morning, with 72,000 troops, Napoleon and Ney set out in pursuit of Wellington, and that night found Wellington's 64,000 British, Hanoverian, Dutch, and Belgian troops camped on the heights of Mont Saint Jean, a mile south of the village of Waterloo and twelve miles from Brussels. Napoleon's army camped a couple of miles to the south of Mont Saint Jean. Twelve miles to the east of Waterloo, Blücher's army had arrived at Wavre, well ahead of Grouchy's pursuing forces.

Although Napoleon learned early on the morning of June 18 of the Prussian presence at Wavre, he counted on Grouchy to prevent Blücher from interfering in his battle with Wellington. He was not aware that Blücher had left an army corps at Wavre to delay Grouchy and was marching with three army corps to join Wellington at Waterloo. Moreover, on June 18 Grouchy continued toward Wavre even after the sound of guns in the direction of Waterloo was reported to him. He wasted his effort in an indecisive battle with the Prussian corps at Wavre that made no difference in the final outcome. But Napoleon also prejudiced the outcome at Waterloo by delaying the opening of the battle there until the ground dried out from an all-night rain; by the time the French commenced their attacks, it was near midday on June 18, and Blücher and Wellington had gained valuable time. By dusk Wellington's army had suffered many casualties and was nearly exhausted under Napoleon's pounding, but it had managed to hold on to its ridge until Blücher's forces arrived. The battle came to a dramatic conclusion when Blücher's Prussians struck the French flank and Wellington's army counterattacked the French front. Swept by panic, the Army of the North fled the field.

Napoleon got away to Paris after Waterloo, and briefly tried to reform his forces to intercept the oncoming Allied army. But public support had vanished. Finding himself increasingly deserted on all sides, Napoleon abdicated his throne on June 22 and fled to the coast. After he surrendered himself to Admiral Sir Henry Hotham, commanding the British naval blockade at Rochefort, the British transported him to permanent exile on the island of St. Helena in the South Atlantic, where he died six years later, in May 1821. The Allies restored Louis XVIII to his throne, imposed a new, harsher peace treaty on France, and kept occupation forces in France for five years. All that the Reign of the Hundred Days and the Waterloo campaign accomplished was to add 50,000 more casualties to the list of two million since 1792.

2

The Nineteenth Century, 1815–71

I. Armies

A. The Long Peace and Military Thought. No wars occurred among the major European powers for almost forty years after Waterloo. Before 1850, the armed violence of the period was mostly internal and associated with liberal revolts or with the early social effects of the Industrial Revolution. The great powers usually settled their differences peacefully through the "Congress System" adopted at the Congress of Vienna. In the 1820s Russia, Austria, and France concerted their efforts to crush insurgencies in Spain and Italy, and Britain made common cause with Russia and France in order to aid the Greek fight for independence from the Turkish Empire. An international fleet under a British admiral fought the last great action under sail when it destroyed an Egyptian fleet off the Greek coast at Navarino in October 1827.

In 1830 a middle-class revolt toppled Charles X, the last Bourbon to rule France, and replaced him with King Louis Philippe of the Orleans dynasty. Although Louis Philippe was a liberal monarch, the conservative governments of Europe accepted the legitimacy of the "July Monarchy." On the other hand, Belgium's secession from the Kingdom of the Netherlands in 1830 almost set off an international war. British diplomacy and a show of force finally secured international recognition of Belgian independence. In 1839 Britain, France, and Prussia signed a treaty to observe Belgium's independence and neutrality, a pact that remained unbroken until the outbreak of World War I in 1914. The Revolutions of 1848 affected all the major powers except Britain and Russia, but were finally unsuccessful except in France where the July Monarchy was replaced by a Second Republic under Louis Napoleon Bonaparte, a nephew of Napoleon I. Tsar Nicholas I was ready to honor the terms of the Quadruple Alliance, signed in November 1815, to wage war in order to prevent any

Bonaparte from holding the French throne, but again British diplomacy maintained the peace when the Second Republic pledged to respect the frontiers set in 1815. In December 1851 Louis Napoleon overthrew the republic with the help of the army, and in December 1852 proclaimed himself Napoleon III, Emperor of the French. The Second Empire lasted until 1870 and Napoleon III's defeat in the Franco-Prussian War.

In regard to military organization, the continental European powers with the exception of Prussia returned to the *armée de métier,* the long-service, professional army, after 1815. Most of these armies were somewhat like those of the pre-1789 era, though more national in character. The officer corps were less exclusively aristocratic, especially in the French army, though in most armies the old nobility tended to dominate the upper ranks. Enlisted men were more commonly recruited from within a country's boundaries than before 1789, and foreign soldiers were usually confined to special units, such as the French Foreign Legion, founded in 1831 for service in Algeria. Conscription was usually handled in such a way that a member of the better-off classes could escape personal military service by either providing a substitute or paying a special "blood tax" that entitled him to exemption. In practice, the main burden of enlisted service fell on the peasant class in the countryside and the working class in the cities. In Russia, where serfdom was not abolished until 1861, peasants could be summoned to the colors for life. In the French and Austrian armies, conscripts and volunteers alike faced a term of service of seven to twelve years.

With 880,000 troops by the middle of the nineteenth century, the Tsar's army was numerically the largest in Europe, but it was also the poorest in quality. The Austrian army's 500,000 troops was also impressive in numbers, but it was beset by ethnic divisions and underfunded. The smaller French army, with 350,000 troops in metropolitan France, was considered qualitatively the best of the European professional armies. Britain was the only major power in these years to rely entirely on volunteers to man its army, the men signing up for twenty-year hitches and serving most of them in overseas posts. Until 1854, the British royal army numbered about 140,000 men.

With the exception of Prussia, the military states of Europe looked to France as the model for military thought until 1870, a reflection of the prestige that the Imperial Army had gained under Napoleon I, which survived even defeat in 1815. In turn, the French army after 1815 was dominated by a school of ideas associated with the writings of General Antoine, Baron de Jomini (1779–1869). Jomini had the distinction of having served as a general officer under both Napoleon I and Tsar Alexander I, having switched sides in 1813, and being Swiss into the bargain. His most influential book on the theory of war was the *Précis de l'Art de la Guerre*

(*Summary of the Art of War*), published in 1836. The *Précis* became a model for European military textbooks, and was widely used for the teaching of military theory in the plethora of military academies which sprouted up over the Western world between 1800 and 1850.

Jomini's approach was to concentrate on the conduct of military campaigns; he claimed that all the great commanders of history, including Napoleon, had been successful through observing certain unalterable principles. The essence of their success, according to Jomini, was their mastery of the lines-of-communication within a given theater of war in such a way that strategic, and then tactical, superiority was obtained. Jomini believed that the great art of war lay in seizing the communications of the enemy without exposing one's own, and that when that goal was accomplished the outcome of the resulting battle was practically decided. In so many words, Jomini was saying that superior strategy insures a decisive numerical and material advantage on the battlefield.

Because Jomini's approach to war was so geometrical, some critics have held that his real idol was not Napoleon but Frederick the Great. They accuse him of being too abstract and too willing to separate the conduct of a particular war from its unique technological, organizational, and sociopolitical underpinnings. On the other hand, practically all commentators have given Jomini credit for distinguishing more clearly than any previous military writer among the factors of strategy, tactics, and logistics, and their relevant roles in the systematic waging of military campaigns. Jomini's influence is still found in the very term "military science" and the emphasis on the teaching of "military principles" in contemporary military colleges. In Jomini's time, of course, such an abstract approach had great appeal in politically conservative countries, which had no reason to celebrate the idea of revolutionary warfare. Nevertheless, it must be admitted that Jomini's influence also served to fix the student's attention on the permanent operating factors of war and not on the element of change which might affect them. This was particularly unfortunate in the rapidly changing circumstances of the mid-nineteenth century.

The other principal military writer of the first half of the nineteenth century was Carl von Clausewitz (1780–1831). Outside Prussia, the impact of his ideas was not really felt until after 1871. Clausewitz served as a junior officer in the disastrous Jena-Auerstädt campaign of 1806, was briefly a prisoner of war, and in 1807 was appointed secretary of the Prussian Military Reform Commission. He lectured at the prototype Prussian war college after it was founded in 1810. When Prussia was dragooned into supporting Napoleon's invasion of Russia in 1812, Clausewitz offered his services to the Tsar. Between 1813 and 1814 he served as a liaison officer between the Prussian and Russian armies. In 1815, having risen to the rank of brigadier general, he served as chief-of-staff of the Prussian corps that fought Marshal Grouchy's forces to a draw at Wavre during the Waterloo campaign. Until a short time before his death from cholera, he spent the final years of his career as head of the Prussian War College, writing in his spare time a philosophical treatise that was published posthumously in 1832 under the title *Vom Kriege* (*On War*). His fame as a military theorist is chiefly based on that work.

In *Vom Kriege*, Clausewitz treats war as a political act distinguished from other political acts by the violence of its means. In theory, war is violence unrestrained; in real life, all sorts of conventions and considerations prevent war from being in practice what it is in theory. Still, with the coming of the Wars of the French Revolution and Napoleon, Clausewitz believed that war in practice had approached that in theory, and what had caused the great change was the eventual involvement of whole peoples, emotionally as well as physically. Such national passions were aroused, Clausewitz believed, that hostile populations not only supported, but also demanded, the goal of total victory. He also believed that in the wake of the "people's wars" of the early nineteenth century it would be harder to restrain the degree of violence employed in future, especially when the issues in any particular war caught the popular imagination. Accordingly, Clausewitz believed that Prussia, and by implication every great power, must prepare in time of peace for a total effort in time of war. He wrote that the "bloody solution" is the "first-born son of war," and that even limited wars may escalate unexpectedly to full-blown struggles. He argued, therefore, that the state must not be left to defend itself with a "dress rapier" if the enemy takes up a "sharp sword."

Unlike Jomini, Clausewitz had little use for universal rules for the waging of war. In his view, every war had its own set of rules or patterns resulting from its political causes, the technology then in use, and, of course, the degree to which it involved the public. In addition, the waging of war could not be separated from the factors of luck and circumstance, and, when a general of Napoleon's stature appeared, even from the influence of genius. While Clausewitz believed that a familiarity with the history of war was essential for the student-soldier, for guides to action in any particular war he preferred empirical observation and common sense. Insofar as land warfare was concerned, he argued that the three great objectives always boiled down to destroying the enemy's armed forces, invading the most vital parts of its territory, and finally breaking its will to resist. Since these goals could be achieved only by combat, or the threat of combat, war remained in essence a phenomenon of violence.

The influence of *Vom Kriege* on military thought is not easy to measure precisely. In the Prussian army, it was studied even before 1871, and, in general, Prussia's waging of the wars of German unification (1864–71) conformed to the Clausewitzian prescription. Certainly, Helmuth von

General Carl von Clausewitz

SOURCE: Walter Goerlitz, *History of the German General Staff, 1657–1945*, trans. Brian Battershaw (New York and London: Praeger, 1953).

Moltke the Elder, Chief of the Prussian General Staff and the great architect of Prussia's victories in those years, shared Clausewitzian views. In other armies, and down to the eve of World War I, Clausewitz's book was usually read in translation and often with an incomplete understanding of its admittedly difficult and sometimes metaphysical language. For the most part, and whether Clausewitz ever intended to have such an effect or not, such reading of *Vom Kriege* promoted a faith that in war moderation was imbecility and maximum violence was the surest road to victory.

    B. The Technological Revolution in Land Warfare.   The revolutionary changes in warfare associated with the French Revolution and Napoleon were mostly sociopolitical and organizational in nature; the changes in technology were secondary. After 1815 and especially beginning about the middle of the nineteenth century, the reverse was true. Changing military technology reflected the facets of the early Industrial Revolution, especially the impact of steam power, mass production through the factory system, and discoveries in metallurgy, chemistry, and physics. The first products of the Industrial Revolution to affect war on land were: (1) the steam railroad; (2) the electric telegraph; and (3) the mass-produced, rifled musket. The first two developments had their greatest impact on strategy; the last had its greatest impact on tactics.

    The steam locomotive marked the greatest revolution in land transportation since the invention of the wheel. As railways were rapidly built across Europe in the 1830s and '40s, military men gradually came to appreciate their military potential. The railroad could move troops and supplies fifteen times as fast as their marching speed, conserving the energies of men and animals at the same time. On the other hand, beyond the railhead, soldiers still marched and draft animals still drew supply wagons. By the mid-nineteenth century military logistics had become an amalgam of new and old technologies. The railhead replaced the fortress-magazine as the collection point for supplies, and local forage remained important to armies beyond a certain distance from the railhead. Railroads in enemy territory had to be repaired and protected as invading armies advanced, and the logistical "trail" tended to increase as communications had to be maintained with the nearest railhead. Thus the layout of the rail systems in a particular country began to assume the role of the "bones" of strategy. Similarly, the electric telegraph permitted instantaneous transmission of messages hundreds of miles between headquarters, yet on the battlefield itself soldiers signaled primarily with traditional drums, bugles, and flags.

    The greatest impact on tactics came about when French Captain Claude Minié perfected the expandable, cylindro-conoidal shaped bullet (the so-called Minié ball) in 1848. This development made the loading of rifled muskets as quick as that of smoothbores. With the addition of percussion-cap ignition (perfected by Joshua Shaw, an American, utilizing fulminate of mercury) to replace the flintlock, the resulting "cap-and-ball rifle" had an accurate range up to five times as far as the smoothbore and reduced misfires to almost none. The new weapon transferred the tactical advantage to the side on defense, which, if troops were wise enough to protect themselves with earthworks, could, with relative impunity, pour a withering fire at a long distance into the traditional mass formations used in the attack. Thus, as a result of a fairly simple set of inventions, rifle fire accounted for about ninety percent of the casualties suffered on American Civil War battlefields. But even more lethal rifles had appeared by 1865, near the end of the war, when a sixth of the Union soldiers had been reequipped with single-shot, breech-loading rifles, and smaller numbers with magazine "repeating" rifles.

The development of field artillery generally lagged behind progress in small arms until after 1871. Half the cannon in American Civil War armies were muzzle-loading smoothbores, and most of the rifled guns still had to be loaded at the muzzle. Rifled shells carried further than spherical-shaped shells from smoothbores, but they lacked reliable fuses and high explosive. Alfred Nobel tamed nitroglycerin with sawdust in 1867, turning it into dynamite, but even dynamite was too sensitive to be employed in standard artillery shells. In the Civil War, if guns were advanced close enough to enemy lines to use canister *à la Napoleon,* their crews were likely to be mowed down by rifle fire. If the guns remained beyond the range of rifle fire, they were not effective supporting weapons for attacking troops. For a time, effective field artillery fire was restricted largely to the defensive. Only the Prussian army really mastered the technique of combining an offensive strategy with defensive tactics, the success of their famed Krupp steel, breech-loading field guns being as much due to better Prussian tactics as to the technical qualities of the guns themselves. On the other hand, by 1861 rifled siege guns had put an end to the relative invulnerability of traditional masonry forts.

The Prussian army aside, military men of the mid-nineteenth century tended to cling to Napoleonic tactical methods long after they were outmoded by developments in rifled arms. This "cultural lag" was due in part to the rapidity with which the wars of the mid-century came in succession, giving even reflective soldiers little time to assess their lessons, and to the fact that no other army of the time had the equivalent of the Prussian War College and General Staff, organizations well suited for the study and rapid application of the lessons learned from experience. Except for the Crimean War and the American Civil War, the conflicts of the mid-century were relatively brief. In the Civil War, the Americans had to learn the lessons of the new warfare the hard way through a four-year ordeal, their armies paying a dreadful price in blood and suffering for the education of their generals. In contrast, Prussia's victories were engineered with a remarkable economy of life, and none of the wars of German unification lasted as long as a year.

C. *The Prussian General Staff, the* Nation-in-Arms, *and the* Kesselschlacht *Doctrine.*   Scharnhorst and his disciples laid the foundations of the modern Prussian general staff system as early as the Napoleonic Wars, and the Prussian General Staff assumed responsibility for developing army doctrine and preparing contingency war plans. It did not, however, have direct control over operations in the field until after the middle of the nineteenth century. The extension of its authority was coeval with the rising influence of Helmuth von Moltke the Elder, Chief of the General Staff from 1857 to 1888. Under his leadership, the General Staff's authority began to widen in 1864 when King William I was impressed with Moltke's advice during the Danish War. On the eve of the Austro-Prussian War in 1866, the king empowered Moltke to issue orders directly to field commanders in the royal name. The successes of the Prussian army in the 1866 war, and again in the Franco-Prussian War of 1870–71, confirmed the supremacy of the General Staff in control of field operations. After the founding of the Kaiserheer (the Imperial German Army) in 1871, the Prussian General Staff widened its responsibilities to include all the land forces of the Second Reich.

The excellence of the Prussian General Staff has been traced to three factors: (1) its members were the best products of the Kriegsakademie (War College), an institution the like of which was found nowhere else in Europe until after 1871; (2) the General Staff officer periodically rotated between duties at general headquarters and service with the headquarters of field armies, corps, and divisions, and thus avoided isolation from the rest of the army; and (3) the separation of duties between the Ministry of War and the General Staff allowed the latter to avoid routine military administration and to concentrate on its missions of revising doctrine and disseminating it, making contingency war plans, and preparing its officers to execute those plans in time of war. The general staffs of other powers before 1871 were deficient in one or more of these factors.

A Prussian officer could take a qualifying examination for entry to the War College beginning with his tenth year of commissioned service, usually when he was a captain or major. No more than 150 officers a year were admitted, and each officer faced a rigorous three-year curriculum which dealt with all aspects of military operations on the levels of the division, the army corps, and the field army. The most promising students at the end of the three years were taken on an annual staff ride under the supervision of the Chief of the General Staff, and, at the ride's conclusion, the Chief chose three or four students for probationary service on the Gen-

Count Helmuth von Moltke, the Elder

SOURCE: Walter Goerlitz, *History of the German General Staff, 1657–1945,* trans. Brian Battershaw (New York and London: Praeger, 1953).

eral Staff. The rest of the War College graduates returned to line duties. Once the probationers donned the distinctive wine-red striped trousers of the General Staff officer, they rotated periodically among the sections of the Great General Staff until they were considered fully qualified. Thereafter, they rotated between general headquarters and the staffs of commanders of divisions, corps, and field armies. The chiefs-of-staff of field commanders bore the same relation to them as the Chief of the General Staff bore to the Prussian king, constitutionally the army's commander-in-chief. Accordingly, their advice was highly valued and bore the authority of the Chief of the General Staff himself. They also served to insure dissemination of changes of doctrine and adherence to war plans. By tradition, General Staff officers maintained a relative anonymity, yet their status and authority within the army was enormous.

The Prussian general staff organization was complemented by the *Nation-in-Arms,* an army organization unique to Prussia until after 1871. After 1815 Prussia retained its practice, developed during the Napoleonic Wars, of using short-service conscripts, reservists, and Landwehr (the national militia) as major parts of the army, the process beginning in 1818. General Leopold von Boyen, then Minister of War and another of Scharnhorst's disciples, secured the king's assent to imposing a liability of three years of compulsory military service on all able-bodied males when they reached age twenty. After the conscripts completed their period of active service, they were required to serve in an army reserve for a further two years, then pass to the Landwehr for varying periods of service according to branch. Sons of the middle class could escape standard enlisted service by volunteering for a year's active duty as officer-candidates, to be followed by direct commissioning in the Landwehr. In the event of war, regiments of the active army, the army reserve, and the Landwehr were to be brigaded together as they had been in the 1813–14 War of Liberation. The peacetime strength of the army was set at 125,000 troops, a number that could swiftly be doubled with the mobilization of the army reserve and the Landwehr. In 1834 compulsory active duty in the army was reduced to two years.

In the 1850s General Albrecht von Roon, by then the Minister of War, reformed the Boyen System at the behest of King William I. Compulsory service had not been strictly enforced in the previous two decades, and the strength of the army no longer corresponded to the growing Prussian population. Roon raised the annual number of conscripts from 40,000 men to 63,000 men, increased compulsory service to three years in the active army and four years in the army reserve, and reduced the status of the Landwehr to that of a second-line reserve of older men. Liberals in the Landtag, Prussia's parliament, opposed these changes because they decreased middle-class influence in the army, increased the importance of the professional and mostly aristocratic regular officer corps, and cost more money. When the Liberal majority in the Landtag blocked further appropriations for army reform, William I appointed Otto von Bismarck, a Junker and a career diplomat, to assume the duties of prime minister in September 1862. Bismarck broke the impasse by claiming that the Constitution of 1850 allowed the government to continue to collect taxes under the old budget whenever the monarch and the Landtag could not agree on a new one. The Liberals railed at Bismarck's parliamentary maneuvers, but the Prussian military victories in 1864 and 1866 made the army so popular that the Landtag saw fit to approve Bismarck's budget manipulations retroactively and to grant the army still more monies. By 1870 Prussia could mobilize half a million troops in two weeks, half of them reservists.

Prussia's heavy reliance on trained civilian reserves made a swift and efficient mobilization system vital to its military success, and Moltke gave much attention to this problem. All contingency war plans had an accompanying set of railroad timetables, and by sending out a single coded order by telegraph from the headquarters of the General Staff at Berlin, he could put into motion a highly complex process with speed and precision across all Prussia. Because every unit knew its assigned role according to the contingency plan indicated, even without knowing the details of the plan as a whole, it could assemble at the designated rail station and be ready for rapid movement to any of Prussia's frontiers. The Prussian railroad authorities worked closely with the Railroad Section of the General Staff, and within hours of the notification of mobilization thousands of troops and animals, together with their arms and equipment, could be poured by rail toward the frontier indicated. When the forces arrived at the railheads, they were fully organized field armies ready for action. Before 1871 no other country in Europe had such carefully developed plans for mobilization, not to mention large numbers of reserves to mobilize. Until it was too late, European advocates of the *armée de métier* failed to realize that the Prussians had managed to combine in their *Nation-in-Arms* large numbers, speed, and quality of performance.

Characteristically, Moltke gave as much attention to the details of strategic and tactical doctrine as he did to those of organization and mobilization. His first experience with the new power of defensive fire came at the Battle of Düppel in 1864, where Prussian troops suffered heavily in their attacks. He quickly surmised from that experience that, in the face of modern firepower, the day of massed frontal attack was over. After the Danish war, Prussian doctrine was revised to emphasize the avoidance of frontal attacks and, where possible, the turning of the enemy's flanks instead. The revised doctrine was employed with qualified success against Austria in 1866, and the experience brought about further changes in Prussian methods. The changes culminated in the doctrine of the *Kes-*

selschlacht, the planned battle of encirclement and annihilation, adopted in 1867. The new doctrine called for strategic maneuvers aimed at encircling large enemy forces, then assuming the tactical defensive in order to allow firepower to destroy the enemy as it strove to break out of the ring. The new doctrine had its greatest success under Moltke at the Battle of Sedan in September 1870, where an entire French army was trapped, its efforts to escape repelled by fire and terrible losses, and its remains finally compelled to surrender. After Sedan, the doctrine of the *Kesselschlacht* had a special place in German military thought, one that lasted even into the era of the Second World War.

II. Navies

Ships being machines, navies even more than armies were technologically transformed between 1815 and 1871. The steam engine began the revolution by gradually replacing sail as the primary means of propulsion, although the process was retarded by the vulnerability of the paddle wheel to enemy fire and the inefficient fuel consumption of the early steam engines. Better engines eventually appeared, and the screw propeller located underwater at the stern of the ship solved the vulnerability problem. The first screw-propelled warship was the USS *Princeton* (1842), designed by the Swedish-American inventor John Ericsson. Ocean-going ships still required sails as late as the American Civil War because of range factors; still, steam power freed the warship to maneuver in battle independently of the wind and to move more safely in and out of port. On balance then, steam improved warships in a tactical sense but robbed them of their former unlimited range-in-space.

On the whole, the effect of steam on commercial naval blockade favored the blockade-runner. During the American Civil War, the Union navy discovered that it took three times as many steam-and-sail vessels to maintain the same blockade as in the age of pure sailing ships because vessels dependent in part on steam had to go back and forth to refueling bases to stock up on coal or wood. Moreover, if the blockade-runner was steam-propelled, its speed was comparable to that of blockading ships, and it was less reliant on the tide than pure sailing ships when trying to get in or out of port.

By the mid-nineteenth century the science of naval gun-making had improved tremendously over that of Nelson's day. Guns with bores as large as 15 inches, weighing forty tons, and firing projectiles that weighed hundreds of pounds, became practical. As the guns and their projectiles grew in size, their lethality was further increased through the use of exploding shells with contact-fuses, harnessing fulminate of mercury for detonators. As individual guns became more destructive, the tendency was to mount fewer but larger guns on warships, a practice that gradually abolished the old distinction between ships-of-the-line and ships-below-the-line, based on the number of guns carried. Around 1870 the most powerfully gunned ships began to be called "battleships."

The new shell guns proved devastating to unprotected wooden hulls in warships. At the Battle of Sinope (1853) on the Black Sea, a Russian fleet, at almost no cost to itself, utterly demolished seven wooden Turkish frigates with shell fire, and in the process killed or wounded 3,000 Turkish sailors. A partial answer to exploding shell was armor protection, but no armored warships (as opposed to armored floating batteries) appeared in time for the Crimean War (1854–56). In 1859 France launched *La Gloire*, the first warship with a wooden hull protected with iron plates, which qualifies as the first true "iron-clad." The plates were 4 1/2 inches thick and proof against existing shell guns. A steam-and-sail hybrid, *La Gloire* was ocean-going and displaced 5,000 tons. In 1860 Britain went France one better when it launched HMS *Warrior*. It had an iron frame, an iron hull, and armor plate over the hull. *Warrior* displaced 9,000 tons, almost as much as a World War II heavy cruiser.

USS *Monitor* and CSS *Virginia* (*née* USS *Merrimac*) of American Civil War fame appeared two years later. The first American armored ships, they were entirely steam propelled, but both had very low freeboards (i.e., the main deck was little more than two feet above the water-line) and very shallow drafts in order for them to operate in rivers and harbors; neither was designed to operate on the high seas. Their engagement at Hampton Roads, just inside Chesapeake Bay, in March 1862, was the first combat between armored vessels in modern times. The *Virginia*, a former Union frigate converted by the Confederates into a harbor-defense vessel, had guns as large as 9-inch in an armored casemate made from converted railroad iron, while the *Monitor*, designed by John Ericsson, was new from the keel up and featured the first revolving armored gun turret. The turret housed two 11-inch guns. *Monitor* and *Virginia* had so much trouble penetrating each other's armor with their guns, even at close range, that *Virginia* resorted to ramming. The more agile *Monitor* avoided serious damage from collision, and the leaking *Virginia* retreated to its base. It was later blown up by the Confederates to keep it from falling into Union hands. During the Civil War, the Confederacy converted, or began work on, fifteen iron-clads, though not all were ever operational. The Union navy commissioned seventy-four iron-clads of various types before the war was over.

But armor, exploding shell, and the large naval gun did not have uncontested sway in the wars of the mid-nineteenth century. They were challenged by the torpedo, both the stationary type and the mobile type. The

La Gloire, 1859, the first iron-clad warship.
Source: Peter Padfield, *The Battleship Era* (New York: David McKay, 1972).

HMS *Black Prince*, c. 1862, similar to HMS *Warrior*, the British
iron-clad riposte to *La Gloire*.
Source: Peter Padfield, *The Battleship Era* (New York: David McKay, 1972).

HMS *Inflexible*, 1881, the last of a type of sail and steam battleship.
SOURCE: Peter Padfield, *The Battleship Era* (New York: David McKay, 1972).

HMS *Devastation*, 1871, the first ocean-going battleship propelled
entirely by steam engines.

stationary torpedo (or mine, as it was later called) had its greatest effect in the defense of harbors and coastal waters. Fuses utilizing fulminate of mercury made the contact mine practical, while the invention of the wet-cell electric storage battery led to the command mine which could be set off from shore by an observer. Even the crude Confederate "keg mine" (a converted wooden barrel) could be dangerous when a ship brushed its detonators. The Confederates pioneered the mobile torpedo as an explosive device carried on the end of a spar and designed to be rammed below the water-line of an enemy ship; it was used by a class of semi-submersibles called "Davids," and by CSS *Hunley,* a true submersible or submarine, which sank USS *Housatonic* while on blockade duty off Charleston, S.C., in 1864. Propelled by a hand-crank attached to a propeller, *Hunley* had drowned both its inventor and several crews in tests before its last sortie, one from which it never returned.

While working for the Austrian navy, Robert Whitehead, an Englishman, invented the first self-propelled, underwater-missile torpedo in 1870. Originally launched from shore, the Whitehead torpedo had a maximum speed of eighteen knots and a range of four hundred yards. Compressed air turned its screw, and its "soft launch" allowed a warhead of dynamite. An ingenious depth-regulator prevented it from plunging or broaching during its run. But the story of the automotive or "fish type" torpedo really belongs to the period after 1871.

The future of *guerre de course* (commerce-raiding) was obscured by the end of the mid-nineteenth century wars. The international Declaration of Paris, made at 1856 at the conference which ended the Crimean War, outlawed the old practice of privateering, for which reason it was not much used by the Confederate States during the Civil War. In addition, even state-owned, steam-propelled commerce-raiders were more tied to their bases and restricted in range than raiders in the sailing age. Still, a dozen Confederate steam-and-sail raiders inflicted considerable damage to the Union merchant fleet during the Civil War, forcing the transfer of many merchant ships to foreign flags. The exploits of these raiders so impressed the British government that it sought to discourage the building of such ships by neutral governments by accepting financial responsibility for the damage done by CSS *Alabama,* a raider built in a British yard and sold to the Confederacy.

III. The Mid-Nineteenth Century Wars before 1861

The effects of the Industrial Revolution were little felt in the mid-nineteenth century wars before 1861. The Mexican War (1846–48) came too early and was fought in an undeveloped region of North America. The

Crimean War (1854–56), the first great war of the period, was also fought in a remote and undeveloped region, and was only slightly affected by the Industrial Revolution. The Great Sepoy Mutiny (1857) in India was important, but mostly for the organizational changes it prompted in the British army. The Franco-Austrian War of 1859, the first war involving the issue of Italian unification, was also the first in which the infantry on both sides were fully equipped with the cap-and-ball rifle and, on the French side, the first in which large numbers of troops were moved by rail during wartime. But the war lasted only four months and involved only two major battles, and the rest of the wars of Italian unification to their close in 1861 had little to teach about the newly emerging patterns of war. Nevertheless, brief examinations of the wars before 1861 provide useful background for understanding the American Civil War (1861–65) and the wars of German unification (1864–71), conflicts in which the new patterns are clearly seen.

The republic of Texas, mostly populated by American settlers, won *de facto* independence from Mexico after a war in 1836, but Mexico never formally recognized Texan independence or the Rio Grande as the boundary of Texas with Mexico. When Texas was granted statehood in 1845 and the United States subsequently claimed the Rio Grande as its boundary with Mexico, war clouds began to gather. Both countries sent troops into the disputed territory just north of the Rio Grande in the spring of 1846, and armed clashes occurred at Palo Alto and Resaca de la Palma in May. These small battles turned out favorably for the Americans, and the Mexican forces were driven south of the Rio Grande.

Upon receiving the news of the fighting just north of the Rio Grande, and at the prompting of President James Knox Polk, the U.S. Congress declared a state of war with Mexico and approved the raising of state volunteer regiments to supplement the regular army of 8,500 troops. The regular Mexican army numbered about 20,000 troops, hence initially outnumbered the American forces, but the United States had a population of 20 million to Mexico's population of 7 million, and was a much more developed country into the bargain.

In the aftermath of the American victories north of the Rio Grande, 4,000 American regular troops commanded by General Zachary Taylor invaded northern Mexico. The arid, desertlike nature of the country created more problems for the American advance than did Mexican resistance, and by the time Taylor's army captured Monterrey in September, his force was only two hundred miles south of its starting point. Early in 1847 Taylor and 5,000 American troops finally got as far south as Buena Vista, where, in the biggest battle of the war, they were attacked by a Mexican army of 15,000 troops under General Antonio Lopez Santa Anna. The Americans fended off the Mexican attacks and claimed a victory, but Taylor's army penetrated no further into Mexico. Except for

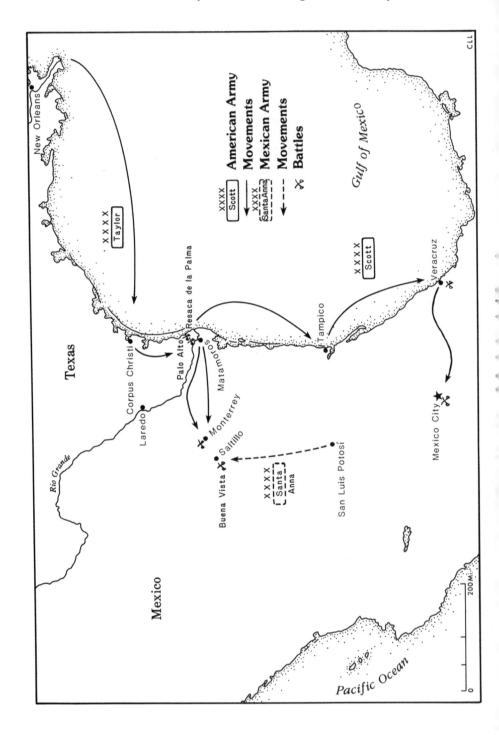

sending troops to Tampico on the coast, it spent the rest of the war screening the border at the Rio Grande.

Meanwhile, another American army of 14,000 troops was assembling at New Orleans under the command of General Winfield Scott. In the absence of a Mexican navy (unless two small converted steamers are counted), the small U.S. Navy had uncontested command of the sea. In March 1847 Scott's army was landed just south of Vera Cruz on the Gulf of Mexico, the first large amphibious assault in the history of the armed forces of the United States. After capturing Vera Cruz, Scott made a daring march toward Mexico City, about two hundred miles away. Halfway to his objective, and after surmounting several Mexican attempts to halt the progress of his army, Scott was stymied when the enlistments of his volunteers ran out and half of his army returned to the coast for repatriation. Scott was forced to drop his communications to Vera Cruz, and his remaining troops lingered between the coast and Mexico City until replacements increased their strength to 10,000 men. With these troops, Scott finally assaulted the approaches to Mexico City and captured it in September.

The Mexican government came to terms with the United States in February 1848 when it signed the Peace of Guadaloupe Hidalgo. The treaty recognized the Rio Grande as the southern boundary of the state of Texas, and, for a sum of $15 million, ceded territories that later became all or part of the states of California, Arizona, New Mexico, Utah, and Nevada. This land-grab cost the lives of 14,000 Americans in uniform, but only 2,000 of them died as the result of wounds received in battle. Disease, exposure, and capital punishment for war atrocities and desertion accounted for the rest. Another 16,000 Americans survived wounds or illness. Mexican losses are uncertain, but probably exceeded the number of American casualties.

The Mexican War was a limited war on both sides; for the United States because it had no need for more than a limited effort to attain its goals, and for Mexico because of governmental incapacity and a lack of resources. Both Taylor and Scott conducted their campaigns more with an eye to occupying places than destroying the Mexican army. (Partisan resistance on the part of the Mexicans was minor in contrast to the guerrilla war mounted against an invading French army of 35,000 troops in the 1860s, one that finally toppled the French-sponsored government of the Archduke Maximilian, and which, along with threats of U.S. intervention, finally led to the withdrawal of the French from Mexico.) The Mexican War demonstrated that Scott was perhaps the ablest American general between the American Revolution and the American Civil War. He remained the commanding general of the U.S. Army until November 1861, when the American Civil War was already underway. Taylor, whom the victories at Palo Alto, Resaca de la Palma, and Buena Vista had made famous, went on to the White House.

The Crimean War was a much larger affair than the Mexican War, and was also the only major amphibious war in Europe of the mid-nineteenth century. Its origins lay in a quarrel between Tsar Nicholas I of Russia and the Sultan of the Turkish Empire as to the administration of the Christian holy places in Palestine. When the Tsar demanded the right to protect Orthodox Christians throughout the Sultan's empire and was refused, he ordered Russian troops to invade the Turkish European provinces of Moldavia and Wallachia (parts of which constitute much of modern Rumania) and Turkish territory in the Caucasus. Turkey retaliated with a declaration of war on Russia. In November 1853 the Russian Black Sea fleet engaged and destroyed the Turkish fleet off Sinope. The governments of Napoleon III and Queen Victoria protested the Russian actions, and, after fruitless negotiations, both France and Britain declared war on Russia in March 1854. When Anglo-French fleets entered the Black Sea, the Russian fleet declined battle and retreated to the shelter of its base at the fortress-city of Sevastopol in the Crimean peninsula. Allied troops landed at Varna (now in Bulgaria) in order to assist the Turks in expelling the Russians from Moldavia and Wallachia, but in the summer of 1854 the Tsar ordered his troops to withdraw to the Russian frontier without a battle. Instead of leaving well enough alone, the Allied governments decided to teach the Tsar a lesson by launching forces into the Crimea and seizing Sevastopol. That decision led unexpectedly to a long and costly war for both sides.

Well over a year after the Tsar had first sent troops into Turkish territory, an Allied expeditionary force of 54,000 troops, about half British and half French, landed on beaches near Eupatoria, north of Sevastopol, in September 1854. Lord Raglan, the British commander-in-chief, was an amiable but bumbling soldier who had last seen action at Waterloo, almost forty years earlier. Devoted to the memory of the Duke of Wellington, who had died in 1852, he seems to have had no ideas of his own. French Marshal Armand Saint-Arnaud had made a reputation fighting natives in Algeria, but he was riddled with cancer and died ten days after the campaign began. Marshal François Canrobert, his successor, was competent but unenthusiastic about the enterprise.

The Allied advance southward toward Sevastopol soon encountered a Russian army, about as large as the Allied army, under General Prince Menshikov on heights above the river Alma. In a battle on September 20, the French bungled a turning movement, while the British engaged the Russians frontally after a clumsy river crossing. Fortunately for the Allies, Russian generalship was even worse than the Allied, and, after heavy casualties on both sides in the Battle of the Alma, the Russian army finally withdrew. The exhausted Allies were slow to pursue. While some 120,000

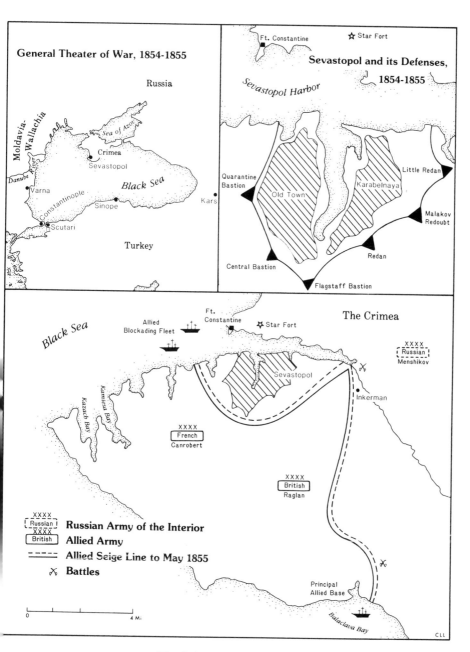

General Theater of War, 1854-1855

Russia

Moldavia-Wallachia

Sea of Azov

Crimea

Sevastopol

Danube River

Varna

Constantinople

Sinope

Scutari

Black Sea

Kars

Turkey

Sevastopol and its Defenses, 1854-1855

Ft. Constantine

★ Star Fort

Sevastopol Harbor

Quarantine Bastion

Old Town

Karabelnaya

Little Redan

Malakov Redoubt

Central Bastion

Redan

Flagstaff Bastion

The Crimea

Black Sea

Allied Blockading Fleet

Ft. Constantine

★ Star Fort

XXXX
Russian
Menshikov

Kazach Bay

Kamiesa Bay

Sevastopol

Inkerman

XXXX
French
Canrobert

XXXX
British
Raglan

XXXX
Russian   **Russian Army of the Interior**
XXXX
British   **Allied Army**
-----   **Allied Seige Line to May 1855**
✗   **Battles**

0   4 Mi

Principal Allied Base

Balaclava Bay

CLL

The Crimean War, 1854–56

Russian soldiers and sailors prepared to defend Sevastopol, the main Russian army withdrew into the interior of the Crimea.

After establishing a base at the Bay of Balaclava, twelve miles south of Sevastopol, the Allied armies began a siege of Sevastopol that lasted a year. The siege was far from watertight. The Allies lacked enough troops to invest Sevastopol completely on its land side, and not even Allied command of the sea prevented reinforcements and supplies from reaching the embattled garrison periodically. The Russians had taken guns from their ships inside the harbor to strengthen their land defenses before scuttling the vessels to block the harbor's mouth, and Colonel Franz Todleben, the chief Russian engineer, designed a formidable system of rifle pits to cover the intervals between redoubts. Though the Russian infantry were only partially armed with the cap-and-ball rifle, the pit-and-rifle combination proved highly effective on defense. Then there was the threat to the Allies from the Russian army in the interior of the Crimea.

That threat first materialized when the Allies nearly lost their base at Balaclava to its attack on October 25, 1854, when most of the Allied troops were in the siege lines around Sevastopol. The British troops defending Balaclava managed to fend off the Russian effort, despite the British blunder immortalized in the poem "Charge of the Light Brigade"—an assault by unsupported British cavalry as the result of a misunderstood order. On November 5, an attempt by the Russian garrison inside Sevastopol to break the Allied line at Inkerman miscarried after a bloody battle fought in darkness and mist. After Inkerman, both sides settled down to a war of attrition.

At the beginning of the winter siege, the Allied forces consisted of 40,000 French troops, 25,000 British troops, and 12,000 Turkish troops. That winter more men on both sides died from disease, bad food, and exposure than from bullets. The French came through best, but scarcely 11,000 British soldiers were fit for duty by the spring of 1855. In the meantime, Nicholas I had died in March, and was succeeded by Tsar Alexander II. After Allied reinforcements arrived, Raglan and Marshal Aimable Pélissier, the new French commander-in-chief, launched an assault on the defenses of Sevastopol in June, only to see it bloodily repulsed. Later that month a despondent Raglan died of dysentery. He was succeeded by General Colin Simpson, a competent if not outstanding soldier.

Over the summer of 1855 Allied strength in the Crimea was raised to 150,000 troops, Sevastopol was more tightly invested, and the muddled British supply and medical situation was improved. On September 8, the Allies launched another major assault, and though the Russians threw back the British attack, the French took the key Malakov Redoubt and beat back all Russian efforts to retake it. The fall of the redoubt doomed the defense of Sevastopol, but did not prevent General Gortschkov, the

Russian commander, from making a successful evacuation of his army to the north. Moreover, the final assault on Sevastopol had cost the Allies 23,000 casualties.

The war dragged on to March 1856, when Tsar Alexander II agreed to the terms of the Peace of Paris. Under the peace, Russia withdrew its claims on Turkey, restored Kars in the Caucasus to Turkish control, and was forbidden to maintain a naval base or a fleet on the Black Sea. The Danube River was internationalized. The Crimean War had finally involved Britain, France, Turkey, and the north Italian state of Piedmont on the Allied side, and over the war's duration the Allies had committed a total of 597,000 troops, of which 309,000 were French, 98,000 British, 165,000 Turkish, and 25,000 Piedmontese. Russia had committed 600,000 troops and would have sent more but for the lack of railroads to the Crimea, which made it difficult to supply even the men who were sent. About 440,000 Russians were casualties. The French and Turkish armies each lost 100,000 men, the British 25,000, and the Piedmontese 5,000. Four-fifths of these casualties were due to disease and exposure.

Essentially, the Crimean War was an old-fashioned struggle with some modern touches. Most Russian infantry were equipped with flint-lock, smoothbore muskets from beginning to end, though the relatively few Russian riflemen protected by earthworks proved highly effective on defense. Todleben's rifle pits foreshadowed the importance of hasty entrenchments in the American Civil War. William Howard Russell's dispatches to the London *Times* went by the Mediterranean submarine electric-cable; for the first time, newspaper readers remote from a theater of war could follow its events within days of their happening. Independent news reporting also proved more truthful than self-serving official dispatches. Russell's revelations about British supply and medical failures influenced Florence Nightingale, the proprietor of a nursing home, to organize female nurses for service in the British hospital at Scutari, where thousands of wretched lay wounded and ill. Nightingale and her nurses not only cut the death rate at Scutari dramatically through simple measures of hygiene and common sense, but their example prodded the British army medical corps to mend its ways. Nightingale's activities also foreshadowed the work of Clara Barton and the U.S. Sanitary Commission in the American Civil War.

Indirectly, the Crimean War contributed to the coming of the Great Sepoy Mutiny in India in 1857. Most of the British regulars in India at the beginning of the Crimean War were siphoned off to the Crimea and not many had returned to India when the revolt broke out. In consequence, there were only 23,000 European soldiers among the 151,000 troops in India at the start of the rebellion, most of them troops of the army of the East India Company. Historians still debate the precise reasons for the revolt, though they involved some mixture of Indian religious and national resentments. In any case, some sepoy regiments turned against their British officers, and whole areas of northern India passed out of British control for months on end. The worst of the revolt took place in the Company's Army of the Bengal, and most of the troops in the other two Company armies remained loyal. Nevertheless, it required the assistance of 40,000 European reinforcements before complete order was restored.

In the aftermath of the Great Mutiny, Parliament abolished both the East India Company and its army; henceforth India was a crown colony. The new Indian Army, a part of the royal army, was supposed to be divided equally between regiments of British regulars and native troops, and the British were to have exclusive control over such technical branches as the artillery. In practice, rather more Indian than British soldiers made up the army through the rest of the century and down to World War I. Its strength hovered around 200,000 troops, hardly too many to police and defend a subcontinent with a population of 250 million by 1914. Still, during World War I and during the interval between the world wars, no serious disloyalty appeared in the native regiments. In World War II, some Indian troops defected to the Japanese, but most served gallantly in the Allied cause, not only for the defense of India and Burma against the Japanese, but in other theaters of war such as North Africa as well. These old Indian regiments also served as the core of the new Indian Army after Britain granted India's independence in 1947.

The Crimean War and the Great Mutiny helped to open the way for British army reforms between 1868 and 1872 when Lord Cardwell was Secretary of State for War. The Cardwell Reforms reduced the regular enlistment from twenty years to twelve years, and allowed up to six of those years to be served in a new army reserve. By the 1880s two-thirds of the British soldiers on their first enlistments were under the shorter term. Cardwell also introduced the linked-battalion system, whereby a regiment kept one battalion in the British Isles as a recruiting and training unit for replacements for its other battalion overseas. In addition, the home battalion was assigned up to three battalions of militia for training, and from which it could draw volunteers in time of war. Cardwell also managed to get parliamentary abolition of the Purchase System in 1872, and thereafter most new regular officers were products of the royal military colleges at Sandhurst (infantry and cavalry) and Woolwich (artillery and engineering). Promotion was based on seniority and merit. Aside from still being entirely a voluntary organization, the remaining chief weaknesses of the British army after 1872 lay in the lack of an organized expeditionary force in the home islands for rapid deployment in overseas emergencies, and a continuing old-fashioned command and staff system.

The Franco-Austrian War of 1859 was the first of the wars which led to the unification of Italy. Count Camillo di Cavour, prime minister of Piedmont, had sought to curry favor with Napoleon III by bringing his country into the Crimean War on the side of France. After the war, he pressed for French support in expelling Austrian control from the Italian provinces of Lombardy and Venetia. Cavour's original aim was to unite northern Italy under King Victor Emmanuel of Piedmont's Savoy dynasty. When Piedmont provoked war with Austria in the spring of 1859, France promptly entered the conflict. Some 128,000 French troops were transported by rail to northern Italy. Once in Piedmont, they joined forces with the 35,000 Piedmontese troops against about 150,000 Austrians. Both sides were well armed with the cap-and-ball infantry rifle, but the French artillery was in advance of the Austrian by having muzzle-loading rifled cannon as well.

The battles of Magenta and Solferino were fought in June 1859, the first being a confused "meeting battle" that led to an Austrian retreat to the other side of Lombardy. The Battle of Solferino almost turned into a bloody stalemate until French artillery weakened the exposed Austrian line to the point where it could be penetrated by a bayonet charge. But French losses at Solferino were very heavy, and a third of the Piedmontese troops were killed or wounded in the fighting. After Prussia threatened to enter the war on the side of Austria, Napoleon III settled for a peace made hastily at Villafranca in July. Under its terms, Austria ceded Lombardy to Piedmont but retained Venetia.

Cavour was disappointed by the terms of the Peace of Villafranca that ended the War of 1859 (he had hoped that the war would expel Austrian power from Italy entirely). Soon after, several other northern Italian states joined Piedmont to form the Kingdom of Upper Italy, dominated by Piedmont. Giuseppe Garibaldi, the famous Italian patriot and guerrilla fighter, led a successful revolt in the south against the Kingdom of the Two Sicilies in 1860, and Piedmontese troops subsequently occupied most of the Papal states. By March 1861 Italy (save Rome under the Pope and Venetia under the Austrians) was effectively united in a kingdom under Victor Emmanuel of the Savoy dynasty.

The War of 1859 cost France 24,600 casualties, most of them suffered in just a month of fighting. On the field at Solferino the French medical corps was so swamped with casualties that some injured soldiers lay on the field for two days before they received attention. Jean Henri Dunant, a Swiss observer who visited the stricken field just after the battle, was so appalled by the sight that he returned to Switzerland and wrote *Un Souvenir de Solferino*. The widely read book shocked European sensibilities, and Dunant went on to help found the Red Cross organization and the Geneva Convention in 1864. The contemporary concern for the rights of wounded and ill combatants, prisoners of war, and noncombatants in war zones dates from that time.

IV. The American Civil War, 1861–65

A. The Opposing Sides.   In 1861 the eleven states of the Confederacy possessed a combined land area equal to that of Western Europe, but only 9 million people lived within that area and just 5.5 million of them were white. As a consequence, the Confederate "garrison" was really too small for the "fortress" it had to defend. The need for military manpower forced the Confederacy to adopt conscription in 1862, and the draft provided about a third of the 900,000 males who served in Confederate gray during the war. Still, the Confederacy never adopted such a sweeping impressment as the French *levée en masse* of 1793, and many Southerners secured exemptions on grounds that they were slave-overseers (plantations were allowed to exempt one overseer for every twenty slaves), newspaper editors, or school teachers. The draft law was tightened in 1864, but many men avoided it illegally. The Confederate forces reached a peak strength of about 600,000 men in 1863, but the number had shrunk to no more than about 150,000 men by April 1865. Perhaps 254,000 Confederates died in line of duty and another 100,000 survived wounds or illness.

The twenty-three states loyal to the Union had a combined population of 22 million people, and the Federal government did not feel the need to resort to conscription until 1863. Then the law permitted substitution or commutation, the latter a fee in lieu of personal military service. These practices promoted such class resentments in the North that the draft was widely evaded and even openly resisted. Draft riots in New York City in the summer of 1863 required 20,000 Federal troops to suppress, a number equal to the Union casualties in the Battle of Gettysburg. Although about two million men wore Union blue at one time or another during the war, only 42,000 of them were conscripts and 178,000 of them were substitutes. Since volunteering was overwhelmingly the main source of Union military manpower, less than a third of the North's abundant manpower was tapped for military service. About 370,000 Union soldiers died during the war, and some 230,000 survived wounds or illness. Counting the losses on both sides (954,000 casualties, of which 624,000 were dead), down to the present no other war has inflicted as many American casualties as the Civil War.

The Southern economy was dominated by a cash-crop agriculture, mainly cotton and tobacco, and, cut off from its natural trading partners in the North, the South had to depend on trade with Europe for most of its manufactured goods. What little heavy industry the South possessed was mostly concentrated at Richmond, Va., only a hundred miles from Washington, D.C., and the *de facto* frontier at the Potomac River. The Tredegar Iron Works and associated industries at Richmond constituted a "Confederate Ruhr," which, like the industrialized Ruhr Valley in Germany, lay almost on the border. Even if the Confederate capital had not been shifted from Montgomery, Ala., to Richmond after Virginia's secession in 1861, the city would have been defended at all costs because of its industrial importance. A lesser but significant area of manufacturing lay in the region around Nashville, Tenn., which, like Richmond, was relatively close to enemy territory.

The Confederacy did surprisingly well in arming its forces throughout the war. In 1861, 300,000 smoothbore muskets and rifled muskets were in the hands of the Southern militia, and 110,000 stands of arms were in Federal armories in the South. With machinery captured at Harpers Ferry, Md., at the beginning of the war, and moved to Richmond and Fayetteville, N.C., many of the smoothbores were converted to rifles. The Confederates captured 120,000 rifles on the battlefield; 400,000 more were imported from overseas. Three hundred heavy naval guns were captured along with the Norfolk navy yard in 1861, and over the course of the war the Tredegar Iron Works turned out 1,099 cannon, more than any single Union supplier in the North. Ammunition production, while not lavish, was adequate. In sum, the Confederacy was never fatally deficient in the numbers or quality of its armaments, though failures of transportation sometimes made it difficult to move them where needed. Even toward the end of the war, the Confederate army was running out of men more rapidly than it was running out of arms or ammunition.

The effect of the Union blockade on the outcome of the war is surprisingly hard to measure. By mid-1862, ten out of thirteen major Confederate ports with rail connections had been captured or effectively neutralized, and the naval blockade of the remaining three—Wilmington, N.C., Charleston, S.C., and Mobile, Ala.—should have been relatively easy. But a Confederate coastline of 3,549 miles offered many havens and inland waterways where certain types of craft could find temporary shelter until a favorable moment to enter port. During the war's course, about 300 steamers challenged the blockade in 1,300 attempts, of which over 1,000 (77%) were successful. Union blockaders captured 136 blockade-runners and destroyed 85 more, for a total of 221 (74%). On average, each blockade-runner survived two round-trips. But the blockade forced goods to be shipped on vessels chosen for speed and shallow draft over carrying capacity, and the average cargo delivered was about four hundred tons. Still, besides providing the Confederacy with 60 percent of its rifled shoulder-arms, the blockade-runners brought in a third of its lead for bullets, the ingredients for three-quarters of its gunpowder supply, nearly all the paper for its cartridges, and all of its cloth and most of its leather for its accouterments. Blockade-runners also brought in critically needed food supplies, especially meat.

Perhaps more important to the blockade's effectiveness on the South's ability to wage war were the Confederate government's mistakes: its failure to regulate cargoes on the blockade-runners until 1864 and the lack of effective government control of the Southern railroads. Until 1864, blockade-runners might bring into the Confederacy anything that suited the financial interests of their owners, however worthless to the war effort. And even the law imposed in 1864 required that only half the cargo had to have military or medical importance. In addition, the Confederate failure to regulate the railroads effectively, and their gradual breakdown from wear and tear as the war progressed, made it difficult to deliver war materials and food from ports to inland locations where they were needed. The classic example is Robert E. Lee's hungry, ragged troops in the trenches before Richmond during the winter of 1864–65. They received only a trickle of supplies, while, two hundred miles away, the warehouses of the port of Wilmington, N.C., were filled with supplies but with no good way to deliver them.

Of the 17,000 officers and men serving in the U.S. Army at the beginning of 1861, many of the officers, but few of the men, were Southerners. A third of the Army's 1,000 officers resigned their commissions in order to serve the Confederacy, but few of the men, many of whom were foreign-born, chose to go South. The difference in background may also explain why only a few of the 8,000 officers and men in the U.S. Navy and Marine Corps joined the Confederate forces.

The U.S. Navy had just 42 warships in April 1861, many of them small and some of them obsolete, but by converting civilian craft and accepting new vessels coming off the ways, it had increased the number of vessels in commission to 264 by December. At the end of the war, the Union navy could boast 671 vessels, manned by 50,000 sailors and marines, and mounting some 5,000 guns. The majority of the U.S. warships were designed to operate in Southern coastal waters and rivers, and the 74 iron-clads represented only a small part of the ships of the Union navy. In addition, few of the U.S. iron-clads were ocean-going at a time when Britain had 40, and France had 35, such ships. Much has been made of the fact that by 1865 the U.S. Navy was the largest in the world, but it was a very specialized navy.

  B. Tactics on Land.   The generals of the Civil War were, for the most part, products of the "Jominian school," and as such they tended to cling to traditional Napoleonic methods and assumptions through most

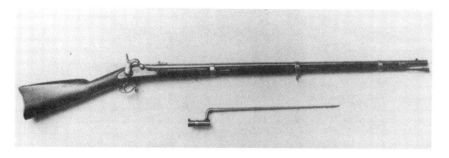

Rifled musket and bayonet, U.S. Civil War.
SOURCE: Bell I. Wiley and Hollis D. Milhollen, *They Who Fought Here* (New York: Bonanza, 1959).

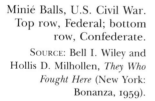

Minié Balls, U.S. Civil War. Top row, Federal; bottom row, Confederate.
SOURCE: Bell I. Wiley and Hollis D. Milhollen, *They Who Fought Here* (New York: Bonanza, 1959).

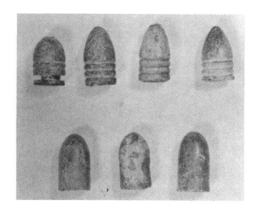

of the war. Almost none of them had foreseen the tactical implications of mass-produced rifled firearms, and most persisted far too long in committing regiments and brigades *en masse* in frontal assaults. A favorite assault formation was a brigade of four regiments, each drawn up behind the next in a column-of-divisions, with intervals of 50 to 150 yards between regiments, each regiment deployed in two ranks. Two companies of the ten companies in each regiment were deployed as skirmishers. In theory, the fire of the skirmishers, and that of the leading regiment, would prepare the way for a breakthrough with the bayonet; in practice, such a formation was woefully vulnerable to defending rifle fire, which often mowed down the attacking "waves" of infantry or forced them to take

Sharps breech-loading rifle, U.S. Civil War.
SOURCE: Bell I. Wiley and Hollis D. Milhollen, *They Who Fought Here* (New York: Bonanza, 1959).

Open breech of the Prussian Dreyse, or "needle gun," mid-nineteenth century.
SOURCE: Harold L. Peterson, *The Treasury of the Gun* (New York: Ridge Press/Golden Press, 1962).

E: A Prussian heavy siege gun
on sloping, traversing runway
F: The Gatling gun
G: A Minié percussion rifle of 1851
H: A Dreyse needle-fire rifle
(Lovell's copy of a Prussian Guard
rifle of 1850)
I: The Chassepot rifle of 1863
J: The Winchester Model 1873 Carbine

Siege gun, Gatling gun, and small arms, mid-nineteenth century.

SOURCE: David G. Chandler, *Atlas of Military Strategy* (New York: Free Press, 1980).

A: The Whitworth 12-pounder rifled breech-loading gun
B: The elevating and laying equipment
C: A section of the breech, showing the vent-piece
D: A Whitworth 12-pounder shell

British Artillery Types, 1850-80

Decade:	Category:	Horse:	Field:	Mountain:	Heavy:
1850s	Smooth-bore, muzzle loading	6pdr. gun	9pdr. gun 24 pdr. howitzer	3pdr. gun 12pdr. howitzer	18pdr. gun 8in. mortar
1860s	Rifled, breech loading	9pdr. gun	12pdr. gun	6pdr. gun	40pdr. gun 8in. mortar
1870s	Rifled, muzzle-loading	9pdr. gun	9pdr. gun 16pdr. gun	7pdr. gun	40pdr. gun 6.3in. howitzer

Mid-nineteenth-century developments in artillery: the Whitworth breech-loader.

SOURCE: David G. Chandler, *Atlas of Military Strategy* (New York: Free Press, 1980).

Confederate 12–pounder howitzer, complete with limber,
U.S. Civil War.
SOURCE: Bell I. Wiley and Hollis D. Milhollen, *They Who Fought Here*
(New York: Bonanza, 1959).

20-pounder rifled Parrott gun, U.S. Civil War.
SOURCE: Bell I. Wiley and Hollis D. Milhollen, *They Who Fought Here*
(New York: Bonanza, 1959).

Imported Confederate breech-loading gun, U.S. Civil War.
SOURCE: Bell I. Wiley and Hollis D. Milhollen, *They Who Fought Here* (New York: Bonanza, 1959).

cover. When defending infantry protected themselves with earthen breastworks or trenches, they were almost invulnerable to frontal attack, even when bombarded by artillery.

The history of the Civil War is replete with examples of costly and usually futile frontal assaults. Robert E. Lee's Army of Northern Virginia launched a vain frontal attack at Malvern Hill on July 1, 1862, in which 5,000 men were lost in two hours of fighting. The casualties at Malvern Hill amounted to a quarter of all those the Confederates suffered over the whole of the Seven Days' Battle; flanking maneuvers on the other days had repeatedly forced the Union army to fall back. Lee did not repeat the mistake at Malvern Hill until a year later at the Battle of Gettysburg and his launching of "Pickett's Charge." In less than an hour, 15,000 attacking Confederate troops sustained 50 percent casualties while failing to penetrate the center of the Union line.

But the Union army had similar experiences. At Cold Harbor in 1864 U. S. Grant lost 6,000 men in a frontal assault on Confederate entrenchments near Richmond. In the same year, during his approach to Atlanta, William T. Sherman lost 3,000 men in less than an hour trying to storm the Confederate defenses at Kennesaw Mountain. One of the rare successful frontal attacks of the Civil War occurred in the Union storming of Missionary Ridge during the Battle of Chattanooga in 1863, but in that case the Confederates had located their rifle pits too far back from the forward slope and the attacking troops used the cover of "dead ground" until they were on top of the defenders.

The main hindrance to a successful frontal attack in the Civil War was, of course, the rifle bullet. The chief surgeon of the Union Army of the Potomac reported that in a few days of fighting in May 1864 his doctors treated one wound from a sword, four caused by bayonets, 749 caused by artillery fire, but 8,218 caused by rifle fire. Moreover, an examination of the dead on the battlefield revealed that the large majority had been victims of the rifle. Still, the vulnerability of attacking troops to rifle fire varied widely with the formation used in the attack. At the Battle of Antietam in 1862 54 percent of the men in the Sixth Wisconsin Regiment who attacked in a column-of-divisions were wounded or killed, but only 5 percent of the men in the same regiment deployed in extended order as skirmishers were casualties. Toward the end of the war, the more veteran soldiers learned to break up their columns-of-divisions into small groups of men, some providing covering fire while others advanced, and all seeking to use cover and to reinforce the skirmish line. If enemy defensive fire proved too intense for forward movement, the soldiers resorted to pick or spade to throw up an earthen-wall of protection. If a soldier was lucky enough to be armed with a breech-loading rifle, he could reduce his vulnerability even in the open by kneeling or lying prone while loading and firing. Even so, and though new offensive tactics reduced casualties, the tactical advantage lay with the defender to the end of the war. Nor were American Civil War armies the only ones in the mid-nineteenth century to be bedeviled by the problems of defensive firepower.

C. Naval Tactics and Coast Defense.   Except for a few ship-to-ship actions on the high seas, such as that between USS *Kearsarge* and the raider CSS *Alabama,* the only tactical actions on water in the Civil War were melées between river and harbor flotillas in which the power of the individual ship counted for more than formation tactics. Since the Union navy had more and better iron-clads in these actions, it usually had the advantage over the Confederate navy. Except for reviving the old tactic of ramming, the Civil War broke no new ground in the art of conducting fleet actions. On the other hand, new ground was broken by the Union navy and army in the art of dealing with coastal defenses; and, in response, the Confederates showed imagination in finding counter-solutions to the revised Union methods for the attack of coasts.

Early in the war, wooden Union steamships successfully ran past Confederate coastal batteries in order to sever Confederate communications, a classic example being that of Commodore David Farragut's Gulf Squadron and its bypassing of the Confederate forts at the mouth of the Mississippi River in April 1862. Farragut relied on darkness, a well-directed fire from his ships on the forts, the speed of his steam-powered vessels, and the harassment of mortar bombs from barges. After bypassing the forts, his ships moved ninety miles up the river to capture almost defenseless New Orleans (with 180,000 people the largest city in the Confederacy). Another favorite tactic was to land rifled guns and, from land platforms, pound the enemy's masonry fortifications at long distance. Union rifled artillery needed just two days to batter Fort Pulaski, near the mouth of the Savannah River, into submission in 1862. Union rifled artillery landed on Morris Island silenced Fort Sumter's batteries when the Federals were attempting to retake Charleston, S.C., in 1863, although Confederate infantry in the fort successfully repelled all efforts by Union infantry to take it by assault.

The Union advantage over Confederate coast defenses tended to fade with time. In many cases, the Confederates managed to counter rifled bolts and shells with earthen mounds in front of the brick walls of masonry forts to absorb their impact. Fort Moultrie, just across from Fort Sumter at the mouth of Charleston's harbor, was fortified in such a fashion; it resisted all Union efforts to silence its batteries. Earthen Fort McAlister on the Savannah River proved more than a match for Union naval bombardments, even by iron-clads. The Confederates also sowed mines at the mouths of harbors and improved their aiming techniques against moving ships. In April 1863, when Admiral Samuel Du Pont's fleet of eight iron-clads tried to break through the entrance of Charleston's harbor, it not only encountered underwater obstructions but had to endure a hurricane of fire from forts around the harbor. The attack failed, several iron-clads were damaged, and the new iron-clad *Keokuk*, pierced by shot and shell some ninety times, sank the next morning off Morris Island. In August 1864 Farragut ordered his squadron "to damn the torpedoes" in order to run by Fort Morgan into Mobile Bay. One of the Confederate mines sank the iron-clad *Tecumseh* within three minutes of exploding. Had the other Confederate mines worked as well, Farragut's daring would have resulted in a massacre of Union ships.

Perhaps the most striking example of the effectiveness of Confederate coast defense was the resistance of earthen Fort Fisher near the mouth of the Cape Fear River near Wilmington, N.C. The largest earthen fort of the war, its garrison repeatedly beat off the attack of superior forces. When it finally fell in January 1865, about 2,500 soldiers and seventy-five guns had held out for three days against the attack of a hundred warships (including 23 iron-clads) under Commodore David Porter and 8,000 Union troops.

Porter's fleet was the largest under the American flag during the whole of the nineteenth century. The cities of Charleston, Savannah, and Mobile never yielded to naval attack, and, in the cases of Charleston and Savannah, neither was captured until its inland communications had been cut by Sherman's army. The city of Mobile, though neutralized as a port in 1864, was not surrendered until after Robert E. Lee's capitulation at Appomattox in 1865 and the end of the war.

  D. Geography and Strategy. The Appalachian mountain chain divided the Confederacy into two major theaters of war, the East and the West. The Eastern theater was essentially a great coastal shelf which, for the most part, lay between the Atlantic seaboard and the Appalachians. Where the mountains dwindled out in northern Georgia, the Eastern theater merged with the Western. South of Virginia, the coasts of the Carolinas and Georgia consisted mostly of swamps and marshes, skirted by barrier islands. Inland, coastal railroads allowed the swift movement of defending troops to any threatened point, thus preventing the easy outflanking of ports such as the British had accomplished during the American Revolution. The Union forces easily overwhelmed the weak defenses of the barrier islands, such as Hilton Head, S.C., the largest island off the Atlantic coast south of Long Island, N.Y., but they found it a different matter to press inland to reach the hundred-mile stretch of railroad between Savannah and Charleston, or to turn the land defenses of either place. They seized the Outer Banks of North Carolina and invaded Pimlico and Albemarle sounds, but they could not advance far into eastern North Carolina.

  In northern Virginia, the coastal shelf narrowed between Chesapeake Bay and the mountains to the west. Richmond was located in this funnel, appearing vulnerable because of its proximity to Washington, D.C., and to the Potomac River. Actually, the hundred-mile corridor between Richmond and Washington was crisscrossed with ridge-lines, forests, and rivers, all easily adapted to defense. Southeast of Richmond, the York and the James rivers flowed into the Chesapeake, but in their upper courses they passed through swamps and forests. When these barriers were defended by the strongest army in the Confederacy, they were formidable obstacles. In addition, Union forces moving down the Shenandoah Valley to the west of the Blue Ridge mountains were moving away from, rather than toward, Richmond. In contrast, Confederate forces going down the Shenandoah in the other direction were potential threats to Washington's communications.

  Beyond the Appalachians, the Western Confederacy stretched to the Mississippi River Valley. The Gulf coast, like the Atlantic coast of the Eastern Confederacy, was not easily penetrable. But unlike the rivers in the Eastern Confederacy, the major rivers in the West served the invader

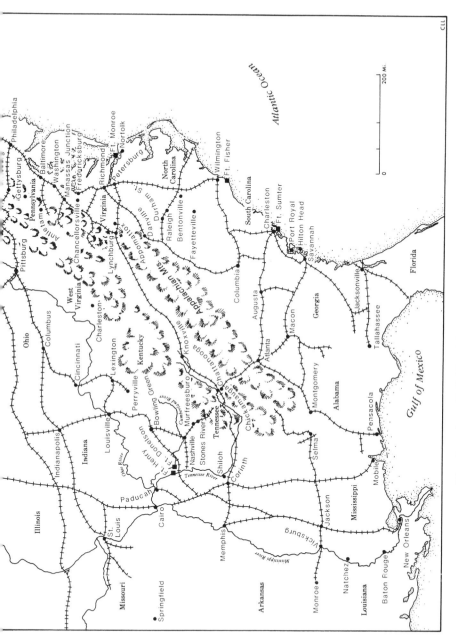

The American Civil War: The Eastern and Western Theaters

better than the defender, especially so when Union forces got footholds south of the Ohio River. From the south bank of the Ohio, Union amphibious forces could move up the Cumberland River to Nashville, Tenn., an area of Southern industry and commerce. Going up the Tennessee, they could reach Pittsburg Landing, twenty miles from Corinth, Miss., on the only continuous railroad in the South from the Atlantic coast to the Mississippi (the Charleston-to-Memphis line). And if Union forces could get control of the Mississippi River over its length, they could isolate the Trans-Mississippi South, primarily Arkansas, Louisiana, and Texas.

The relatively fragile nature of the Western Confederacy, compared to that in the East, explains in part why Union leaders gradually grasped that the solution to the Eastern problem lay not in breaking through its front door in Virginia, but in driving through its back door in Georgia. A drive from Chattanooga, also on the Charleston-to-Memphis line, to Atlanta and thence to Savannah or Charleston, would sever away the Western Confederacy and open the way for an attack on the Carolinas and Virginia from the south.

E. The Strategic Direction.   Given the Confederacy's limited resources, President Jefferson Davis believed that the goal of Southern independence would be best served by a strategy which conserved those resources as much as possible and at the same time encouraged foreign intervention. His strategic thinking was therefore similar to that of George Washington in the American Revolution. Davis called for an active defense of Confederate territory to beat off invasions and to preserve as much territory and population as possible until foreign intervention occurred, and he accepted a voluntary embargo on cotton shipments to Britain and France during the first year of the war in order to pressure them into intervening on behalf of the Confederacy. Industries of both countries were heavily dependent on Southern cotton; for instance, twenty percent of the British population drew its income from the making of cotton textiles. But the embargo turned out to have no positive results for the Confederacy. Britain and France had foreseen the threat to their cotton supply, each had an eighteenth-months' supply on hand when the war broke out, and, while some unemployment as a result of the embargo was suffered in Britain especially, both countries found alternative sources of cotton in Egypt and India. After the embargo was lifted, Britain especially traded with the Confederacy and did a thriving business with blockade-runners coming to the Bahamas. (Charleston was only 550 miles from Nassau, and Wilmington, N.C., only slightly further.) The embargo only served to prevent trade in the first year of the war when the Union blockade was at its weakest.

Robert E. Lee represented the other principal school of Confederate strategy. Placed in command of the most important of the Confederate armies beginning on June 1, 1862, Lee had no faith in foreign intervention or in a purely defensive strategy. He believed that the war could only be won by carrying it to the soil of the North and there winning Napoleonic-style victories over the Union armies. His ultimate objective was to break the Northern will to continue the war. But Lee's strategy did not accord with the tactical trends at the time. In his two great forays into the North—the first leading to the Battle of Antietam in 1862 and the second to the Battle of Gettysburg in 1863—the results were tactically indecisive and almost ruinous to the Confederate army in their human cost. After Gettysburg, Lee abandoned his earlier strategy and adopted a strategy of actively defending Confederate territory, one that he knew was likely to fail eventually if the Union managed its resources well and was willing to pay a high price for the extinction of Southern independence. Perhaps there was no good strategic choice for the Confederacy, given its circumstances and the patterns of mid-nineteenth century warfare, even though Southern valor and determination managed to drag out the war for four years.

The Union did not lack for strategic options at the beginning of the war, but it lacked a management for an effective central direction of its war effort. Old General Winfield Scott, the commanding general until his retirement in November 1861, wisely urged the build-up of very strong forces and then a concentration of effort against the most vital areas of the South. But Scott's scheme was largely ignored, and the early Union efforts went after too many things at once and often with unprepared forces. From November 1861 to February 1862, General George McClellan tried to command an army in the field and act as general-in-chief at the same time. From then into the summer of 1862, President Lincoln and Edwin M. Stanton, Lincoln's secretary of war, tried to function collectively as the Union high command. When that experiment failed, General Henry W. Halleck was brought in from the Western theater to serve as general-in-chief, but, though an able administrator, he did not turn out to be the strong strategist that Lincoln needed. The problem was finally solved in March 1864, when Lincoln appointed U. S. Grant as general-in-chief and secured his promotion to lieutenant general (the first Union officer to hold that rank since Scott's retirement). A little more than a year after Grant's appointment, the concerted operations of the Union forces brought about the final fall of the Confederacy. Had an effective Union high command existed at the beginning of the war, perhaps the conflict would have been shortened by years.

F. The Eastern Theater to May 1864. In July 1861 35,000 semi-trained Union troops under General Irvin McDowell tried to seize Richmond by an overland march from Washington, D.C., only to be

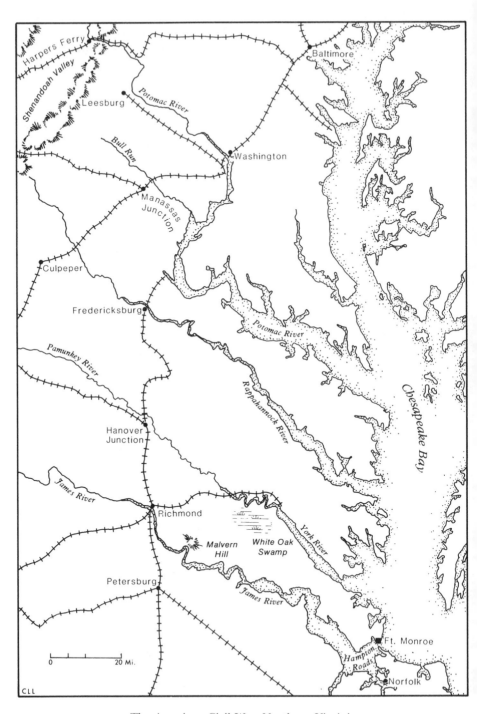

The American Civil War: Northern Virginia

routed on the banks of Bull Run just twenty miles southwest of Washington by a like number of Confederate soldiers under generals Joseph E. Johnston and P. G. T. Beauregard. After McDowell's army fell back on Washington, Lincoln appointed McClellan as commander of the principal Union army in the East, the "Army of the Potomac," as McClellan dubbed it. He remained in personal command of that army even after the duties of general-in-chief were entrusted to him in November 1861.

In early 1862 McClellan moved 90,000 troops of his army to Fort Monroe at the tip of the peninsula between the York and James rivers on Chesapeake Bay, and tried to approach Richmond from the coast via Yorktown. By then Beauregard had been transferred to the Western theater, and Johnston, in command of 60,000 troops, fought delaying actions on the peninsula as his army slowly retreated toward Richmond. On May 31, the Confederates launched a counteroffensive at the Battle of Fair Oaks (Seven Pines), only to be repelled with heavy loss; Johnston himself was seriously wounded in the fighting. On June 1, 1862, Robert E. Lee succeeded Johnston in command of the troops defending Richmond, and the same day he designated his command the Army of Northern Virginia.

In the wake of the Confederate defeat at Fair Oaks, Lee ordered the digging of extensive fortifications around Richmond and called up reinforcements from other parts of the South. McClellan failed to press his advantage by attacking in the meantime in the belief that the Confederate army at Richmond was much stronger than was the case. Meanwhile, a detached Confederate corps in the Shenandoah Valley under General Thomas J. ("Stonewall") Jackson inflicted defeats on small Union forces attempting to invade this Southern "grain basket," and finally caused Lincoln to divert reinforcements there instead of sending them to McClellan. Jackson's corps then moved by rail to join Lee's army at Richmond, and by June 25, 1862, Lee stood at the head of 80,000 troops, the largest army he was ever to command, and one only marginally smaller than McClellan's army.

In the Seven Days' Battle (June 26–July 1, 1862), the Lee-Jackson team outmaneuvered McClellan every day but the last, and forced McClellan's army to withdraw to a position on the James River dominated by Malvern Hill. Then, with no Union flank to turn, Lee tried to break through the Union center, losing 5,000 men to no purpose. McClellan's army fell back to an even stronger position around Harrison's Landing and the campaign was at a stalemate. Lincoln ordered 60,000 troops from the Shenandoah Valley concentrated at Manassas Junction, two miles south of Bull Run, under General John Pope, in order to approach Richmond from the north while McClellan's army kept Lee's army tied to the James, but Lee apprehended the danger. He sent Jackson's corps, and eventually most of his army, to deal with Pope, and, with the coming of word that Jackson was on the loose, Lincoln became preoccupied with the safety of Washington. Instead of allowing McClellan to seize the offensive against Lee's weakened forces on the James, Lincoln ordered McClellan's army withdrawn by water to the area around the capital, where it was to cooperate with Pope's army. While McClellan's army was moving to Washington by the circuitous water route, and was temporarily out of the campaign, Jackson's corps got into Pope's rear and burned his supply base at Manassas Junction. Pope's army finally cornered Jackson's outnumbered forces on the edge of the old Bull Run battlefield in late August, but by then the rest of Lee's army, moving by rail and foot marches from the James, had arrived to strike Pope's command in flank and rear. In the Second Battle of Bull Run (or Second Manassas), Pope's unsupported army was badly defeated. McClellan's army arrived only in time to cover its retreat into Washington and to secure the capital.

Having thrown the Union forces in the East on the defensive, Lee seized the initiative in September 1862 by leading 57,000 troops across the Potomac and into the Cumberland Valley, west of the Blue Ridge mountains, in an invasion of Maryland. His strategy was to use the mountain range as a shield to conceal his movements until his army recrossed the Blue Ridge and threatened Washington's communications. Lee hoped to force the Union army to come from behind its fortifications and to risk a decisive battle in the open. But faulty Confederate security allowed McClellan to learn that Lee had temporarily divided his army, leaving a part under Jackson to besiege a Union garrison at Harpers Ferry while the rest marched toward Chambersburg, Md. With unusual vigor for him, McClellan seized the offensive, pushed his troops across the mountains, and cornered part of Lee's army near Sharpsburg, on the banks of Antietam Creek.

By September 17, the day of the Battle of Antietam, all but one division of Jackson's corps had managed to reach Sharpsburg from Harpers Ferry. Even so, Lee's army, with 47,000 men against McClellan's 90,000 troops, was heavily outnumbered. It barely managed to repel a series of Union attacks until late in the day, when General A. P. Hill's division arrived from Harpers Ferry just in time to repel the last Union assault. Antietam, the bloodiest single day's battle of the war (12,000 Confederates and 15,000 Union soldiers were killed or wounded), ended in a tactical draw, but it amounted to a strategic victory for the Union. A day later Lee ordered his army to withdraw to Virginia. Encouraged by the outcome, five days after the battle Lincoln issued the Emancipation Proclamation. In effect, the proclamation expanded Union war goals to include abolition of slavery in states in rebellion against the Union, a measure that reduced the danger of foreign intervention, won support for the war among the abolitionists, and opened the way for recruitment of black soldiers. Eventually, 186,000 African-Americans served in Union blue.

In the wake of Antietam, Lee withdrew the Army of Northern Virginia to a defensive position at Fredericksburg, Va., on the Rappahannock River, a point equally distant from Washington and Richmond. Lincoln appointed General Ambrose Burnside to relieve McClellan of command of the Army of the Potomac in November 1862, and Burnside's troops tried to make a frontal attack on Lee's position in December. The Battle of Fredericksburg ended in a bloody Union failure, costing the Army of the Potomac 12,000 men in the process, more than twice as many as the 5,000 casualties suffered by Lee's army. Subsequently, General Joseph Hooker relieved Burnside of command of the Army of the Potomac.

In the spring of 1863 Hooker's army of 107,000 troops tried to turn Lee's position at Fredericksburg when a part of it crossed the Rappahannock and the Rapidan, a tributary, near Chancellorsville. Having plunged into an area aptly called the Wilderness, Hooker's forces created a strong defensive position facing toward Fredericksburg. Unknown to Hooker, an unprotected wagon road led around his army's right flank and, on May 2, Jackson's corps used the road to work its way into Hooker's rear. A Confederate surprise attack at dusk routed one Union corps and threatened to cut off the Union line of retreat across the river. But, on the eve of final success, Jackson was fired on by mistake by his own troops and badly wounded. As the Confederate attack lost its momentum, Hooker managed to reorganize his forces and avert the worst disaster. After beating off more Confederate attacks on his position during subsequent days, he removed his army from the Wilderness on May 4. Still, in the Battle of Chancellorsville, he had lost 17,000 men to Lee's loss of 13,000, and failed to breach the line of the Rappahannock. On the other hand, the fruits of the Confederate victory were offset in part when the critically wounded Jackson died on May 10; no other Confederate general serving under Lee proved as able as he.

The climax of the war in the East approached in June 1863, when Lee assembled 75,000 troops and launched his second invasion of the North. As in 1862, his army crossed the Potomac and marched up the Cumberland Valley, using the Blue Ridge as a screen, but this time it crossed Maryland to reach southern Pennsylvania. Detachments recrossed the mountains to raid Harrisburg and York preliminary to a decisive battle with the Army of the Potomac, but Lee's army was moving blind. General J. E. B. Stuart's cavalry, detached at the beginning of the campaign as a diversion, had failed to reunite with Lee's army, and, in Stuart's absence, Lee was in ignorance of Union movements. Yet the Army of the Potomac was also in difficulty. Just five days before the pivotal battle of the war in the East, Hooker resigned his command after a quarrel with Lincoln over

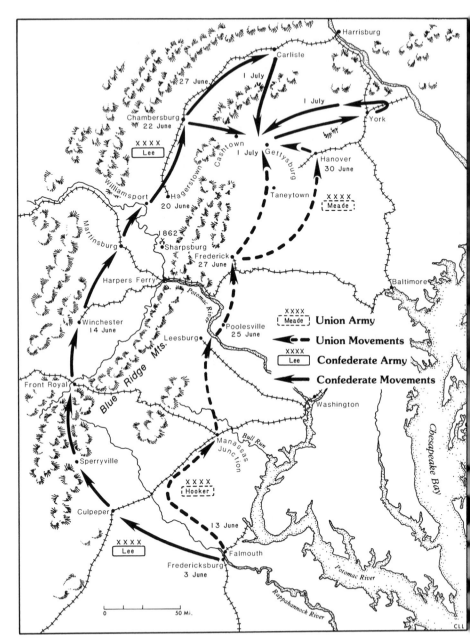

The American Civil War: The Gettysburg Campaign, 1863

strategy. Lincoln appointed General George Meade, one of Hooker's corps commanders, to Hooker's place, but no one could be sure how well the untested Meade would perform against the greatest of the Confederate generals.

The Army of the Potomac followed Lee's army into Pennsylvania. A Confederate division was surprised to run into the Union vanguard near the crossroads town of Gettysburg, ninety miles from Washington, on July 1. As the scattered Confederate corps rushed to concentrate at Gettysburg during the day, the Union troops were driven back to heights behind the town, but a Confederate failure to press their advantage allowed Meade's men to consolidate a defensive position during the night. By the morning of July 2, both armies were largely assembled. Meade's 90,000 troops remained on defense as, for two days running, Lee's forces attacked the left, right, and center of the Union position, the final effort culminating in "Pickett's Charge" on July 3. By that night the battle was at a tactical stalemate, but in over three days of fighting Lee had lost 23,000 men to no purpose. Meade had lost 20,000 men in same period, but his position was secure and he could more easily make up his losses. Meade's army remained on the defensive during the lull on July 4, and that night Lee's army began its retreat to Virginia. In the Battle of Gettysburg, Lee failed to find that Napoleonic victory which he had hoped would bring about Southern independence, and greatly weakened his army in the process.

Gettysburg, like Antietam, was a tactical draw but a strategic victory for the Union, and with long-lasting effects. Although Lee's army still had enough strength to beat back Union advances into northern Virginia during the rest of 1863, and both armies finally came to rest in camps there for the winter, the Army of Northern Virginia no longer had the capacity for decisive offensive action. By then it was also becoming clear that the war was being won for the Union by its armies in the West. Lee's army in Virginia continued to fight resolutely at the front door of the Confederate mansion for nearly two more years, but its rooms were being destroyed one by one in Lee's rear. When the front door at Richmond finally collapsed in the spring of 1865, there was little behind it left to defend.

G. The Western Theater to May 1864.   In 1861 General Albert S. Johnston, commander-in-chief in the Western Confederacy, tried to guard against Union invasions from the Ohio Valley and down the Mississippi by creating a chain of forts and camps along the major waterways and railroads leading into the South. Further west, weaker Confederate forces tried to gain control of Missouri and to hold Arkansas.

But the fate of the western Confederacy really rested on the theater between the Mississippi River Valley and the western Appalachians, and there Johnston's cordon-defense proved only as strong as its weakest links. In early February 1862, Union gunboats and 40,000 troops on steamers under General U. S. Grant easily captured Fort Henry after floodwaters of the Tennessee River made the fort undefendable. Grant's army then marched the twelve miles to the rear of Fort Donelson on the Cumberland River. There, and in concert with Union gunboats, Grant's army trapped and then compelled the surrender of a Confederate army under General Simon Buckner that may have numbered 17,000 troops. The surrenders of forts Henry and Donelson knocked the center out of Johnston's strategic line of defense, and marked the beginning of the rise of Grant's star in the West.

Soon after Grant's victories at Henry and Donelson, Union forces under General Don Carlos Buell were able to occupy Nashville, Tenn., and Grant's army pushed up the Tennessee River as far as Pittsburg Landing, only twenty miles from Corinth, Miss., the vital rail junction on the Charleston-to-Memphis line. But on orders from General Henry Halleck, then Grant's superior, Grant's army went no further and awaited the arrival of Buell's army of 40,000 troops, marching overland from Nashville, before attempting to push on to Corinth.

The Union delay allowed Albert Johnston and P. G. T. Beauregard, Johnston's second in command, time in which to concentrate 40,000 Confederate soldiers at Corinth for a counteroffensive to destroy Grant's army at Pittsburg Landing before Buell's army could arrive. The Johnston-Beauregard plan almost worked. Early on the morning of April 6, 1862, the Confederate attack caught Grant's army by surprise while it was camped around Shiloh Church. The Confederate assault nearly drove the Union forces into the Tennessee during the course of the day, but Johnston was mortally wounded in the fighting and a stubborn Union resistance broke the Confederate momentum. On the Union side, General William T. Sherman distinguished himself in helping to direct the defense until Grant could assume the chief command, an event that would lead to a close partnership between the two generals. The fighting of the first day ended in a stalemate with the Federal forces managing to maintain a foothold on the banks of the Tennessee River.

Meanwhile, Buell's army arrived on the opposite bank, and that night Buell's reinforcements joined Grant's army in its beachhead. On April 7, Grant seized the offensive and by the end of the second day of battle his attack had recovered most of the ground lost by the Union forces the previous day. Though both armies were exhausted by the end of the second day of fighting, and the Confederates had suffered the loss of fewer men (10,000 to the Union loss of 13,000) in two days of battle, the combined forces of Grant and Buell heavily outnumbered Beauregard's remaining Confederates. Beauregard judged his army to be in no condition to resume the contest, and ordered his troops to begin a withdrawal to Corinth under cover of darkness. The Battle of Shiloh ended in a tactical draw, but it was clearly a strategic victory for the Union.

The super-cautious Halleck did not press the Union pursuit of the Confederate army after Shiloh, and delayed the final push on Corinth until 110,000 Federal soldiers had been assembled for the purpose. Faced with such overwhelming numbers, on May 31 Beauregard gave up the rail junction without a fight and withdrew his troops to Tupelo, Miss. In early June, Memphis fell to Union forces which had fought their way down the Mississippi. Together with the fall of New Orleans to David Farragut's fleet in the Gulf of Mexico on May 1, the combined effect was to leave only Vicksburg and Port Hudson as the remaining Confederate links to the Trans-Mississippi South.

The splitting of the Confederacy down the length of the Mississippi River might have been accomplished during the rest of 1862 had the Union forces remained concentrated on that objective, and had not Confederate cavalry raids under generals Nathan Bedford Forrest, John Hunt Morgan, and Joseph Wheeler constantly disrupted Union supply lines. But with Halleck's approval, Buell's army moved lethargically eastward down the Charleston-to-Memphis rail line in the direction of Chattanooga, leaving Grant too few troops to protect his communications adequately and at the same time make much progress in an overland advance into Mississippi. Even though the Confederates had been defeated in Missouri, and lost part of Arkansas after the Battle of Pea Ridge (March 1862), Confederate forces under generals Sterling Price and Earl Van Dorn moved across the Mississippi to join in the defense of the new front along the Tennessee-Mississippi state line. In late June, President Jefferson Davis appointed General Braxton Bragg to replace Beauregard as commander-in-chief of the Confederate armies in the Western theater. In contrast, when, a month later, Halleck was ordered east to become the Union general-in-chief, no single Federal commander was appointed to take charge of all the Union forces in the West.

Bragg decided to divide his forces, leaving part of them under Van Dorn and Price to defend northern Mississippi, and moving with the rest from Tupelo to Chattanooga by rail, using a roundabout route through Mobile. Though Van Dorn and Price managed to limit Grant's further movements south, and even launched an offensive to recover Corinth in October, their offensive efforts finally failed. In turn, Grant's overland advance on Jackson, Miss., in order to get into the rear of Vicksburg, was thwarted when Van Dorn's forces burned his supply depot at Holly Springs in December 1862.

Progress was discouraging for President Lincoln in eastern Tennessee as well. In September 1862, under Bragg's personal command, 40,000 Confederates launched a sudden offensive from Chattanooga through eastern Tennessee and Kentucky that imperiled the strategic flank and rear of Buell's army. Buell's army rushed northward by way of Nashville in order to protect its communications to Louisville, its main base of supply on the Ohio, and the two armies finally collided in a confused battle at Perryville in October. Buell narrowly won a victory over the Confederates and Bragg's army was forced to retire to a defensive position near Murfreesboro, Tenn., where he could block the route to Chattanooga. But Buell's brush with near-disaster caused Lincoln to replace him with General William S. Rosecrans, and Chattanooga, another key rail center on the Charleston-to-Memphis line, remained untaken.

The President urged Rosecrans to get his army moving on Chattanooga at the earliest opportunity, but Rosecrans was as deliberate as Buell and his communications across Tennessee—frequently raided by Confederate cavalry—about as insecure. Not until the turn of the year did Rosecrans's army engage Bragg's in the Battle of Murfreesboro (or Stones River). But between the end of December and the first few days of 1863 the attacks and counterattacks of the two sides inflicted perhaps 24,000 casualties, slightly more than at Shiloh. Yet, although Stones River was perhaps the bloodiest battle west of the Appalachians during the war, its results were barren. Both armies were so injured in the outcome that neither was capable of seizing the offensive again for months.

In December 1862 Grant abandoned his overland drive toward the center of Mississippi and shifted his lines of communication to the Mississippi River. He focused his aim on the capture of Vicksburg by water, but for months none of his stratagems worked. A landing at Chickasaw Bluffs just above Vicksburg was repelled in December 1862; an effort to penetrate the watery maze of the Delta to reach Vicksburg by the Yazoo River also failed in early 1863; and an attempt to dig a canal through the peninsula where the Mississippi looped in front of Vicksburg, and thus to bypass the fortress, was also abandoned. Finally, in April 1863, Grant hit on the strategy that broke the deadlock.

Grant caused part of his army to move down the west bank of the Mississippi to a point below Vicksburg, and, from that point, it was transported to the other side of the river by vessels which had run by the Vicksburg batteries at night. But, instead of attacking Vicksburg from the south, as General John C. Pemberton, the Confederate commander, expected, Grant took a leaf from Scott's book in the Mexican War, dropped his communications to the river, and struck out for Jackson, Miss., the rail junction and Confederate supply center, fifty miles to the east of Vicksburg. The sudden arrival of the Union army there enabled it to seize the center intact and to resupply itself at Confederate expense for an advance on Vicksburg's rear. Pemberton's attempt to drive Grant's army off Vicksburg's communications was defeated at Champion's Hill, and the Vicksburg garrison was forced back into its works. Grant reestablished contact with the rest of his forces on the Mississippi and imposed a tight siege. Pemberton was finally compelled to surrender the fortress and his 20,000 starving men on July 4, 1863. Port Hudson fell four days later. Thereafter, the entire length of the Mississippi lay in Union hands, and the original Confederacy was split in half.

In September 1863 Rosecrans's army at last maneuvered Bragg's army out of Chattanooga and the Confederate army withdrew across the state line into Georgia. But the arrival of General James Longstreet's corps from Lee's army enabled Bragg to launch a surprise counteroffensive and to defeat Rosecrans's army at the Battle of Chickamauga Creek. Thanks to a rear-guard action by troops under General George Thomas (the "Rock of Chickamauga"), Rosecran's defeated army managed to get to Chattanooga and to deny Bragg's forces entry. Still, Rosecrans's army was soon under siege and seemed likely to share the fate of Pemberton's Confederate army at Vicksburg.

Lincoln dealt with the crisis by appointing Grant to command an army of relief. Grant assembled forces from armies in the West and reinforcements sent by Meade from the East. He managed to arrange a line of supply and reinforcement across the Tennessee River to the Union army inside Chattanooga, and he replaced Rosecrans with Thomas as its commander. While the Union army inside Chattanooga was being strengthened, Bragg weakened his army by sending off Longstreet's corps to Knoxville, where it besieged another Union force. The scene was set for a Confederate disaster. In the three-day Battle of Chattanooga in late November 1863, Grant's army broke through Bragg's weak siege lines and forced the Confederates to make a hasty withdrawal into Georgia. The relief of Chattanooga set Lincoln's stamp of approval on Grant.

During the relative lull in the West during the rest of 1863 and into the spring of 1864, Grant and Sherman prepared for a massive offensive into Georgia. Meanwhile, Lincoln chose Grant to serve as general-in-chief of the Union armies in March 1864. Grant turned over chief command in the West to Sherman, and subsequently placed his headquarters with Meade's Army of the Potomac in the East. But before leaving the Western theater, Grant worked out with Sherman the main lines of their joint strategies for simultaneous offensives, beginning in May 1864.

H. The Final Campaigns, May 1864–April 1865. After his appointment as general-in-chief of Union armies, Grant adopted a plan for ending the war that was both simple and sensible. Meade's army, increased to 134,000 men, would attempt to drive Lee's army back on Richmond and prevent any transfers of its forces to the West. Sherman's army, numbering

100,000 troops, would launch a drive from Chattanooga to Atlanta, and thence to either Charleston or Savannah on the coast. If the drive was successful, it would divide the South again and permit Sherman's army to threaten the Carolinas and Virginia. Lesser Union forces would maintain pressure wherever they could. At some point, Grant reasoned, the over-stretched Confederate resistance would collapse.

Within the same twenty-four hours in early May 1864, both Meade's and Sherman's offensives got underway. In the East, and by fighting terrible battles in the Wilderness, at Spottsylvania Courthouse and Cold Harbor, Meade's army lost 60,000 men but reached the vicinity of the field of the old Seven Days' Battle by early June. Moreover, Lee had lost a third of his 60,000 men in the fighting. Blocked north of the James, Grant prepared a pontoon bridge in secret, and at mid-month the Union forces suddenly crossed the river and made a rush to seize Petersburg, a rail center south of Richmond. The Union army's crossing of the James caught Lee by surprise, but he managed to rush troops to Petersburg in time to block the way. On July 30, the Union forces exploded a giant mine under the Con-federate entrenchments in hopes of creating a breach in Lee's defenses at Petersburg, but the follow-up attack was botched and the Battle of the Crater ended in a stalemate. In August, Grant's forces managed to cut the Weldon-to-Wilmington railroad, and Lee was thereafter unable to use the railway from Wilmington closer than sixteen miles to Richmond. From that point wagon trains had to carry supplies to Richmond by a circuitous route.

In the fall of 1864 a diversion by General Jubal Early's small Confeder-ate army in the Shenandoah Valley did not shake Grant's determination to maintain his grip on the Confederate positions at Richmond and Peters-burg. A Union army under General Philip Sheridan ran Early's force to earth, destroyed it, and then devastated the Shenandoah Valley. Grant's forces in the East could not break the Richmond-Petersburg lines until the spring of 1865, but in the meantime neither could Lee send reinforce-ments from his army to stop Sherman's advance in the Deep South.

General Joseph Johnston commanded the 60,000 Confederate troops attempting to contain Sherman's drive from Chattanooga to Atlanta in the spring and summer of 1864. By falling back from one defensive position to another, and by forcing Sherman's army to make detours, Johnston delayed the Union advance until it reached Kennesaw Mountain. There on June 27 the Confederates inflicted a bloody repulse when Sherman unwisely launched a frontal assault on a prepared position. The Union advance was temporarily stymied in the wake of the battle, but Sherman finally managed to maneuver Johnston's army back into the defenses of Atlanta. President Davis, disillusioned with Johnston's generalship, appointed General John Bell Hood to replace him on July 18.

Hood's strategy of rash attacks on Sherman's army to prevent it from encircling Atlanta failed of their purpose and nearly gutted Hood's army in the process. By the end of August, the Confederate ranks had been reduced to 20,000 men and the city was clearly doomed. Hood withdrew his forces from Atlanta at the beginning of September, and Sherman secured his first prize of the campaign. After unsuccessfully raiding Sherman's communications between Atlanta and Chattanooga, Hood's army moved through Alabama in order to attack Sherman's rail communications across Tennessee. Sherman relied on General George Thomas's 40,000 troops in Tennessee to deal with the problem, and they eventually destroyed Hood's force at the Battle of Nashville in December 1864.

Even before Hood's threat in Tennessee was eliminated, Sherman convinced Grant not to delay a march through central Georgia. In mid-November 1864, after destroying much of Atlanta, Sherman's army dropped its communications and commenced its "March to the Sea." By living off the country, the 60,000 Union troops fed themselves while systematically devastating almost everything in their path. A small Confederate army under General William Hardee delayed Sherman's capture of Savannah until December 21, then retreated toward Charleston. After seizing Savannah, Sherman spared it from destruction in order to use it as a base for his march north. He resupplied his forces from the sea and, in January 1865, turned to the task of removing the Carolinas from the war.

Sherman's army invaded South Carolina by a route that simultaneously took it to Columbia, the state capital, and severed Charleston's inland communications. Faced with potential encirclement, Hardee was compelled to abandon Charleston on February 17. Union forces on the sea islands, which had laid siege to the port for the better part of four years without success, occupied it without resistance. When Sherman's army occupied Columbia, Sherman intended to burn only its public property, but on the night of February 17–18 two-thirds of the city was destroyed by fires set by unruly troops and mobs. Sherman's army then moved toward Fayetteville, N.C., intending to link up with other Union forces which had captured Wilmington, N.C., the last functioning Southern port, on February 22. Sherman's army fought its last major action of the war when it drove General Joseph Johnston's 20,000 Confederates from its path at the Battle of Bentonville, near Goldsboro, N.C., on March 19–20.

After linking up with Union forces coming from the sea, Sherman's army moved on to seize the state capital at Raleigh. Sherman was preparing for a drive into Lee's rear in Virginia when, in early April, Grant's attacks finally broke Lee's lines at Five Forks near Petersburg. Lee abandoned Richmond and Petersburg, and withdrew the remains of his army toward Lynchburg, Va., a remaining base of supply. After replenishing his army, he hoped to link up with Johnston's forces at Greensboro, N.C., and to continue resistance. But Lee's plan was thwarted when, a few days later, his army's way to Lynchburg was blocked at Appomattox Courthouse, Va., by General Philip Sheridan's cavalry. As over 100,000 Union troops closed around the remaining 26,000 troops of the Army of Northern Virginia, many of them hungry and half-armed, Lee finally surrendered to Grant on April 9. Johnston surrendered his army to Sherman at Durham Station, N.C., later that month, effectively removing the last significant Confederate resistance. By the time of the two surrenders, there was very little left in the South to defend.

V. The Wars of German Unification, 1864–71

The final wars of the mid-nineteenth century were associated with the process of unification of the states of Germany under the monarchy of Hohenzollern Prussia. None of the three conflicts lasted as long as a year, even though the wars of 1866 and 1870 opposed major powers. During the Austro-Prussian War (1866) occurred the greatest battle of the nineteenth century—Königgrätz or Sadowa—in which more men fought than even at Leipzig, the greatest battle of the Napoleonic Wars. The number engaged at Königgrätz was more than twice the number of men who fought at Gettysburg, the greatest battle of the American Civil War. The chief reasons for these quick German victories were the excellence of the Prussian General Staff, the soundness of the Prusso-German *Nation-in-Arms,* and the comparative mediocrity of the opposing armies.

  A. The Wars with Denmark and Austria, 1864–66.   When the King of Denmark refused to allow the provinces of Schleswig and Holstein, his personal possessions since the Congress of Vienna, to join the Germanic Confederation despite their large German populations, the Confederation declared war on Denmark. Both Prussia and Austria put armies into the field, but the small Danish army, armed with cap-and-ball rifles, put up a brave resistance in a fortified position at Düppel on the Jutland peninsula. As mentioned earlier, it was from that experience that Helmuth von Moltke the Elder, Chief of the Prussian General Staff, first gained insight regarding the effects of the new firepower on tactics. The combined strength of the Austro-Prussian powers finally proved too much for Denmark, however, and the Danish king was compelled to accept the inclusion of Schleswig and Holstein in the Germanic Confederation under the administration of Austria and Prussia.

  By 1866 Prussia's prime minister, Otto von Bismarck, was ready to risk war with Austria in order to expel it from the Germanic Confederation, a first step toward extending Prussian domination over Germany. Bismarck

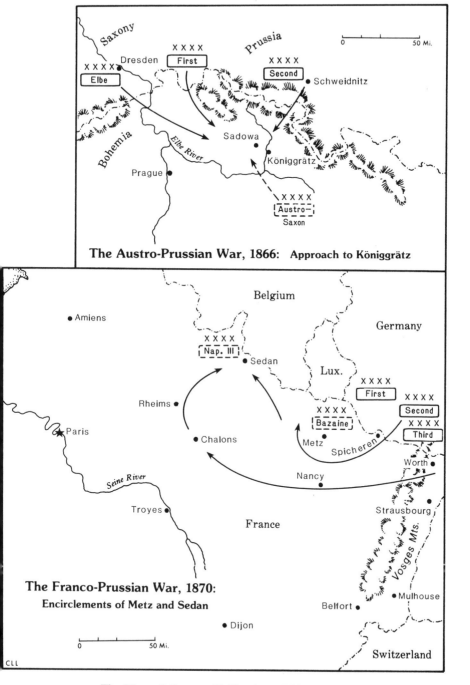

The Austro-Prussian War, 1866: Approach to Königgrätz

The Franco-Prussian War, 1870:
Encirclements of Metz and Sedan

The Wars of German Unification, 1866 and 1870

manufactured a quarrel with Austria over the administration of Schleswig-Holstein, and so provoked the Habsburg government that in June the other German states sided with Austria in declaring war on Prussia. France and Russia declared their neutrality as the result of Bismarckian diplomacy, but the new Kingdom of Italy lined up with Prussia in hopes of gaining the province of Venetia from Austria as an outcome of the war.

Superficially, the Austrian and Prussian armies seemed well matched, each being able to mobilize about 500,000 troops initially. Austria's artillery was nearly all rifled, if still muzzle-loading, while half the Prussian field guns were smoothbore muzzle-loaders and half Krupp steel, rifled, breech-loading guns. Austria's infantry were armed with the Lorenz cap-and-ball rifle, while the Prussian infantry were the first to be generally armed with a breech-loading rifle, the Dreyse or needle gun (so-called for its long firing-pin). The Lorenz had superior range and accuracy over the Dreyse, but the Dreyse could be loaded and fired by troops kneeling or lying down, and thus soldiers using it presented a more difficult target. Austrian cavalry was considered better than the Prussian. Taken in all, Prussia did not have a great technological advantage over Austria. The Prussian edge lay in Prussia's *Nation-in-Arms,* an excellent General Staff, a sound doctrine of war in the *Kesselschlacht,* and the fact that Bismarck's diplomacy insured that Austria would have to fight Prussia and Italy simultaneously and with only weak support from its German allies.

At the outbreak of the war, the Prussian General Staff implemented its contingency war plan, and three field armies, totaling 250,000 troops, took the field against Austria and its ally Saxony. The rest of the Prussian army overawed other German states and stood guard against foreign intervention. In contrast to the smooth Prussian mobilization, the Austrian mobilization was disorderly and slow, and further confused by the Italian declaration of war. Lieutenant Field Marshal Ludwig von Benedek was belatedly appointed to command Austria's Northern Army assembling in Bohemia, a force of about 230,000 troops, but it was still not ready for action when, on June 16, the Prussian Army of the Elbe invaded the territory of the King of Saxony and forced his army of 32,000 troops to retreat into Bohemia. Benedek hastened to join his forces with the Saxons near Königgrätz, a key rail junction fifty miles south of the Prussian border, but, meanwhile, the Prussian First Army absorbed the Army of the Elbe as it advanced across the low mountains shielding Bohemia and approached Königgrätz from the northwest. The Prussian Second Army approached from the northeast. Benedek deployed his combined forces of 262,000 troops around the village of Sadowa, west of the river Elbe (rather than east of it as Moltke had expected), and on the morning of July 3, exactly three years after the Battle of Gettysburg, the First Army under Prince Frederick Charles unexpectedly collided with the front of the Austrian army in a heavy fog and thus commenced a major battle. Though outnumbered, the First Army held out for most of the day, until the Second Army arrived to inflict a fatal thrust into the flank of the Austro-Saxon forces. Benedek managed to cover the retreat of his army across the Elbe with cavalry charges, but he had lost 44,000 men and the morale of his troops was shattered. The Prussian losses came to just 9,000 men. Within a few days, the Habsburg government asked for an armistice, and the Peace of Prague, signed in August, ended the so-called Seven Weeks' War. Meanwhile, the Austrians had hurled back an Italian invasion of Venetia, but the province was lost to Italy under the terms of peace.

The most interesting combat between the Italians and Austrians took place not on land but at sea when, on July 20, 1866, Admiral Wilhelm von Tegetthoff's Austrian fleet engaged the Italian fleet of Admiral Count Carlo di Persano off the island of Lissa in the Adriatic Sea. Tegetthoff put his seven inferior iron-clad warships and fourteen wooden warships in a "V" formation and charged the center of the Italian line, sailing in line-ahead and at right angles to the Austrian fleet. In the confused melée that followed, the large Italian armored ship *Re d'Italia* was rammed and sunk, and Austrian gunfire fatally damaged two smaller Italian iron-clads. A total of 667 Italian sailors were killed and 39 were injured. Tegetthoff lost no ships and his casualties were limited to 38 killed and 138 wounded. In the absence of a more recent fleet action to study until 1893, the Battle of Lissa and its supposed lessons influenced naval architects and tacticians for almost thirty years, causing them to build warships with rams and making provision for ramming tactics long after the prospect of getting close enough to ram had passed.

The Peace of Prague dissolved the Germanic Confederation and henceforth excluded Austria from German affairs. In 1867 the Protestant German states north of the Main River were united with Prussia in the North German Confederation, headed by King William I of Prussia, while the Catholic German states south of the Main signed treaties of defensive alliance with the North German Confederation. That same year, Emperor Francis Joseph of Austria was forced to appease the Magyars of Hungary by reorganizing the Habsburg domains into the Dual Monarchy of the Austro-Hungarian Empire. The two parts of the empire were joined only in the person of the monarch, a common army, and a common foreign office. Down to the early twentieth century, the friction among the differing ethnic groups of the empire further weakened the military potential of Austria-Hungary. In contrast, first the union of the north German states under Prussia in 1867, and then the unification of all Germany under the Hohenzollern dynasty in 1871, confirmed the fact that the seat of power in Central Europe had shifted from Vienna to Berlin. Indeed, Imperial Germany was to emerge as the single strongest military state in Europe.

B. The Franco-Prussian War, 1870-71. Emperor Napoleon III was deeply troubled by the outcome of the Austro-Prussian War and the emergence of the powerful North German Confederation on the eastern borders of France. Accordingly, Napoleon directed a reform of his military forces, accepting a proposal in 1868 by Marshal Adolphe Niel, Minister of War, which called for the number of conscripts entering the French army each year to be greatly increased, a four-year active duty military obligation imposed on some, and on others a stint of five months on active duty to be followed by a long period in the army's reserve. Those men allowed exemption from either form of service would be required to enroll in a *Garde National Mobile,* a semi-trained militia, somewhat like the German *Landwehr.* Had the reform gone as intended, and had the Franco-Prussian War not come sooner, by 1875 the Imperial French Army would have consisted of an active and reserve force of 800,000 troops, backed by a *Garde Mobile* of 500,000 men. In reality, the reform had scarcely got underway by the outbreak of the Franco-Prussian War in 1870, and the only French force that counted at its outbreak was a relatively small *armée de métier* of 350,000 troops.

Napoleon III also tried to reform French armaments before 1870. French infantry were equipped with the Chassepot, a better breech-loading rifle than the Prussian Dreyse, and the *mitrailleuse,* an early machine-gun mounted on an artillery carriage, and similar to the Gatling gun of the American Civil War. The *mitrailleuse* was expected to give the French a great technological advantage over the Germans, but it was kept so secret that few French commanders had any idea how to get the most out of it; in the Franco-Prussian War, the weapon was kept back with the artillery and usually out of range of the enemy. In contrast, and while the Prussian army had no counterpart to the *mitrailleuse,*it had equipped its artillery entirely with improved Krupp steel, breech-loading field guns, whereas the French still relied upon muzzle-loading artillery. But France's military inferiority to the North German Confederation in 1870 was not primarily technological. The fatal weaknesses in the French army were a flawed command and staff system, a poor system of mobilization, lack of reserves, and an unsuitable doctrine of war.

The genesis of the Franco-Prussian War was a quarrel between Napoleon III and William I of Prussia over the candidacy of William's cousin to the vacant throne of Spain. In July 1870, when pressed by Napoleon's ambassador to withdraw the candidacy and to forswear any future Hohenzollern claim, William broke off the interview. Bad feelings had been aroused in both France and Germany over the issue, and apparently Napoleon believed that he had no choice but to declare war or lose face with the French people. Bismarck had been seeking an excuse for war with France as a means of bringing the south German states into union with the north, and he was not a little pleased when Napoleon III declared war on the North German Confederation on July 19. The French initiative made France appear as the aggressor, and thus made the intervention of other powers on the side of France less likely. It also triggered the defensive alliances between the North German Confederation and the German states south of the Main. The wave of nationalism which swept over Germany in the summer of 1870 enabled Bismarck to move forward swiftly with the final steps of political unification.

By the end of the first week in August 1870 Moltke had assembled 500,000 German troops in three armies on the French frontier. In contrast, the French had managed to get only two army corps to the frontier area, and they were separated by the line of the Vosges mountains. Further west, Marshal François Bazaine was laboriously cobbling together an army at Metz from 180,000 troops gradually arriving from all over France. Between Metz and Paris another army of 124,000 troops was also being assembled. Moltke seized the initiative on August 6 when two German armies attacked the lone French army corps on Spicheren Heights, overlooking Saarbrücken, while a third German army attacked the French corps on the other side of the Vosges at Wörth (Fröshwiller). The two French army corps were compelled to retreat, two German armies penetrated the Lorraine Gap, then the Germans wheeled to encircle Metz.

Bazaine's army tried to retreat before its line of retreat was severed, but its attempts were beaten back at the battles of Mars-la-Tour and Gravelotte, and it found itself under siege inside Metz. Meanwhile, as the third German army probed further west, Napoleon III, mortified by the defeats at the frontier, took personal command of the army at Chalons-sur-Marne, and, with the assistance of Marshal Patrice MacMahon, he tried to bring relief to the army in Metz by approaching from the direction of the Belgian border. But the movements of Napoleon III's army played into German hands. The third German army followed the French army north, while one of the two German armies at Metz peeled off in order to close on its front. Finally, about 250,000 German troops encircled Napoleon III's army near the small town of Sedan. On September 1, the Germans executed a perfect *Kesselschlacht* as their infantry and artillery fire mowed down 20,000 French soldiers trying to break out of the ring around them. On September 2, Napoleon III surrendered himself and the rest of his army—104,000 troops—in the biggest capitulation in the field in modern times.

Following their victory at Sedan, the German forces began an advance on Paris. While they were on the way, a revolution in Paris toppled the government of the Second Empire and established a republican-dominated Government of National Defense. General Louis Trochu, formerly one of Napoleon III's generals, headed the new government, but its real driving force was Léon Gambetta, Minister of the Interior. He encouraged Trochu to defend Paris with its regular garrison, the Parisian National Guard, and the forts that encircled the city, while Gambetta and a delegation of the government went to Tours in order to direct a *levée en masse* and to build new armies. France still had its ports; its navy was still intact; and it could import weapons and other items of war. It was vital, however, that the defense of Paris and Metz tie down so many Germans that Moltke could not attempt to occupy the rest of France for a few months.

In fact, Moltke was alarmed by the new French strategy. Though he staged artillery bombardments of Paris after German troops encircled the city, he relied on hunger to force its capitulation, and that would take time. Bismarck was afraid that if the war dragged on, other countries, concerned for the balance of power if France were completely defeated, might be inclined to intervene. Paris, a city of two million people in 1870, could not be taken either easily or rapidly, and the siege of Metz also tied down many German troops. In addition, the only functioning railroad from Germany to Paris, via Strasbourg, was barely able to meet the German need in munitions, let alone food and fodder; accordingly, the German troops and their animals around Paris had to live off the country.

Fortunately for the Germans, Bazaine unexpectedly surrendered his 180,000 troops at Metz on October 31, a month before it was thought his supplies would run out, and during November the Germans were able to regroup in time to beat off the attacks of the new French armies in the south and west. They also repelled a sortie by the French garrison inside Paris. In December, the logistical situation for the Germans eased, and Moltke was able to concentrate a million German soldiers on French soil. By then, too, it was becoming clear that the German *Nation-in-Arms* had been more than a match for either the French *armée de métier* or armies raised by the French *levée en masse*.

On January 17, 1871, William I of Prussia was crowned Kaiser (Emperor) of Germany at Versailles, and the Second Reich was born. Paris surrendered ten days later, and a general armistice went into effect on January 30. A French National Convention meeting at Bordeaux approved a new government led by Adolphe Thiers and empowered it to make peace with the Second Reich. Just after the Germans carried out a victory march through Paris in early March and then left the city, radicals seized control of the Paris Commune (the city government) and refused to recognize the new French government, seated at Versailles, or any peace it might make with Germany. Bismarck consented to the return of French troops to restore order by force, and more Frenchmen died in the suppression of the Commune than during the German siege of Paris. The last vestiges of resistance were being stamped out in the French capital when, on May 10, 1871, the Peace of Frankfurt was signed. Under the peace treaty, France lost the provinces of Alsace-Lorraine to Germany, had to submit to German occupation of fortresses in eastern France until a war indemnity was paid off, and, of course, had to recognize the unification of Germany under the Hohenzollern dynasty. The last German soldier left French soil in 1873. The war had cost France 238,000 casualties, while Germany's losses came to 133,750 men.

3

The March toward
World War, 1871–1914

I. Armies

A. *The Spread of the German System and the Technology of Land Warfare.* In the years after 1871 France, Italy, Austria-Hungary, and Russia followed Germany in adopting the *Nation-in-Arms* and the German-style war college and general staff. The size of the major European armies kept pace with the growing populations and national budgets. Defense expenditures also provided for the training, arming, and equipping of reserves. As the proficiency of the general staffs increased across Europe, ever-larger numbers of men could be mobilized in less time. The mobilization plans dovetailed with the initial offensive plans of each army in such a way that the early movements were foreordained. Their complexity was such that, once mobilization was begun, it could not be stopped or altered extensively without risking chaos. Long before 1914 European governments had come to view general mobilization as tantamount to an act of war, and thus in any diplomatic crisis there was always the danger that one side or the other might "panic forward."

France made a heroic effort to keep up with German military development before 1914, and despite a smaller continental population. In 1872, it imposed universal liability to compulsory service on all Frenchmen of military age, and by 1880 most of its young men were required to perform three years of active service in the army, followed by four years in the army's reserve. In the 1890s the size of the French and German mobilizable armies was about the same, a million men apiece, but after the turn of the century the German edge in population (60 million Germans to 44 million French by 1914) made it impossible for France to keep up in total numbers. In order to narrow the German advantage in numbers as much as possible, in 1905 France reduced active service to two years and speeded up the formation of the reserve. By 1914 four out of every five eligible young French males were being called up for service in the army. In contrast, Germany summoned only half of its eligible manpower pool, leaving the rest—the *Ersatz Reserve*—to be trained in the event of war. In August 1914 France mobilized 1,650,000 troops and sixty-two infantry divisions; Germany mobilized 1,850,000 troops and eighty-seven infantry divisions. But whereas Germany had a large, if untrained, *Ersatz Reserve* for further army expansion, France had few more young men to call up. Hence, in a prolonged war, heavy French losses would affect not only the strength but the quality of the French army.

With a population of 150 million by 1914, Tsarist Russia had no difficulty in finding enough men for the army, but training them, arming them, and mobilizing them in event of war were quite different matters. Despite French financial loans, Russia remained industrially backward compared with the other great powers, while Russian distances and lack of enough railroads forced the army to take up to forty days in order to mobilize all of its 3 million troops and 114 infantry divisions. Even then, not all of these forces could be concentrated in European Russia, and they did not compare with the German or French troops in the quality of their arms and equipment. The Austro-Hungarian and Italian armies could each field 1.25 million men by 1914, and, like the German and the French armies, they could mobilize in about two weeks. But the Austro-Hungarian army was plagued with ethnic divisions, and the Italian army had never shown much military prowess since Italy's unification. Still, the total mobilizable strength of the five largest armies in Europe in 1914 came to about 9.5 million men, easily the largest number of troops ready to take the field to that time in history.

In the 1880s European armies began to reequip their infantry with the repeating magazine rifle and smokeless-powder ammunition. By 1914 the typical bolt-action, repeating rifle held three to nine rounds in its magazine. By working the bolt the soldier could jack a fresh cartridge into the chamber once every three seconds. The insertion of rounds into the magazine was also a matter of a few seconds. Under conditions of good visibility, the army rifle was dangerous to a thousand yards. Even more dramatic in its effect was Hiram Maxim's water-cooled machine-gun, developed in the 1880s. Using belts of ammunition, the Maxim gun could fire four hundred rounds a minute, yet was light enough for a crew of three soldiers to carry its parts and ammunition from place to place, and it could be fired from a prone or sitting position. Though the Maxim gun and its imitators were still too heavy for easy use on offense by 1914, they made ideal defensive weapons.

In the period between 1871 and 1914 artillery made great strides. Nitrocellulose (gun cotton) replaced black powder as the propellant, and trinitrophenol (picric acid) and trinitrotuolene (TNT) were excellent high explosives. The invention of the field telephone made it possible for forward observers to exploit the increasing range of the guns, now measured in miles, and thus gun batteries could be sited well in the rear of engaged infantry. The first field piece with a recoil piston was the French 75-mm gun, introduced in 1897. By absorbing the gun's recoil, the piston allowed the French 75 to fire as many as seven 18-pound shells in a minute and hit targets as far away as seven miles. The caliber of siege guns rose dramatically before 1914. "Big Bertha," the giant siege howitzer unveiled by the Germans at the beginning of the Great War, had a 420-mm caliber (16.8 inches) and could hurl a 2,200 lb. shell up to nine miles in order to smash concrete forts. Advances in artillery by 1914 had increased the depth as well as the devastation of the battlefield.

The hot-air balloon had been used for aerial observation as far back as the Wars of the French Revolution, but tethered balloons had their limits, and free balloons could not be steered. This situation began to change at the beginning of the twentieth century with the advent of both the dirigible (a steerable lighter-than-air craft, using hydrogen gas for inflation and gasoline engines for power), and the gasoline-engined airplane. Count Ferdinand von Zeppelin's work put Germany in the lead in development of dirigibles by 1914, and by then most armies had a few primitive airplanes. In the 1911–12 Italian invasion of Turkish Libya, a few planes were even used as platforms—not very effective ones—from which to hurl grenades on enemy forces below. Similar experiments were carried out with airplanes in the Balkan Wars of 1912–13. Still, down to 1914 no army saw the real potential in airpower beyond observation and scouting.

One of the great weaknesses of the mass armies of Europe by 1914 lay in their logistics. The automobile and the motor truck were still in their infancies, and beyond the railroad the troops marched and supplies were hauled for the most part in horse-drawn wagons. The mobilized German army in 1914 used 726,670 horses and 150,000 wagons, but fewer than 5,000 automobiles and motor trucks. Its animals consumed 14,533,400 pounds of fodder a day, or enough to fill up 581 boxcars or 7,266 horse-drawn wagons. The need for ammunition competed for space with food and fodder in the supply columns to an increasing degree, and, as a consequence, no army in motion could meet all its needs from supply from the rear further than about fifty miles from the nearest railhead. At the same time, huge numbers of troops and horses also found it more difficult to meet their needs for food and fodder from local requisition, especially if they could not camp for a prolonged period. On the other hand, if they camped too long in one place, they might exhaust local forage.

The other great weakness of the mass armies was in signal communication, chiefly because the available means depended on potentially vulnerable land lines. The telephone had joined the telegraph as an instrument of strategic control from a central headquarters by 1914, but both telephone and telegraph lines might be severed, or they might not be advanced with sufficient speed to keep higher headquarters in contact with troops in movement. The best solution, wireless telegraphy, was short-ranged and unreliable in 1914, and the voice radio was not perfected until after World War I. In consequence, mass armies in motion were harder than ever before to control from the rear, and errors in movement might develop a kind of slow but irresistible momentum of their own. Like the fictional Dr. Frankenstein, the general staffs of Europe had created monsters that they could scarcely control and whose movements at a distance were difficult to gauge.

   B. The Alliance Systems and Contingency War Plans.   One of the significant developments after 1871 was the formation of alliance systems to bolster the security of the European great powers. The alliances were indefinite in duration and amounted to mutual defense pacts. The process began in 1879 when Germany and Austria-Hungary concluded the Dual Alliance, expanded in 1881 to include Italy and thereby converted to a Triple Alliance. Subsequent quarrels between Austria-Hungary and Italy over their Adriatic frontier robbed the Italian addition of much vitality, but the Dual Alliance cemented the ties between Germany and Austria-Hungary, the so-called Central Powers of Europe. Bismarck's diplomacy kept Russia and France from forming an alliance to counterbalance the Central Powers until after Bismarck's retirement in 1890, but in 1894 the autocratic empire of the Tsar and the democratic republic of France put their ideological differences aside by forming the Dual Entente. Britain remained officially aloof from either alliance system to the turn of the century, but the growth in German naval power and overseas imperialism left Britain's leaders uneasy about the intentions of Kaiser William II. In 1904 Britain settled its colonial differences with France with the *Entente Cordiale,* and thereafter Britain and France engaged in joint defense planning for the contingency that Britain might intervene in a war between France and Germany.

   Both of the major alliance systems in Europe were allegedly defensive in purpose, but their existence made it more likely that a quarrel between any two members of the opposing systems might end by dragging all the major powers into war. Under the direction of Helmuth von Moltke the Elder, the German General Staff drew up contingency plans for a two-front war with Russia and France as early as 1879. Upon Moltke's retirement in 1888 and General Alfred von Waldersee's accession to his post, the German war plan continued to call for a concentration of German forces in East Prussia, and then, in conjunction with Austro-Hungarian forces, the carrying out of a *Kesselschlacht* against the Russian forces in

Poland. While the battle of encirclement and annihilation in Poland was underway, the General Staff counted on German forces and fortifications in the West to secure Germany from French invasion. Once the Russian forces were so mangled that they posed no offensive danger to Germany, Moltke planned to shift the mass of the German forces to the West in order to deal with France. But even if the *Kesselschlacht* in Poland were successful and the German forces were reconcentrated in the West, neither Moltke nor Waldersee thought that Germany could win a quick and decisive victory over a mobilized French *Nation-in-Arms.* They believed that the war would have to be ended through diplomacy. In short, the main objective of their war plans was to insure the safety of the Second Reich and to provide German diplomats with good bargaining chips at the peace table.

A main shift in German strategy came in 1891 when Waldersee was succeeded as Chief of the German General Staff by Alfred von Schlieffen. The young, headstrong Kaiser William II had fired both Bismarck and Waldersee in the first three years of his reign, and Schlieffen found himself free to depart from the more cautious military aims of his predecessors. Schlieffen sought a strategy whereby German forces could quickly defeat France before Russia had time to mobilize and intervene; then he proposed to concentrate in the East for a more prolonged but successful war against Russia. If Schlieffen's strategy was successful, Germany would be left in a position where it could dictate terms of peace to its enemies. But in the face of French border defenses and a powerful French *Nation-in-Arms,* a strategy of striking first in the West had little likelihood of success if the German offensive was launched headlong at the French frontier. Moreover, such an approach conflicted with German military doctrine. Schlieffen concluded that the best prospect for a quick German victory over France was to strike through neutral Luxembourg, Belgium, and Holland in order to outflank and then encircle the French armies at the German frontier. If the French *Nation-in-Arms* could be destroyed in a giant *Kesselschlacht* within forty days of the outbreak of war, the victorious German forces could then be moved by rail to the East to join with the Austro-Hungarian armies against Russia. Schlieffen realized that a German attack through neutral Belgium might provoke Britain into entering the war in fulfillment of its pledges under the Treaty of 1839, but he also knew that a British expeditionary force was bound to be small. He believed that any British force sent to the continent could either be swept up in the encirclement which destroyed the French armies, or penned up helplessly along the coast until the Germans had time to dispose of it. Schlieffen did not expect effective resistance from the armies of Holland and Belgium.

In the final version of Schlieffen's plan before his retirement in January

Count Alfred von Schlieffen

SOURCE: Walter Goerlitz, *History of the German General Staff,*
1657–1945, trans. Brian Battershaw (New York and London:
Praeger, 1953).

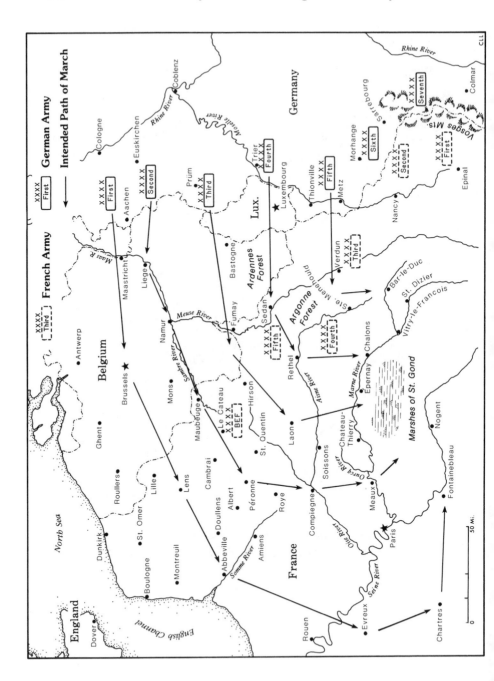

1906, he called for a mobilized German army of ninety infantry divisions, twelve more than the German army then possessed, to be divided among eight field armies. One of these armies containing ten divisions would be posted in the East as a hedge against an unexpected early Russian offensive, while seven armies containing eighty infantry divisions would be sent to the Western front. Two of the armies in the West, composed of ten infantry divisions and forming the German left wing, would guard the frontier with France in Alsace-Lorraine; the other five armies and seventy divisions, comprising the German right wing, would carry out the invasions of Holland, Belgium, and Luxembourg, and finally thrust into northern France into the rear of the French armies. The front of the right wing's advance would eventually extend as far west as the English Channel. Such was the version of Schlieffen's plan inherited by Helmuth von Moltke the Younger, nephew and namesake of the first Moltke, and Chief of the German General Staff from 1906 through the opening campaign of World War I.

The younger Moltke accepted the plan in principle, and by 1914 he had achieved an expansion of the army to eighty-seven of the ninety divisions that Schlieffen had called for. But Moltke also made important changes in Schlieffen's plan. He allocated nine divisions to the Eighth Army in East Prussia, twenty divisions to the two armies which were to defend Alsace-Lorraine (twice as many as Schlieffen had specified), and assigned only fifty-eight divisions, not seventy, to the five German armies on the right wing in the West. The ratio of forces between right and left wings in the West was changed from seven to one to less than three to one. In addition, Moltke canceled the planned invasion of Holland, a change that caused three of the five German armies on the right wing to crowd together in 1914 at the Liège Gap in order not to violate the neutrality of the so-called Dutch Maastricht Appendix. Yet when these armies deployed in the plains of Belgium, their front was barely broad enough to envelop Paris, much less to reach the Channel as Schlieffen had intended.

Critics have tended to fasten the blame for the failure of the Schlieffen Plan in 1914 on the pre-war changes made by Moltke, but in reality any version of the plan was risky. The combined French, British, and Belgian armies had almost as many divisions in the West as the Germans, while the Germans underestimated the logistical difficulties that their armies would face west of the river Meuse. The Germans never expected that the French would be able to correct the error in the original deployment of their forces in the time it took for the German armies to enter northern France, yet the French accomplished that very thing in 1914. When the German armies closed in for the final battle, they encountered not the enemy's rear but its front. True, had seventy divisions borne down on the Allied line, which extended no further west than Paris, they might have outflanked it; but it is also true that German logistics in 1914 were not even adequate to support the fewer than sixty divisions on the right wing. Indeed, had the campaign not taken place in August-September 1914, when there was an abundance of local forage in the plains of Belgium, German logistics might have faltered sooner than they did.

Whatever the faults of the Schieffen Plan, it was more imaginative than the French Plan XVII adopted after 1911. Plan XVII was a product of the French pre-war obsession with the offensive, and its underlying assumptions were in part derived from misapplied lessons from Ardant du Picq's *Battle Studies,* published after its author was killed in the Franco-Prussian War. Du Picq's book was based on questionnaires filled out by combat veterans at du Picq's request, and from the answers to his probing questions about the nature of combat, du Picq concluded that the factor of morale was dominant in success or failure on the battlefield. A later generation of French officers convinced themselves that high morale was associated with seizing the offensive, and Ferdinand Foch, professor at the French War College early in the twentieth century, developed syllogistic arguments which seemed to prove that improvements in firepower had benefited offense over defense. By 1914 French heads and field manuals were chock-full of aphorisms praising the offensive and denigrating defense.

The French obsession with seizing the offensive at the beginning of the war did not blind the French General Staff to the danger of a German flanking attack through Belgium, but the debate in their councils boiled down to whether the Germans would strip their frontier of troops in order to risk a wide envelopment west of the Meuse, or follow a more cautious course and use fewer troops to carry out a narrow envelopment through the Belgian Ardennes and Luxembourg. General August Michel, the French commander-in-chief designate in 1911, believed that the Germans would gamble everything on a wide envelopment and that, in such a case, the French army should deploy most of its forces at the Belgian frontier. The "Young Turks" on the General Staff argued to the contrary that the Germans were only planning a narrow envelopment and that the danger could be averted without abandoning plans for an early invasion of German territory. The "Young Turks" won out, General Joseph Joffre replaced Michel as commander-in-chief, and the details of Plan XVII were worked out in the final years before 1914.

Plan XVII called for the mobilization of fifty divisions in five armies, four of which were to invade Alsace-Lorraine and the German Rhineland beyond. The fifth army was to stand guard against a German flanking movement through Luxembourg and the Belgian Ardennes. Only twelve divisions, formed from older reservists, were to be held back around Paris as a general reserve; and, by accident, the same divisions, and reinforcements from North Africa, were the first forces available to Joffre when France was faced with a wide-front envelopment from Belgium in 1914. On that account, and because the French offensive into Alsace-Lorraine smashed itself to pieces on German fortifications and defensive fire, the modified Schlieffen Plan that Moltke executed in 1914 might have worked had its logistics not been faulty and had the French General Staff not performed something like a miracle by a rapid redeployment of the French armies to face the danger from Belgium.

The Russian war plan was predicated on the French need for early action in the East in order to draw off as many German divisions as possible. The *Stafka,* the Russian high command, showed great powers of self-denial in agreeing to the French pre-war demand that a Russian offensive aimed at German soil would be launched within two weeks of mobilization. Two Russian armies composed of twenty divisions would attempt to encircle the German forces in East Prussia. Within a month of the beginning of mobilization, the Russians would launch forty divisions in four armies against the Austro-Hungarian frontier. But forty days would pass before all of Russia's 114 infantry divisions could be deployed, and, while the early Russian offensives of 1914 did help to insure France's survival, the Tsar's armies never fully recovered from the effects of the Russian defeats resulting from them.

Count Franz Conrad von Hötzendorff, the ambitious chief of the Austro-Hungarian General Staff, planned to concentrate fifty infantry divisions in Galicia for Austria-Hungary's part of the *Kesselschlacht* in Poland, which the German General Staff had never informed him had long since been canceled. But other Austro-Hungarian plans called for a different deployment in event of war with the Balkan state of Serbia on Austria-Hungary's southern frontier, or in the event of war with Italy. As matters turned out, in 1914 the Austro-Hungarian army started to concentrate against Serbia, then had to carry out a hasty deployment against the Russian danger. It too never fully recovered from the effects of the battles of 1914. Italy declared its neutrality in 1914, then entered the war on the Allied side in 1915, hence its pre-war plans had no relevance to the situation at the outbreak of war.

Until 1911 the British were unsure whether to commit an expeditionary force to the continent independently of the French, or to send it to fight alongside the French armies. Advocates of the "Blue Water" strategy argued that the British Expeditionary Force (BEF) would have more effect as a distraction to the Germans by landing on either the Belgian coast or on the German Baltic coast. But most army leaders shared the view of the French General Staff that it was vital for the BEF to be at the side of the French armies for the opening battles. This "Continental School" won out over the "Blue Water School," and the BEF (six infantry divisions and a cavalry division in 1914) was assigned to occupy a position just west of the Meuse on the northwestern flank of the French Fifth Army watching the Belgian Ardennes. If the Germans tried a narrow envelopment through the Ardennes, as the French expected, they would find themselves blocked to their front by the French Fifth Army and outflanked to the west by the BEF. In reality, of course, the BEF's position put it squarely astride the path from Belgium that three German armies would take in 1914.

    C. The Anglo-American Military Experience to 1914.   The United States and Britain were unique among the world's major powers before 1914 in that neither imposed compulsory military service or maintained a *Nation-in-Arms*. In both countries, military service was voluntary. Until 1890 the United States was preoccupied with westward expansion across the North American continent and the final conquest of Indian territory, a task chiefly left to a small professional army. In the 1880s Congress approved the Endicott Plan for repairing America's crumbling and obsolete seacoast fortifications, but so little money was actually appropriated by Congress that not much was accomplished before the outbreak of the Spanish-American War in 1898. At the war's outbreak, the regular army numbered 27,865 officers and men, and the organized militia of the several states—the army's only uniformed reserve—was understrength and poorly prepared for war. Further, constitutional uncertainties about compelling Guardsmen to serve abroad forced the War Department to enlist volunteers from the militia as individuals, along with civilian volunteers, in United States Volunteer regiments under their own officers. The regular army was also expanded by taking in volunteers. The resulting mobilization process was so confused and hectic that, after 1898, it served as a major impetus for the first major American military reform since the Civil War.

    The chief architect of American military reform at the turn of the century was Elihu Root, Secretary of War from 1899 to 1904. The Root Reforms included: (1) a quadrupling of the authorized strength of the peacetime army to 100,000 officers and men; (2) the creation of an Army War College and a modernized General Staff; and (3) federal aid to the organized state militias, now officially called the National Guard, in hopes that they would serve as a pool of trained volunteers in time of war. The Root Reforms were, in certain respects, an attempt to compromise the views of the regular military establishment and the defenders of the tradition of the organized militia. The professional military's view had been influenced for many years by General Emory Upton's *The Military Policy of the United States* which, among other things, advocated the largest possible cadre of professional soldiers in skeletonized regiments in time of peace. In time of war, these regular army regiments under professional officers could be filled out with civilian volunteers. The leaders of the National

Guard preferred the creation of independent volunteer regiments drawn from the Guard and serving under their own officers, which would fight alongside, rather than as part of, the Regular Army. Neither the Army nor the National Guard had a good solution to the problem of getting Americans to volunteer for peacetime training, but in *laissez faire* America the idea of compulsory military service was anathema. The regular army's greatest progress after the Root Reforms was in completing a modern system of seacoast fortifications at home and overseas, and in creating separate field and coast artilleries for more effective specialization.

The British army remained largely unchanged from the time of the Cardwell Reforms (1868–72) down to the Second Anglo-Boer War (1899–1902). Problems of rapid expansion and heavy initial defeats in South Africa revealed the need for change. The Haldane-Esher Reforms, carried out just after the Boer War, were the counterpart to the Root Reforms in America. They included: (1) creation of a British Expeditionary Force in the home islands for quick deployment overseas in future emergencies; (2) consolidation of the militia and other voluntary military bodies into the Territorials, an organization roughly similar to the U.S. National Guard but assigned to regiments of the British regular army for training and mobilization; and (3) establishment of an Imperial General Staff and a modern war college. Britain, like America, rejected any form of compulsory peacetime military service, but by 1914 the Territorials provided fifteen partially trained and equipped reserve divisions. Moreover, unlike the U.S. National Guard down to 1916, Territorials could be compelled to serve overseas in time of war. But beyond the Territorials and a small army reserve, the regular British army's expansion in wartime required taking volunteers straight from civilian life. Even in World War I, Britain resisted general conscription until 1916.

II. Navies

A. *The Challenge of the* Jeune École *to 1889.*   From 1871 to 1889, the most formidable challenge to the old concepts of sea power was presented by the *Jeune École* ("Young School") of the French navy. Led by Admiral Théophile Aube, this school of thought predicted that mines and automotive torpedoes would make effective blockade impossible in future, and would rob the battleship of its traditional value as the chief means of commanding the sea. The reasoning of the *Jeune École* was persuasive to a French government already saddled with the expense of maintaining an army organized as a *Nation-in-Arms* and which saw little value in a navy except in a war with Britain. France could hardly expect to rival Britain in battleships while carrying the burden of great land armaments aimed at Germany; and a fleet built around torpedo-boats, mines, coast defenses, and commerce raiders would be much less expensive than one created around battleships. The high point for the *Jeune École* in France came in January 1886, when Aube was appointed Minister of Marine and stopped all battleship building in favor of a French navy built for *guerre de course.*

The claims of the *Jeune École* alarmed even the British admiralty and raised the question whether command of the sea based on the battleship was out of date. In 1885 some members of the naval establishment admitted that the battleships then under construction might be the last ever to join the British navy. Between 1885 and 1888, however, the Admiralty carried out extensive studies and tests and, in the latter year, concluded that, while the fleet must be extensively redesigned and strengthened to meet the new threat, the battleship remained the *sine qua non* of naval supremacy. The British Naval Defense Act of 1889 reflected both renewed confidence in the battleship and the fact that only a "balanced fleet" could meet a variety of threats satisfactorily. Huge sums of money were provided the navy in order to restore the "Two-Power Standard," a British navy that was at least as large as the next two navies combined (at the time, the navies of France and Russia). The new battleships were to be completely steam-propelled and their large guns supplemented with numerous, relatively small-caliber, quick-firing (QF) guns suitable for defense against torpedo-boats. In addition, a new class of "torpedo-boat-destroyers," also armed with QF guns and torpedoes, was created for the purpose of screening larger ships. When the British commissioned the first destroyer in 1893, they set off a wave of destroyer-building in all navies. Finally, the British dealt with the problem of commerce raiders by constructing numerous armored cruisers, ships fast enough to run down enemy ships and with more than enough power and armor to destroy them. Altogether, the Naval Defense Act of 1889 provided for the construction of seventy ships in five years.

British faith in the battleship and in a "balanced fleet" served to influence other navies to follow suit. Even the French navy moved in that direction after Aube left office. Moreover, the French strategic position changed. The last crisis between Britain and France occurred over rival claims to the Sudan in 1898, but, after the French backed down in order to curry British favor, Anglo-French relations began to improve. The last outstanding colonial differences between Britain and France were amicably settled under the *Entente Cordiale* of 1904, following which the French and British began joint defense planning. Well before 1914 the French navy could afford to leave the problem of an ever-increasing German navy to the British, and to concentrate on naval supremacy over Italy in the Mediterranean Sea and over Austria-Hungary in the Adriatic. By the outbreak of World War I, the ideas of the *Jeune École* seemed largely irrelevant even to the French fleet.

>   *B. The Mahanite School of Naval Power, 1890–1914.*   Next to
Britain's example, perhaps the writings of Captain Alfred Mahan of the
United States Navy did more than anything else to encourage navies to
return to traditional concepts of sea power. While servng as a professor at
the U.S. Naval War College, founded in 1884, Mahan published his
lectures in book form in 1890 under the title *The Influence of Sea Power
upon History, 1660–1783*, and thereby put himself on the way to be
proclaimed as a "Jomini of the sea." The central theme in Mahan's book,
and in the other books by his hand which followed, was that unchanging
principles govern the conduct of war at sea as much as on land, and that
certain natural factors largely determine the fitness of a state to be a sea
power. These natural factors, according to Mahan, were a state's
geographical position, its physical conformation, the extent of its
territory, the size and character of its population, and the character of its
government. According to Mahan, Britain's rise to naval predominance
was no accident, but rather an inevitable result of the natural factors
being more favorable in its case than in the cases of its rivals. The force of
these factors had manifested itself in Britain's unceasing urge for overseas
empire, a merchant fleet to link that empire's trade with the mother
country, and a great battle fleet which supported, and was supported by,
the wealth of that empire. In Mahan's view, overseas imperialism and
great sea power were concomitants.

Mahan's drawing of a connection between sea power and overseas
imperialism could not have been better timed. The forty years after 1871
saw the greatest Western overseas expansion since the eighteenth century,
and most of its thrust was aimed at undeveloped regions in Africa and
Asia, where the prospects of markets and sources of raw materials served
to lure the industrial powers of Europe. Mahan's thesis that great navies
and imperialism combine to produce, rather than to consume, great
wealth helped to produce "navalism," or the uncritical demand for naval
power. Mahan's writing influenced even continental European countries,
none more so than Imperial Germany. Kaiser William II was so enamored
with Mahan's first book that he caused translated copies to be placed in
every ship of his navy. He was so conditioned by the Mahanite view that by
the turn of the century he had fallen under the influence of the wily
Admiral Alfred von Tirpitz, who served successively as chief-of-staff of the
Supreme Naval Command (1892), secretary of state for naval affairs
(1897), and admiral of the fleet (1911–16). Aided by the preachments of
Mahan and the Kaiser's own visions of Germany as a world power, Tirpitz
had little difficulty in convincing William that the German navy should be

placed on the same secure financial basis as the army. Navalist propaganda by the Navy League and imperialist associations helped to lobby the German people in favor of a great High Seas Fleet. The Fleet Laws of 1898 and 1900 marked the passage of Germany to the status of a great naval power.

Once Germany committed a substantial part of its national wealth to its navy, the German battle line soon exceeded in size that of any other European naval power save the British. But there is also irony in the fact that with its resources divided between a great army and a great navy, Germany was never likely to overtake Britain's naval lead. Tirpitz rationalized his next largest fleet with the so-called "Risk Theories." He maintained that strict naval equality with Britain was unnecessary because Britain's much larger overseas empire forced a greater dispersion of its fleet over the globe. Should Britain try and succeed in destroying the rising navy of its new rival, it could do so only at the risk of such naval losses as would make it vulnerable to the attack of other naval powers. Germany's new and elaborate coastal defenses on the North Sea would make a direct British attack and close blockade of the German High Seas Fleet extremely hazardous. Britain would therefore be more respectful of Germany's ambitions overseas in time of peace, and less effective against Germany in time of war.

Tirpitz's Risk Theories proved as hollow as any of the other pre-war military rationalizations. Britain solved the problem of concentrating most of its fleet on the North Sea by reaching diplomatic agreements with potential overseas rivals. Its agreement with the United States over the Caribbean Sea and the right of the United States to build an isthmian canal across Central America opened the way for the British West Indian fleet to be withdrawn to home waters. The Anglo-Japanese Treaty of 1902 protected British interests in the Far East against the rising power of Japan. And deals struck with France in 1904 and with Russia in 1907 removed still more obstacles to "bringing the legions home." By 1914 most of Britain's battleship strength was based only three hundred miles from Germany's North Sea coasts. Moreover, the peculiar geography of the North Sea eliminated any British need for a close blockade of German ports. By controlling the Channel at one end and the passage between Scotland and Norway at the other, the British navy could impose a "distant blockade" far from Germany's coastal defenses. The result of William's big-navy policy was a fleet large enough to antagonize Britain, but too small to make it either respectful in peace or vulnerable in war. Perhaps a more careful reading of Mahan's work would have revealed to the Kaiser that no European land power since the seventeenth century had successfully competed with Britain for naval supremacy.

Outside Europe, however, the naval picture was indeed changing. The

United States and Japan were respectable—and still growing—naval powers at the turn of the century. As early as 1890 the United States had become the world's leading industrial power. In 1898 it annexed the Hawaiian Islands, two thousands miles from its Pacific shores, and acquired the Philippines in the Far East from Spain at the end of the Spanish-American War. President Theodore Roosevelt was no less a big-navy man than the Kaiser, and, as a close friend of Mahan, Roosevelt steadily pushed the expansion of the American fleet. By 1914 the American navy was the third largest in the world after the British and German. Japan rose to fourth place after knocking Russia out of the lists in the Russo-Japanese War (1904–5). The rise of the United States and Japan as naval powers was the principal reason that Britain abandoned the Two-Power Standard before 1914 to concentrate on naval supremacy over Germany.

C. Technical Developments in Navies, 1890–1914.   The British battleships built under the Naval Defense Act of 1889 typically displaced about 13,000 tons, carried four 12-inch guns in two large turrets, and were armed with as many as ten 6-inch and 4-inch QF guns as secondary batteries. Armor thickness at belt-line was a maximum of 24 inches. The largest guns could hit a target 6,000 yards distant, or six times further than the range of existing torpedoes. HMS *Cossack*, the first torpedo-boat-destroyer launched by Britain in 1893, displaced only 420 tons and carried two 3-inch QF guns as well as torpedoes. By 1914 the average destroyer's displacement had risen to 1,000 tons, and the newer destroyers carried four 4-inch guns and 21-inch torpedo tubes. Destroyers might do up to 35 knots, and their mission had been expanded from screening the large vessels of their own fleet to attacking large ships in the enemy's fleet whenever they could get within torpedo range. Armored cruisers, typically carrying 8-inch and 6-inch guns, completed the most important ships of the fleet.

In 1906, a revolution in battleship design took place when Britain launched HMS *Dreadnought,* the first of the "all big-gun ships," which lent its name to the generic type of future battleships. The designers of the *Dreadnought* had dispensed with secondary batteries in favor of arming it with ten 12-inch guns in five turrets. Instead of the "hail of fire" achieved by the older battleships with large guns of different caliber, which often made accurate observation of the fall of shot difficult, the *Dreadnought* improved "spotting" through firing salvos by groups of guns of the same caliber. The result was that under conditions of good visibility, the *Dreadnought* could lay down an accurate fire to 13,000 yards (6.5 nautical miles) and overwhelm any conventional battleship before it could get within range to reply. The *Dreadnought* also had steam-turbine engines in place of piston-driven engines, the first large warship so equipped. It burned a

HMS *Dreadnought*, 1906, the first "all big-gun battleship."
Source: Peter Padfield, *The Battleship Era* (New York: David McKay, 1972).

combination of oil and coal, and used four screws instead of two. Despite its 11 inches of armor at belt-line and a total displacement of 17,800 tons, it reached a speed of 21.5 knots on its trials, or six knots faster than existing battleships. In short, the advent of the *Dreadnought* made all previous battleships obsolete.

Admiral Sir John ("Jackie") Fisher, First Sea Lord at the time of the launching of the *Dreadnought*, was the person most responsible for its development. A naval officer with an unconquerable faith in big ships and big guns, Fisher also pushed the development of the battle cruiser, a ship with the same firepower as a dreadnought battleship but achieving greater speed and range through reduced armor. The first pair of British battle cruisers—HMS *Invincible* and HMS *Inflexible*—were launched in 1907. In 1911 another leap forward was taken with HMS *Thunderer*, a dreadnought battleship with a complete director fire-control system. All the heavy guns of the vessel were laid and trained by gun crews who never saw the target, but simply followed orders from a fire-control director station on the foremast. The operator of the director sight was in an elevated aiming position where he could see much further over the horizon than the gun crews and was less likely to be blinded by smoke or spray. He could cause salvos and broadsides to be fired as needed, and, by observing the pattern of falling shells around the target, he could adjust it until it was on the target. With the advent of HMS *Queen Elizabeth,* a dreadnought battleship launched in 1913, director-controlled fire could be delivered accurately to 20,000 yards (10 nautical miles). The *Queen Elizabeth* displaced 27,000 tons, carried eight 15-inch guns, and was a completely oil-burning vessel. It had a speed of 25 knots, and each of its 15-inch shells weighed almost a ton.

Britain did not retain a monopoly on the dreadnought design for long. Germany and other naval powers began laying down both dreadnought battleships and battle cruisers, and a so-called dreadnought race developed between Germany and Britain in the years just before World War I. Until 1914 the British and German admirals thought of little else but big ships and big guns. At the end of the race in August 1914, Britain had twenty-two dreadnought battleships and battle cruisers in commission and thirteen building or under trials. Germany had fourteen dreadnought battleships and battle cruisers in service, and seven more were under construction. On average, the British ships carried guns of larger caliber than the German, but the German ships were better armored. Still, with the numerical advantage lying with the British fleet, the German High Seas Fleet had no choice but to adopt a Fleet-in-Being strategy at the beginning of World War I.

The naval obsession with dreadnoughts before 1914 obscured important improvements in the submarine, still considered a kind of "thinking mine" and useful only for coast defense. The French *Gymnote,* launched in 1888, was the first submarine commissioned in any European navy, but the great breakthrough in submarine development came subsequently with the inventions of the gyro compass and periscope for underwater navigation, and the diesel engine for surface propulsion. The diesel engine was more efficient and safer than existing gasoline engines, and could be used to charge the electric storage batteries which powered the electric motors used underwater. Britain did not commission a submarine until 1902, but, with ninety-seven of the craft in 1914, the British submarine fleet was the largest in the world on the eve of World War I. The average British submarine displaced 540 tons when submerged. France, the United States, and Russia, in descending order, had the next largest number of submarines. Germany, the fifth-ranked submarine power in 1914, had forty-five of the craft, but fewer than half were designed to operate beyond the North Sea. Only by accident of circumstance after the outbreak of war did the German navy discover that the submarine's true vocation was *guerre de course.* Before the First World War was over, the commerce-raiding submarine had upset many Mahanite assumptions about naval power and the command of the sea.

III. The Wars, 1871–1914

Most of the wars of this period were connected with Western imperial expansion. Some of them were waged against older empires such as the Ottoman Turkish, the Chinese, and the Spanish, while still others were aimed at the primitive or less developed societies in Africa and Asia. The motivation for Western imperialism in this period has been attributed to "Gold, God, and Glory," or economic, missionary, and prestige factors. Thanks to steam power, preserved foods, and advances in medicine—as well as to superior arms, equipment, and organization—the Western countries could project their power into regions heretofore almost inaccessible to them. For example, in 1870 90 percent of the great continent of Africa was still unexplored and unmapped by Europeans; by 1914 all of Africa, except for the black states of Liberia and Ethiopia, was controlled by European powers. The story was similar in Southeast Asia where only Thailand (Siam) escaped Western domination before 1914.

A. The Russo-Turkish War and Tensions among the Great Powers, 1877–78. Complaints by Balkan Christians of Turkish abuse gave Tsar Alexander II an excuse to launch in 1877 still another of the many Russo-Turkish wars. Although the Russian armies outclassed the Turkish, they were brought up short by repeating rifles in Turkish hands at the siege of Plevna, where they required months of effort and suffered heavy casualties in order to break Turkish resistance. The Russian Black Sea fleet, revived after 1870, claimed to be the first to sink an enemy warship with a Whitehead automotive torpedo, though the first confirmed sinking with a Whitehead did not take place until 1891 when a Chilean torpedo-boat sank the iron-clad *Blanca Encalada* after it was seized by mutineers. The Russian victory over the Turks in the Balkans almost set off a new "Crimean War" among the great powers; Bismarck, however, hosted an international conference at Berlin at which the matter was settled peacefully.

The Congress of Berlin in 1878 created an independent Rumania (which ceded the province of Bessarabia to Russia), Bulgaria, and Montenegro, while requiring Turkey further to grant full independence to autonomous Serbia. But the Tsar was angered when the Congress awarded administrative control over the provinces of Bosnia and Herzegovina to Austria-Hungary, and thereby made the Habsburgs rivals of the Romanovs for influence in the Balkans. Because the Tsar blamed Bismarck personally for this outcome, tensions between Russia and Germany increased to the point where Berlin and Vienna found it prudent to conclude the Dual Alliance in 1879. But Bismarck had no intention of tying Germany's interests to Austria-Hungary's ventures in the Balkans, or of allowing Russia to drift into the arms of France. He worked diligently to improve relations among Germany, Russia, and Austria-Hungary through the Three Emperors' League and ultimately a secret Reinsurance Treaty with Russia which guaranteed that Germany would never support Austria-Hungary in an offensive war against Russia. Bismarck was largely successful in his diplomacy until William II came to the throne in 1888. The new Kaiser compelled Bismarck to retire in 1890 and allowed the Reinsurance Treaty with Russia to lapse. Four years later, Russia concluded a defensive alliance with France.

   B. The Overseas Colonial Wars.   Britain and France waged more overseas colonial wars between 1871 and 1914 than any other colonial powers, though Italy and Germany were involved in some lesser conflicts in Africa and Asia. Often the native armies or tribal hosts were superior in numbers to the invading Western armies, but they were usually inferior in weapons and organization. The essential problem for Western forces was to bring about native subordination at the lowest possible cost and in a manner likely to insure permanent pacification.

   In general, Western armies were best suited for set-piece battles, where their superior firepower made short work of attacking hordes armed with spears or primitive flintlocks, but this was not always the case. The Zulu host in South Africa proved to be brave, numerous, and well led. In 1879, when General Lord Chelmsford invaded Zululand with 8,500 British and Kaffir (native) troops, 20,000 Zulus outmaneuvered his army, isolated a detachment at Isandhlwana, and overwhelmed it, leaving only fifty European soldiers and three hundred Kaffirs alive. Few of the Zulu warriors in that battle had any weapon more deadly than the *assegai* or throwing spear. (In comparison, in 1876 perhaps 1,800 Sioux warriors wiped out fewer than three hundred cavalrymen under George Custer at the Battle of the Little Big Horn, the biggest victory ever achieved by the Plains Indians in North America, and at least some of the Indians were equipped with repeating rifles.) Chelmsford's army was compelled to retreat after Isandhlwana, but six months later it reinvaded Zululand and crushed the Zulu host at a pitched battle near Ulundi, the Zulu capital. The power of the Zulu nation never recovered from that defeat.

   The British also had their share of trouble in North Africa after they established a protectorate over Egypt in 1882 in order to protect their interests in the Suez Canal, opened in 1869, and to collect debts owed by the Khedive of Egypt. The British inherited Egypt's war with the Dervishes of the Sudan, and in 1883 an Egyptian army advised by General William Hicks invaded the Sudan, only to be wiped out in the sands of the Khordufan desert. The Dervishes laid siege to the Egyptian garrison at Khartoum, commanded by British general Charles "Chinese" Gordon, and, after 317 days, broke through Khartoum's defenses to massacre the garrison and its commander in 1885. The British abandoned their efforts to conquer the Sudan for thirteen years, but in 1898 an Anglo-Egyptian army of 25,000 troops under General Horatio Herbert Kitchener drove up the Nile to crush a Dervish host of 40,000 men at the Battle of Omdurman. An Italian army of 15,000 troops invading Ethiopia in 1896 had not been so lucky. It was routed at Adowa by Abyssinian tribesmen in the worst defeat suffered by any Western colonial army before 1914.

Among the ablest of the British imperial generals were Garnet Wolseley and Frederick Roberts. Wolseley won a reputation in the Ashanti Wars of West Africa in the 1870s, and he commanded the expedition to Egypt in 1882 with brilliance. (*Pirates of Penzance*'s "very model of a modern major general" was inspired by Wolseley.) Roberts first won fame in the Second Afghan War when, in 1880, he led a relief expedition to besieged Khandahar. In the Second Anglo-Boer War (1899–1902), he was to rally a defeated army and lead it forward to victory. Perhaps the best of the French colonial generals were Joseph Gallieni and Louis Lyautey. Gallieni is best remembered for his vital role as military governor of Paris in the crisis of 1914, but he first achieved reputation as a colonial soldier and administrator in Tonkin China (northern Vietnam) in the 1890s. Lyautey also served in the construction of the French colony of Indochina (Vietnam, Laos and Cambodia), in Madagascar, and was the dominant figure in the French conquest of Morocco in 1912. The greatest of the German colonial commanders was General Paul von Lettow-Vorbeck, whose operations with black troops in German East Africa during World War I repeatedly confounded the best efforts of the British to defeat him.

No colonial foe proved more difficult for the British to defeat than the white South Africans known as the Boers. This hardy people were descended from the Dutch who settled Cape Colony in the seventeenth century and found themselves under British rule at the end of the Napoleonic Wars. After Parliament outlawed black slavery throughout the British empire, many Boers trekked into Natal where they defeated the Zulu chieftain Dingaan and his warrior host at the battle of Blood River in 1838. When Britain annexed Natal in 1843, some Boers migrated across the Drakensburg range to found the Orange and Transvaal republics. These farming republics were threatened again when gold and diamonds were discovered on their territory and a host of British prospectors and mineral companies rushed to the Rand. In 1881, Boer militia, well armed with modern rifles, beat back the invasion of a small British army under Gen-

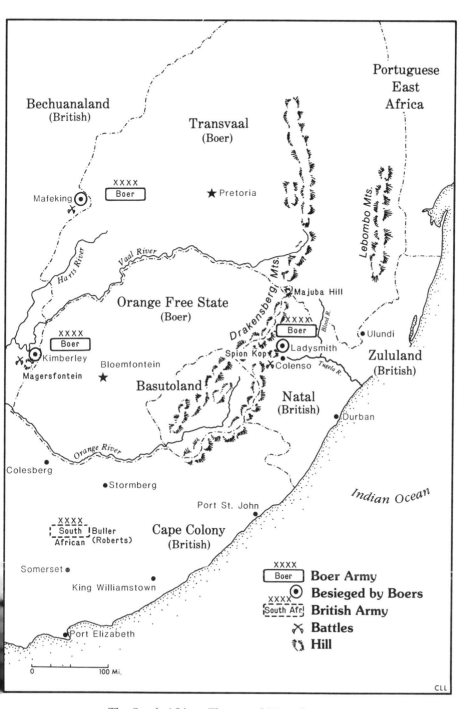

The South African Theater of War, 1899–1902

eral Sir George Colley in the First Anglo-Boer War. Colley lost his life at the British defeat at Majuba Hill, the first successful white colonial resistance to British regulars since the American Revolution a century earlier.

The Second Anglo-Boer War (1899–1902) broke out when negotiations between President Paul Krueger and the British governor of Cape Colony collapsed in October 1899. Rather than await British invasion of their territories, the Boer militia—45,000 strong—invaded British Rhodesia, Natal, and Cape Colony, imposing sieges on the British garrisons at Mafeking, Ladysmith, and Kimberley. No more than 15,000 British troops were in South Africa at the outbreak of war. When 47,000 British reinforcements arrived in South Africa under General Redvers Buller, they were heavily defeated in their attempts to raise the sieges of Kimberley and Ladysmith at the battles of Magersfontein, Colenso, and Spion Kop (December 1899–January 1900). Roberts then relieved Buller of command, and the strength of the British forces was eventually raised to 250,000 troops. During 1900 Roberts's forces relieved Kimberley, Ladysmith, and Mafeking, and then went on to capture the Boer capitals at Bloemfontein and Pretoria. After the regular Boer armies were broken up, Roberts passed command to Kitchener and returned to Britain in January 1901, where he was personally decorated by Queen Victoria a few weeks before her death.

But the Boer War was not over. Boer commandos launched a hit-and-run guerrilla war by horseback across the veldt that the British required the better part of two years to suppress. Kitchener resorted to the very un-Victorian tactics of burning Boer farms, imprisoning Boer populations in concentration camps, and crisscrossing the veldt with block houses and barbed wire barriers. His systematic sweeps through Boer country foreshadowed American "Search and Destroy" tactics during the Vietnam War nearly seventy years later. A fifth of the Boer population in the concentration camps died of disease, bad food, and poor sanitation. By the time the last commando surrendered, the war had cost the lives of 25,000 Boers (in a population of less than a million people), as well as 22,000 Britons and 12,000 black Africans.

The regular side of the Boer War revealed once again that in the face of modern rifled arms, armies must practice dispersion, cover, and concealment, and avoid frontal attacks wherever possible. The British army shifted to khaki-colored uniforms in order to blend in with the countryside in the manner of its Boer enemy. Early British defeats were attributed in part to outdated assault formations, which even included movement of artillery within range of Boer marksmen. The British were so impressed with the accuracy of Boer rifle fire that after the Boer War the British infantry were given the most intensive training in marksmanship of any army in Europe. As a result, the accuracy of British rifle fire was second to

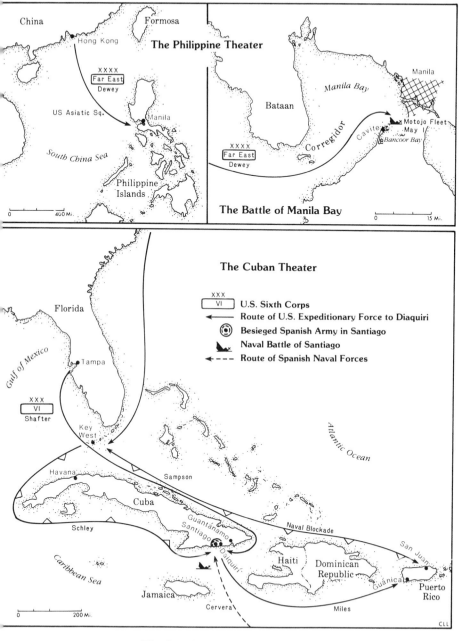

The Spanish-American War, 1898

none by 1914, something the Germans learned to their cost on more than one occasion in the opening battles of World War I. The Boer War also demonstrated the need for centralized imperial war planning on the British side, and thus contributed to the creation of an Imperial General Staff as well as to all the other Haldane-Esher reforms already discussed.

Coincident with the Boer War and just after the Spanish-American War, the Americans had their first experience with a guerrilla war overseas. Emilio Aguinaldo led the Philippine Insurrection against American rule, and the Filipinos offered such resistance that eventually the Americans had to employ 65,000 regular troops and 35,000 short-term volunteers to put it down. By the time President Theodore Roosevelt declared the insurrection at an end on July 4, 1902, the Americans had suffered 10,000 casualties, or twice as many as they had suffered in the Spanish-American War. With the outbreak of the Boxer Rebellion in China (1900), American troops joined those of other powers in an international expeditionary force to relieve the besieged legations at Peking (Beijing). Some American troops remained in China until 1938 as part of a larger international force to garrison the Tientsin-Peking railroad. The American acquisition of the Philippines and participation in the Boxer Rebellion had the effect of making the United States a new power in the Far East, with great consequences for itself and the Pacific region.

C. The Spanish-American War, 1898.   American involvement in the Far East came about by the unlikely route of conflict with Spain over its island territory of Cuba. U.S. interest in the Caribbean was connected with prospects of Latin American trade and the need for an isthmian canal across Central America, but American attention was drawn to Cuba by a long revolt against Spanish rule and the Spanish measures for crushing it. Americans were horrified by newspaper accounts of the Spanish policy of *reconcentrado* (herding the rural population into concentration camps so that they could not aid the guerrillas), though the Spanish measures were no more cruel than some to be used by the British in the Boer War or by the Americans themselves during the Philippine Insurrection. Public tensions produced by "Yellow Journalism," especially the competing Pulitzer and Hearst newspaper syndicates, were heightened in February 1898 by a mysterious explosion that sank the U.S. battleship *Maine* while on a visit to Havana, and by the De Lome Letter episode, in which the Spanish minister to Washington seemed to insult President William McKinley. McKinley ordered Admiral William T. Sampson's North Atlantic Squadron to begin a blockade of Cuban ports on April 21, and on April 25 Congress declared a state of war with Spain.

The United States had all the advantages at the outbreak of war. The U.S. Navy boasted six battleships, two armored cruisers, ten protected (partly armored) cruisers, and a number of gunboats against a Spanish fleet of five cruisers, a few destroyers, and some lesser craft. While the Spanish army had 100,000 troops in Cuba and 20,000 troops in Puerto Rico, they were diseased and harried by guerrillas, as were the Spanish troops in the Philippines. The U.S. Army of 28,000 officers and enlisted men was too small to serve other than as a cornerstone for the wartime army, but the principal operations against Cuba were relatively near American shores, and Spain was far away from all its territories in jeopardy.

The war began over the Cuban issue, but the first blow was struck far across the Pacific on May 1 at Manila Bay in the Philippines. There Commodore George Dewey's cruiser squadron annihilated the decrepit Spanish fleet in a morning's fighting after steaming from Hong Kong, where it had been on an official visit. The attack was not improvised; it had been planned in advance in the event war broke out between Spain and the United States, the cable at Hong Kong keeping Dewey apprised of events. A simple order from Washington was all that was necessary to get Dewey's force in motion. However, American troops to occupy the Philippines did not arrive for another two months, the cruiser *Charleston*—escorting a convoy of reinforcements—capturing Spanish Guam on the way.

Dewey's attack on Manila Bay was about the only thing that went as intended at the outbreak of war. Nelson Miles, Commanding General of the U.S. Army, favored a plan of systematically preparing 80,000 regulars and volunteers for tropical warfare, then landing them near Havana in October at the end of the rainy season, following up the invasion of Cuba with the seizure of Puerto Rico. But Russell Alger, Secretary of War, was under pressure from President McKinley and the public to begin operations at once; accordingly, training camps were hastily erected at Chickamauga, Mobile, and Tampa Bay, and a hard-pressed War Department sought to arm and equip an influx of volunteers quickly. Amid a near-chaotic mobilization, word was received that Admiral Pascual Cervera's naval squadron had left Spanish waters for the Western hemisphere, possibly to bombard American cities along the Atlantic coast, protected only by crumbling pre–Civil War fortifications. While the navy formed a fast squadron under Commodore Winfield S. Schley to intercept Cervera's force in the North Atlantic, the army turned its attention to throwing up improvised seacoast fortifications. All this activity proved pointless when Cervera's force turned out to be heading across the South Atlantic in order to approach Cuba from a southerly direction. The Spanish fleet finally took shelter in the port of Santiago on May 19. Belatedly, Sampson and Schley reunited their squadrons at Key West and finally imposed a blockade on Santiago beginning on May 27.

The arrival of Cervera's fleet at Santiago shaped the further direction of

American strategy so far as Cuba was concerned. On June 10, a few hundred U.S. Marines seized Guantanamo in order to provide Sampson's fleet a coaling station near Santiago, and on June 21 the first 17,000 troops of General William R. Shafter's V Corps landed at Daiquiri. Santiago's garrison of 25,000 Spanish troops withdrew behind their fortifications as the American army approached the rear of the port, and the first major landfighting of the war—indeed about all that occurred in Cuba—took place on July 1, when U.S. troops attacked the outer line of Spanish defenses at San Juan Hill and El Caney. Theodore Roosevelt, who had resigned his post as Assistant Secretary of the Navy in order to become a lieutenant-colonel in a volunteer cavalry regiment, was prominent in the fighting at San Juan Hill. At the end of the day, the Spanish troops had fallen back on their final line of defense around Santiago. On July 3, Cervera's squadron attempted to get to sea before the port fell, but, with a force of four battleships and a cruiser, Commodore Schley made short work of the Spanish fleet. All of Cervera's ships were sunk or driven ashore. A fortnight later, the remaining 22,000 Spanish troops in Santiago surrendered to Shafter. Before July was out, General Miles had carried out an unresisted American invasion of Puerto Rico, and in August the Spanish government requested an armistice. The war had cost the United States 5,000 casualties, three-fifths of them fatal, and most of them caused by disease and bad food. As the result of what John Hay, the American Secretary of State, called a "splendid little war," Cuba received its independence, and Puerto Rico and the Philippines became American territories.

D. *The Sino-Japanese and Russo-Japanese Wars.*   Two Far Eastern wars at the turn of the century marked the rise of Japan to great power status, the Sino-Japanese War (1894–95) and the Russo-Japanese War (1904–5). As the first Asian state in recent times to modernize, Japan escaped the fate of China and other Far Eastern states which were being increasingly eroded and overwhelmed by Western imperialism. Before the end of the nineteenth century, Japan had a modest but modern industrial base, a *Nation-in-Arms* army (since 1885 mostly modeled on the German), and a modern navy with its larger ships built in the West. Japan was eager to share in the spoils of the disintegrating Chinese empire, and in 1894 it found a pretext for war through a Japanese-fomented rebellion in Korea, a client-state of China. When Japanese troops landed in Korea to support a puppet regime, China declared war on Japan on August 1.

The war was hardly a challenge to Japan. The decrepit Chinese army and navy were speedily defeated—the naval battle off the mouth of the Yalu River being the first large fleet action since Lissa—and Japanese troops overran Korea, southern Manchuria, and, across the Yellow Sea, the Shantung peninsula and its port of Weihaiwei. In 1895, when Japan

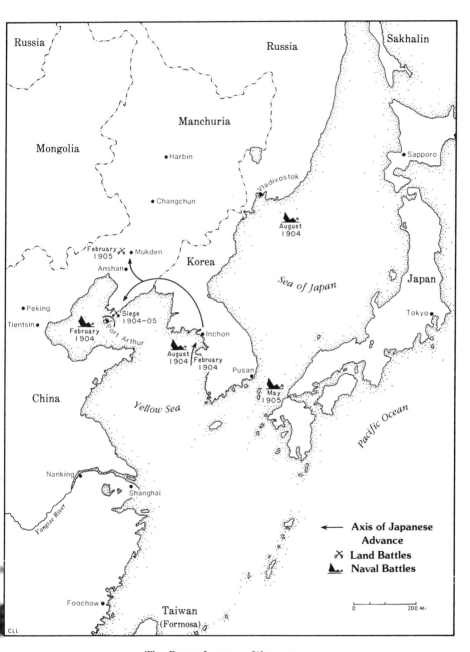

The Russo-Japanese War, 1904–5

demanded the cession of these territories and more, Russia, Germany, and France—each jealous of its own interests in the Far East—threatened to intervene unless Japan submitted to a revision of terms. Japan finally abandoned its earlier demands and accepted the island of Taiwan (Formosa), the Pescadores, and a war indemnity from China. Much to Japanese chagrin, the Germans subsequently moved into China's Shantung peninsula, and in 1896 China granted Russia the right to extend its Trans-Siberian Railroad to Vladivostok through central Manchuria in return for a Russian loan to pay off the Chinese indemnity to Japan. In 1897 Russia acquired the right to extend a spur of that line—known as the Chinese-Eastern railroad—from Harbin south to Port Arthur at the end of the Laiotung peninsula. In 1898 Russia acquired a long-term lease on the naval base at Port Arthur and the neighboring commercial port of Dairen. Russia thus gained a dominating position in Manchuria, warm-water ports on the Yellow Sea, and a base for possible expansion into Korea, about as close to Japan as Cuba is to the United States.

But Britain was also disturbed by Russian expansion in the Far East; as discussed earlier, it was eager to shift much of its naval power to European waters in order to offset Germany's growing naval power. Its solution was the Anglo-Japanese Treaty, signed in 1902. The treaty guaranteed Japanese respect for Britain's interests in the Far East in return for Britain's intervention on Japan's side if Japan became involved in war with a coalition of powers, and Britain's benevolent neutrality should Japan engage a single foreign power. The treaty freed Japan to risk war with Russia, and Tokyo promptly demanded a renegotiation of the Russian position in Manchuria and increased security for Korea. When these negotiations faltered, Japan resorted to war in 1904.

At the outbreak of war, Russia appeared to have the advantage. Tsar Nicholas II had a million troops on active duty and 2.5 million reservists. His navy was then the third largest in the world, and included fifteen battleships, nineteen cruisers, and thirty destroyers. In contrast, the mobilized Japanese army had 800,000 troops, and the Japanese navy only six battleships, twenty-five cruisers, twenty-one destroyers, and thirty-nine torpedo-boats. But, as Alfred Mahan was fond of pointing out, all of Japan's large warships had been built in Europe, and moreover, geography often vitiates apparent strength. Only 300,000 Russian troops were in Manchuria when the war began, and they were dependent for supply and reinforcement on a single-track Trans-Siberian railroad that stretched over 5,000 miles to European Russia. The Russian Far Eastern fleet was composed of seven battleships, eleven cruisers, and eight destroyers, but at the outbreak of war all of the battleships and destroyers were at Port Arthur, four of the cruisers were at Vladivostok, and one cruiser was at Inchon, Korea. Since international treaties prevented the Russian Black

Sea fleet from passing through the Dardanelles, only the Russian Baltic fleet was free to sortie to the Far East, assuming it could solve the logistical problems of a voyage of 18,000 miles without overseas coaling bases. In short, Japan had local superiority in land and naval forces at the beginning of the conflict and was likely to keep it as the war continued.

Admiral Heihachiro Togo's Combined Fleet commenced hostilities on February 8, 1904, with a surprise attack against the Russian fleet at anchor in Port Arthur and the Russian cruiser at Inchon. The attack with gunfire and torpedoes put two Russian battleships and a cruiser out of commission at Port Arthur and eliminated the cruiser at Inchon. With the Russian cruisers at Vladivostok frozen in until spring, Japanese command of the sea was assured. The Japanese army was free to invade Korea, southern Manchuria, and eventually to impose a siege on Port Arthur. In March, Admiral Stephan Makarov and the Russian fleet at Port Arthur sortied against Togo's blockade, but returned to port after a mine sank the Russian flagship and took Makarov's life. Admiral Vilgelm Vitgeft, Makarov's successor, made another sortie in August with six battleships, four cruisers, and eight destroyers only to meet with a humiliating defeat in the Battle of the Yellow Sea. Though Togo's fleet had previously lost two of its battleships to mines, it proved superior to the Russian in both its speed and accuracy of fire. Vitgeft was killed, and only five battleships, a cruiser, and three destroyers managed to get back to Port Arthur. In the same month, a Russian sortie from Vladivostok had led to the loss of two of four cruisers at the hands of another Japanese force. In January 1905 the Russian garrison and fleet at Port Arthur surrendered, half of the 65,000 Russian soldiers and sailors defending the port casualties by the end of the fighting.

In February 1905 300,000 Japanese troops engaged 350,000 Russian troops near Mukden, a key rail center in Manchuria, in the biggest battle in history before 1914. The battle front eventually stretched to twenty miles. Both sides employed entrenchments, barbed-wire barriers, repeating rifles, machine-guns, hand grenades, and rapid-fire artillery and high explosive shell. The battle raged on indecisively for ten days, then the Japanese finally outflanked the Russians and compelled their withdrawal. The defeated Russians had suffered 89,000 casualties, but the victorious Japanese had suffered the loss of 70,000 men. Still, the battle left southern Manchuria securely in the hands of the Japanese.

The last Russian hope for victory in the Far East lay in Admiral Zinovi Rozhdestvenski's fleet, which had left the Baltic in October 1904. Accompanied by a train of coal colliers, and covertly resupplied by the French overseas colonies on the way as it worked its way to the Far East, it was in the Indian Ocean in early 1905 when it learned of the fall of Port Arthur. Rozhdestvenski then set a new course for Vladivostok, recoaling for a final time near Camranh Bay, French Indochina, in May. It steered north toward Tsushima Strait between Japan and Korea, where Admiral Togo's fleet lay in waiting. Superficially, the Russian fleet was more powerful—eight battleships, seven cruisers, seven destroyers, and four old iron-clads—to Togo's force of four battleships, eight cruisers, fourteen destroyers, and thirty-nine torpedo-boats. But the Japanese were rested and ready, while months at sea had left the Russian vessels fouled and slow moving, and their crews exhausted.

When the Battle of Tsushima Strait was joined on May 27, Admiral Togo's fleet—using the advantage of two columns of ships, accurate gun-fire, and superior speed—sank or captured five Russian battleships, four cruisers, and two destroyers. A Russian cruiser and two destroyers reached Vladivostok, but the remaining Russian vessels fled to neutral ports. Of the 13,000 Russian sailors involved, 4,830 lost their lives. Togo's losses came to three torpedo-boats, minor damage to larger vessels, and 117 sailors killed or wounded. Such a one-sided victory at sea had not been seen since Trafalgar.

The peace treaty which ended the Russo-Japanese War was mediated by the United States and signed at Portsmouth, New Hampshire, in September 1905. By its terms, Japan acquired Port Arthur, the Laiotung peninsula, the Chinese Eastern railroad as far north as Mukden, the southern half of Sakhalin Island off Russia's Pacific coast, and effective control over Korea (formally annexed by Japan in 1910). The Russians, however, were able to resist Japanese demands for a war indemnity. Military and naval observers concluded from the events of the war that a future great conflict elsewhere would be, like the Russo-Japanese War, violent but relatively brief. Moreover, they held that the war demonstrated the side which attacked first would have a clear advantage. Hence, force in being, rather than potential strength, was likely to count most in future great wars. There was no opportunity for them to reconsider their verdict before the guns of August 1914 commenced the First World War.

E. The Final Wars and Crises before 1914.   In 1905 the First Moroccan Crisis erupted when Britain and France agreed that Morocco would be in the French sphere of influence. The German government was angry that Berlin had not been consulted, and a German challenge to the settlement seemed likely to lead to war. But Britain firmly supported France at the Algeciras Conference in 1906, and Germany backed down. In 1908 an even greater crisis broke out when Austria-Hungary formally annexed the territories of Bosnia and Herzegovina in the Balkans without consultation with Tsarist Russia. The Russian and Serbian governments were outraged, the latter because it dreamed of Serbia becoming the hub of a future Yugoslavia ("south Slav state") that included Bosnia and

Herzegovina. This time, Germany supported Austria-Hungary's action; the Tsar's government, still recovering from the effects of the Russo-Japanese War and a mass revolt inside Russia in 1905, backed down. The Bosnian Crisis subsided.

In 1911 a Second Moroccan Crisis was peacefully ended when France ceded some minor territory in Africa to Germany, but in the same year Italian forces invaded Turkish Libya and achieved an easy victory. Turkey's apparent military weakness encouraged the Balkan League (Serbia, Montenegro, Greece, and Bulgaria) to attack Turkey's remaining territories in Europe in the First Balkan War (1912); then quarrels over the spoils brought about a Second Balkan War (1913) between Bulgaria and the rest of the League. Only a partial solution to the Balkan crisis was reached at the London Conference by establishing the new state of Albania on the Adriatic Sea. The Serbian government at Belgrade remained bitter over Austria-Hungary's maneuvers to prevent Serbia from getting access to the Adriatic, and, in turn, Vienna had come to view Serbia as a threat to the integrity of the Slavic parts of the Austro-Hungarian empire. By the beginning of 1914 these developments, and a strident nationalism surging across Europe, made the maintenance of general peace very precarious; that year the march toward world war reached its destination.

4

The First World War, 1914–18

I. The Outbreak and the Stalemate of 1914

A. The Outbreak of War. The Great War, as the generation between 1914 and 1939 would call it, was precipitated by the assassination of the Archduke Francis-Ferdinand, heir to the Austro-Hungarian throne, on June 28, 1914, while he was making a state visit to Sarajevo in Bosnia. After arrest of the assassin and investigation of the crime, the Austro-Hungarian government placed responsibility on Serbia, and succeeded in getting German support for a punitive policy against the Balkan state. In late July, Vienna issued an ultimatum to Belgrade, which, had all its points been agreed to by the Serb government, would have jeopardized Serbia's independence and sovereignty. When Belgrade refused to comply with all the Austro-Hungarian terms, Austria-Hungary declared a state of war with Serbia on July 28.

Tsar Nicholas II's government viewed Austria-Hungary's actions toward Serbia as unwarranted, and resented Germany's support of Austria-Hungary's actions. On July 30, the Tsar ordered general mobilization of the Russian army against Austria-Hungary and Germany. Berlin demanded that Russia cease mobilization on pain of war, and inquired of Paris where France stood in the quarrel. The French government replied ambiguously that it would consult its own interests, but ordered general mobilization of the French army on the afternoon of August 1 as a precautionary measure. Within the hour of the French order, Kaiser William II ordered German mobilization against both Russia and France. By the night of August 1, a state of war effectively existed between Germany and Austria-Hungary on the one hand and Russia and France on the other.

At the outbreak of war, General Helmuth von Moltke the Younger, Chief of the German General Staff, ordered the implementation of his revised version of the pre-war Schlieffen Plan. On August 2, German troops occupied Luxembourg, and on August 3 special German units at the frontier launched attacks on the Belgian forts around Liège, gateway to the Belgian plains. Germany's violation of Belgium's neutrality provoked a strong protest from the British government, which, under the Treaty of 1839, was a guarantor of Belgian neutrality and independence. London warned Berlin that Britain could not fail to take action if the Germans persisted with their invasion of Belgium. Berlin rejected the British demand for withdrawal of German troops, pleading the excuse of "military necessity" and expressing the hope that Britain would not go to war over a "scrap of paper." The tactless German reply did much to stir up a war fever among the British people, and at midnight on August 4 Britain declared a state of war with the German empire.

B. The Opening Battles and Stalemate in the West, 1914. Except for the German occupation of Luxembourg and German attacks on Liège, the first two weeks of August 1914 were taken up in the West with the completion of the mobilizations of opposing forces. By mid-month General Joseph Joffre, the French general-in-chief, had concentrated 1,060,000 troops in eastern France and divided them into five armies. Three armies, composed of 600,000 men, were to attack the German frontier in Alsace-Lorraine and invade the German Rhineland. The Fourth Army, 160,000 men, was to invade the southern tip of the Ardennes forest in Belgium, and the Fifth Army of 240,000 men was to attack down both sides of the Meuse River into the northern Ardennes. As a further precaution against a German turning movement against the Allied left, the British Expeditionary Force (BEF), under General Sir John French, took position to the west of the Meuse and on the flank of the Fifth Army. On the German side, 1,360,000 troops were deployed in the West in seven armies, 320,000 of them in two armies to protect the border with France, but over a million troops in five armies to carry out the great encirclement of French forces at the Franco-German frontier by a wide envelopment through Belgium.

The outcome of the Battle of the Frontiers (August 16–23) was a victory for the Germans. The three French armies trying to break into Alsace-Lorraine were repelled in their attacks, and, in a week's time, the French army suffered 300,000 casualties. The French pre-war illusions about the irresistibility of the offensive were wiped out in a trice by withering German defensive fire. Meanwhile, the Belgian army of 115,000 troops was compelled to abandon the defenses of Liège after monster German siege guns demolished the Belgian concrete forts and German infantry infiltrated the gaps between them. The Belgian army retreated toward Brussels and then Antwerp. After detaching troops to follow the Belgian army, the German First, Second, and Third armies advanced through central Bel-

Artillery of the World War I era: the French 75-mm gun
and British 18-pounder gun.
SOURCE: John Batchelor and Ian Hogg, *Artillery* (New York: Ballantine, 1972).

Artillery of the World War I era: the German 21-cm howitzer.
SOURCE: John Batchelor and Ian Hogg, *Artillery* (New York: Ballantine, 1972).

gium, then pivoted south toward the French frontier west of the river Meuse. On the inside of the German wheel, the Fourth and Fifth armies advanced through the Belgian Ardennes and Luxembourg respectively, pivoting on the fortified area of Metz-Thionville. At first unaware of the huge size of the German right wing entering Belgium, the French Fourth and Fifth armies, plus the BEF, advanced headlong into the wall of oncoming German forces and were almost enveloped before they recognized the danger. Then they began a fighting withdrawal to French territory.

The Allied defeat in the Battle of the Frontiers opened Joffre's eyes to the fact that, pre-war French predictions to the contrary, the Germans were attempting a wide-front envelopment of French forces through Belgium, and at least three German armies were west of the Meuse. In order to thwart German intentions, a new front of Allied armies had to be formed facing north, while at the same time the French frontier had to be protected from attacks by the German armies in Alsace-Lorraine. Joffre arranged for the French First and Second armies to man the fixed defenses at the frontier, where they subsequently beat off the attacks of the German Sixth and Seventh armies, while he regrouped the Third and Fourth armies between the fortress-city of Verdun and Rheims. With reserves and drafts from the other armies, he created a new Ninth Army (so designated to confuse the Germans) under General Ferdinand Foch in order to extend the new line further toward Paris. The gap between the Ninth Army and Paris was to be filled by the BEF and the Fifth Army, as they retreated from Belgium. Finally, he formed a new Sixth Army from the collection of reserve divisions at Paris and troops arriving from North Africa. He entrusted its command to General Joseph Maunoury and stationed it north of Paris. General Joseph Gallieni, the military governor of Paris, rushed the defenses of the city to completion. The new line of Allied forces ran from Verdun down the axis of the Marne valley to Paris, a distance of 150 miles. Joffre lacked enough forces to extend the line beyond Paris to the English Channel, and he could only hope that the Germans lacked the forces for a turning movement west of Paris.

The Allied redeployment took a little over a week to accomplish, and was possible because of the excellent rail network between the Franco-German frontier and Paris and the relative slowness of the German advance through Belgium. Not only was the German advance hindered by logistical difficulties inherent in all mass armies in 1914, but its problems were compounded by the resistance of a bypassed Belgian garrison at Namur which kept the direct rail line from Liège into northern France closed until late August. The same line, where it entered northern France, was blocked again by a bypassed French garrison at Maubeuge. In consequence, the Germans had to forward supplies to their First and Second armies by a rail dog-leg north to Brussels, then south again through Mons and Cambrai. The German First Army, on the outside of the wheel, ran so short on food and fodder that instead of resting at night between marches, its troops had to scramble about the countryside looking for sustenance for men and animals. Some of its troops, and some of the troops of the German Second Army, the next in line on the wheel, entered the Battle of the Marne having been unfed for two days.

Still, the German armies might have summoned up enough strength to swing slightly west of Paris and to envelop Joffre's new line of resistance had not other factors intervened. First, there was an unexpected early Russian offensive against East Prussia and the German Eighth Army stationed there. The danger was such that Moltke felt compelled to detach two German army corps from the German armies in the West to assist the Eighth Army. The detachment, in turn, forced a contraction of the front of the German armies on the right wing in the West, and further reduced any chance that Paris could be outflanked. Then General Alexander von Klück, commander of the German First Army, made matters worse when he caused his troops to veer to the southeast in an effort to trap the BEF before it could withdraw below the Marne. The attempt failed and the First Army's new direction insured that it would cross the Marne well east of Paris. Klück was unaware of the existence of the French Sixth Army, just north of Paris, or that his army's new axis of advance would expose its flank and rear to attack once it was south of the Marne.

General Gallieni, the military governor of Paris, was first to grasp the significance of intelligence reports about the German First Army's change in direction. He urged Joffre to withdraw all his armies except the Sixth to well below the Marne in order to draw the whole German right wing into a potential trap. Joffre quickly agreed, and his new orders were for his armies to continue their retreat well south of the Marne until September 6 when Joffre judged the enemy would be well into the trap. Then, while the Sixth Army struck into their rear, the rest of the Allied armies would turn and counterattack against the German front.

The Gallieni-Joffre plan might well have worked had not Manoury, commander of the Sixth Army, misjudged the position of the German First Army. On September 5, and twenty-four hours too soon, he launched the Sixth Army's attack when two of Klück's four corps were still north of the Marne. Klück promptly wheeled the corps above the Marne to intercept and delay the French attack and recalled the other two corps to come to their assistance. This fighting on the river Ourcq began the action that the next day expanded into the full-blown Battle of the Marne. By the night of September 6, a general action was underway all the way from Paris to Verdun.

The premature attack of the French Sixth Army ruined Joffre's plan to draw the German right wing into a trap, but it opened another possibility

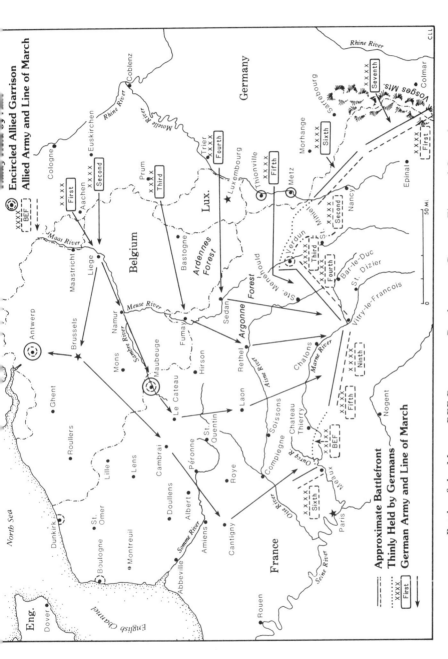

Battle of the Marne: BEF Penetrates Gap between German First and Second
Armies, September 9, 1914

to the Allies. The concentration of the German First Army against the French Sixth in the direction of Paris left a gap of about twenty miles between the German First and Second armies. As it happened, this gap was opposite the axis of approach of the BEF as it moved toward the Marne. But General French, the BEF's commander, was not aware that a gap existed, and he was puzzled why his troops failed to make contact with major enemy forces as they probed northward. His caution increased as his troops approached the Marne. Meanwhile, on the German side, both Klück and General Karl von Bülow, commander of the German Second Army, were acutely aware of the gap and the danger to both their armies should the BEF penetrate it. To make matters worse, Moltke's headquarters, moved to Luxembourg, had lost contact with the headquarters of the First and Second armies. Moltke dispatched Lieutenant-Colonel Richard Hentsch by automobile to find the headquarters of the First and Second armies, assess the situation, and issue orders on the spot if there was no time to refer to Moltke.

Hentsch arrived at Second Army headquarters in the afternoon of September 8, when the Battle of the Marne was approaching its climax. He conferred with Bülow, then drove on to First Army headquarters to talk with Klück's chief-of-staff. The situation seemed critical. With telegraph and telephone lines to Luxembourg down, there was no time to contact Moltke, and Hentsch himself made the decision. He instructed the headquarters of the First and Second armies that if the BEF crossed the Marne the following day, they were to commence a general withdrawal until the gap was closed.

Hentsch's decision proved crucial for the outcome of the Battle of the Marne. On the morning of September 9, General French, by sending a few British patrols over the river, unwittingly decided the outcome of one of the greatest battles in history. Both Klück and Bülow ordered their troops to break off action and commence a retreat. On September 10, the German Third Army, which had meanwhile decimated the attacks of the French Ninth Army on its front, was forced to conform to the retrogressive actions of the two armies on its right; that evening, Moltke, who had finally learned of Hentsch's actions, affirmed a general withdrawal of German armies on the right wing as circumstances compelled. The retreat of the German First, Second, and Third armies continued for forty miles until they reached the Aisne River, while the nearly exhausted French and British forces slowly followed. Moltke had a nervous breakdown during the withdrawal, and his secret resignation led to the appointment of a new Chief of the German General Staff, General Erich von Falkenhayn, formerly Minister of War, who officially took up his new duties on September 14, the same day that the German armies reached the Aisne.

Elated by their victory at the Marne, the Allied commanders launched

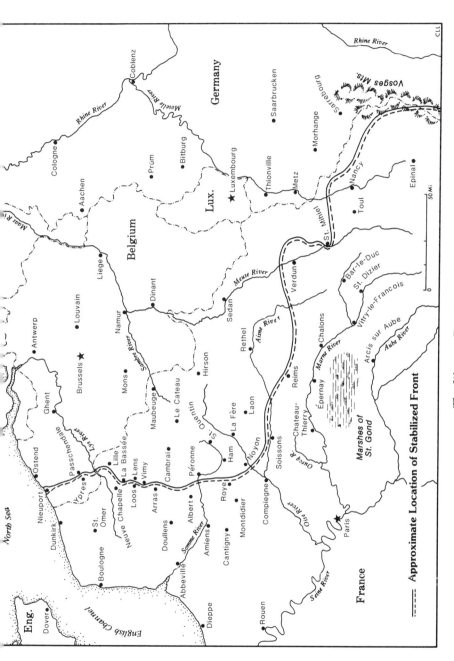

The Western Front, 1915–16

The map shows the Western Front with locations including North Sea, English Channel, Germany, Belgium, France, Luxembourg (Lux.), and England (Eng.). Cities and features labeled include: Rhine River, Coblenz, Cologne, Aachen, Moselle River, Prüm, Bitburg, Saarbrucken, Morhange, Vosges Mts., Sarrebourg, Luxembourg, Thionville, Metz, Nancy, Toul, Epinal, Liege, Namur, Dinant, Sedan, Verdun, St. Mihiel, Bar-le-Duc, St. Dizier, Vitry-le-Francois, Arcis sur Aube, Aube River, Meuse River, Aisne River, Rethel, Laon, Reims, Chalons, Marne River, Epernay, Marshes of St. Gond, Ourcq R., Oise River, Seine River, Rouen, Dieppe, Paris, Chateau-Thierry, Soissons, Noyon, Compiegne, Montdidier, Cantigny, Royé, Ham, La Fère, St. Quentin, Péronne, Albert, Amiens, Abbeville, Somme River, Doullens, Arras, Cambrai, Lens, Loos, La Bassée, Neuve Chapelle, Lille, Vimy, Ypres, St. Omer, Boulogne, Dunkirk, Nieuport, Ostend, Passchendaele, Lys River, Ghent, Antwerp, Brussels, Louvain, Mons, Maubeuge, Le Cateau, Hirson, Sambre River, Dover, Boulogne, Meuse R., Rhine River.

==== **Approximate Location of Stabilized Front**

50 Mi
0

attacks on the German positions at the Aisne only to discover that against a continuous front they could make no headway. Meanwhile, Falkenhayn was seeking to regain the initiative. The unoccupied terrain west of Compiègne offered a possibility for turning the Allied flank, and the same idea in reverse occurred to the Allied generals. Leaving part of their forces to hold the trench-lines established along the Aisne, both sides began shifting troops to the west in hopes of outflanking one another. While this was going on, the Belgian army broke out of its besieged position at Antwerp and made its way down the coast. It finally linked up with the BEF which had leap-frogged the French armies to its left. This misnamed "Race to the Sea" reached its climax when troops of the opposing armies reached the beaches just north of Nieuport on October 10. The Germans then tried to break through the Allied line further inland at Ypres, but to no avail. When the Germans suspended their last attacks on November 11, it was four years to the day before the armistice of 1918. A deadlocked front stretched some 450 twisting miles from the North Sea to the neutral Swiss frontier. For this indecisive result in the West, France paid the price of 950,000 casualties, the Germans 700,000 casualties. About two-fifths of the original BEF and the Belgian army had been killed or wounded.

C. The Opening Battles and Stalemate on the Eastern Front, 1914.   In compliance with its pre-war pledges to aid the French by launching an early offensive against German territory in the East even before the Russian army completed mobilization, the Russian General Staff assembled General Pavel von Rennenkampf's First Army at Vilna and General Alexander Sampsonov's Second Army at Warsaw during the first two weeks of August 1914. The Russian plan called for the First Army to invade East Prussia from the east in order to hold the attention of the defending German Eighth Army, while the Russian Second Army struck from Poland into its rear. Soon after the Russian First Army crossed the frontier in mid-August, it inflicted a repulse on the Eighth Army's counterattack at Gumbinnen. When the Eighth Army's commander and chief-of-staff telegraphed Moltke that only an abandonment of East Prussia and a retirement west of the river Vistula could save their army, Moltke relieved them of their posts. He recalled General Paul von Hindenburg from retirement to command the Eighth Army, and he transferred General Erich Ludendorff from the Western Front to serve as Hindenburg's chief-of-staff. The Hindenburg-Ludendorff team arrived at East Prussian headquarters on August 23, by which time Colonel Max Hoffmann, the Eighth Army's chief of operations, had worked out a plan for the Eighth Army to redeploy rapidly by rail to deal with the threat posed by Sampsonov's army. Hindenburg and Ludendorff, who had

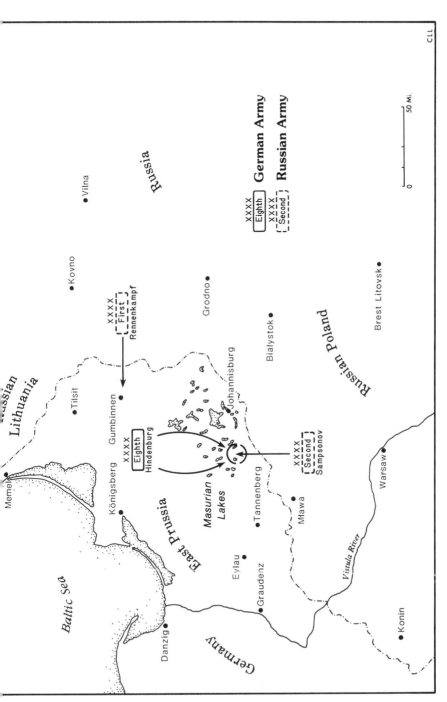

The Battle of Tannenberg, 1914

developed a similar plan while on their way to their new headquarters, quickly approved Hoffmann's arrangements.

The rapid German redeployment by rail was not detected by Rennenkampf's army, which remained stationary while working on logistical problems, and Sampsonov was unaware that he was leading his army into a trap when it pushed into East Prussia in late August. The resulting battle of Tannenberg (August 26–30) was to be the only *Kesselschlacht* (battle of encirclement and annihilation) of World War I, but it was a brilliant German success. Almost 100,000 Russian soldiers in ten divisions were killed or captured. Then the Eighth Army again redeployed rapidly by rail to intercept the advance of Rennenkampf's army. The Germans outflanked the Russian First Army at the Battle of the Masurian Lakes (September 9–12) and forced it to withdraw to the Russian frontier. The second battle had been won before the German retreat to the Aisne in the West had been completed, and Hindenburg and Ludendorff emerged as the first major German heroes of the war.

The Russians had better luck against the Austro-Hungarians. Franz Conrad von Hötzendorff, the Austro-Hungarian chief-of-staff, made the mistake of dividing his forces for an invasion of Serbia, and was unable to reconcentrate them on the Polish frontier before the Russians assembled. As a result, four Russian armies got the better of three Austro-Hungarian armies in the Battle of the Galician Frontier (August 23–September 1), and by late September the Austro-Hungarian armies had been driven back a hundred miles to the line of the Carpathian Mountains. The Germans came to the rescue of the Austro-Hungarians when a new German Ninth Army, under General August von Mackensen, joined the Eighth Army in the East and launched an invasion of Poland. The Russians had to take the pressure off the Austro-Hungarians in order to deal with these attacks, and, while they finally contained the German advance, by the end of 1914 they had lost half of Poland and a million men. The first five months of the war cost the Austro-Hungarian Army 750,000 men, while on the Eastern Front the Germans suffered 200,000 casualties in 1914. Still, the East was another deadlocked front, one that stretched for 950 miles from Memel to the frontier of neutral Rumania. Neither the Russian nor the Austro-Hungarian army ever fully recovered from the effects of the opening battles in 1914, and neither was there any prospect of a quick end to the war on the Eastern Front.

D. The War at Sea, 1914.   The German High Seas Fleet braced itself for a British attack on its anchorages on the North Sea in August-September 1914, but none came. Admiral Sir John Jellicoe, commander of Britain's Grand Fleet, moved his dreadnoughts to war stations at Rosyth, Scotland, and Scapa Flow in the Orkney Islands. The British Channel

Fleet, composed of old battleships, closed off the other exit from the North Sea. The British then declared a "War Zone" in the North Sea and a distant blockade on Germany's ports. Only then did Germany's leaders begin to realize how dependent the Second Reich was on foreign raw materials and even foodstuffs. As events were to reveal, Germany had the capacity to last about four years if the blockade was not lifted sooner.

With assistance from the British navy, the French fleet in the Mediterranean quickly bottled up the Austro-Hungarian navy in the Adriatic Sea, but two German ships—the battle cruiser *Goeben* and the cruiser *Breslau*—cruising in the Mediterranean at the outbreak of war, fled to Constantinople, where they were interned by the Turks. After the Ottoman Empire entered the war in November 1914 on the German side, the two ships, complete with their original German crews, were recommissioned in the Turkish navy and soon proved more than a match for the five old Russian battleships on the Black Sea.

In the Far East, Admiral Count Maximilian von Spee took his cruiser squadron from Shantung to the German bases in the Marshall and Caroline Islands in the Pacific, and then launched attacks on Allied shipping along the South American coasts. On November 1, his squadron defeated a pursuing British cruiser force off Coronel, Chile, but in December the British had their revenge when all of Spee's ships but the *Dresden* were sunk by British battle cruisers in the Battle of the Falkland Islands. The *Emden*, earlier detached from Spee's squadron, and the *Dresden* were run down and destroyed during 1915. Though a few other German surface raiders appeared at sea during the rest of the war, the main burden of carrying on the German *guerre de course* fell to the submarine.

The German discovery of the submarine's potential as a weapon for commerce raiding was accidental. In 1914 the U-boat's greatest achievement was in a coast defense encounter in which the U-9 sank three British cruisers in less than an hour. In retaliation for the British declaration of a "War Zone" in the North Sea, in 1914 the German admiralty declared a "War Zone" around the British Isles in which its submarines might attack any Allied vessel without warning. But with only twenty-one U-boats with range enough to operate beyond the North Sea, and only a third of them on station at a time, the German declaration at first seemed little more than a gesture. By 1915 the German "War Zone" had taken on real substance as submarines proved unexpectedly effective against the slow-moving merchant ships on which Britain had to depend for its imports and exports. The German admiralty ordered the building of more and longer-ranged submarines, and it took a new interest in the heretofore despised doctrines of *guerre de course*. By the end of the war, Germany had commissioned 345 submarines, manned by 10,000 sailors, and the lowly U-boat proved to be one of the most effective weapons in the Kaiser's arsenal.

II. The Search for Victory, 1915–16

A. Allied Strategy and Operations, 1915.   By 1915 British councils were divided between "Westerners" and "Easterners." The "Westerners," led by General French, commander of the BEF, called for British concentration of effort on the Western Front in France. The "Easterners," led by Winston Churchill, First Lord of the Admiralty, despaired of a decisive success against the deadlocked front in France. They favored a concentration of effort against Germany's new ally, the Ottoman Empire, and establishing a line of supply from the Mediterranean to southern Russia in order to sustain the lagging Russian armies, already suffering from a dearth of arms and munitions. The strategic problem was complicated for the British by their unprecedented effort to expand their land forces, as well as to equip the volunteer forces of Canada, Australia, and New Zealand. Field Marshal Kitchener, called from retirement to serve as Secretary of State for War, promised to create an army of thirty-seven divisions by the end of 1915. David Lloyd George soon headed a new Ministry of Munitions to deal with the British and Allied munitions crisis. The final decision was to give priority to the Western Front, but to launch lesser operations in the Middle East, relying heavily there on Dominion forces and the troops of the Indian Army, and giving priority to opening a new line of supply for the Tsar's hard-pressed armies.

The biggest Allied effort in the Middle East in 1915, and the largest amphibious assault carried out in World War I, ended as a disaster for the Allies. In early 1915 British warships tried to knock out the Turkish shore batteries blocking the straits of the Dardanelles, preliminary to linking up with the Russians on the Black Sea. When the naval effort failed, an amphibious force of mostly Australian and New Zealand troops tried to occupy the key Gallipoli peninsula. But the bungled Allied landings lost the element of surprise, and Turkish troops, advised by German General Liman von Sanders, kept the Allied forces bottled up within their beachheads for months. Every attempt to break out resulted in slaughter. By the time the Allied forces withdrew from Gallipoli at the end of 1915, they had suffered 300,000 casualties. The British and French navies had lost several old battleships to the fire of shore batteries, submarines, and mine fields into the bargain. An Allied effort through Greece to aid Serbia against a German, Austro-Hungarian, and Bulgarian invasion came too late, and, though the Allies kept their foothold in Greece, the Germans contemptuously referred to the Allied forces there as their "armed prisoner-of-war camp." The British beat off a Turkish attack on Egypt from Palestine, but a British drive from the head of the Persian Gulf into Mesopotamia (Iraq) bogged down. On balance, Allied operations in the Middle East in 1915 were costly failures.

Allied spirits rose when in May 1915 Italy entered the war against the Central Powers and launched offensives over the river Isonzo at the head of the Adriatic Sea against the Austro-Hungarian frontier. But the narrow coastal shelf left little room for maneuver and the offensives soon bogged down in the face of defensive firepower. For the next three years, the Italian armies would make repeated efforts to break the stalemate, using up a million men in the process, but, until nearly the end of the war, getting no nearer the objective of Trieste than when they had started. With the stiffening of German reinforcements, the Austrians not only held their line, but in 1917 launched a counteroffensive that drove the Italian forces back fifty miles. The Austro-German bombing of small Italian towns behind the front, and the resulting panic of their populations, inspired General Giulio Douhet, the most radical of the post-war advocates of air power, to believe that the destruction of civilian morale might be the key to breaking stalemates on the ground in future wars. Actually, in a theater as deadlocked as any in World War I, Italian morale declined for a variety of reasons.

Allied performance on the Western Front in 1915 was disappointing. General French's offensives at Neuve Chapelle, La Bassée, and Loos gained little ground and almost used up the last of the "Old Contemptibles," the original soldiers of the BEF. The attacks against the German entrenchments also took a large toll of the Territorials and the first of Kitchener's volunteers. Near the end of 1915 General Sir Douglas Haig relieved French of command of the BEF, but he would prove to have no more strategic or tactical insight, though he managed to hold his command to the end of the war. As for France's army, it called up older men in order to expand to 102 divisions during the year, but Joffre squandered much of the new strength in offensives at Artois and in the Champagne. In point of casualties, 1915 was the worst year of the war for the French: 1,450,000 men killed, wounded, taken prisoner or missing. In the seventeen months since the war began, the French had suffered a total of 2,400,000 casualties.

B. German Strategy in 1915. Like the British councils, the German leaders divided among "Westerners" and "Easterners." Falkenhayn, Chief of the General Staff, was a "Westerner" who believed that German strength should continue to be concentrated primarily against the Allies on the Western Front. He recognized Russia's material weaknesses, but he also believed that an extensive invasion of Russia would be a prolonged affair. He therefore favored a concentrated effort to knock France out of the war first. In contrast, Hindenburg and Ludendorff, the leading "Easterners" and in supreme command on the Eastern Front by 1915, favored an early concentration of effort against

Russia to knock it out of the war before giving primacy to eliminating France. The Kaiser finally decided that forces should be transferred to the Eastern Front and that four German armies in the East (the Eighth, Ninth, Tenth, and Eleventh, amounting to sixty-five divisions), would be permitted to try to force Russia from the war by the end of the year. The reduced German forces in the West would launch only local offensives and stand mainly on the defensive.

The German effort in the East was only partially successful. The Germans took Warsaw and nearly all of the rest of Poland not occupied during 1914, and by October 1915, when the effort was called off, the battle line ran from just west of Dvinsk south through the Pripet Marshes. Still worse for the Russians, they had lost two million men during 1915 and Grand Duke Nicholas had been discredited as the army's commander-in-chief. Tsar Nicholas II assumed personal command of his armies, despite the fact that further defeats would tend to discredit him and that his new duties would require him to be away from his capital at St. Petersburg most of the time. Still, Hindenburg and Ludendorff had failed to remove Russia from the war in 1915.

Left with only limited forces in the West during 1915, Falkenhayn confined the German armies there to local offensives around Ypres, including the first use of poison gas on the Western Front. On April 22, German troops released clouds of chlorine gas from cylinders in the front lines which drifted with the wind toward the Allied trenches. French Algerian troops fled at the approach of the gas clouds, thus creating a gap through which the Germans might have broken through. But nearby Canadian troops rushed into the breach and held the line, and they also withstood a second German gas attack on April 24. The Germans believed that they had not used enough gas to be decisive in both attacks, and prepared to use poison gas on a larger scale in the summer of 1915. By then, however, the element of surprise had been lost. The Allies had equipped their troops with gas masks and other anti-gas equipment, and were preparing to use poison gas against the Germans. Gas-filled artillery shells became the favored means of delivery by both sides as the war went on, but, though poison gas of several lethal types were employed, the new weapon did not prove decisive. If anything, gas made the deadlock worse by burdening both sides with additional equipment to counter it. Moreover, twelve times as many men were killed by shell-fire alone as by poison gas during the war.

C. *The War at Sea, 1915.*   Sixty-eight new German U-boats were added to the Kaiser's submarine fleet during 1915, against the loss of twenty-three. Meanwhile, U-boats sank an impressive million tons of Allied shipping in the War Zone. But on May 7 a German U-boat sank the trans-Atlantic passenger liner *Lusitania* off the Irish coast without giving warning, and over a thousand passengers and crew, among them 128 Americans, were killed. The unannounced nature of the attack was clearly in violation of international law governing the conduct of *guerre de course,* and President Woodrow Wilson strongly denounced the German action. After three more American lives were lost on the *Arabic* to a German attack in August, the United States seemed on the point of severing diplomatic relations with Germany. But the Kaiser's government made the "Arabic Pledge," promising that no more liners would be attacked in the War Zone without prior warning. Still, a new crisis arose in 1916 with the sinking of the French steamer *Sussex* and the injury to three Americans. In order to avoid a break with the United States, the Kaiser made the "Sussex Pledge," affirming that German submarine warfare would be carefully restricted in future to insure neutral rights. In protest against the "Sussex Pledge," Admiral Alfred von Tirpitz resigned as head of the German navy, but not until early in 1917 did Germany go over to unrestricted submarine warfare again. The final U-boat campaign nearly won the war for Germany, but proved fatal when it provoked the United States into entering the war on the Allied side.

D. The War on Land, 1916. Falkenhayn's faith in victory over France was given full sway in February 1916, when the biggest German offensive of the war to that time was unleashed against French lines around Verdun. Falkenhayn hoped for either a breakthrough or a battle of attrition that would hurt the French army more than the German. General Henri Pétain, placed in charge of the defense of the threatened sector, pledged, "They shall not pass." In August, Falkenhayn admitted his failure to the Kaiser, who appointed Hindenburg to succeed him as Chief of the General Staff and Ludendorff to serve as Hindenburg's deputy. The French kept the battle going, hoping to regain lost ground, and when it finally ended, ten months after it began, it had cost the Germans and the French 362,000 and 332,000 troops respectively. Joffre was blamed for the near-disaster at Verdun in the battle's early stages, and was replaced with General Robert Nivelle as French commander-in-chief. French casualties for the whole of 1916 came to 950,000 troops.

Britain adopted general conscription for the first time in its history in January 1916, and New Zealand followed suit. An Australian referendum on conscription rejected the draft. Canada adopted conscription, but officials were afraid to enforce it vigorously in the French province of Quebec. The British and Dominion conscript armies could not be made ready for service before 1917, and General Haig believed that the existing combination of regulars, Territorials, and volunteers could win a decisive victory on the Somme in 1916. For a week prior to the attack on July 1, 850 British

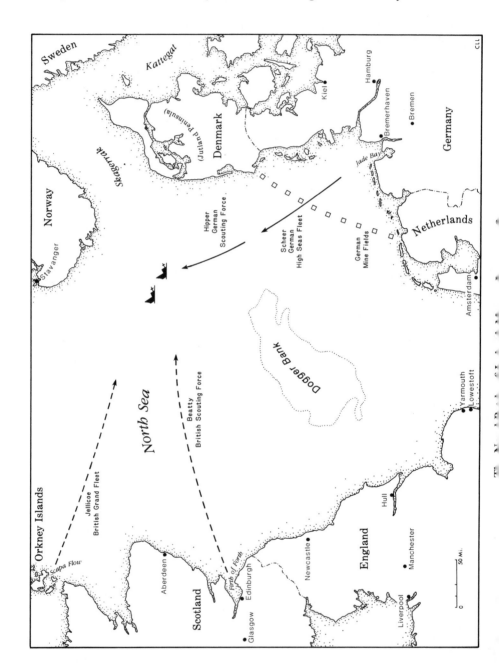

guns hammered an eighteen-mile stretch of German trench line; then 100,000 British troops went forward, only to suffer the worst single day's defeat in the history of the British army. Before noon some 60,000 casualties had occurred without a dent in the German line. Haig's repeated attacks on the Somme from July 1 through November 14, the official end of the offensive, resulted in a total of 400,000 British casualties in 140 days of fighting. By the end of the offensive on the Somme, the regular-Territorial-volunteer British army was about used up, and the vast majority of troops in the British armies of 1917–18 were conscripts.

When Nivelle took command of the French army, he was told confidentially that the new levies might represent the "last army of France." By the beginning of 1917 France had run through about half the young men in the country. But Nivelle optimistically prepared a new French offensive on the Aisne for April 1917. In the East, the Russian offensive, directed by General Aleksi Brussilov, against the Austro-Hungarians was at first successful and even encouraged Rumania to throw in its lot with the Allies. But a German army under Falkenhayn—who had accepted a field command after his relief as Chief of the General Staff—crushed the Rumanian army, and the Russian offensive was finally contained. By the fall of 1916, German intelligence had indications that the Tsar's armies were demoralized and close to collapse.

In the Middle East, 1916 was a mixture of Allied successes and failures. The British drove the Turks from the Sinai Desert and placed themselves on the borders of Palestine, but a British drive from the Persian Gulf into Mesopotamia ended in a humiliating defeat on the Tigris River at Kut, where some 14,000 British troops surrendered to the Turks in April. Still, Major T. E. Lawrence, using his mastery of Arabic, was making progress in arousing the Arab tribes against their Turkish masters, though it was 1917 before the war in the Arabian Desert would begin to have important results.

    E. The War at Sea, 1916.   German U-boats sank two million tons of Allied shipping in 1916, but the great drama of the year was the only sortie of the German High Seas Fleet far into the North Sea during World War I. Admiral Reinhardt von Scheer, commander of the fleet, hoped to court action with Admiral David Beatty's Scouting Force without risking a fleet action with Admiral Jellicoe's Grand Fleet, but British radio intelligence alerted Jellicoe that Scheer's forces were going to sea at the end of May. Accordingly, Jellicoe's fleet sortied to intercept Scheer's fleet, and late in the afternoon of May 31, on a latitude with the Danish peninsula of Jutland but in the center of the North Sea, the Grand Fleet and the High Seas Fleet engaged in the greatest naval battle in history to that time. The Battle of Jutland involved 254 ships, the whole displacing

1,600,000 tons. The most powerful ships in Jellicoe's fleet were thirty-seven dreadnought battleships and battle cruisers; the most powerful in Scheer's were twenty-one battleships and battle cruisers. In a battle obscured by smoke and darkness, the Grand Fleet lost three battle cruisers, three cruisers, and eight destroyers (110,980 tons and 6,784 men), while the High Seas Fleet lost a pre-dreadnought battleship, a battle cruiser, three cruisers, and ten destroyers (62,233 tons and 3,039 men). Much of the British loss in tonnage was due to defects in the three lost battle cruisers. Though Scheer claimed a victory on points, it was his fleet that fled to port on June 1, leaving Jellicoe's fleet in command of the North Sea. The British distant blockade of German ports remained intact and, after Jutland, it was clear that a German victory at sea—if there was to be one—would have to be accomplished by the submarine and *guerre de course.*

  F. The Rise of Air Power.   Though both the airship and the airplane began their careers in World War I as observation and scouting craft, they made the transition to weapons-platforms in a remarkably short time. In January 1915 German zeppelins based in Belgium began a strategic bombing campaign against the British Isles and especially against London. The typical airship could carry 5,000 lbs. of bombs, but accuracy of bombing was poor and the craft was vulnerable to bad weather. In the span of two and a half years, zeppelins made 208 sorties against England, dropped 196 tons of bombs, killed 557 Britons and injured 1,360 more. Eighty zeppelins and 1,600 crewmen were lost in these raids. In June 1917, twin-engine Gotha and Giant airplanes took over the strategic air war. Each airplane was capable of carrying 1,000 lbs. of bombs, and by November 1918 seventy-three tons of bombs had been dropped on England, killing 860 Britons and injuring another 2,060. The main effect of the strategic bombing was to lower civilian morale, already weakened by food shortages and the horrendous casualties suffered by the British armies on the Western Front.

  The German air raids on the British Isles had an important influence on British thinking about the organization of air power. Until 1918 Britain had followed the practice of other countries in dividing aviation between the army and the navy. But neither the British army's Royal Flying Corps (RFC) nor the navy's Royal Naval Air Service (RNAS) was willing to take primary responsibility for the defense of Britain's skies. The problem was referred to a special committee, headed by Field Marshal Jan Christian Smuts, which, after studying the matter, concluded that all British aviation ought to be combined in a Royal Air Force (RAF), divided into specialized commands for particular air power missions. In April 1918 the RFC and RNAS were merged as the RAF, and a new Air Ministry was founded. The

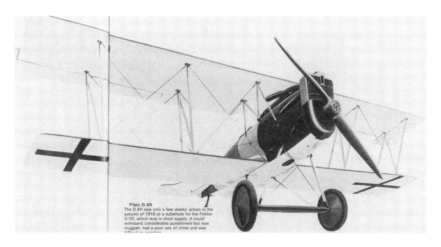

The Pfalz D.XII, German pursuit plane, World War I.

SOURCE: John Batchelor et al., *Air Power: A Modern Illustrated Military History* (New York: Exeter Books, 1979; in association with Phoebus Company/BPC Publishing, London).

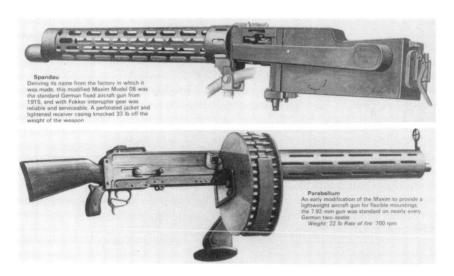

German aerial machine guns, World War I: the fixed-mounted synchronized Maxim-Spandau and the flexibility mounted Maxim-Parabellum.

SOURCE: John Batchelor et al., *Air Power: A Modern Illustrated Military History* (New York: Exeter Books, 1979, in association with Phoebus Company/BPC Publishing, London).

RAF was headed by Hugh Trenchard, former head of the RFC. The RAF assigned pursuit squadrons to the Home Defense Air Force, tactical squadrons to the support of the army and navy, and even created a special force of Handley-Page bombers for long-range bombardment of Germany from airfields in eastern France. In embryo, the 1918 organization foreshadowed future RAF organization, especially the Fighter Command and the Bomber Command of World War II.

The pursuit plane was the most glamorous type of aircraft to appear in World War I and is the ancestor of the modern fighter plane. The pursuit plane evolved from the scouting and observation airplanes, types which were increasingly armed to attack or defend themselves from their counterparts in the opposing air forces. The pursuit plane became a specialized type when, in 1915, Anthony Fokker, a Dutch designer working for the Germans, developed the synchronized machine-gun, which could be safely fired through a spinning propeller. The pilot could aim the gun by aiming the airplane, thus increasing the probability of hits. After Allied planes were also equipped with synchronized machine-guns, the age of great aerial "dog-fights" over the Western Front began. By 1916 as many as a hundred planes at a time dueled over the Western Front for aerial supremacy, and, as parachutes were absent until nearly the end of the war, pursuit pilots came back with their planes or not at all. "Aces," or pilots who had downed five or more of the enemy's machines, were good newspaper copy, and governments used aerial heroes for propaganda and to bolster public morale. But combat flying of any kind was extremely hazardous, and there was a high rate of attrition in all types of airplanes. Assemblies of engines, doped canvas or linen skin, and external struts and wiring, the relatively fragile airplanes of World War I were consumed rapidly in combat and in training accidents. Though some 30,000 airplanes designed for combat were produced during World War I, only 8,000 Allied and 3,300 German combat aircraft were still in service at the end of the war.

The internal organization of air units was much the same from country to country during World War I. The typical pursuit squadron consisted of eighteen planes and twenty-five pilots, supported by about 150 ground personnel. Bomber and observation squadrons usually had twenty-five aircraft and fifty crew, counting observers and gunners. Several squadrons composed a group, several groups composed a wing, and several wings composed an air division. The authorized strength of the 1918 French air division was 432 pursuit planes and 193 bombers and observation planes. Usually, one or more air divisions were assigned to the support of a field army, but resources were a limiting factor. An air officer was assigned to the field army's staff to coordinate air operations with those of the ground forces.

In terms of aircraft performance, the Fokker D-VII pursuit plane, introduced in 1918, had a maximum speed of 118 mph in level flight. The French Nieuport 17, with a maximum speed of 110 mph, was also popular with its pilots. The Spad, with a speed of 119 mph, was so successful that over 5,000 of the type were built. The British Sopwith Camel flew at 115 mph, and 5,490 copies were made for the army and navy. Most airplanes in World War I were bi-planes, but the synchronized machine-gun was introduced in a monoplane, and the Fokker Dr.I was an excellent tri-wing fighter. All these airplanes were small machines by the standards of today's aircraft.

The British Royal Naval Air Service was the largest and best equipped of its type in the world at the beginning of the war, yet its assets consisted of just thirty-one seaplanes, forty land-based airplanes, and seven airships. It had no aircraft carriers and no plans to carry airplanes to sea in other types of warships. Soon after the war began, however, the British converted three small cross-Channel steamers into seaplane carriers, the planes being hoisted over the side for takeoffs and being hoisted back aboard after landing on the sea. In December 1914 these carriers launched nine Short seaplanes against the German naval bases in the Helgoland Bight, but four aircraft were lost and not much damage was done to the bases. In mid-1915 HMS *Campania*, the first carrier in history capable of launching aircraft from a flight-deck, joined the fleet, but its planes had to land on water and be hoisted back aboard. *Engadine*, sister ship of *Campania*, served in the Jutland campaign but had no influence on the outcome. The first carrier that could both launch and recover airplanes from its decks was HMS *Furious*, a battle cruiser converted into an aircraft carrier in 1917. Its takeoff and landing decks were on different levels. Finally, in August 1918, HMS *Argus* joined the British fleet as the first aircraft carrier which could both launch and recover airplanes from a single flight-deck; it was the prototype of the carriers used in the Second World War.

G. The Development of Armored Fighting Vehicles.   Although a few armies had armored cars propelled by gasoline engines before 1914, the history of the tracked armored fighting vehicle (AFV) began when British Colonel Ernest D. Swinton conceived of a "Machine-Gun Destroyer" while watching tractors powered by gasoline engines towing heavy artillery behind the Western Front early in the war. Swinton imagined a machine with treads which could negotiate broken ground, smash through barbed wire, and roll over trenches. It would be protected by armor thick enough to deflect small-arms fire and and shell fragments. Swinton offered his idea to the British War Office, but it paid little attention. Apparently, Winston Churchill, the First Lord of the Admiralty, rescued the idea from oblivion by forming a Landships Committee in the Admiralty. After the

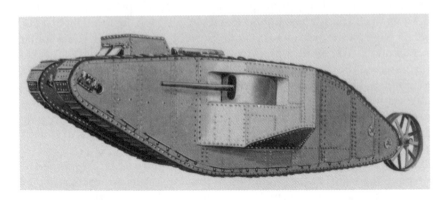

British Mark I, the first type of tank introduced on the
Western Front, 1916.

SOURCE: Kenneth Macksey and John H. Batchelor, *Tank: A History
of the Armoured Fighting Vehicle* (New York: Charles Scribner's Sons, 1970).

army joined the project, Swinton was recalled to become its secretary. In
order to protect secrecy, the early "landships" were covered with
tarpaulins when moved on flatcars between factory and proving ground,
their covers marked "Water Tank" to delude enemy spies. The nickname
"tank" stuck even after the "landship" went into action in September
1916.

Though the British successfully tested a mechanical test-bed dubbed
"Little Willie" in December 1915, the first tank committed to combat was
the "Mother" Mark I of 1916. The Mark I had less than half an inch of
armor thickness for protection, and its 105–horsepower gasoline engine
could move it at a maximum speed of four miles an hour. Requiring a
crew of nine to man it efficiently, it was armed with two 6-pounder naval
guns and four machine-guns. Its rhomboidal shape, so characteristic of
many World War I tanks, enabled a track running around the outside of
the frame to drag it across trenches and shell-holes up to ten feet in
diameter. Because its stated purpose was merely to smash a gap in enemy
lines through which conventional forces could advance, this early tank was
provided with a range of only twenty-three miles. The Mark I was thirty-
two feet in length, almost fourteen feet in width, and just over eight feet in
height.

Unknown to the British, the French had also launched a program to
develop tracked AFVs. Their first machines were designed to fit a sugges-
tion of Colonel Jean Estienne of the artillery that armored, self-propelled
guns should be developed. The French mated existing American-made

Holt tractors used for towing guns with armored boxes carrying the French 75-mm gun. The Schneider CA-1 of this version weighed 14.6 tons, had a 70-hp engine, a speed of 5 mph, and an inch of armor protection. When first put into action in 1917, however, it proved to have poor trench-crossing abilities. When the French and British discovered that each was working independently of the other on AFVs, they agreed that tanks would not be introduced to battle until large numbers of reliable machines were available, something that would be impossible for either country before mid-1917.

Unfortunately for the Allies, the secret of the tank was compromised by General Haig in September 1916, when he ordered the thirty-six Mark I tanks available to be thrown into his flagging offensive on the Somme. Some of the machines failed to start, others mired down in the muddy morass produced by weeks of shelling, and still others suffered from mechanical malfunctions that caused them to break down. But the handful that reached enemy lines made a powerful impression before they too were put out of action. Many German troops panicked at the sight of the puffing monsters, and Haig was so impressed that he urged the War Office to increase the number of tanks on order from 150 to 1,000. On balance, however, the unveiling of the tank in 1916 was a mistake. Attacks with large numbers of tanks were many months away, and, by tipping the secret to the Germans, the British allowed them time to develop anti-tank weapons and tactics that might have been absent in the battles of 1917 and 1918. Among the German measures were anti-tank traps and direct-fire artillery. These measures did not completely neutralize the tank when it was introduced in large numbers, but they may have prevented tanks from being the decisive weapons in World War I that their designers had hoped for.

The first successful tank attack in history came at Cambrai in November 1917. Colonel J. F. C. Fuller, chief-of-staff of the British Royal Tank Corps, planned the attack very carefully, choosing a place in the line with hard, chalky ground, eschewing a preliminary artillery bombardment that might have alerted the Germans to the coming attack, and employing 371 of the improved Mark IV tanks. The sudden tank assault in thick fog caught the Germans by surprise, unhinged the local German defense, and, before day's end, had resulted in a British gain of four miles. But by then nearly all the tanks were out of action from one cause or another, and, in any case, the infantry and cavalry proved unable to keep up with the armor and to exploit the gap in a decisive fashion.

Fuller was among the few soldiers who looked beyond the tank as merely a hole-punching device which would allow other arms to practice mobile warfare. He envisioned machines capable not only of creating gaps but of rapidly exploiting them to strike decisively into the enemy's rear areas. The British Whippet tank, available in large numbers by 1918, was a move in that direction. Weighing only fourteen tons, the Whippet had twice the speed of the British heavy tanks, and had much better range into the bargain. After still more experience was acquired in Allied operations in 1918, Fuller composed a "Plan 1919," which envisaged using heavy or battle tanks for smashing holes in the enemy's front, then the dispatching of relatively light and fast tanks to plunge deep into the enemy's rear areas in order to overwhelm its headquarters and support facilities. In primitive form, "Plan 1919" was the concept for the decisive use of armored forces still twenty years in the future.

By the end of the Great War, Britain had built 3,000 tanks of all kinds, and the French had built 2,000. Though it cannot be said that the tank won the war for the Allies in 1918, it may be said that it played an important role in breaking the trench deadlock on the Western Front and, in combination with other arms, was a significant factor in the success of the final Allied offensives. The tank, like the airplane, however, required another two decades of technical and doctrinal development before it came into its own. As for the Germans, they entered the field of armored warfare only after the British revealed their tanks on the Somme, and they were further hindered by the Allied naval blockade which was slowly starving German industry of raw materials for war production of all kinds. The German A7V tank was hastily designed and inferior to the British Mark IV, and the Germans never had more than forty tanks at one time or place. The Germans ended up pursuing a different avenue for solving the problem of the deadlocked front, and tanks played no great role in their 1918 offensives which came so close to winning the war on the Western Front.

III. The Years of Decision, 1917–18

A. The 1917 U-Boat Campaign and America's Entry into the War. Commencing on February 1, 1917, German submarines operating in the War Zone around the British Isles dropped all restrictions on their operations and began an unprecedented attack on the shipping of belligerent and neutral countries alike. This action was bound to lead to war between Germany and the United States, but the German government had made its decision to go over to unrestricted submarine warfare out of two considerations. The first was the belief that unless Britain's blockade on Germany was broken and Britain was defeated within the next two years, Germany would be starved into submission in any case. The second was the fact that only a submarine campaign which included neutral shipping bound for the British Isles could possibly starve Britain into surrender before Britain's surface blockade could do the same to Germany. Admiral Henning von Holtzendorff, chief of the German

U-boat command, was confident that if his U-boats could operate without restrictions, they could drive Britain out of the war within a year and at the same time prevent the United States from affecting its outcome even if it chose to enter the war on the Allied side.

The first attacks under the new policy fell on Allied merchant vessels, but on March 12 the American steamer *Algonquin* was torpedoed and sunk near the British coast. A week later three more American merchant vessels were torpedoed and sunk in the War Zone. President Wilson, who only a few months before had attempted to mediate a "peace without victors," declared that the world had to be made safe for democracy. At his bidding, on April 6, 1917, the Congress of the United States declared a state of war with Germany.

Until April 1917, the United States had taken only modest measures for military preparedness. The Wilson administration had adopted a policy of "a navy second to none," but nearly all the new naval building planned was in battleships and battle cruisers. When the United States entered the war, the U.S. Navy was weak in destroyers and other antisubmarine craft. Although the U.S. Navy put the 1916 program on the shelf and switched its priorities to antisubmarine warfare, the main responsibility for defeating the U-boat offensive fell to the British navy. In the first months of 1917, however, the British navy was clearly failing in that task. Between February 1 and May 31, U-boats sank 1,175 ships, whose combined tonnage came to 2.5 million, or more than the German submarines had sunk in all of 1916.

The U-boat's effectiveness was partly due to the refusal of the British admiralty to adopt convoy in place of its "Defense of Routes" strategy, under which British destroyers and other antisubmarine craft patrolled the sea lanes and attacked any U-boats they encountered. Adopting convoy meant that the flow of material and food into Britain from overseas would be hindered: first when merchant ships must delay sailing until they could be formed into groups large enough to justify escorts, and second at voyage's end, when they all arrived at one time, resulting in unloading delays. Until 1917 the trade-off between sinkings and the maintenance of the general flow of trade had been favorable.

Admiral William S. Sims, appointed commander of the U.S. naval forces operating in European waters, soon added his voice to those of a minority of officers in the British admiralty who favored convoy despite the economic drawbacks. Their pressure, and the terrible shipping losses between February and the end of May 1917, at last convinced the British admiralty to experiment with using convoys for ships bound for British ports. Almost magically, the number of sinkings declined. The admiralty then extended escort protection to ships leaving port, and finally to Allied ships in the Mediterranean. In all cases the pressure eased. The effectiveness of the convoy system lay in the fact that it forced U-boats to make attacks in the presence of warships designed to destroy them. The knowledge that a swift counterattack awaited any transgressor made U-boat commanders more cautious. The number of U-boat sinkings also increased dramatically. Of the 345 U-boats commissioned by Germany in World War I, 178 never returned to base, and half of the 10,000 sailors who crewed Germany's submarines were lost with them. Still, before the German U-boats were finally defeated, they had sunk 12 million tons of Allied shipping and another 2 million tons of Allied warships. But the Allies managed to build or add 13 million tons of shipping (a million more than the Germans sank) during the war, and, because large numbers of American troops did not begin crossing the Atlantic until after December 1917, no American troop ships were sunk on their way to Europe. Only three such transports were sunk on return voyages.

Despite the Allied victory over the submarine by the end of 1917, it remained to be seen whether the United States could make a difference in the outcome of the land war in Europe. The National Defense Act of 1916 had defined the country's land forces as the regular army, its reserves, the National Guard when in federal service, and a so-called National Army to be raised by Congress in time of war. But on April 6, 1917, the regular army had 108,399 officers and men, the reserves 16,767, and the National Guard 181,620. The National Army existed only on paper. Nor did the United States have stockpiles of arms and equipment ready to equip a large army, if one could be created.

Newton D. Baker, Wilson's Secretary of War, had been convinced by the War Department's General Staff that the manpower problem could be quickly solved only by resorting to general conscription. General Enoch Crowder, the Army's Judge Advocate General, had developed a plan that would in effect make the National Army described in the National Defense Act of 1916 a force of conscripts through a *levée en masse*. Won over by Baker, Wilson supported the plan before Congress, and that body, swept up by the country's enthusiasm for the war, enacted the Selective Service Act on May 18, 1917. The law, which applied to all males between twenty-one and thirty-five years of age, was administered through local boards of citizens, a feature that may have made it more palatable to the American people, and compliance with registration and induction was good. Though the Navy and the Marine Corps remained volunteer organizations, the Army and the National Guard used conscripts whenever they failed to recruit to strength through volunteers. Eventually, in August 1918, the Army Chief-of-Staff consolidated the regular army, reserves, National Guard, and National Army into a single United States Army. Approximately 4 million men served in the USA, of whom 2,180,296 entered by way of the draft. Since 2 million American troops were serving in Europe by the end of the war, the number of conscripts only slightly exceeded the number who actually served at or near the front. About 800,000 men served in the United States Navy and Marine Corps.

Selective service supplied enough men for a large army, but it could not provide them with training or equipment. The United States was the world's leading industrial power, but little had been done prior to 1917 to prepare its industry for wartime production. The Americans were to learn that it took a year to plan and retool, and still another year before much could flow from the production lines. In the crisis of the World War, a two-year delay was inadmissible. And with so many raw recruits and so few experienced soldiers to train and lead them, the training problem, like the production problem, seemed almost insurmountable over the short haul.

Fortunately for the United States, it could fall back on the resources of its Anglo-French allies for solving both problems with relative speed. The United States undertook to provide the American Expeditionary Force (AEF) with most of its small arms and clothing, while Britain and France undertook to meet its demands in heavy arms and in most other items of equipment. Thus, the AEF adopted the French 75-mm gun as its basic artillery piece, and only a hundred of the 2,250 field guns it used in France were made in the United States. Similarly, although some 5,000 American pilots and other aircrew served in forty-five combat squadrons on the Western Front, nearly all of the 1,029 airplanes they used were of European manufacture. Most of the 250 tanks used by the AEF were provided by the European allies. And, of the 18 million tons of supplies and equipment used by the AEF in Europe, 10 million tons were purchased there.

The solution to the training problem was to give American recruits basic instruction in the United States and then more advanced training under European instructors in Europe. Junior officers were turned out *en masse* in as little as three months by officer candidate schools, and by the Reserve Officer Training Corps (ROTC), established under the 1916 National Defense Act, under which college campuses helped to meet the need.

General John Pershing, commander-in-chief of the AEF, had never commanded more than 16,000 troops at a time before 1917, but none of the other 5,175 regular army officers in April 1917 was more qualified. Pershing had become famous in 1916 while commanding an expedition into Mexico in pursuit of Pancho Villa, the revolutionary leader and border-raider, but it was a long step from chasing Mexican bandit-revolutionaries to commanding a mass army in Europe. Pershing and the other American commanders and staff officers had to work at a frantic pace in order to prepare themselves, as well as their forces, for the challenges of a great war in Europe. While General Peyton C. March soon assumed the duties of Army Chief-of-Staff, and largely directed the mobilization of the land forces, Pershing and the AEF staff proceeded to Europe to establish an American headquarters and organize the arrival of American troops. Still, a year after the United States formally entered the war, the American presence in France consisted of only 320,000 troops and four combat-ready army divisions. Just eight months later, the AEF's strength had swelled to 2 million men and forty-two divisions, and twenty-four more army divisions were training in the United States. The AEF played a vital role in the final successful outcome of the war, though the effectiveness of the American intervention was very much due to splendid American-European cooperation.

B. *The Russian Collapse, the French Mutiny, and New German Methods of Land Warfare.*   Before American strength could help bring about an Allied victory, the Allies in Europe came very close to losing the war. In February 1917 the war-weary soldiers and workers in Petrograd (formerly St. Petersburg) turned on the monarchy and toppled it. Nicholas II and his family were placed under arrest, and political power was divided between the Petrograd Soviet (Council) of Workers and Soldiers, and the Russian Duma (parliament). Alexander Kerensky, a moderate socialist, became head of the new Russian republic. By the summer of 1917 the Russian army was disintegrating before the advancing Germans, and, by fall, V. I. Lenin, the Bolshevik leader recently returned from exile, had seized leadership of the Petrograd Soviet. In early November, Lenin led ten thousand armed followers in an overthrow of the Kerensky government. Lenin's peace negotiations with the Central Powers finally resulted in the Treaty of Brest-Litovsk in March 1918, which surrendered Poland and a large slice of western Russia, but which confirmed Lenin's grip on power.

Events on the Western Front in 1917, particularly in France, also favored the Central Powers. In preparation for their concentration of effort in the East in 1917, and meanwhile to strengthen their defensive positions in the West, in early 1917 the Germans chose to shorten and strengthen their lines, creating a formidable system of defense that could be successfully held by fewer troops. Accordingly, they withdrew from the westernmost bulge of their line, along a fifty-mile front from Arras to Soissons, twenty-five miles to the rear. There they created a position in depth which they called the Siegfried Zone, but which came to be known to the Allies as the Hindenburg Line. The two hinges of the line, Arras in the north and the Chemin Dames-Aisne River in the south, were precisely where the British and French were to launch their initial offensives in 1917. In consequence, Nivelle's offensive on the Aisne in April-May consumed 200,000 Frenchmen to no purpose, and set off the event called the Great Mutiny. Soldiers in fifty-four divisions—about half the army—followed the Russian example in setting up Soldiers' Councils and engaging in sit-down strikes. A frightened French government relieved Nivelle as general-in-chief and appointed Pétain—the hero of Verdun—to his place. Pétain's appointment had a calming effect on the French army. He acted quickly to bring about needed reforms in food, health, recreation, and leave policies. Most important, he placed a temporary moratorium on French offensives. By summer the French army had recovered its discipline and a measure of its morale, but the Great Mutiny gave the Germans reason to hope that French army was fragile and, in future, might collapse under heavy blows.

A third reason for German optimism was their growing confidence in a new system of infantry-artillery assault tactics. The new doctrine called for intense, accurate, but relatively brief preliminary barrages, followed by the attack of specially trained *Sturmtruppen* (Storm Troops), armed with the new air-cooled machine-guns, trench mortars, hand-grenades, flame-throwers (introduced by the Germans at Verdun), and conventional weapons. The Storm Troops sought to penetrate weak places in the enemy's front-line trenches, encircling strong points, and finally linking up to create a gap which could be exploited by the regular German infantry. Meanwhile, German artillery hammered all approaches in order to prevent enemy reinforcements from reaching the front.

Before committing the German army entirely to Storm Troop tactics in the West, Hindenburg and Ludendorff gave them a test on the Italian front in October-November 1917. On October 24, six German and six Austro-Hungarian divisions used the new methods to shatter the Italian front at Caporetto in twenty-four hours. Many Italian troops were caught in local encirclements after the front had been penetrated, and other Italian troops were so demoralized that they fled the battlefield. The Austro-German offensive ground forward for fifty miles before logistical problems brought the drive to a close in mid-November. After losing 320,000 troops, the Italian army was so weakened and unnerved that it was a year before it had the capacity to attack.

The Caporetto campaign erased any lingering German doubts that they had found an answer to the problem of breaking a continuous front, though the experience also showed that logistics still posed a problem for long-range penetration during the phase of exploitation. But time was running out for Germany because of the Allied blockade, and the new system offered the German High Command the greatest prospect for a victory in the West during 1918. On January 1, the High Command published *The Attack in Position Warfare,* which became the basic doctrinal document for the German offensives launched during 1918. Upon the success of that doctrine and a concentration of forces in the West, Hindenburg and Ludendorff were prepared to stake the fate of the Second Reich.

C. British Failures and Successes in 1917.   The French failure on the Aisne and the resultant mutiny, already discussed, placed an even greater burden on the British in supporting the Western Front. Fortunately for the Allies, the new British conscript armies were joining Haig's BEF, but their general-in-chief continued to show little imagination or insight in the methods of assault. In April 1917 the Canadians captured Vimy Ridge near Arras as part of an operation to draw German attention from the Aisne where Nivelle's offensive struck shortly after, but beginning in July the BEF was hurled into an offensive around Ypres that in many ways resembled the unfortunate Somme offensive of the year before. Again the bloody and muddy fighting achieved small gains, although the offensive dragged on into November. The ultimate objective, Passchendale village, fell on November 6, but this was just four air-line miles from the point where the BEF attack had begun in July. British casualties came to 240,000. Haig's reputation was somewhat restored by the successful tank attack at Cambrai in the same month that Passchendale fell, but even that success resulted in only local gains.

The greatest British successes on land in 1917 occurred in the Middle East. In 1916 the British forces in Egypt had managed to occupy the northern Sinai Desert and to bring Palestine into striking range. General Sir Edmund Allenby then succeeded to the command of the Egyptian Expeditionary Force (EEF), and, in the latter half of 1917, Allenby's forces drove the Turkish army from Palestine and captured Jerusalem. Turkish rule in the Arabian Desert also collapsed as the tribes there, fighting under the direction of British Major T. E. Lawrence, rebelled against their Turkish overlords. A British student of Middle Eastern archaeology before the war, Lawrence drifted into partisan warfare thanks to his knowledge of Arabic. The renewed British drive from the head of the Persian Gulf also made progress in 1917. In March, British troops under General Frederick S. Maude finally captured Baghdad and created the potential for a linkup with Allenby's forces, an event that might sever Turkey from most of its Middle Eastern empire. But a final victory over Turkey would mean little if the Allies were defeated in Western Europe in 1918, and by that spring that possibility was by no means out of the question.

D. The Ludendorff Offensives, March-July 1918.   By March 1918 the German High Command had concentrated 210 German divisions on the Western Front with an infantry strength of 1,559,000 men. Opposed to these forces were 164 Allied divisions with an infantry strength of 1,245,000 men. The Germans decided to make their first effort against the British line on the Somme in hopes of severing contact between the British and French armies and then rolling the Anglo-Belgian armies into the sea. Ludendorff, who largely planned and directed the final German

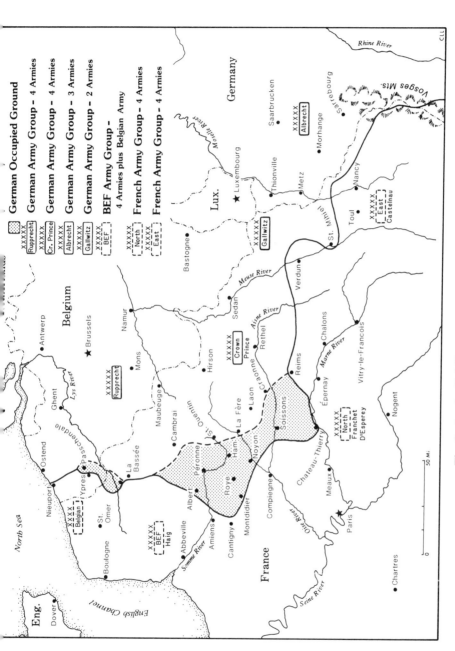

The Ludendorff Offensives, March 21–June 4, 1918

offensives of the war, massed sixty-seven divisions and three thousand guns for an attack on a British front held by twenty-six divisions and fewer than a thousand guns.

The first of the Ludendorff offensives began at dawn on March 21 with a tremendous artillery bombardment, followed by the advance of Storm Troops. By afternoon the Germans had penetrated the front of the British Fifth Army in many places, and whole British battalions had been surrounded or annihilated. As Haig's reserves withered away, the Germans advanced in the general direction of Amiens, a key rail junction and the last stop but one (Abbeville) down the valley of the Somme before reaching the sea. The situation was so critical for the Allies that on March 26 their highest political and military leaders met at Doullens to consider emergency measures. Haig agreed to a French general serving as the Allied generalissimo in return for French reinforcements on the Somme. The chosen Allied commander-in-chief was General Ferdinand Foch, then the French representative on the Allied War Council which had been formed in November 1917 in consequence of the Caporetto disaster. Foch took up his new duties in April 1918, just as sixteen French divisions arrived on the Somme to aid in the defense against Ludendorff's offensive. German logistical problems, as well as stiffening Allied resistance, gradually brought the German drive to a halt short of Amiens. Ludendorff shifted the weight of his offensive further north to the Lys, but by the end of April it was clear that the Allies had frustrated his attempts to drive a wedge to the sea.

In the lull that followed Ludendorff's first offensive, the Allies braced themselves for a renewed German onslaught toward the Channel. Ludendorff had, however, decided on a change in direction. During May, he secretly concentrated forty German divisions opposite the Allied line on the Aisne, held by only eleven French and five battle-weary British divisions. On May 27 a second Ludendorff offensive was unleashed in this sector that shattered the Allied line in less than a day of fighting. As the Germans surged through the gap toward the Marne, Foch rushed reinforcements to shore up the shoulders of the breakthrough, but by early June he lacked reserves, except for uncommitted American troops, for sealing the bottom of the sack. Up to that point General Pershing had been willing to commit only a few American divisions to major fighting, for he wished to conserve his forces until he could field a complete American army. Foch appealed to Pershing to abandon his policy for the time being and send at least two American divisions to the most threatened points along the Marne. Pershing quickly agreed and dispatched the Third Division to hold the crossing at Château-Thierry and the Second Division (with the U.S. Marine Corps Brigade attached) to hold adjacent ground to the west, including Belleau Wood. The German attack at Château-Thierry was soon repulsed, but a three-week battle took place for the ground to the west before the Germans abandoned their effort to reach the Marne. At the farthest point of the German advance, their troops were only thirty-seven miles from Paris. In early July Ludendorff shifted his attacks to the flanks of the forty-mile salient created in the Allied line, but the French held at Soissons and elsewhere. By mid-July the Germans had exhausted their reserves of men and materiel, and the crisis for the Allies had passed.

Since mid-March 1918 the Ludendorff offensives had conquered ten times as much ground as all of the 1917 Allied offensives on the Western Front combined, and they had inflicted the loss of 800,000 Allied troops. But the Germans had failed to knock the Allies out of the war on the Western Front, had suffered a million casualties of their own (among them many of their elite Storm Troops), and were incapable of launching further offensives. In contrast, the Allied armies were on the rebound by midsummer. American troops were arriving at French ports by July at the rate of 200,000 men a month, and Allied factories were rapidly making up for the materiel lost in the German spring and summer offensives. Foch sensed that at last the Allies might have the necessary forces for final victory on the Western Front.

E. Foch's Offensives to the End of the War, July–November 1918. Until Foch's appointment as Allied generalissimo, command arrangements between the French and British armies had been on a voluntary basis. After the Doullens conference, Foch had authority for centralized planning and execution of all Allied operations on the Western Front, an arrangement to which the Americans adhered, as well as more forces with which to execute them as time wore on. Yet his method was to persuade rather than to order other Allied commanders to follow his strategic plans. In this he was quite successful. Accordingly, to a large extent the final Allied strategy which won the war on land in Western Europe in 1918 was Foch's alone.

Foch's strategy was to use the ever-increasing Allied superiority in forces in a series of shifting attacks, each of which was aimed at a local goal and was well within the logistical capabilities of his armies. Much like Grant's final strategy against the Confederacy in 1864–65, Foch's strategy in the summer and fall of 1918 aimed at using a constantly increasing superiority in resources at multiple points to wear down enemy resistance and finally inflict a fatal crack in the enemy's defenses.

The first of Foch's offensives was aimed at eliminating the dangerous German salient to the Marne, a task carried out by mostly French troops from July 18 to August 3. By the end of the offensive, the Germans had withdrawn to their original positions on the Aisne, and, as a reward for this success (which had not cost too many Allied casualties), the French parlia-

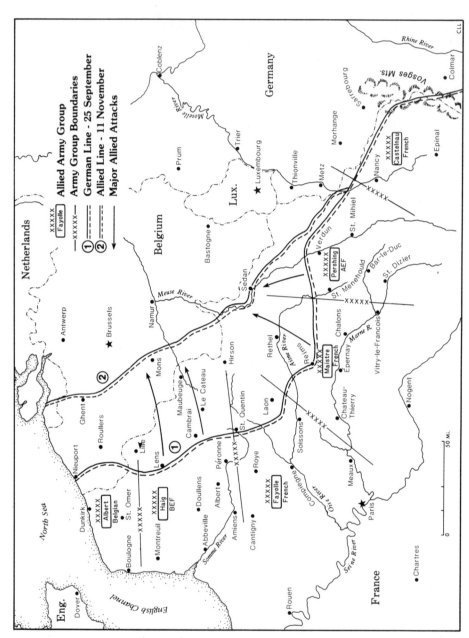

The Western Front, 1918: Final Allied Offensive, September–November

Map labels and legend:

Legend:
- XXXXX Fayolle — Allied Army Group
- —xxxxx— Army Group Boundaries
- ① German Line - 25 September
- ② Allied Line - 11 November
- Major Allied Attacks

Netherlands

Belgium

Lux.

Germany

France

Eng.

North Sea

English Channel

Rhine River

Moselle River

Meuse River

Aisne River

Marne R.

Oise River

Somme River

Seine River

Vosges Mts.

Coblenz
Prum
Trier
Luxembourg
Bastogne
Sedan
Namur
Antwerp
Brussels
Ghent
Roullers
Nieuport
Dunkirk
Boulogne
Dover
Mons
Maubeuge
Cambrai
Le Cateau
Lille
Lens
St. Quentin
Péronne
Albert
Doullens
Montreuil
St. Omer
Abbeville
Amiens
Cantigny
Roye
Laon
Hirson
Rethel
Rheims
Soissons
Compiègne
Meaux
Paris
Rouen
Chartres
Château-Thierry
Epernay
Chalons
Vitry-le-Francois
Nogent
St. Dizier
Bar-le-Duc
St. Menehould
Verdun
St. Mihiel
Metz
Thionville
Morhange
Nancy
Sarrebourg
Epinal
Colmar

XXXXX Albert Belgian
XXXXX Haig BEF
XXXXX Fayolle French
XXXXX Maistre French
XXXXX Pershing AEF
XXXXX Castelnau French

50 Mi.

CLL

ment voted Foch a marshal's baton on August 6. By then Ludendorff had concentrated his reserves in the Aisne sector in anticipation of further Allied attacks in this region, but Foch was about to unleash his first surprise.

On August 8, General Haig launched an offensive in Flanders with eighteen Allied divisions (seven British, five Australian, four Canadian, and one American), led by an armored force of 414 tanks. The assault broke through the enemy's lines and set off such a stampede of German troops to the rear that Ludendorff called August 8 the "Black Day" of the German army. For a time it seemed that Haig's offensive could not be contained, and by September 3 it had recovered all ground lost to the Germans since March 21. When at last it came to a halt, the Germans had concentrated their forces heavily in this region. And by the time Haig's drive ended, the American First Army—a force of six oversized divisions—was ready for commitment.

Once again Foch shifted his assault to an unexpected quarter, this time to erase a small salient near Verdun at Saint-Mihiel. This operation would give Pershing and his staff much needed experience in the conduct of large operations, as well as reduce a vulnerable point in the Allied line. To insure American success, Foch reinforced the attack with six French divisions, 3,000 guns, 2,200 airplanes, and 267 tanks. The drive, launched on September 12, wiped out the salient in four days, and again left the Germans wondering where the next Allied blow would fall.

By late September, Foch was ready to carry out his most daring move of all. Instead of another single-front drive far from the point of the previous one, Foch had acquired enough forces to risk two simultaneous offensives at relatively remote points. These drives were intended to put the Germans on the horns of a dilemma; if they concentrated enough reserves to stop one of the drives, they would probably lack the forces to contain the other. Foch's "Victory Offensive," as he called it, began on September 26 when 660,000 French troops and 220,000 American troops attacked north from the Verdun salient down the valley of the Meuse River and into the Argonne forest. The drive had as its ultimate goal the severing of the lateral railroad that ran along the southern fringe of the Ardennes forest further north, without which Ludendorff would have great difficulty in shifting reinforcements from one threatened point to another. As Foch expected, German resistance in the Argonne was fierce; Ludendorff gave top priority to holding the Meuse-Argonne region. After a month of intense fighting, the Allied drive had advanced only ten miles from its starting point. But German concentration in the Argonne sector tipped the balance in Flanders, where Haig renewed his attack and the weaker German forces there were compelled to fall back. As early as September 29, Hindenburg told the Kaiser that German prospects were grim if the Allies could keep up the pressure.

As the German armies slowly yielded ground on the Western Front, Germany's allies began to collapse. In the fall of 1918 Allenby's army in Palestine invaded Syria, captured Damascus, and advanced as far as Aleppo. The desperate Turkish government accepted Allied armistice terms on October 30, and Turkey left the war. The almost-forgotten Allied army in Greece launched a probe into the Balkans in late September, and, much to its surprise, it found the troops of the Central Powers in its path were abandoning all resistance. The Italian army had its one great victory of the war when its troops broke through enemy lines at Vitorio Veneto and eventually advanced to Trieste, the goal of its first offensive in 1915. The collapse of the Austro-Hungarian army was accompanied by internal revolution in the Habsburg empire which brought down the monarchy. Vienna and Budapest severed relations, Austria capitulating to the Allies on November 3, and Hungary on November 6.

By the time Austria-Hungary left the war, Foch's offensives had driven the German armies far back into Belgium, Haig's forces having occupied about half the country. Further east, the American forces had expanded into two field armies—the First and Second—and Pershing had become the equivalent of an army group commander. Some of the American forces were approaching Sedan and the southern fringes of the Ardennes. Foch's armies consisted of 220 divisions (106 French, 60 British and Dominion, 42 American, 12 Belgian, 2 Italian, and 2 Portuguese), while the German armies in the West had dwindled to the equivalent of 80 full-strength divisions. Ludendorff resigned as Hindenburg's deputy on October 27, and General Wilhelm Groener succeeded to his post. On the German home front, there were severe food shortages, and German factories were running out of raw materials from which to produce armaments. German discipline commenced a fatal internal breakdown when, on November 3, sailors of the High Seas Fleet refused an order to put to sea against the Allied blockade and instead raised the standard of revolt. Civilian disorders followed in Munich and then Berlin. The Reichstag took control of foreign policy from the Kaiser, with whom the Allied governments had refused to negotiate, and the last stumbling block to an armistice was removed on November 9 when the Kaiser abdicated the throne of Germany and fled to neutral Holland. Philip Scheidemann, head of the Socialist Party—the largest in the Reichstag—assumed power and proclaimed Germany a republic. A German delegation from the new government in Berlin was received by Foch in his railway car at Compiègne, and the terms of the armistice were hammered out. All German troops were to be withdrawn behind their pre-war borders, Foch's armies were to occupy the German Rhineland, the German fleet was to be interned at Scapa Flow pending a final peace treaty, and specific quantities of arms, railroad engines and cars, and motor trucks were to be surrendered to the Allies so as to insure the impossibility of renewed German resistance. The Armistice went into effect at 11:00 a.m. on November 11, 1918, with German armies still on foreign soil but with little question that, had the war lasted much longer, the Allied armies would have invaded Germany within a matter of a few weeks.

After the war, German ultranationalists made much of the fact that the home front collapsed even while the German army was still on foreign soil, and the new German republic bore the onus of the armistice as well as the signing of the Peace of Versailles in June 1919. But by the time of the Paris Peace Conference—the greatest diplomatic assemblage since the Congress of Vienna in 1814–15—had begun its deliberations in January 1919, a host of new European states had emerged from the rubble of the former Hohenzollern, Romanov, and Habsburg empires: Finland, Latvia, Estonia, Lithuania, Poland, Czechoslovakia, and Yugoslavia, and a great change had taken place in the political order of Europe for which the victors were only partly responsible. The Middle East was also in turmoil as a result of the war and Turkish collapse, and Russia (not invited to the conference) was involved in civil war. In addition, the war's financial and human costs dwarfed those of any previous conflict. The direct financial costs have been put at $180,500,000,000 in 1918 dollars, and the indirect costs at $151,612,500,000, but these sums would have to be multiplied many times to reach the equivalent in contemporary dollars. But most impressive—and depressing—are the casualty lists, which speak for themselves: some 10 million dead and 20 million wounded or ill as the result of the war. And the general peace achieved at such a price lasted scarcely more than twenty years.

5

Between the World Wars, 1919–39

I. The Failure of the Treaty Approach

The years between the world wars saw the greatest effort to that time to control armaments and to discourage war through treaty. The approach varied in form all the way from the dictated armament clauses in the Treaty of Versailles with Germany to the voluntary renunciation of war as an instrument of national policy under the Paris Peace Pact of 1928. The greatest practical progress in limiting armaments during the interwar years was made through naval treaties, though ultimately even those efforts failed of their purpose. The fault lay not with the treaty approach itself, or even with the terms of the treaties, but with the unwillingness of Nazi Germany, Fascist Italy, and Imperial Japan to abide by the *status quo* after World War I. Their revisionist policies in the 1930s finally resulted in a global war even worse than the first World War.

In June 1919 a German delegation was summoned to the Palace of Versailles outside Paris to sign, not to negotiate, a treaty of peace with Germany's enemies in World War I. Although the Imperial German government that had waged the war had been replaced by the democratic Weimar Republic, the peace terms were no less severe for that fact. They stripped Germany of its overseas empire and a seventh of its territory in Europe. The Germans had expected the loss of Alsace-Lorraine to France, and the small territorial losses to Belgium and Denmark were tolerable, but they resented the large loss of territory in the east to the new state of Poland. In addition, the Saarland was transferred to France for fifteen years, its return subject to a local plebiscite. Under the War Guilt Clause, Germany was also saddled with a heavy reparations bill. The German Rhineland was converted into a demilitarized zone in which Germany was forbidden to station troops or build fortifications, but in which the Allies could station troops for up to fifteen years. Germany was also denied membership in the new League of Nations, founded at the Paris Peace Conference.

The Treaty of Versailles placed limitations on the German armed forces of special relevance to the study of the patterns of war. The post-war German army was reduced to the status of an *armée de métier* (professional army) of 100,000 soldiers serving under long-term enlistments. All German military service had to be voluntary, and neither an army reserve nor any paramilitary organizations were permitted. The army was denied tanks, poison gas, heavy artillery, and air forces, and it was not supposed to have any form of the traditional General Staff. The German navy was limited to 15,000 sailors, six old pre-dreadnought battleships, six light cruisers, twelve destroyers, and twelve torpedo boats. The remainder of the High Seas Fleet, interned at Scapa Flow since the end of the war, was to be divided among the Allies. (Much of it was scuttled by its crews at Scapa Flow when the terms of the peace treaty were learned.) The pre-dreadnought battleships could be replaced by ships displacing no more than 10,000 tons and carrying guns no larger than 11-inch in caliber. (Only three replacements conforming generally to the treaty were built between the world wars—*Admiral Scheer, Admiral Graf Spee*, and *Deutschland*—and dubbed "pocket battleships" by the press.) An Inter-Allied Military Control Commission (IMCC) was to make periodic inspections in order to insure that Germany was complying with the armament provisions.

In the long run, the enforcement of the Treaty of Versailles rested upon cooperation among the United States, Britain, and France, but that cooperation proved weak in the post-war period. The U.S. Senate rejected the treaty because it committed the United States to membership in the League of Nations. The state of war between the United States and Germany was ended by a joint resolution of both houses of Congress, and in 1921 the American garrison in the Rhineland was withdrawn. Relations between Britain and France withered after Germany defaulted on reparations payments in 1923 and French troops occupied the Ruhr in retaliation. By then the British government had come to realize that a revitalized trade with Germany was worth more to Britain's economy than reparations. The Ruhr Crisis ended in 1924 when American loans under the Dawes Plan allowed Germany to resume reparations payments to France. In 1925 the government of Gustav Stresemann in Germany signed the Pact of Locarno, voluntarily recognizing Germany's new frontiers in the West and promising not to change those in the East by force. In 1926 France sponsored Germany's admission to the League of Nations, and Britain withdrew its troops from the Rhineland. The Young Plan of 1929 made it easier for Germany to continue to pay reparations, and in 1930 the last French troops in the Rhineland were withdrawn. In the same year, the IMCC made its final report on German armaments and was dissolved. The

onset of the Great Depression caused Germany to default on its repara-
tion payments in 1932, and that summer a final settlement was made. But
in January 1933 Adolf Hitler and the Nazi Party came to power in Germany, and the era of the Third Reich began. In October 1933 Hitler took
Germany out of both the League and the World Disarmament Conference, and it was widely rumored that Nazi Germany was covertly
rearming.

In 1921–22, representatives of several powers met in Washington, D.C.,
in order to seek a settlement in the Pacific and to head off the danger of a
new naval race. Three treaties emerged from the conference: the Nine-
Power Treaty reaffirmed international support for the "Open Door" policy toward China; the Four-Power Treaty obligated the United States,
Britain, France, and Japan to respect each other's territory in the Pacific
and the Far East, and limited fortification in the Pacific basin; and, most
important, the Five-Power Treaty (or Washington Naval Treaty) imposed
limits on the world's leading navies.

The Washington Naval Treaty—signed by the United States, Britain,
Japan, France, and Italy—defined all warships larger than 10,000 tons
displacement with guns larger than 8-inch in caliber as "capital ships," and
provided, with a few specific exceptions, that no capital ship could exceed
35,000 tons displacement or carry larger than 16-inch guns. A ceiling of
525,000 tons was placed on each of the capital fleets of the United States
and Great Britain, and 310,000 tons on that of Japan (the so-called 5–5–3
ratio). France and Italy were each restricted to 178,000 tons of capital
ships. A "battleship-building holiday" was to go into effect for ten years,
though some capital ships under construction could be completed. Except
for specific cases, no aircraft carrier was to exceed 27,000 tons displacement. The United States and Britain were each allowed 135,000 tons in
aircraft carriers, Japan was allowed 80,000 tons, and France and Italy were
each allowed 60,000 tons. Though no agreement was reached on ratios for
cruisers, "heavy cruisers" would carry 8-inch guns, "light cruisers" 6-inch
guns. No agreement was reached on submarines, save that they would not
be employed as weapons of *guerre de course* (France abstained from this
pledge). Among the vessels exempted from the limits of the treaty were the
British battle cruiser *Hood,* which displaced 40,000 tons (the largest warship in the world for most of the interwar period), the American aircraft
carriers *Lexington* and *Saratoga* (originally intended to be battle cruisers),
each of which displaced 33,000 tons when completed in 1927, and the
Japanese carriers *Kaga* and *Akagi,* also converted ships, each of which,
when completed, displaced 30,000 tons.

At the London Naval Conference of 1930, the United States, Britain,
and Japan reached agreement on a ratio for cruisers of 10–10–7, and they
placed a limit of 57,000 tons on their respective submarine fleets. They

also extended the "battleship-building holiday" for another ten years. But Japanese militarists increasingly controlled Japan's policies after 1930, launching an invasion of Chinese Manchuria in 1931 and turning it into the puppet state of Manchukuo, and causing Japan to leave the League when that body found Japan guilty of aggression. In December 1934 Japan served the required two-year notice of withdrawal from the limitations of the Washington and London naval treaties, and all multilateral treaty limitations expired on December 31, 1936.

Meanwhile, the Italian invasion of Ethiopia in 1935 led to Italy's condemnation by the League and Benito Mussolini's withdrawal of his country from that body. In March 1935 Adolf Hitler disavowed the armament limitations of the Treaty of Versailles, and Britain's government resigned itself to German rearmament. It believed that it had headed off another Anglo-German naval race of the sort that had occurred before World War I when, in June 1935, Hitler signed an Anglo-German Naval Treaty which limited the German surface navy to 35 percent of the British and accepted parity in submarines. Hitler really gave away nothing by signing this treaty, since it would be many years before the reviving German navy approached the level of 35 percent of the British navy in surface ships or reached parity with Britain in submarines. In the meantime, the treaty helped to convince British leaders that they could do business with Hitler.

British and other Western European leaders hung on to the delusion that Hitler's aims were limited into the late 1930s, despite disturbing developments. In early 1935, a plebiscite in the Saarland led to its return to Germany, a legal action under the Treaty of Versailles; but in March 1936, in violation of the treaty, German troops marched back into the demilitarized zone of the Rhineland. Britain was unwilling to take action, and France was unwilling to risk war with Germany without Britain's support. The Germans then began building the so-called West Wall—a line of fixed defenses along Germany's western frontiers—the strongest segment being the Siegfried Line, opposite the French frontier. Though the Siegfried Line was not finished in September 1939, it served as a psychological as well as a physical barrier to French attack when Germany attacked Poland. Thus, one by one, the "bonds of Versailles" on Germany were stripped away. Meanwhile, in 1936, Hitler and Mussolini had pledged through the Axis Pact that Nazi Germany and Fascist Italy would support each other's foreign policies.

In 1937 the Far East took the limelight when Japan launched an undeclared war on China, referred to as the "China Incident." Over the next three years, Japanese armies occupied much of eastern China and imperiled the interests of other powers in the Far East, in clear violations of the Nine-Power and Four-Power treaties made in Washington after World War I. In early 1938, Hitler's actions shifted the focus to Europe again when his threats forced Austria—a landlocked country of only 6 million people—to accept union with Nazi Germany. Later that year, Hitler demanded cession of the Sudetenland, whose German population constituted almost a fifth of the 15 million people who lived in Czechoslovakia. Prague called on its alliance with France for protection, but both Paris and London were appalled at the prospect of war over the Sudetenland issue and finally accepted proposals for a four-power meeting at Munich in September 1938. The upshot was that Prime Minister Neville Chamberlain of Britain and French Premier Édouard Daladier of France agreed with Hitler and Mussolini that the Sudetenland would be transferred to Germany in return for Hitler's pledge that he would seek no more territorial changes in Europe. When Chamberlain returned to London, he thought he had brought with him "peace in our time."

Actually, the Munich Pact whetted Hitler's appetite for more territory and made Hitler and Mussolini contemptuous of the Anglo-French leadership into the bargain. Hitler's triumph at Munich led to a renamed "Czecho-Slovakia," and Poland further weakened the shrinking Czech state by seizing disputed territory. In March 1939 Hitler cast aside his pledge made at Munich and ordered German troops to occupy all of what remained of former Czechoslovakia, and also Lithuania's port of Memel. In April Mussolini, encouraged by the success of his Axis partner, ordered the invasion of Albania on the Adriatic Sea.

Axis aggression finally discredited the Anglo-French policy of appeasement, and London and Paris shifted belatedly to a policy of deterrence. Britain adopted the first military conscription in its peacetime history, and both Britain and France pledged aid to Poland, Rumania, and Greece against future Axis aggression. But in May 1939 Hitler and Mussolini made the Pact of Steel—a full-fledged military alliance—and that summer Hitler began to make demands on Poland. Both Germany and the Anglo-French powers began to court Soviet Russia, but Hitler proved to be the more skillful bidder. On August 23, the Nazi-Soviet Pact was signed. In the wake of the Nazi-Soviet Pact, Britain and France made a military alliance with Poland in a last effort to deter Hitler, but the Führer was not impressed. The peace of Europe was doomed. Treaties for peace had been replaced by pacts for war.

II. Armies

The principal topic of debate in the more advanced armies between 1919 and 1939 concerned the future of motorization and of armored warfare. Conservative soldiers held that the heavy tank was essentially an infantry-support weapon, while the light tank and armored car were properly assigned to the cavalry for reconnaissance missions. Since conservatives held the upper hand in the British, French, and American armies after World War I, armor in each of these armies was divided between the infantry and cavalry branches. But whereas the French army shared with the other mass European armies the problem that motor resources were too scarce to dispense completely with horse-drawn vehicles for supply, the smaller Anglo-American armies were able to motorize their logistics almost entirely by 1939. The motor truck replaced the horse-drawn wagon as the chief vehicle in their supply columns.

Since completely motorized supply columns were unavailable to them, the French and the other continental armies had the choice of either mixing what motorization they possessed with horse-drawn vehicles and distributing it evenly throughout the entire force, or concentrating it in a completely motorized *corps d'élite* within an otherwise traditional mass army. Down to 1939, the French army chose to motorize completely only a few light mobile divisions and to distribute any excess motorization among the infantry divisions as far as it would go.

All three of the French generals-in-chief between the world wars were cautious in their attitude toward the organization of armor and motorization, and they generally favored a strategic defense for France in the event of another war with Germany. Henri Pétain, who had made his reputation with his unconquerable defense of Verdun in World War I, continued to believe in the power of defense over that of the attack. Not only was he relatively indifferent to developments in motorization and armor, he may have played a decisive role in the French decision in 1930 to build a powerful line of fixed fortifications across the hundred-mile-wide Lorraine Gap, the traditional gateway from Germany into France. Though the Maginot Line was named for André Maginot, the minister of war when the credits were voted by the French parliament, it was really Pétain's monument.

General Maxime Weygand, Pétain's successor at the head of the French army, took more interest in armor and motorization than did Pétain, but French doctrine continued to stress that only traditional combinations of infantry and artillery could conquer and hold ground in a decisive fashion. Under Weygand, the French continued the practice of distributing heavy tank battalions piecemeal among the infantry divisions. Weygand did concentrate the French army's light tanks and armored cars in *Divisions Légère Méchanique* (DLMs) in anticipation that these divisions could carry out armed reconnaissance into Belgium in the event that France ever had to counter a reenactment of the German Schlieffen Plan, but once contact with the enemy was made and the battle developed, Weygand planned for his army to go on the defensive in the Belgian plains and to immolate German attacks with its firepower. General Maurice Gamelin, who succeeded Weygand at the head of the French army, did not challenge the ideas of his predecessors down to 1939, the French war plan calling for the active army to serve as a *force de couverture* (covering force) for the mobilization of the reserve, and the mobilized mass army remaining on the defensive until its German opponent made some move, either against the Maginot Line or through Belgium.

Among the critics of conservative thinking between the world wars were the British general J. F. C. Fuller, British captain B. H. Liddell Hart, and Colonel Charles de Gaulle of the French army. Of the three, Fuller, who had served as chief-of-staff of the Royal Tank Corps in World War I, had the most extensive experience with armored operations. He believed that a relatively small but armored, all-motorized army could overwhelm a much larger army composed of the traditional branches. He visualized tanks of great speed and range penetrating the enemy's front and overrunning its centers of command, creating paralysis among its forces. For his part, Captain Liddell Hart visualized armored divisions composed of tanks and motorized infantry, which could make deep penetrations to sever enemy communications and to carry out strategic encirclements. De Gaulle, serving in a mass army, proposed to his superiors the creation of armored divisions with as many as five hundred tanks apiece, manned by 100,000 professional soldiers. These armored divisions could serve not only as weapons of offense, but also as a mobile reserve with which to mount counterattacks against the enemy's breakthroughs of the continuous front. But the British and French high commands paid little attention to the ideas of Fuller, Liddell Hart, and de Gaulle between world wars.

Soviet Russia was a potential customer for new ideas on armor and motorization after it survived a civil war and the forced-draft industrialization imposed by Joseph Stalin, Lenin's successor in power. Marshal Mikhail Tukhachevsky, the Red Army's commander-in-chief in the 1930s, carried out a number of experiments with armored, motorized, and airborne forces. But Tukhachevsky's career and innovation in the Red Army were cut short by Stalin's great purges of his real and imagined enemies, and the Russian generals who survived the purges became almost slavish adherents to Stalin's ideas on war. Stalin relied on sheer quantities of armament to offset their mediocre quality. Russian armored organization and tactics, as well as the quality of Russian equipment, lagged well behind the German by 1939.

There is some irony in the fact that Germany, denied armored fighting vehicles by the Treaty of Versailles in 1919, and really without them until after 1933, should have developed the most advanced ideas on armored, motorized warfare of any army on the European continent by 1939. Actually, the Treaty of Versailles stimulated Germany's interest in mobile forces by denying it fixed fortifications on its western frontiers and a traditional mass army. General Hans von Seeckt, Chief of the Army Command to 1926, encouraged experiments with infantry carried by motor trucks and using trucks to tow artillery, and, after his retirement, the Troop Office (the disguised Army General Staff) set up a special section in 1928 to study the theoretical possibilities in armored warfare. Major Heinz Guderian, formerly an officer of light infantry, became familiar with the ideas of Fuller and Liddell Hart through their books and articles, and in 1929 he hit upon his own conception of an armored or panzer division.

Essentially, Guderian's panzer division was an armored-mechanized-motorized task force, in which mobile infantry, artillery, engineers, and supply units were combined with a brigade of tanks in order to allow the tanks to fight with full effect. Guderian recognized that such panzer divisions might serve to revive the traditional German doctrine of the *Kesselschlacht,* or battle of encirclement and annihilation, and thus lend decisiveness to ground warfare of the future. He also grasped the importance of the radio for command and control of rapidly moving forces. Guderian's ideas were supported by his superior General Oswald Lutz, later the first general-in-chief of German armored forces, though Lutz retired before the outbreak of World War II. Lutz and Guderian took the opportunity to impress Hitler with exercises of motorized troops, and in 1935 the Army High Command (OKH) created three panzer divisions on an experimental basis. Despite the fact that these early armored formations were equipped with only the PzKw. I light tank, they looked so promising that by September 1939 their number had been increased to six panzer divisions and a panzer brigade. By then the principal German tanks were the PzKw. I and the somewhat better PzKw. II, about 300 to a division, but they were soon replaced by the excellent PzKw. III and PzKw. IV as Germany's main reliance. The best of the German tanks were good compromises of speed, range, protection, fire-power, and versatility, as suited their roles and missions. They stood in contrast to the overly specialized Anglo-French tank designs with their inadequate systems of command and control.

In addition to the panzer divisions, the German army had two other types of all-motorized divisions by 1939. The four "light divisions" combined regiments of motorized infantry with a light tank battalion per division, and represented a compromise between the panzer division and the French DLM. Six motorized infantry divisions completed the *corps d'élite* of the German mass army of slightly more than a hundred divisions on the eve of World War II. The German infantry divisions, which made up the vast majority of German divisions of all types, were not greatly different in organization and capacities from those of 1918. Still, with the close air support of the Luftwaffe (the German air force), this combination of new and old style forces constituted the essence of the *Blitzkrieg* ("Lightning

War") which Hitler unleashed on Europe in 1939 and which soon laid more of Europe at Hitler's feet than at any man's since Napoleon.

No such blitzkrieg vision inspired the American army between the world wars. Part of the problem was that the army was starved for funds; in addition, few army leaders foresaw another major American commitment to Europe. Moreover, a war in the Pacific with Japan would require different kinds of land forces than would a continental ground war in Europe. Still another hindrance was the National Defense Act of 1920, which arbitrarily defined tanks as weapons of infantry and armored cars as weapons of cavalry. An Experimental Mechanized Force (EMF) in 1928, modeled on a similar British experiment in 1927, never came to much, in part because it was forced to use outdated and obsolete World War I equipment. Though General Douglas MacArthur, while serving as Army Chief-of-Staff in 1934, set up a mechanized cavalry brigade by transferring tanks from the infantry (he called them "combat cars" in order to get around the 1920 Act), the result was more like the French DLM than the German panzer division. The American army did not hit on the right organization until the German panzers rolled over France in 1940. Within a few weeks of the French defeat, the Americans had cobbled together the First Armored Division. Fortunately for the Americans, it was not too late to change tank designs, and mass production began on the M-4 Sherman, like the best of the German designs, a good compromise on speed, range, protection, firepower, and versatility. Nor did the Americans neglect the radio as an indispensable tool for the command and control of armored forces.

Neither Japanese armor nor armored organization was outstanding when, in 1938–39, they encountered the Red Army in Manchurian border clashes. But the demonstrated inferiority of Japanese machines and organization came too late to result in major policy changes before the outbreak of the war in the Pacific. Moreover, in that contest, amphibious mechanization was more important than armor designed for continental warfare, and Japan could not compete with the United States in those resources in the long run.

III. Navies

Because of the impact of the treaty limitations already discussed, many of the world's battleships and battle cruisers were aging by the time naval rearmament got underway in the 1930s. In addition to age, most of the older warships had been designed and built when airpower was in its infancy, and it was not always practical to reconstruct them against the new threats of the aerial bomb and torpedo. Accordingly, the new battleships that appeared in the late 1930s and early 1940s were in fact a quantum leap over the so-called treaty battleships in dreadnought design. Among the new dreadnoughts were such ships as USS *North Carolina* with a speed of thirty knots, nine 16-inch guns, horizontal sloped armor to deflect aerial bombs, and numerous dual-purpose 5-inch and other anti-aircraft guns. The most impressive of the World War II dreadnoughts were the Japanese *Yamato* and *Musashi*, at 70,000 tons displacement the largest such ships ever built. Each had a main battery of nine 18-inch guns capable of hurling 3,200-pound shells up to twenty miles. Besides anti-aircraft guns, each was protected by an 8-inch-thick steel deck impervious to bombs weighing less than a ton and dropped from below 10,000 feet. Armor protection at belt-line was 19 inches thick. While both ships were to be sunk by air power during World War II, it took fleets of aircraft to sink them.

When the Second World War broke out in September 1939, none of the new dreadnought battleships was in service. Germany's *Bismarck* was not ready until the spring of 1941, and *Tirpitz*, its sister ship, was not ready before early in 1942. Both vessels displaced about 45,000 tons and carried 15-inch guns. Since two battleships do not make a battle line, both were used as surface raiders in World War II. In 1939, the Germans possessed *Scharnhorst* and *Gneisenau*, battle cruisers displacing nearly 35,000 tons apiece but armed with 11-inch guns like those of Germany's three "pocket battleships." All five ships were used in World War II as surface raiders. In 1939, France had seven battleships, but only five were suited for fleet actions. *Dunkerque* and *Strasbourg* carried 13-inch guns, and were designed to counter raids on shipping by the German ships armed with 11-inch guns. Italy had four battleships and two more under construction. Japan had ten battleships and battle cruisers, but the most recent had joined the fleet in 1921, and Japan's two super-battleships were still under construction. Britain had fifteen battleships and battle cruisers, but the newest had joined the fleet in 1925. In September 1939, the United States had fifteen battleships, but the newest—*West Virginia*—had joined the fleet in 1923. New American battleships were building, but by December 1941, only *North Carolina* had joined the fleet and *Washington* had just completed trials. Both displaced 35,000 tons and carried 16-inch guns. All the battleships attacked at Pearl Harbor on December 7, 1941, were old.

Among the European powers, only Britain and France possessed aircraft carriers between the world wars, and France had only *Béarn*, launched in 1927. The German carrier *Graf Zeppelin* was laid down in 1935 but was never completed, and the Luftwaffe absorbed the fledgling German naval air arm. Five of Britain's six carriers in 1939 were modernized vessels from World War I, and three new carriers were under construction.

Part of the relative indifference of continental European navies to aircraft carriers had to do with the belief that carrier forces would be no match for land-based aircraft in European waters. But even Britain's carrier forces also suffered from organizational and technical weaknesses; by 1939 they lagged behind the American and Japanese naval air services in both numbers of aircraft and in performance, and, in addition, British carriers based only about half as many planes on the same tonnage as their American and Japanese counterparts. For instance, in December 1941, nine British carriers based 450 aircraft when seven American carriers based 500 planes and nine Japanese carriers based 700 aircraft. On the other hand, Britain was first to build a carrier with an armored flight deck, a reflection of the British proper appreciation of the dangers that aerial bombs would pose to the carrier.

Cruiser design varied among the world's three largest navies. The American and Japanese navies preferred fewer heavy cruisers armed with 8-inch guns to a larger number of light cruisers armed with 6-inch guns. The British view was just the opposite. The difference was explained by the Royal Navy's need to protect the largest merchant marine in the world, one spread all over the globe. The threat from surface attack could be best done with a greater number of light cruisers. In September 1939, only fifteen of Britain's fifty-seven cruisers were heavy cruisers, and some of the others were classified as antiaircraft cruisers and armed with 5-inch dual-purpose guns. But not even the British cruisers with 8-inch guns were a match for the five German ships armed with 11-inch guns in 1939, and, in gunned ships, only Britain's battleships and battle cruisers had any chance against *Bismarck* and *Tirpitz* when the German vessels were used as surface raiders. Therefore, after the outbreak of war, Britain had no choice but to escort all important convoys with battleships, battle cruisers, and aircraft carriers, as well as antisubmarine craft—a tremendous strain on British resources. Fortunately for the British, all of the large German warships were never available at one time for commerce-raiding. On the other hand, the German occupation of Norway and France in 1940 gave the Germans far better bases for a surface *guerre de course* than they enjoyed in World War I. Part of the British solution to the problem of powerful surface raiders was air attack on their bases before they could put to sea, a kind of resurrection of the old close blockade.

Destroyers developed in diverse directions before 1939. Large destroyers, displacing up to 3,500 tons and carrying 5-inch guns, were launched for service with the battle fleets. Smaller destroyer escorts, corvettes, and frigates served to protect merchant ships from submarines. Antisubmarine warfare got a tremendous boost from the development of sonar ("asdic" in the British navy), an acronym for "sound navigation and ranging." The device could detect and track underwater craft by bouncing sound waves off their hulls and measuring the echoes returned. Combined with the traditional depth charge, sonar made antisubmarine craft a far greater threat to the submerged submarine than in World War I. On the other hand, the American and British navies, the first to possess sonar, were somewhat complacent that the device would largely negate the threat of submerged submarine attack against merchant fleets. Actually, far more destroyer escorts and sonar sets were needed than were available at the outbreak of World War II. Also, new submarine tactics—such as the night surface attack—sometimes rendered sonar useless. Eventually antisubmarine craft had to be equipped with both sonar and radar, and supplemented by land-based and sea-based aircraft, in order to deal adequately with the submarine threat.

Soviet Russia led the world in the number of submarines in service in September 1939—perhaps 150—but most of them were small craft intended for coast defense. Italy ranked second with 104 submarines, but they were designed for operations in the Mediterranean Sea and lacked great range. With 100 submarines, the U.S. underwater fleet was third in size, but, in line with American opposition to submarine *guerre de course* dating back to World War I, American submarines were intended for coast defense and operations with the battle fleet. However, the prospect of operations in the great distances of the Pacific Ocean led the United States to emphasize range in its submarines. France had 78 submarines, including the huge and long-ranged submarine cruiser *Surcouf* (9,000 tons displacement, two 8-inch guns, and carrying a catapult-launched seaplane). Japan had 59 submarines, which, like the American, were built for range but not commerce-raiding. Britain and Germany tied for sixth place with 57 submarines apiece in September 1939, but only Germany's U-boats had been designed with commerce-raiding in mind.

Between the world wars, German naval leaders had given much thought as to how to conduct a future *guerre de course,* even though they also hoped eventually to build a "balanced fleet" capable of commanding the sea. The relative paucity in submarines in September 1939 was due both to the lateness of German rearmament and to Hitler's earlier assurances to Admiral Erich Raeder, commander-in-chief of the navy from 1928 to 1943, that Germany would not face war for many years. After 1933, Raeder opted to give priority to building larger warships over submarines because they took longer to complete. When war came much sooner than Raeder had been led to believe, Admiral Karl Dönitz's submarine fleet was excellent in many respects but still small in numbers. Still, the U-boat command faced up to the task of waging *guerre de course,* even when Hitler was slow to place priority on building more submarines.

Though type XX was the most numerous submarine in the German navy, type IX-B sank more merchant tonnage than any other single type in the world during the Second World War. When submerged, the IX-B displaced 1,200 tons, had a surface speed of 18 knots on diesel engines, and an underwater speed of seven knots when powered by electric motors. It was armed with 21-inch torpedoes and a 4-inch deck gun, and, later, an antiaircraft gun. But the problem of insufficient numbers of U-boats was not overcome until 1942, by which time the Allied antisubmarine fleet was swelling. A total of 1,178 submarines served Germany during World War II, but, for all the damage they did, they never severed the Allied sea lanes. In contrast, some 300 American submarines waged a *guerre de course* against Japan's merchant fleet which brought it to the point of collapse. To be sure, the Japanese merchant fleet was far smaller than the Allied merchant fleets which Germany's submarines had to attack, and there were far fewer antisubmarine craft in the Japanese navy to counter the American submarine threat.

Faced with the prospect of a war in the Pacific, both the United States and Japan took more interest in the problem of amphibious assault than did other countries. On the American side, beginning in 1927, the Joint Army-Navy Board sanctioned efforts by the U.S. Marine Corps to find a satisfactory doctrine. In the early 1930s, the Marine Corps issued the *Tentative Manual for Landing Operations,* which became the "bible" of American amphibious assault doctrine in World War II, and created the Fleet Marine Force (FMF) to operate as an integral part of the fleet for the purposes of capturing advanced bases. The Marine doctrine covered all aspects of amphibious assault, including command relationships between land forces and the supporting fleet, ship-to-shore movement and communications, air and gunfire support, and amphibious logistics. No other country in the world, except Japan, had such an advanced doctrine by 1939. Japan came up with similar solutions, and was slightly in advance of the United States in the design of landing craft before World War II. The U.S. Army, which had neglected the issue of amphibious assault between world wars, adapted the Marine doctrine to its own purposes and organization in 1941. Thanks to a sound doctrine developed between the world wars, most of the prototype equipment necessary for amphibious assault had been developed by the United States by the time it entered World War II. Thus, there was no great delay in deciding on the mass production of such designs as the bow-ramped Landing Craft Infantry (LCI), the Landing Ship Tank (LST), and the amphibious tank and personnel carrier. Although the U.S. Marine Corps numbered only 18,000 troops in September 1939, and had no more than 50,000 troops by December 7, 1941, the Corps was prepared to serve as the cornerstone of the greatest amphibious assault force of the Pacific War. By 1945, at its peak strength, the Marine Corps numbered 485,000 men, six amphibious-assault divisions, and several supporting air wings.

IV. Air Forces

Land-based air power was the focus of heated debate between the world wars. Airpower enthusiasts such as General Giulio Douhet of Italy and General William ("Billy") Mitchell of the United States believed not only that air forces would dominate future land and sea operations, but that strategic air power might strike the vital centers of the enemy homeland and bring about the rapid collapse of the opposing society. More conservative military thinkers believed that air power would be important in future wars, but that it would be exercised in forms familiar from World War I.

In 1922, just after Benito Mussolini became Fascist dictator of Italy, Douhet became the Italian minister for air. His book *Command of the Air* (1921) had brought him to the attention of a government interested in overhauling Italian military power. Douhet was instrumental in organizing an independent Italian air force—the Regio Aeronautica—but his plans for making it an offensive striking force at the expense of the Italian army and navy aroused so much opposition that he finally resigned his post and returned to writing on air power. In the aftermath, the Italian air force developed into a mediocre air service of about 1,500 combat aircraft by 1939, one equipped to support the surface forces and to carry out high-level pattern bombing designed to close the central Mediterranean to enemy naval forces. It never met Douhet's requirement for an air force capable of long-range strikes against the urban centers of other European countries.

Billy Mitchell served as assistant chief of the Army Air Service for operations in France during World War I, during which time he came into contact with Hugh Trenchard and witnessed with approval the creation of the Royal Air Force in 1918. After the war, Mitchell returned to the United States with the conviction that his country should have an independent air force as well. In 1921, he rigged the celebrated "battleship bombing tests" of that year in such a way that they were more useful for propaganda for airpower than as tests to show how well dreadnoughts would stand up to aerial bombing under combat conditions. Still, the sinking of the old German battleship *Ostfriesland* greatly impressed the American public. Mitchell's intemperate criticisms of American military and naval leadership in 1925 led to his court-martial and five years' suspension from the service. He resigned his commission and spent his final years until his death in 1936 writing and speaking on airpower issues as he understood them.

Under less abrasive leaders than Mitchell, the Army Air Service made slow but steady progress during the interwar years. In 1926, the AAS was retitled the Army Air Corps, a step toward autonomy, and in 1933 its mission was expanded to include coast defense. In 1935, its combat components were placed under a single headquarters, and in the same year the new four-engine B-17 Flying Fortress was test-flown. Originally designed as a long-range coast defense bomber, the B-17 was easily adapted to the role of a strategic bomber. The B-17, and the later four-engine B-24 Liberator, were equipped with the Norden bomb sight, the best high-level optical aiming device to appear in World War II. Still, the AAC remained a relatively small organization down to the fall of France in June 1940. Then, at the urging of President Franklin D. Roosevelt, Congress untied the nation's purse strings and Army air planners made preparations for an Air Corps of 400,000 men and 7,800 airplanes by June 1942. Meanwhile, in June 1941, the AAC was subsumed under the Army Air Forces (AAF), General Henry H. Arnold to serve as both head of the AAF and as Assistant Army Chief of Staff for Air. By December 7, 1941, the AAF had a strength of 354,000 men and 2,864 aircraft. In the fewer than four years following the attack on Pearl Harbor, the AAF reached a strength of 2,400,000 men and 41,163 aircraft (13,930 of them four-engine bombers), the mightiest air force in the world.

Until 1933, Germany got around prohibitions in the Treaty of Versailles on air forces to a degree by exchanging technical knowledge on aircraft with Soviet Russia in return for the use of an airfield near Lipetsk, where 180 German pilots had graduated by 1933. In some cases, German officers took up sport plane and glider flying in order to acquire aviation experience. German aircraft companies learned much of military importance while building civilian aircraft of all kinds. And the pilots and ground crews of Lufthansa, the German national airline, had skills which could be applied to military aviation. Still, down to Hitler's accession to power, no real plans existed for a German air force. Hitler gave responsibility for building the Luftwaffe (the German air force) to Hermann Göring, second only to Hitler in the Nazi Party and a pursuit pilot in World War I.

Göring created the upper echelons of the Luftwaffe by transferring officers from the army and the navy to the new air force, and by commissioning civilian aviators. Officially, the Luftwaffe did not come into being until March 1935, at which time Göring, until then minister for aviation, took on the added title of commander-in-chief of the air force. Göring was an empire builder rather than a man of ideas, however, and it was General Walther Wever, the first chief of the Luftwaffe's general staff, who wanted an air force capable of launching independent air operations, as well as supporting the army and the navy. Wever commenced work on a four-engine, long-range bomber similar to the American B-17, but his death in an aerial accident in 1936 removed his influence from the highest circles of the air force. His successors as chief of the air force's general staff were more interested in Ernst Udet's proposals for dive bombers and other specialized aircraft for support of the army and the navy. Head of the technical office of the Luftwaffe, Udet was a former pursuit pilot turned post-war stunt flyer. Subsequently, work on the four-engine bomber was canceled, and the emphasis was shifted to the development of aircraft such as the famous Junkers 87 Stuka, the gull-winged, fixed-gear plane that almost symbolized the blitzkrieg for a generation. The excellent Messerschmidt Bf 109 fighter held the world's speed record before the war, but it had a combat radius of only 125 miles. The Dornier 17 and the Heinkel 111 were twin-engine bombers which, like the Ju-87 dive bomber, had a combat radius of about 500 miles. None of the German bombers were heavily armed or armored, but the doctrine of the Luftwaffe emphasized surprise attacks to destroy the enemy air forces on the ground, not extended air-to-air combat. Germany had about 3,000 combat aircraft by September 1939, the most powerful air force on the continent of Europe at the time, but one weak in reserves of pilots and aircraft.

Whatever the shortcomings of the Luftwaffe by September 1939, it was far superior in performance and capabilities to any other air force in Europe at the time except, perhaps, the British. The French Armée de l'Air had received its independence in 1933, but remained very much tied to the army's preoccupation with surface warfare and was less than half as numerous as the Luftwaffe as late as the campaign in the West in 1940. Most of its aircraft did not compare with their German counterparts. The Soviet air forces, organically part of the Red Army, numbered 10,000 aircraft, the most numerous in Europe by 1939, but, for the most part, they were of obsolete design when in June 1941, Germany attacked Russia. Newer Soviet aircraft were coming off the assembly lines, but in the early phases of the Russo-German War the Russians were distinctly inferior to the Germans in the air. The other European air forces, save the British, hardly counted as rivals to the Luftwaffe.

As early as 1936, the British Air Staff selected four-engine bomber designs for mass production whenever money became available, and these designs evolved into the Stirling, Halifax, and Lancaster bombers. These bombers could carry from six to nine tons of bombs as far as a thousand miles and return to base in England. Not many of the new bombers had been produced by the outbreak of war in September 1939, or, indeed, until 1941. In the meantime, the British relied upon two-engine bombers of mediocre qualities for strategic operations. But fear of attack on the British Isles by the Luftwaffe resulted, before the war, in priority being placed on the development of formidable fighter-interceptors such as the Hurricane and the Spitfire. Britain also made more progress than any other power in developing an early warning system based on radio detection and ranging (radar). Twenty radar stations monitored the European approaches to England by September 1939, and more were under construction. By the summer of 1940, British radar could detect and track aircraft as far away as seventy-five miles, and Fighter Control, using voice radio, could vector the aircraft of Air Marshal Hugh Dowding's Fighter Command to intercept enemy planes before they could reach their targets. In September 1939, Britain had 2,000 combat aircraft, of which 750 were fighters.

Save for a few special naval air squadrons, Japan's land-based aviation was organically part of the army, and, as such, it developed only short-ranged aircraft and no strategic bombers. The Japanese Zero fighter was superior to the American P-40 Tomahawk in 1941, and Japanese twin-engine bombers were about as good as their American counterparts, the B-25 and the B-26, but Japan could never compete with the United States in the production of numbers of aircraft and aircrew in a long war. Whereas the United States introduced a variety of new aircraft in large numbers after December 1941, Japan was hard pressed to mass-produce existing types. Accordingly, Japanese performance fell off as the war lengthened. In 1939, Japan had about 2,000 land-based, combat aircraft.

Experiments with airborne landings began soon after World War I in Italy, where General Allesandro Guidoni took a special interest in landing soldiers by parachute. By 1927, nine-man squads were training by jumping from Italian transports on a regular basis. But the promising Italian airborne program went into decline in 1928 when Guidoni was killed in a parachute accident, and it was not until 1938 that Air Marshal Italo Balbo reestablished a parachute-training school, this time in Italy's colony in Libya. Even so, Italy carried out no significant airborne operations in World War II. The Soviet Union founded a parachute-training school in 1930, and in army maneuvers in 1935 some 1,500 troops went into action from the air. In the maneuvers of 1936, 5,200 Soviet troops were parachuted into action. By 1939 the Red Army claimed to have five airborne brigades and 50,000 paratroopers.

Inspired by what they had seen at the Russian maneuvers in 1935, German military observers urged the Luftwaffe and the German army to develop airborne forces. In January 1936 Göring ordered the formation of a parachute battalion in the Luftwaffe, and about the same time the German army created its own airborne unit. A struggle ensued as to whether Germany's fledgling airborne forces should belong to the air force or to the army, but Göring was finally triumphant in July 1938, when all parachute and glider troops were concentrated in General Kurt Student's Seventh Air Division of the Luftwaffe. The Luftwaffe also created the Twenty-Second Air-Landing Division, a force to be ferried to its objective and then landed in aircraft. By September 1939, Germany claimed 12,000 troops had been trained for airborne assault by parachute or glider.

Neither the U.S. Army nor the British army took much interest in airborne forces between the world wars. The first simulated American airborne assault took place on maneuvers in 1932 and consisted of a single infantry company landed behind "enemy lines." Little more was done with the idea down to the outbreak of World War II. The British gave parachute training to a few soldiers before 1939, but nothing resembling airborne forces existed in the British army before the summer of 1940. Then, in the wake of the successful German airborne landings in Norway and the Low Countries, both the United States and Great Britain took an intense interest in developing airborne forces of their own. By the end of the war, three American and three British airborne divisions, composing an Allied airborne army under General Lewis Brereton, were serving in Europe. In practice, as many as three Allied airborne divisions were used in combat operations at one time. The largest German airborne operation of the war—that against Crete in May 1941—involved one division delivered by parachute and glider and another division landed in airplane transports. The Russians never carried out an airborne operation with more than one division at a time, and the Japanese never employed more than one brigade delivered by parachute at a time.

The performance of air forces of all kinds in World War II depended heavily on the technical means at hand. By 1939, airplanes had come a long way from the relatively primitive machines of World War I. The latest aircraft had fuselages of sheet metal, cantilever wings (struts and supporting wires located inside the "skin" of the wings), enclosed cockpits with more sophisticated instruments, oxygen masks for high altitudes, retractable landing-gear, voice radio, and instrument landing systems. The latest pursuit planes could fly in level flight at speeds up to 350 mph; bombers were fifty to a hundred miles an hour slower. There were numerous twin-engine and tri-engine aerial transport aircraft. The twin-engine C-47, the American "workhorse" transport of World War II, could haul about three tons of supplies or thirty troops over distances of up to five hundred miles. The German DFS-320 glider carried up to fifteen soldiers. Aerial navigation was by dead reckoning, corrected by ground observation and sometimes by radio direction-finding and celestial "fixes." Ground-attack aircraft were often provided with armor protection for the pilot and vital parts of the aircraft, and sometimes with self-sealing fuel tanks against leaks caused by small arms fire or shell fragments. By the eve of World War II, the last of the bi-planes were fast disappearing from military air fleets, and the monoplane ruled the skies in the Second World War.

V. Electronic Warfare

Electronic warfare played a major role in World War II and in a variety of forms. Radar, originally used for early warning and fighter-control, could also direct the fire of ships at sea in darkness and in all kinds of weather. Toward the end of the war, airborne radar aided the accuracy of the bombardier even when he could not see the target visually. Another radar application was in the proximity or variable time (V-T) fuse. By constantly measuring the distance between the shell and the aircraft being fired upon, the fuse determined the optimum moment for the shell's detonation. Since most shells brought down or damaged aircraft not by direct hits but from shell fragments, the V-T fuse proved greatly superior to either chemical or mechanical fuses for antiaircraft shells. In fact, the proximity fuse was found to multiply by five times the lethality of the antiaircraft artillery shell. The V-T fuse was given much of the credit for the high percentage of German V-I "buzz bombs" (pilotless cruise missiles) downed when Hitler's new weapons were launched against England in 1944, and the V-T fuse played an equally important role in helping American ships in the Pacific to fend off Japanese *Kamikaze* or suicide-plane attacks in 1944–45. Anglo-American fears that Germany and Japan might learn the secrets of the V-T fuse from a dud caused a prohibition on using V-T fused shells for surface-to-surface artillery until late in the war. Then V-T shells played a significant role in helping to repel the German Ardennes offensive in 1944, and in defeating Japanese forces on Luzon and Okinawa, where aerial bursts were especially effective.

An enormous increase in the use of the military radio took place between world wars. No other signal means had the radio's range, flexibility, and speed. But messages cast into the ether were easily intercepted by enemy radio monitoring and therefore depended upon encoding for their security. The most sophisticated encoding device between the world wars was the German Enigma machine, a kind of complex electric typewriter which substituted other letters for the originals but never the same letter twice. Yet when an encoded message was received, it could be swiftly deciphered by typing it back into another machine with its rotors set in a prearranged fashion. German confidence in Enigma was such that all high commands used variations of the machine well before the war, and Japan even acquired still other variations for both its armed forces and its diplomatic service.

Polish intelligence made the first progress in breaking Enigma's secrets even before 1939, but not enough to save Poland from defeat. With the aid of the Poles who escaped to France and England with Enigma counterpart *Wicher* machines, still more penetration was made before the fall of France in 1940. But it was not until the summer of 1940 that the British Operation Ultra finally penetrated the secrets of the Luftwaffe's Enigma. By 1944, the British could read messages from the Enigma machines of any of the German armed forces and Hitler's headquarters. The American counterpart to Ultra was Magic, which concentrated on Japanese radio traffic. By

December 1941, the Japanese diplomatic code known as Purple had been penetrated by the U.S. Army Signal Service, though nothing in the final messages between Tokyo and its embassy in Washington, D.C., indicated where the first blow would be struck in the Pacific war. The Office of U.S. Naval Intelligence broke a Japanese naval code sufficiently in April 1942, to allow U.S. commanders in the Pacific to anticipate the Japanese drives into the Coral Sea and against Midway, and to a degree those American victories resulted from intelligence coups.

But radio intelligence successes were not always on the Allied side, and sometimes radio intelligence was ignored. A major German success was penetration of the American Black Code even before the United States formally entered the war but after American aid began to flow to Britain. Messages to Washington from the American military attaché in Cairo often contained information of value to the Germans about British forces in the Western Desert. Then, after Ultra deciphered the order of battle for the German surprise invasion of Russia in 1941, Stalin ignored the offering because he thought it was some kind of British trick to foment war between Soviet Russia and Nazi Germany. In still another case, British agents captured in the Netherlands were used by the Germans to radio false and misleading information back to Britain. The list is long, and it suffices to say that the battle for information was continuous, sometimes favoring the one side, sometimes the other, and only toward the end of the war clearly favoring the Allied powers. Still, Ultra and Magic, taken together, were perhaps the most important intelligence operations of the war, and highly influential to its outcome.

VI. The Wars between the World Wars

None of the wars between 1919 and 1939 gave much indication of the direction that World War II would take. They were either civil wars in which the forces involved were not well equipped, or between states of such unequal military capacity that no firm conclusions could be drawn. None of them provided an illuminating test of the new German conception of mass and mobility for decisive battle in the Napoleonic tradition which would so revolutionize warfare in the first phases of World War II, and none of them settled the debates over the proper role of air power, motorized, and armored forces.

The Russian Civil War began in the summer of 1918 when former tsarist generals and admirals led rebellions against Lenin's government. In March 1918, Lenin moved his capital from Petrograd (Leningrad) to Moscow for reasons of security, and most of the civil war's campaigns occurred in the Baltic territories, in southern Russia, and in Siberia. Britain and France openly aided the so-called White forces, while the more ambivalent United States landed troops at Murmansk and sent troops to Vladivostok to check Japanese ambitions in the Far East. The Workers' and Peasants' Red Army (shortened to the Red Army) had only been founded in January 1918, and numbered just 100,000 men when it faced its first great challenge. Leon Trotsky, Lenin's commissar for war, has been called the "Red Carnot"—a reference to Lazare Carnot, the organizer of the armies of the French Revolution—and there are points of similarity in their methods. Trotsky put his considerable organizing talents into building an army of workers and peasants through propaganda and compulsion, and he used former tsarist officers for technical positions when they could not be filled adequately otherwise. He insured the army's loyalty through a political commissar system similar to that of the deputies-on-mission of the French Revolution. Trotsky also founded schools for junior officers, which, by the end of 1919, had insured that four-fifths of the Red Army's officers came from worker and peasant backgrounds. At its peak strength, in January 1920, the Red Army may have had 600,000 troops, but several million men served in it at one time or another during the civil war.

The crest of the fortunes of the White forces was reached in 1919 and thereafter began to subside. A new danger was posed in 1920 when the new state of Poland attacked Russia in the west and, aided by Ukrainian nationalists, seized Russian territory as far east as Kiev. When a Red Army offensive drove the Polish army almost back to the gates of Warsaw, French supplies and the advice of French general Maxime Weygand helped the Poles to repel its attacks and to drive it further east. The Peace of Riga in March 1921 finally left Poland with a large strip of territory that Soviet Russia considered to be properly its own. But by the end of the war with Poland, the last of the White armies in the Crimea had been defeated and the Soviet regime was secure. Possibly more Russians, Poles, Balts, and Ukrainians were victims of the Russia's civil war than died in World War I. In any case, the Red Army emerged from the ordeal with a tradition of endurance in the face of adversity.

When the Chinese monarchy collapsed in 1911, a period of prolonged strife began in China that was to last nearly forty years. In 1921, Sun Yat-sen founded the Kuomintang (National Democratic) Party and established a shaky central government, but much of China was really ruled by local generals called "war lords." The Nationalist government established ties with the Soviet government, and Soviet military advisers helped to establish Whampoa military academy in 1924. Upon Sun's death in 1925, General Chiang Kai-shek, superintendent of Whampoa and a close associate of Sun, assumed leadership of the Nationalist government. Sun had tolerated a wide array of different ideologies in the old Kuomintang, but under

Chiang the Nationalist government moved to the right and ruthlessly purged leftist elements of the old party. A Marxist faction under Mao Tse-tung and Chu Teh retired to the hill country between Hankow and Canton, where they organized a peasant guerrilla war against Chiang's regime. In 1927, Chiang's armies defeated the independent war lords of the Yangtze valley, and in 1928 they seized Peking (Beijing), the traditional Chinese capital. In the early 1930s, they defeated Mao's forces in southern China so severely that they were compelled to undertake the "Long March" northward in 1935 to find safety at Yenan in Shensi province.

Chiang's efforts to unite China under his leadership were complicated by Japanese intervention, first by their invasion of Manchuria in 1931, and then by an undeclared war on China in 1937. Chiang's armies were no match for the Japanese, which captured Peking, Shanghai, and much of the populated region of southern China. In December 1937, the Japanese captured Nanking, the Nationalist capital, and in 1938 Chiang moved his capital to Chungking in the remote province of Szechuan, bordering Tibet. The Japanese empire in China was populated by 170 million people, more than twice the number of Japanese living in the home islands. Still, Japan was unable to terminate the "China Incident," and Chiang's government received aid and encouragement in its resistance from Britain, the United States, France, and the Soviet Union. In northern China, Mao's Communist armies also continued to resist the Japanese, and, further complicating matters, in 1938 and 1939 the Japanese engaged the Soviet forces in serious border clashes in Manchuria. The largest of these battles, fought in 1939, was at Khalkhin-Gol. It ranged a Japanese army of 75,000 troops, 180 tanks, 500 guns and 450 aircraft against a Russian army of 100,000 troops, 498 tanks, 750 guns and 580 aircraft. The battle ended in a victory for General Georgi Zhukov, the Russian commander, and in its aftermath Japan's militarists lost interest in expanding Japanese territory at Russian expense.

The Italian invasion of Ethiopia in 1935 miscarried at first, but in March 1936, a new Italian offensive with tanks, poison gas, and airplanes routed the primitive army of Haile Selassie, and the capital of Addis Ababa was occupied in May. But by far the most serious war involving European powers in the 1930s was the Spanish Civil War. It commenced in July 1936, when elements of the regular army led by General Francisco Franco and other Spanish generals rose against the left-leaning Spanish republic founded in 1931. Franco's forces, called the Nationalists, quickly seized the most important provinces of Spain in the north save Catalonia, but they failed to take either the capital at Madrid or most of southern Spain. The Loyalist supporters of the republic included a minority of the regular forces and the militia. When both sides discovered that they lacked the means to win the war without outside help, the Nationalists appealed to

Fascist Italy and Nazi Germany, while the Loyalists appealed to the Soviet Union and to the democracies of Britain, France, and the United States.

The three democracies ended up taking official positions of neutrality and nonintervention, though thousands of their citizens—Communists, socialists, and liberals—volunteered to serve the Loyalist cause in "international brigades." Soviet Russia sent minor contingents of armor and aircraft, as well as military advisors, to the Loyalist side, but not on a scale that compared with the aid rendered the Nationalists by Fascist Italy and Nazi Germany. Mussolini's government was the most responsive to Franco's pleas, finally sending 50,000 troops, 750 planes, and many tanks and other war material. Hitler dispatched 16,000 troops and military technicians, a Condor Legion of 200 aircraft, and a few battalions of tanks. While the Germans gained some practical experience in the war in Spain and tested out some of their new weapons there, the conditions were not conducive to any real test of the blitzkrieg doctrine.

Even with foreign aid, the Spanish Civil War became a long-drawn-out struggle of attrition. The mountainous nature of much of the country favored defense; despite repeated Nationalist attacks, Madrid did not fall to Franco's forces until March 28, 1939. Among the more modern aspects of the war were the Condor Legion's indiscriminate bombing of the Basque town of Guernica on April 26, 1937 (an attack that may have killed 5,000 people, and that inspired Pablo Picasso to produce one of his most famous paintings), and the airplane-tank spearheads in the Nationalist drive down the Ebro valley in 1938. At peak strength, the Nationalist army numbered perhaps 700,000 men, the Loyalist army about 600,000. The Loyalists were increasingly short of arms and equipment toward the end of the war, while the Nationalists steadily improved their position in this regard. By the spring of 1939, as many as 600,000 people had died from the war's effects, half of them on the battlefield and at least 100,000 as victims of atrocities. The balance perished from famine and disease.

6

The Second World War, 1939–45

I. Hitler's War, 1939–41

A. *The German Armed Forces to the Eve of War.*   From the time Adolf Hitler took power in 1933, he was determined to carry out a German expansion over central and eastern Europe (including western Russia) that would establish the dominion of the *Herrenvolk* ("master race"), as Hitler conceived people of Germanic origin to be. The Greater Reich of which he dreamed would be independent of overseas resources and based on the enslavement of the Slavic peoples, the union of all ethnic Germans, and the annihilation of "inferior races," especially the Jews. With the resources and *Lebensraum* ("living space") afforded by a centralized eastern European empire, Hitler believed that his Greater Reich could last a thousand years. He recognized, of course, that the realization of his dream of continental expansion would require the ruthless use of force and an especially powerful army designed for offensive operations.

Hitler's dream also required armed forces responsible to his will. Because they were opposed to Hitler's policies, Field Marshal Werner von Blomberg, the Minister of War, and General Werner von Fritsch, Commander-in-Chief of the Army, were dismissed in 1938. At that time, Hitler replaced the Ministry of War with the Oberkommando der Wehrmacht (OKW or High Command of the Armed Forces), with himself as Oberbefehlshaber (Commander-in-Chief), and made the high commands of the Army (OKH), the Navy (OKM), and the Air Force (OKL) subordinate to the OKW. General Wilhelm Keitel was appointed as Hitler's deputy in the OKW. Hitler appointed General Walther von Brauchitsch as the new Commander-in-Chief of the Army, a talented soldier but one unlikely to stand up to Hitler in a difference of opinion. In August 1938, General Franz Halder succeeded General Ludwig Beck, another opponent of Hitler, as Chief of the OKH General Staff. At least covertly, Halder was more willing than Brauchitsch to oppose Hitler, and he involved himself in the so-called Green Plot to remove the Führer from power during the height of the Sudetenland Crisis in 1938. But both Halder's opposition and the plot were quickly abandoned after Hitler's triumph at the Munich Conference. Willingly or unwillingly, most German soldiers went along with Hitler's leadership until nearly the end of the war.

Between 1933 and March 1935, the German army expanded by taking volunteers, and by the latter date it had reached a strength of 500,000 men and twenty-one divisions. Then, beginning with Hitler's proclamation of compulsory military service in March 1935, the German army returned to its traditional form as a *Nation-in-Arms*. With all able-bodied males of military age being made liable to service in both the active army and its reserve, the army's further expansion was very rapid. On the eve of war in September 1939, the army had reached a mobilizable strength of 2 million men, and could deploy 58 active divisions and 51 reserve divisions. But the speed of German military expansion under Hitler had been achieved at a price. All of the army's reserve divisions were traditional infantry with little or no motorization, and only the men in eighteen of those divisions had passed through the required two years' active training in the army. The men in the rest of the reserve divisions had been trained on weekends and in summer camps, and, until shortly before the war, were classified as Landwehr (militia). Of the 58 divisions in the active army, all were well trained but only 16 were fully motorized (6 panzer, 4 light divisions, and 6 motorized infantry divisions), the rest being traditional infantry divisions. Thus, the panzer and other all-motorized divisions composed a relatively small *corps d'élite* of an army that otherwise relied for transportation on the railroad, what motorization was left over from the all-motorized divisions, horse-drawn vehicles, and its legs.

Since so much of the German army of 1939 was composed of unmotorized or semimotorized divisions, its successful invasion of enemy territory, like that of the German army of 1914, was contingent on capturing enemy rail facilities and resources as it advanced, and defeating the enemy decisively not far from its bases of supply. What differentiated the army of 1939 from that of 1914 was that the later model had a powerful armored-motorized spearhead with a range of about 250 miles, and a strong supporting tactical air force. With those advantages, the army of 1939 proved capable of reviving the dormant *Kesselschlacht* doctrine of the nineteenth century, and, in the guise of the *Blitzkrieg* ("Lightning War"), and within certain limits, it applied it successfully in the early stages of the Second World War.

Heinrich Himmler's Schutz Staffel (SS), the "Defense Corps" of the Nazi Party, was not oriented to a combat role in September 1939, and in the Polish campaign of that month furnished a single motorized regiment. The Waffen SS (Combat SS) was not founded until 1940, and, during the May–June campaign of that year against France and the Low Countries, it provided the army with only three all-motorized infantry divisions. The Waffen SS continued to expand, however, and in 1944 it reached a strength of 500,000 troops. Throughout its career it furnished 38 divisions for ground operations, some of the divisions armored. Though the Waffen SS gave Hitler well-equipped and fanatically loyal troops, they made up only a relatively small part of the German forces upon which Hitler relied in his effort to dominate Europe. By way of comparison, the German army at its peak strength in World War II had 7 million troops and over 300 divisions. The value of the Waffen SS to Hitler's aims notwithstanding, final German victory hinged primarily on the performance of the German army and its supporting air force.

B. *The War from Poland to the Channel, September 1939–June 1940.* The bloodless German conquests of Austria and Czechoslovakia in 1938–39 gave the OKH (Army High Command) an opportunity to detect weaknesses and to correct deficiencies in the German army. By September 1939 the OKH had confidence in its active divisions and in the best of its reserve divisions, but it had doubts about the readiness of the rest. When it became clear in the summer of 1939 that a two-front war with the Anglo-French powers and Poland was on the horizon, Brauchitsch and Halder decided to deal with this problem by adopting a plan of mobilization that took an unusual form. The *Wellen* ("waves") system called for two separate but simultaneous mobilizations, a faster one for the active divisions and the best of the reserve divisions, and a slower one for the rest, and with a different mission for each "wave." The divisions intended for the attack on Poland would be ready for action and concentrated on the Polish frontiers at the end of four days. The rest of the reserve divisions would be mobilized by the end of fourteen days, and, stiffened by twelve active infantry divisions, mostly deployed in the defenses of the Siegfried Line facing the French frontier. If both the Polish and Anglo-French mobilizations took the usual two weeks to complete, the OKH hoped that Poland could be attacked and struck down before it was fully ready to defend itself and before the Anglo-French armies were ready to attack Germany's western frontiers. Once Poland was conquered, it was possible that London and Paris would accept the *fait accompli* and make peace with Germany. The only remaining danger would be intervention on behalf of Poland by Soviet Russia.

The danger of Soviet intervention to defend Poland was removed by the signing of the Nazi-Soviet Pact on August 23, 1939, a measure by which Hitler not only removed a potential enemy, but gained a temporary ally.

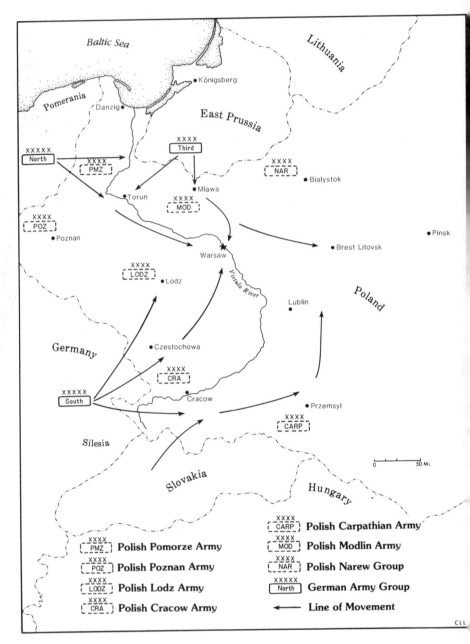

The German Attack on Poland, September 1939

When Hitler ordered general mobilization on August 26, the OKH put the *Wellen* system into effect, and the subsequent mobilizations of the best divisions in the army, both active and reserve, went forward smoothly and swiftly. By the night of August 31, a total of 1,512,000 German troops and 62 divisions had concentrated on the Polish frontiers. In contrast, Poland, which did not begin mobilization until August 29, had only about two-thirds of its 600,000 active and reserve troops and thirty-five divisions in position. The Anglo-French mobilizations did not get underway until after the German attack on Poland had commenced, and, as the OKH had anticipated, they were not completed until the campaign in Poland was nearly over.

The first blitzkrieg of World War II got underway about dawn on September 1, 1939. A German air assault on Polish airfields, heralding the ground attack, was only partially carried out because fog kept part of the Luftwaffe grounded in the early hours of the campaign, but within three days some 2,000 German warplanes had destroyed most of the Polish air force of a thousand aircraft. Only 240 Polish planes were modern by German standards, hence most were vulnerable both in the air and on the ground. Meanwhile, German armored-motorized forces broke through the weak Polish frontier defenses at many points, spearheading the drives of Army Group North (Fedor von Bock) consisting of two armies and 23 divisions, and that of Army Group South (Gerd von Rundstedt) composed of three armies and 39 divisions. By September 9, when German motorized forces reached the defenses of Warsaw, *Kesselschlachten* (battles of encirclement and annihilation) were fast eliminating the trapped enemy forces in western Poland. The large Polish garrison at Warsaw put up such stubborn resistance that the Germans were obliged to lay siege to the city, battering it with siege guns and air attacks. On September 17, the day before the last organized Polish resistance collapsed everywhere in western Poland save at Warsaw, the Red Army attacked eastern Poland and drove forward to link up with the Germans. Finally, the Polish garrison at Warsaw—some 120,000 troops—laid down its arms and surrendered to the Germans on September 27. Except for some minor mopping-up operations against isolated pockets of resistance, the campaign was at an end. The speed with which a nation of 30 million people had been brought to its knees led newsmen to dub the German method "lightning war," although it was really an updated version of the *Kesselschlacht* doctrine dating back to the nineteenth century. As for German casualties, Hitler admitted to only 10,000 killed and 40,000 wounded.

Britain and France declared war on Germany on September 3 in fulfillment of their pledges to Poland, but their mobilizations were completed much too late to affect the outcome of the Polish campaign. As the Allies deferred any future offensive operations, Hitler had ample time to shift most of his best troops to the western frontiers of the Reich. Meanwhile, Hitler and Joseph Stalin divided up their Polish booty between them. The part of Poland occupied by the Germans, which included Warsaw, had a population of 22 million, including 3 million Jews. Accordingly, the Nazi policies of ethnic persecution and genocide were carried out in this zone with particular savagery. When Hitler ordered the implementation of the "Final Solution" in 1941, Himmler chose Poland as the site for some of the most notorious of the German "death camps," including Auschwitz and Treblinka. Polish Jews constituted half the 6 million Jews who died at Nazi hands, easily the largest national group. The fate of the 8 million Poles in the Soviet zone was slightly better, but Stalin caused some 10,000 captured Polish commissioned and noncommissioned officers to be executed in the Katyn forest near Smolensk. Their graves were discovered by the Germans when they invaded Russia in 1941.

While the war lulled in the West during the fall and winter of 1939–40, Stalin ordered the Red Army to occupy the Baltic states of Latvia, Estonia, and Lithuania. In November 1939 the Red Army attacked Finland in order to revise the Finnish-Soviet frontier, one that on the Karelian isthmus between the Baltic Sea and Lake Ladoga came within a few miles of Leningrad. The Finnish army put up a surprisingly effective defense, aided by the Mannerheim Line on the Karelian isthmus, and Finnish units operating in the winter snow outmaneuvered Russian invasions north of Lake Ladoga. The Russians did not crack Finnish resistance until Stalin had committed 500,000 troops, 1,000 tanks, and 800 aircraft against a Finnish army that never exceeded 175,000 men and nine divisions. The "Winter War" ended on Stalin's terms in March 1940, but the Red Army emerged from the episode with a diminished reputation, something not lost on Hitler. Still, Hitler, preoccupied by operations in the West, raised no protest when Stalin extorted the province of Bessarabia from Rumania in June 1940, thereby placing the Red Army uncomfortably close to the oil fields around Ploesti, Germany's chief oil supply in Europe. One reason for Hitler's tolerance was that Stalin continued to fulfill his pledges to deliver Russian grain and oil to the Third Reich, thereby helping to undermine the effects of the British naval blockade.

Though before the outbreak of the war the Pact of Steel had forged a formal military alliance between Nazi Germany and Fascist Italy, Mussolini declared Italy's neutrality at the outset of hostilities in September 1939. He told Hitler that Italy was not sufficiently supplied with raw materials to risk war with Britain and France. Even without assistance from Italy, Hitler was eager to launch an offensive in the West before the end of 1939, but bad weather and the pessimism of his generals finally persuaded him to postpone an attack until the spring of 1940 when the German forces would be expanded and strengthened. As for the Allies, they were glad to

gain time in which to increase and strengthen their forces before a decisive struggle with Germany. It was taken as a positive sign in March 1940,
when Paul Reynaud replaced Édouard Daladier as French premier; before
the war, Reynaud had been one of the few French politicians to take
seriously Charles de Gaulle's warnings about the importance of motorized
and armored forces. In any case, a long lull had settled over the Western Front, and bored newsmen dubbed the situation the Sitzkrieg or Phoney War.

At the outbreak of war, the British Home Fleet took up its war station at
Scapa Flow and once again the North Sea became a declared war zone.
Thanks to the raw materials that Nazi Germany could draw from eastern
Europe and Russia, the British economic blockade was not as effective as
it had been against the Germany of World War I. But Hitler worried about
the security of iron-ore shipments from neutral Sweden, shipments vital to
German steel production. In warm weather the shipments came by the
safe route across the Baltic Sea, but in winter much of the Baltic route was
blocked by ice and shipments of iron ore for Germany had to go by rail to
Narvik in Norway, then by sea through the neutral coastal waters of Norway and Denmark. Hitler feared that eventually the British navy would
ignore Norwegian and Danish neutrality in order to stop the iron-ore
traffic, and thus deal a heavy blow to German war production. In addition,
Admiral Raeder pressed him to acquire naval bases beyond the North Sea
for surface raiders, and the Norwegian fjords seemed ideal for such a
purpose. The possibilities for surface raiding had been demonstrated by
the damage inflicted on British merchant shipping by *Admiral Graf Spee*
before the pocket battleship had been trapped at Montevideo on the
South American coast and scuttled in December. Hitler's thoughts about
Denmark and Norway came to a conclusion in February 1940, when British destroyers violated Norway's waters in order to intercept the German
supply ship *Altmark*. The British move was not made to stop iron-ore
shipments, but to liberate British prisoners on *Altmark* earlier transferred
from *Admiral Graf Spee*. The *Altmark* affair highlighted the danger to Germany's iron-ore supply from Sweden, and Hitler resolved to carry out
invasions of both Denmark and Norway before launching his offensive in
the West.

The "Phoney War" ended suddenly on April 9, 1940, when the
Germans launched Operation Exercise Weser, the invasion of Denmark
and Norway. The sudden thrust of a German motorized brigade into Jutland resulted in the occupation of the Danish peninsula within five hours,
a strange contrast to the extended Danish resistance there to the Austro-
Prussian armies in 1864. The German airborne capture of the bridges
leading from Jutland to the Danish islands made resistance on them hopeless as well, and Copenhagen announced a general Danish surrender on

the first day of the campaign. Simultaneous to the German occupation of Denmark, German destroyers landed troops along the Norwegian coasts as far north as Narvik, and German airborne troops descended on Norwegian airfields inland. In these operations, the Germans were aided by intelligence of Norwegian defenses provided by Major Vidkun Quisling, whose name became a byword for traitor in Allied countries during World War II. Except in the far north of Norway, where the remains of the small Norwegian army held out in hopes of Anglo-French aid, resistance to the Germans collapsed quickly.

After the British recovered from their surprise at Hitler's audacity, the Home Fleet struck back with vigor. A British expeditionary force of 60,000 troops landed in Norway after the recapture of Narvik on April 17. But the Germans held command of the straits between Jutland and Norway, and were able to funnel six infantry divisions into southern Norway. They also flew in Luftwaffe squadrons to operate from captured Norwegian fields. The Home Fleet soon learned of the dangers of operating in coastal waters within range of enemy land-based aviation when some of its ships were heavily attacked. But the German navy also took heavy losses at British hands. Still, in early June the British were compelled to withdraw their expeditionary force from Norway, and by the end of the campaign the Royal Navy had lost an aircraft carrier, two cruisers, nine destroyers, and six submarines. The German navy lost three out of eight cruisers (the *Königsberg* having the distinction of being the first large warship ever sunk in combat by carrier-based airplanes), twelve out of twenty destroyers, and four submarines. In addition, *Scharnhorst*, *Gneisenau*, and *Lützow* (the renamed pocket battleship *Deutschland*) had been damaged. Temporarily, the German navy was reduced to one operational warship larger than a cruiser. But Hitler had achieved his goal of securing Germany's access to the iron ore of Sweden, and Raeder's surface warships had their bases beyond the North Sea. Even before the campaign in Norway was over, Chamberlain's government had resigned in favor of a new cabinet headed by Winston Churchill. As it happened, Churchill took up his duties as prime minister on May 10, the day that Hitler launched his offensive in the West.

By May 10, 1940, the Germans had massed 136 army divisions in the West, including 10 panzer divisions and 6 motorized infantry divisions, 2,600 tanks, and 3,700 aircraft. The ground forces were divided among three army groups and an OKH reserve. From north to south, the army groups consisted of Army Group B (Bock), composed of two armies and 29 army divisions (including 3 panzer divisions and 2 motorized infantry divisions), and supported by the Luftwaffe's airborne division and its air-landing division; Army Group A (Rundstedt), composed of five armies and 45 divisions (including 7 panzer divisions and 3 motorized infantry divi-

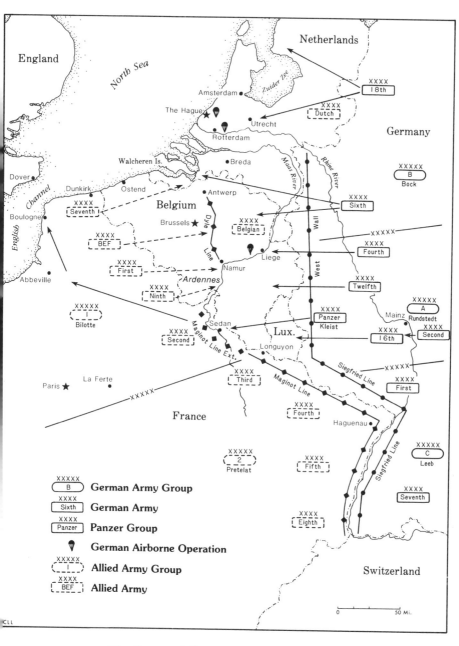

England

North Sea

Netherlands

XXXX
18th

Germany

Amsterdam
Zuider Zee

The Hague
Utrecht

XXXX
Dutch

Rotterdam

Breda

Maas River

Rhine River

XXXXX
B
Bock

Walcheren Is.

Dover

Dunkirk
Ostend

Antwerp

Belgium

XXXX
Sixth

English Channel

Boulogne

XXXX
Seventh

Brussels

Dyle Line

XXXX
Belgian

XXXXX

XXXX
Fourth

West Wall

XXXX
BEF

Liege

Abbeville

XXXX
First

Namur

Ardennes

XXXX
Twelfth

XXXX
Ninth

XXXXX
I
Bilotte

Sedan

XXXX
Panzer
Kleist

XXXXX
A
Rundstedt

Mainz

XXXX
Second

Lux.

XXXX
16th

XXXX
Second

XXXX
Maginot Line Ext.

Longuyon

Siegfried Line

XXXXX

La Ferte

Paris

XXXX
Third

Maginot Line

XXXXX

XXXX
First

XXXX
Fourth

Haguenau

France

XXXXX
2
Pretelat

XXXX
Fifth

Siegfried Line

XXXXX
C
Leeb

XXXX
Seventh

XXXX
Eighth

XXXXX
B German Army Group

XXXX
Sixth German Army

XXXX
Panzer Panzer Group

German Airborne Operation

XXXXX
I Allied Army Group

XXXX
BEF Allied Army

Switzerland

0   50 Mi.

CLL

The German Offensive in the West, May 1940

sions); and Army Group C (Wilhelm von Leeb), composed of two armies and 20 infantry divisions, serving in the Siegfried Line. Rundstedt's armored and motorized divisions were divided between a panzer group under General Ewald von Kleist (Panzer Group Kleist) and a separate panzer corps. Heinz Guderian, the pioneer of the panzer division organization, was by 1940 a general and commanded one of the panzer corps in Panzer Group Kleist. The balance of the German divisions in the West were kept in the large OKH reserve.

Opposed to the Germans on May 10, 1940, were 108 French army divisions in northern France, including 3 DLMs or light mechanized divisions, 10 motorized infantry divisions, and 3 *Divisions Chirasée* (DCs), the French version of armored divisions, and organized after the Germans had demonstrated the advantages of armored concentrations in the Polish campaign. A fourth DC was still forming under General Charles de Gaulle on May 10. But Maurice Gamelin, the French general-in-chief, had an imperfect understanding of the DC's proper role, and they were also inferior to the German panzer divisions in organization, equipment, and doctrine. In addition, only 800 of France's 3,000 tanks were in units larger than battalions. The British Expeditionary Force (BEF), commanded by General John, Lord Gort, was composed of 10 motorized infantry divisions but possessed only a single tank brigade. A British armored division was forming in England, but it had to be committed in piecemeal fashion after the battle had begun, and did not affect the outcome. The German advantage on the ground extended to the air where the 3,700 German aircraft not only vastly outnumbered the 1,400 French and 400 British planes based in France, but, for the most part, they were technically superior as well. Most of the British Hurricane and Spitfire fighters, the only types in the same class as the German Messerschmidt Bf 109, were behind radar protection in England. The German offensive included the Netherlands and Belgium, but the Dutch could mobilize only 5 divisions, the Belgians 10 divisions, and both the Dutch and Belgian armored forces and air forces were inconsequential.

The German offensive was led off by massive German air attacks on airfields in Holland, Belgium, and eastern France. Most of the Allied planes caught on the ground were destroyed within a day. German airborne troops seized strategic places on the Dutch and Belgian frontiers, including the fortress of Eben Emael at the Liège Gap, ahead of Army Group B's advancing ground forces. The overwhelmed Dutch army surrendered after only five days of resistance. The Belgian army made a hasty retreat to the Dyle River where it awaited help from the Anglo-French armies. On the first day of the offensive, Gamelin ordered Allied Army Group One—consisting of three French armies and the BEF, and nearly all the Allied motorized forces—to implement Plan D (an advance to the

General Heinz Guderian
SOURCE: Matthew Cooper, *The German Army, 1933–1945:
Its Political and Military Failure* (New York: Stein and Day, 1978).

Dyle) in the belief that the Germans were executing a broader version of the Schlieffen Plan attempted in 1914. But the Allied wheel into Belgium left a weak pivot at the Ardennes, opposite to which lay Rundstedt's powerful Army Group A.

Spearheaded by Panzer Group Kleist and a separate panzer corps, Army Group A began its advance through the Ardennes on the first day of the offensive. This advance was, in fact, the master-stroke of the German operation called Case Yellow. Case Yellow used Bock's forces invading Holland and northern Belgium to lure the Allied left wing into making a hasty advance, the BEF and two French armies advancing to the west of the Meuse and one French army entering the northern Ardennes. The form of the Allied advance left a weak link between the French Ninth Army in the northern Ardennes and the static French Second Army manning the Maginot Line Extension, actually a line of weak fixed defenses just west of the Meuse facing the southern Ardennes. The German plan, approved personally by Hitler, had only been adopted after long debate and Guderian's assurance that German armored-motorized forces could cross the southern Ardennes swiftly and quickly penetrate the French defenses along the Meuse. The plan aimed at positioning Rundstedt's forces so that they could drive westward across the communications of Allied Army Group One as it engaged in a frontal battle with Bock's forces in Belgium and thus achieve a *Kesselschlacht*.

In the event, German armored-motorized forces crossed the Ardennes so swiftly that Guderian's corps reached the Meuse at Sedan about noon on May 12. The Maginot Line Extension at that point was manned by inferior French reserve divisions without adequate air defenses, and their line was penetrated on May 13. With pontoon bridges across the Meuse, Rundstedt's forces began to drive west on May 14, Panzer Group Kleist in the lead. The armored-motorized spearhead encountered hardly any opposition as it rolled westward, except for a weak Allied counterattack at Arras, and it reached Abbeville near the sea on May 20. Behind the spearhead, a corridor was being formed by German infantry divisions marching west, utilizing the captured French rail system to aid in their supply, and blocking any retreat by Allied Army Group One or any attempt of Allied troops below the developing encirclement to come to its aid. After capturing Abbeville, the German armored spearheads moved north, capturing one port after another, until it became clear that it was only a matter of time before Army Group One and the Belgian army beside it would be completely encircled and destroyed. Fortunately for the Allies, a German delay in seizing Dunkirk allowed Gort, the BEF commander, to insure it was occupied in force by British troops, and subsequently Operation Dynamo, an evacuation by sea, got underway utilizing almost every sort of craft in the Royal Navy and the civilian fleet. Operation Dynamo finally

German PzKw. III, one of the best tank designs of
World War II.

SOURCE: Kenneth Macksey and John H. Batchelor, *Tank: A History
of the Armoured Fighting Vehicle* (New York: Charles Scribner's Sons,
1970).

saved 338,000 Allied troops, about a third of them French (the Belgian
army surrendered to the Germans), but nearly all their arms and equipment were abandoned. By the close of the "Flanders *Kesselschlacht*," as the
Germans called it, they claimed that they had killed or captured 500,000
troops and destroyed the equivalent of about forty divisions.

As the Allied disaster in Belgium was unfolding, Maxime Weygand
relieved Gamelin as French general-in-chief on May 18. While the
Germans were preoccupied with carrying out the final phases of the battle
of encirclement and annihilation in Flanders, Weygand used the time to
redeploy 40 of his remaining divisions across northern France in order to
contain the German drive south soon to come. But this Weygand Line was
almost denuded of supporting air power and armor, and its divisions were
no match for the combined forces of Rundstedt's and Bock's army groups.
When the Germans started southward on June 5, the Weygand Line crum-
bled within a week. On June 10, Mussolini, sensing the certainty of
France's fall, abandoned his neutrality and declared war on both France
and Britain. Still, 10 French divisions on the Italian frontier beat back all
the attacks of the Italian army until the armistice. Meanwhile, Reynaud's
government had fled to Tours and Paris was declared an "open city" in
order to prevent its destruction. On June 14, and for the second time in
seventy years, Paris felt the tread of German boots. As the Germans pene-

trated deeper into France, Reynaud's government fled to Bordeaux, where on June 16 it resigned to make way for a new government under old Marshal Pétain. Pétain immediately asked for armistice negotiations, and his emissaries were received at Compiègne in the same railroad car in which Foch had humbled the German representatives in November 1918. An agreement was reached and on June 22 a general armistice went into effect between French and German forces. Fighting between the French and Italians ceased two days later. In just six weeks, the German army and air force had defeated one of Europe's mightiest armies and extended Hitler's control over most of Western Europe. His empire then extended from central Poland to the Channel, and well into Scandinavia.

C. From the Armistice of Compiègne to the Battle of Moscow, June 1940–December 1941. The Armistice of Compiègne in June 1940 divided France into a German-occupied zone in northern France that included Paris and a strip of territory along the Bay of Biscay to the neutral Spanish frontier, and an unoccupied zone in southeastern France, under Pétain's government, with a capital at Vichy. Hitler had allowed a measure of French sovereignty to survive lest the French fleet and overseas territories rally to Britain and remain in the war. Churchill's fear that Hitler would somehow get control of the French fleet—interned in North African ports—caused him in July 1940, to order naval attacks on major French naval units at Mers-El-Kebir (near Oran) as a preventive measure. The French vessels that survived that attack fled to Toulon. French soldiers who got away to Britain before the armistice of 1940 rallied around Charles de Gaulle in the Free French Movement, but most of France's forces overseas recognized the Pétain government and obeyed its orders. Vichy France maintained a precarious official neutrality in the war until November 1942, when Anglo-American forces invaded Morocco and Algeria. Then Hitler ordered all of France occupied and Pétain's government interned. Hitler's attempt to seize the French fleet at Toulon was foiled when its crews scuttled their vessels. Pétain's attempt at collaboration with Nazi Germany from 1940 to 1942 would earn him French imprisonment after the war until his death in 1951.

After the armistice with France in 1940, Hitler hoped that Churchill's government in Britain would also come to terms with him. He told his generals that all he demanded was a free hand on the continent, and, in fact, he was so eager to get on with German eastward expansion that on July 21 he gave his first instructions to the OKW for preparations for an invasion of Russia in 1941. But when Churchill made clear Britain's intent to continue the war against the Axis powers, Hitler ordered preparations for Operation Sea Lion, an invasion of England, in the summer of 1940. When German studies showed that such an invasion would be impossible unless the Luftwaffe could guarantee no interference from the British fleet and the Royal Air Force, the plan for an invasion began to hinge on the Luftwaffe's ability to eliminate the RAF. As head of the Luftwaffe, Hermann Göring pledged that the RAF Fighter Command, the main hindrance, would be crushed within two weeks of the beginning of unlimited air operations over the British Isles. Operation *Adler Angriff* (Eagle Attack), the German air offensive, would employ 3,000 aircraft, a third of them fighters.

Except for aerial skirmishes over the English Channel and adjacent ports commencing on July 10, the so-called Battle of Britain took place as a series of air combats over Britain from August 12 to September 27, 1940. Initially, the Germans were opposed by a thousand Spitfire and Hurricane fighters, some older and semi-obsolescent fighter aircraft, and a pool of 1,500 RAF fighter pilots. But RAF Fighter Command, aided by Fighter Control, radar, and Ultra (the code-breaking operation against Enigma), proved almost impossible to surprise on the ground, and, in the air, the best of the British fighters quickly exploited the weaknesses of the German bombers. The Messerschmidt Bf 109, the only German fighter in the same class as the Hurricane and Spitfire, lacked sufficient range to escort German bombers to all targets in England, and unescorted bombers proved too weak in armor protection and defensive guns to withstand the fierce British air attacks. Over the six weeks of the Battle of Britain, the Luftwaffe lost 1,400 aircraft (including 668 fighters) and about 2,000 aircrew, to a RAF loss of about 700 fighters and 618 pilots. British factories turned out new fighters about as quickly as they were lost, hence the real strain on Fighter Command was in pilot replacements. But the Germans could not make up either aircraft or aircrew losses, and, after September 27, Göring terminated Operation Eagle Attack. Hitler ordered Operation Sea Lion postponed until 1941, but he eventually discarded the plan to invade England altogether.

In the fall of 1940, Göring turned to a protracted program of night bombing of British cities, the so-called Blitz—a strategy that was less costly in planes and crews than the daylight air offensive, though bombing accuracy was poor. By indiscriminate attacks on Britain's cities, especially London, Göring hoped to weaken morale and damage the economy. The raids continued until the spring of 1941, when most German air units were transferred to meet more pressing needs in other theaters of war. During the Blitz, a raid sometimes involved up to 200 bombers and delivered 600 tons of high explosive bombs and incendiaries. The single most destructive of these raids occurred on the night of November 14, 1940, when 450 German bombers dropped 500 tons of bombs and incendiaries on the city of Coventry. Hundreds of Britons perished in the bomb blasts and flames, and the center of the city was destroyed. But the favorite German target was London, with an area so huge that it was easy to find. About half of the 50,000 Britons killed and 60,000 wounded during the Blitz lived in the greater London area. When the Germans sought to improve the accuracy of night bombing by the use of radio navigation beams, the British tried, with some success, to hinder their efforts by employing electronic countermeasures (ECM). Antiaircraft artillery and eventually night fighters were pressed into service, and, in 1941, some of the British night interceptors were equipped with an early version of airborne radar to aid them in locating German aircraft. Though the night bombing was an ordeal, the British people endured and the British economy never faltered for that reason. Moreover, the RAF Bomber Command hit back at targets in Germany during the Blitz, giving Hitler a taste of the much greater Allied strategic bombing effort against Germany to come in later years.

Less spectacular than the Blitz, but more menacing to Britain's survival over the long run, was the German *guerre de course* at sea. Between October 1940 and May 1941, Admiral Raeder sent a battleship, two battle cruisers (as the British designated *Scharnhorst* and *Gneisenau*), and two "pocket battleships," as well as a heavy cruiser and six converted merchantship-raiders, into the North Atlantic by way of the Arctic Ocean and the Denmark Strait between Greenland and Iceland. All of these ships operated from the new German bases in Norway, and forced the British to detach battleships and battle cruisers to escort their most important convoys. But the day of the German surface raider in the Atlantic was relatively brief. Ships which put back into French ports, such as Cherbourg and Le Havre, ran the risk of being damaged by British air attacks while in port, and the British gradually became more efficient in tracking down the raiders at sea. Though the new battleship *Bismarck* sank the battle cruiser *Hood* just south of the Denmark Strait in May 1941, within days *Bismarck* too was destroyed 700 miles from the safety of the port of Brest by shells and torpedoes of British battleships and carrier-borne aircraft. The loss of the great ship on its maiden voyage led Hitler to forbid the sending of any more large warships into the Atlantic. Raeder confined the sorties of his remaining large ships to the waters off Norway, especially against the convoys bound for the Russian Arctic ports after June 1941.

Admiral Dönitz's U-boat command proved to be more of a long-term threat than surface raiders in the Atlantic. Between September 1939 and June 1941, the Germans built 96 new submarines, while losing 41. Over the same period, U-boats sank 4 million tons of shipping, and German surface raiders one million tons, or about a fourth of the Britain's pre-war total. As the British were able to build or acquire only 2.2 million tons of new merchant ships in this period, they were left with a net loss of 1.8 million tons, or a figure not quite equal to a seventh of the tonnage of their prewar merchant fleet.

Meanwhile, the war was spreading, and not entirely due to Hitler's initiatives. As early as the summer of 1940, Mussolini ordered his forces in Libya to invade British Egypt. But the September invasion by the Italian Tenth Army and 135,000 troops was soon stopped by the 30,000 troops of the Western Desert Force under General Richard O'Connor, a part of General Archibald Wavell's Middle East Command. The frustrated Mussolini then ordered his forces in Albania to invade Greece in October, only to see the small Greek army defeat them and drive them back into Albania. In mid-November, Admiral Sir Andrew Cunningham's fleet based on Alexandria, Egypt, made a daring raid into the central Mediterranean in order to launch strikes from aircraft carriers at the Italian fleet anchored in the Bay of Taranto. Three out of four Italian battleships there were sunk or disabled. The crowning blow for the Italians in 1940 came on December 9, when the Western Desert Force routed the Italian Tenth Army in Egypt and drove it pell-mell back into Libya. The British victory at Sidi Barrani was followed by another at Beda Fomm on Libyan soil in February 1941, after which the Italian Tenth Army hardly existed. At the price of 500 Britons killed and 1,400 wounded, O'Connor's force had destroyed ten Italian divisions and killed or captured 150,000 Italian troops. Such a one-sided desert victory would not be seen again until Operation Desert Storm in 1991.

Had O'Connor's Western Desert Force been permitted to drive on after the Battle of Beda Fomm to capture the major port of Tripoli, the war in North Africa might have been over in a few more weeks. But Ultra warned Churchill that Hitler was preparing a Balkan blitzkrieg and that Greece would need all the help it could get. Accordingly, the Western Desert Force was ordered to halt its move westward, and its best units and equipment were withdrawn to Egypt to form an expeditionary force to be sent to Greece. Two inexperienced British divisions with old equipment under General Philip Neame occupied Cyrenaica (eastern Libya) to provide a secure flank for Egypt. The British did not expect any further trouble from the Axis forces in that direction, but they might have thought again had they known in February 1941 that a Deutsches Afrika Korps (DAK or German Africa Corps), composed of a German panzer division and a light division, was on its way to North Africa under General Erwin Rommel.

Hitler's decision to send help to the Italians in North Africa and to launch a blitzkrieg in the Balkans was largely motivated by his desire to secure the German southern flank before beginning the German invasion of Russia in June 1941. He also feared that, from British bases in Greece, the RAF could launch air strikes at the oil fields at Ploesti in Rumania. Only Greece and Yugoslavia refused his invitation to join the Axis alliance in the spring of 1941, and neither their forces nor the British expeditionary force sent from Egypt to Greece were any match for the two powerful

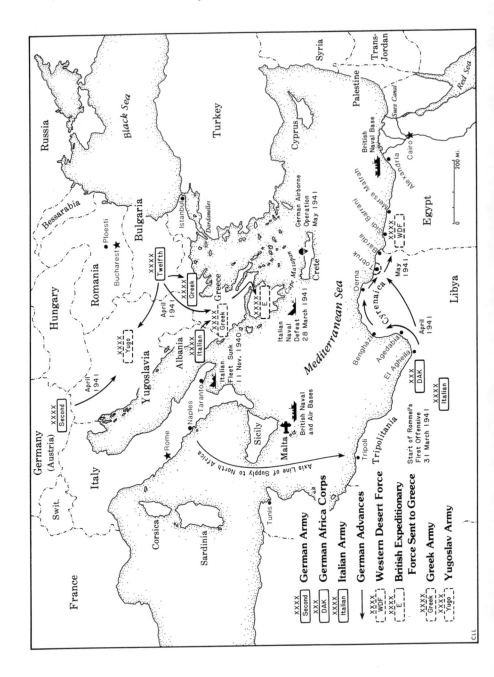

German armies assembled to execute operations Twenty-Five (Yugoslavia) and Marita (Greece). Accordingly, when the German blow fell in April 1941, Allied resistance speedily collapsed. The most populated parts of Yugoslavia were overrun by the Germans in five days, and the Anglo-French defense of upper Greece lasted only a little longer. By early May, the Germans had captured Athens and the British expeditionary force was evacuating through the port of Piraeus. But hardly had the British withdrawn their forces to the island of Crete than, later in May, the Germans launched their biggest airborne operation of the war (Mercury). The airborne invasion of Greece was successful, but the two German divisions involved lost so many men and airplanes that the German airborne capacity for future operations was almost nil for months to come.

Meanwhile, at the end of March, Rommel had at his disposal a German light division—the first of the DAK to join the Italian forces in Tripolitania (western Libya)—and with these forces he decided to launch an offensive against the British in Cyrenaica on his own authority even before the arrival of his panzer division. The unexpected Axis attack surprised and routed Neame's Western Desert Force from El Agheila eastwards, and, except for four British brigades which sheltered in the bypassed port of Tobruk, the British fled behind the Egyptian frontier in April. O'Connor, who had rushed from Egypt to restore order in the early phase of Rommel's offensive, was captured along with Neame during the British retreat. Only lagging Axis logistics and the threat from Tobruk to Rommel's rear prevented the Axis forces from invading Egypt. After Rommel's offensive ground to a halt, Churchill gave top priority to rebuilding the Western Desert Force.

The high point of the European war in 1941, however, was Hitler's invasion of Russia. That spring, a total of 3.3 million German troops and 142 divisions assembled in eastern Europe for Operation Barbarossa. The forces included 19 panzer divisions, 14 motorized infantry divisions (including 3½ Waffen SS divisions), 4 light divisions, 2 mountain divisions, a cavalry division, and 102 infantry divisions. Hitler also assembled 3,350 tanks, 7,000 pieces of artillery, 600,000 motor vehicles in addition to the tanks, 625,000 horses, and over 100,000 horse-drawn wagons. But the diversion of Luftwaffe planes to the Mediterranean, and earlier aircraft losses in the Battle of Britain, resulted in only 2,250 German aircraft being available for the invasion of Russia. The Germans estimated that the Red Army had 178 divisions, 10,000 tanks, and 7,000 aircraft in western Russia, but they thought the quality of German forces would more than offset Russian numbers, given the element of surprise. Hitler predicted that the only hard fighting would be over within a month.

The greatest land war ever fought began at 3:30 a.m. on June 22, 1941, with a tremendous German pre-dawn barrage laid down on Russian fron-

Operation Barbarossa: The German Plan of the Invasion of Russia, June 1941

tier positions. At first light, the Luftwaffe delivered massive air attacks on Soviet airfields within range. Within twenty-four hours, an estimated 2,000 Russian planes were destroyed on the ground. Russian air losses mounted so rapidly over the next several weeks that the Luftwaffe enjoyed complete command of the air. On the ground, Army Group North (Leeb), composed of two armies, a panzer group, and 26 divisions, swept into the former Baltic states and headed for Leningrad. Army Group Center (Bock), composed of two armies, two panzer groups, and 32 divisions invaded Russian Poland and White Russia in the direction of Moscow. Army Group South (Rundstedt), consisting of 3 armies, a panzer group, and 35 divisions, struck into the Ukraine and advanced toward the Dnieper. As logistics permitted, the balance of the German divisions in the East were sent forward as reinforcements. Rumania, desirous of regaining Bessarabia, entered the war with 12 divisions. Finland attacked with 16 divisions in order to recover the territories lost to Russia in the Winter War of 1939–40.

The greatest of the early German successes was on Bock's front, where, by the end of the encirclement battle of Minsk-Smolensk in August, a total of 475,000 Soviet troops, 4,530 tanks, and 3,400 pieces of artillery had been destroyed or captured. But forty-seven days of incessant marching and fighting had taken their toll, and German infantry divisions especially were showing signs of exhaustion. The OKH ordered Army Group Center to halt, rest its infantry, and repair its logistics before attempting to move toward Moscow. The panzer groups with Army Group Center were to conserve their resources for a final great battle at the Russian capital. But Hitler had other ideas. He proposed that while Bock's group rested, its two armored groups—under Hermann Hoth and Heinz Guderian—would be temporarily assigned to aid the other army groups. Hoth's group would assist Army Group North, encountering stubborn resistance before Leningrad, and Guderian's panzers would aid Army Group South, also meeting tough resistance in the Ukraine. Brauchitsch and Halder opposed Hitler's proposal because it would add wear and tear on the armored-motorized groups even before the drive on Moscow began, and because it would delay the start of Bock's drive beyond the time necessary for the infantry divisions of his army group to recuperate. Hitler insisted on having his way, however, and the two panzer groups were detached. Hoth's panzer group aided Army Group North in sealing in the defenders of Leningrad, and Guderian's armor aided Army Group South to achieve the greatest *Kesselschlacht* ever when 665,000 Russian troops were encircled, killed, or captured at the Battle of Kiev. But most of the Russian troops lost in the south turned out to be ordinary infantry of the sort most easily replaced by the *Stafka* (the Soviet High Command); the better Soviet armored and motorized forces escaped the trap. Though Rundstedt's

Soviet T-34 tank, perhaps the best medium tank of World
War II.
SOURCE: Kenneth Macksey and John H. Batchelor, *Tank: A History
of the Armoured Fighting Vechicle* (New York: Charles Scribner's Sons,
1970).

army group moved on to capture Rostov, the Soviet forces in his front
remained formidable.

As the OKH feared, by the time Hoth's and Guderian's panzer groups
had rejoined Army Group Center for Operation Typhoon, the drive on
Moscow, their men were tired and their equipment worn. Bock's advance
began with a 40 percent shortage in tanks and a 30 percent shortage in
trucks. Still, the Luftwaffe ruled the skies, the weather was fair, and a
faulty Russian deployment in a defensive position resulted in another German *Kesselschlacht* at the Battle of Vyazma-Bryansk in October. A total of
663,000 Russian troops, a thousand tanks, and 5,000 pieces of artillery
were destroyed or taken. Elated, Hitler announced to the German people
that the decisive battle of the Eastern campaign had been won. But to his
surprise, the Red Army was still not broken, and Vyazma-Bryansk turned
out to be the last great German victory by encirclement of the war.

After the Battle of Vyazma-Bryansk, the fall rains began, turning the
unpaved Russian roads into quagmires. As wheeled vehicles mired down,
Army Group Center's advance came to a halt. The grip of the mud was
not broken until a freeze on November 7, but the dash of cold weather
was a portent of the approach of winter. While the Germans were temporarily immobilized, Stalin and his generals completed the defenses of Moscow. These defenses amounted to five fortified lines collectively fifty miles
deep, and containing 1,428 artillery emplacements, 75 miles of barbed
wire, and vast numbers of tank traps and mine fields. General Georgi
Zhukov, the former Chief of the Soviet General Staff, assumed personal

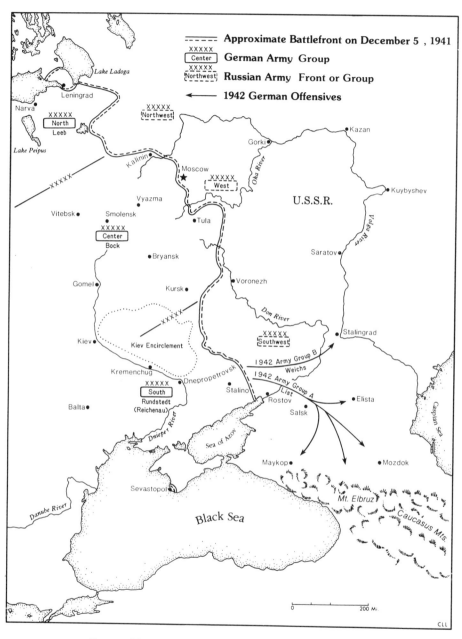

Approximate Battlefront on December 5 , 1941

XXXXX
Center — **German Army Group**

XXXXX
Northwest — **Russian Army Front or Group**

← **1942 German Offensives**

Eastern Front: Maximum Line of German Advance, 1941

command of the group of armies assembled to defend the capital, including 18 fresh divisions from the Far East.

The Battle of Moscow began on November 16, when Bock's army group first encountered the outer line of Moscow's defenses. Though the German armored groups tried to turn the city's defenses north and south, every approach was blocked. The German frontal attack took such heavy losses that Bock likened it to the brutish chest-to-chest struggle of the 1914 Battle of the Marne. By early December, some of the German infantry divisions involved in the battle were ninety miles from the nearest functioning rail-head, and lack of fodder as well as the effects of winter weather caused thousands of draft animals to die. The lack of enough antifreeze immobilized many German motor vehicles and aircraft. By December 5, the German offensive had ground to a halt. Hitler gave permission for Bock to regroup before resuming the attack, but, before Bock could do so, the Russians seized the initiative on December 6. Zhukov unleashed a powerful counteroffensive that sent the Germans reeling back some fifty miles before it was finally contained a few days later. The Battle of Moscow sputtered to a close as a clear strategic defeat for the Germans. Moreover, the OKH reckoned that, since November 16, Army Group Center had suffered 250,000 casualties (55,000 dead) from wounds and the cold, and, over the whole of the Eastern Front since June 22, the Germans had lost 750,000 men, 75,000 motor vehicles, and 180,000 draft horses. Still worse, the quick victory on which Hitler was counting had proved impossible, and a long struggle in the East was in prospect.

Almost simultaneous with the German setback in Russia, bad news for Hitler poured in from North Africa. In November 1941 the new British Eighth Army (which subsumed the Western Desert Force), placed under General Sir Alan Cunningham by General Sir Claude Auchinleck, the new British general officer commanding in the Middle East, had launched Operation Crusader in order to raise the siege of Tobruk. Rommel skillfully parried Cunningham's attacks, but in December Auchinleck assumed personal command of Eighth Army and his attacks compelled Rommel to abandon his siege of Tobruk and to retire his Panzer Army Africa (which included the DAK) and their Italian allies deep inside Cyrenaica. Fortunately for Rommel, the arrival of a shipment of tanks at Benghazi in January 1942 allowed him to launch a counteroffensive, and by early February the Eighth Army had been driven back to El Gazala, not far from Tobruk. Still, the Desert War was at a stalemate, and the prospect there was for another struggle of attrition that the Axis forces were ill equipped to maintain.

Next to the German defeat at Moscow, the most serious event for Hitler in 1941 was the Japanese attack on Pearl Harbor on December 7 and the opening of the Pacific War. Though Germany and Italy were committed to come to Japan's aid under the Tripartite Pact of September 1940 only if Japan were attacked, Hitler and Mussolini took their respective countries into war with the United States before the year was out. Perhaps war between Nazi Germany and the United States was inevitable in any case. As a massive supplier of war material to Great Britain under Lend-Lease, the United States had taken further steps against Germany's interests by allowing its warships to escort British merchant vessels partway across the Atlantic in an undeclared naval war against German U-boats. By the beginning of 1942 World War II had become a group of interlocking conflicts on a global scale.

II. The European War, 1942–45

A. *From Moscow to Sicily, January 1942–July 1943.*   In the immediate aftermath of the German reverse at Moscow in December 1941, Brauchitsch submitted his resignation as Commander-in-Chief of the German army and Hitler appointed himself to that position. He also decreed that the OKH would henceforth have responsibility for the Eastern Front and the OKW would assume responsibility for any others. Of course, Hitler was effectively supreme commander at both headquarters, located near each other in East Prussia as the war went on.

Winter weather forced a suspension of major operations on the Eastern Front until the spring of 1942, by which time the effects of climate and battle had raised the total of German casualties on the front to over a million men. Nevertheless, Hitler did not despair of a final victory over Stalin. At the Führer's direction, the OKH planned an offensive intended to overrun the Russian oil fields in the Caucasus and to undermine both the Red Army and Soviet industry. After preliminary operations, the main German effort was launched on June 28 and immediately created a great gap in the Russian front in the south. Of the reorganized German forces carrying out the offensive, Army Group A advanced 300 miles before a combination of fierce Soviet resistance and German logistical problems brought it to a halt almost in sight of the Russian oil fields. Army Group B, protecting Army Group A's northern flank, advanced toward the Volga, but its Sixth Army was engaged in a street-by-street battle for Stalingrad by late summer. Halder urged Hitler to allow General Friedrich von Paulus, commander of the Sixth Army, to break off the battle and withdraw his army from the dangerously exposed salient, but Hitler's reaction was to dismiss Halder as chief of the OKH General Staff on September 24. General Kurt Zeitzler, Halder's deputy and successor, shared Halder's opinion of the situation at Stalingrad, but obeyed Hitler's orders to continue the deadlocked battle there until late in November. Then a powerful

Russian offensive north and south of Stalingrad encircled the Sixth Army inside the city and severed its communications. Though Hitler promoted Paulus to field marshal in order to encourage his determination to continue the fight, all German attempts to relieve his army or to supply his forces by air were unavailing. On January 31, 1943, Paulus and his remaining 91,000 troops surrendered. His was the first German army to surrender in the field since the Napoleonic Wars. Hitler's battle for Stalingrad had cost his forces some 300,000 men.

The Battle for Stalingrad turned out to be the point-of-return for the Red Army. Except for the abortive German offensive at Kursk (Operation Citadel) in July 1943—the largest armored battle of the war, involving perhaps 6,000 AFVs—the Red Army kept the initiative on the Eastern Front for the rest of the war. As the Russian offensives slowly drove the Germans westward, the only realistic German hope lay in a gradually narrowing front and shortening lines-of-communication. At some point, these factors might enable Hitler's forces to impose a stalemate in the East. Even for this strategy to work, the Germans would also have to be able to beat off any Anglo-American attack on Hitler's empire in Western Europe.

The year 1942 was also the turning point of the war in North Africa. That spring, Field Marshal Albert Kesselring, German Commander-in-Chief, South, managed to bring enough air power to bear on Malta that British air submarine attacks from the island on Axis shipping to North Africa were temporarily suppressed. In addition, from November 1941 to February 1942, the British navy suffered heavy losses in both the Mediterranean and in the Far East in capital ships and aircraft carriers. Kesselring had concentrated two German and two Italian airborne divisions on the island of Sicily for a descent on Malta (Operation Hercules), but Hitler hesitated to give the order for fear the Italian navy would not carry out its part in the operation. Rommel lost patience and on May 26, 1942, launched a new offensive with Panzer Army Africa against the British position at El Gazala (Operation Theseus). His attack defeated the British forces and enabled his forces to seize Tobruk, and with supplies captured there the Axis forces were able to press on into Egypt. Hitler, pleased with Rommel's success, decided that the proposed airborne invasion of Malta could be canceled. He also ordered Kesselring to send much of his air force to the Eastern Front in order to support the German offensive there.

By July 1942 Auchinleck had withdrawn the British Eighth Army to a good defensive position at El Alamein, the terminus of the desert railroad from Alexandria, eighty miles to the east. Between July 3 and July 21, the Eighth Army beat off a series of Axis attacks on the position at El Alamein, and Rommel suspended further attacks until Panzer Army Africa could be resupplied and repaired. During the lull until August, Churchill relieved Auchinleck, abolished the Middle East Command, and created a new Near East Command in its place. He appointed General Sir Harold Alexander to head the Near East Command, and General Bernard L. Montgomery assumed command of the Eighth Army. Thus Rommel faced new British commanders when he launched a final effort to get by the position at El Alamein (the Second Battle of El Alamein or Alam El Halfa Ridge). The rejuvenated Eighth Army fought Panzer Army Africa to a draw in late August and early September.

By then Rommel realized that a tremendous build-up of Allied forces was going on, while his own forces, far from their main base at Tripoli, were dwindling. In addition, the British Tenth Submarine Flotilla had returned to its bases on Malta and, joined by 250 British aircraft, had resumed attacks on Axis shipping between Italy and Tripoli. Rommel saw no alternative but to request permission to withdraw behind the Libyan frontier and establish a defensive position in Cyrenaica. Hitler refused the request.

By the last half of October, the Eighth Army had reached a strength of 200,000 troops, 750 aircraft, 1,000 tanks, and as many pieces of artillery. Its troops were well supplied with food, water, fuel, spare parts, and ammunition. In contrast, Panzer Army Africa had 100,000 ill-supplied troops, 675 planes (275 German), 500 tanks (211 German), and 500 guns. Montgomery felt great confidence in the outcome when he launched Operation Lightfoot on October 23 in the Third Battle of El Alamein. For thirteen days British armor and infantry, assisted by British planes and artillery, systematically hammered Panzer Army Africa to fragments until, on November 3, Rommel ordered what remained to begin a withdrawal to Libya. When his army crossed the frontier on November 8, only half of his original force of German troops and a fifth of his Italian troops were still with him. His armored component was down to thirty tanks. The triumphant Montgomery and the Eighth Army followed Rommel's retreating forces in a leisurely pursuit.

On the day that the remains of Panzer Army Africa crossed the frontier into Libya, Hitler learned that about 100,000 Anglo-American troops had invaded the Vichy French territories of Morocco and Algeria in Operation Torch. Clearly the Allies intended to catch Rommel's forces between the jaws of a closing vice. After token resistance, the Vichy French forces in Morocco and Algeria surrendered to the Allies on the orders of Admiral Jean-François Darlan, the Vichy minister of defense, who happened to be in Algeria at the time. Hitler retaliated by ordering German occupation of both Vichy France and its remaining North African territory of Tunisia. The relatively short distance between Italy and Tunisia made it a potential safe haven for the retreating Panzer Army Africa, while the province could be occupied ahead of time by troops of General Hans-Jürgen von Arnim's Fifth Panzer Army. After Panzer Army Africa completed its withdrawal into southern Tunisia in January 1943, it was reorganized as the Italian First Army (including the DAK) under Rommel's command. The Italian First Army manned the Mareth Line—old French fortifications facing the Libyan frontier—while the Fifth Panzer Army defended northern Tunisia. After troops under U.S. General Dwight D. Eisenhower, the Allied Commander-in-Chief for Operation Torch, had made contact with Montgomery's Eighth Army, General Alexander assumed command of the new Allied Eighteenth Army Group, composed of the British First and Eighth armies, the U.S. II Corps, and a French corps. Eisenhower remained as supreme commander for Allied ground, air, and sea forces.

In mid-February 1943 Rommel and Arnim launched a spoiling offensive, Rommel directing an armored raid toward Kasserine Pass which mauled elements of the inexperienced U.S. II Corps. Eisenhower relieved the commander of the II Corps and appointed General George S. Patton, Jr., to his place. Just after the raid, on February 23, Rommel was made Commander-in-Chief of all Axis forces in Tunisia, then titled Army Group Africa. But his subsequent offensive against the Eighth Army at Medenine on March 6 went badly. Depressed, exhausted, and in ill health, Rommel turned over command to Arnim and flew back to Germany for medical treatment. He never returned to North Africa. Arnim's forces, fifteen divisions (eleven German, four of them panzer divisions), were confronted by twenty Allied divisions (most of them British), and by Allied command of the air and sea. Gradually, Allied attacks compressed the Axis foothold in Tunisia. Tunis, the major port, fell on May 7, and the last organized Axis resistance ceased on May 13. In all, the Allies had inflicted 300,000 Axis casualties, while suffering 75,000 casualties in the process. The Italian navy, fearful of the Anglo-American sea and air power, made no effort to evacuate Axis forces before the surrender.

After a respite of two months following the Axis surrender in Tunisia, the Allied forces in the Mediterranean launched an invasion of Sicily (Operation Husky). The invasion was carried out by the Fifteenth Army Group (Alexander), composed of Montgomery's Eighth Army and the new U.S. Seventh Army under Patton. Each side initially committed nine divisions to the battle, but the Allied forces were supported by 3,350 planes against 1,400 Axis planes (half of them German), and the Allies again possessed command of the sea. Still, the stubborn German defense of the so-called Messina Corner delayed Montgomery's straightforward advance across the island toward the narrows between Sicily and Italy. This defense was partially overcome by a daring motorized run by Patton's forces around the western end of the island via Palermo. Yet the Allies failed to block the narrows in time to prevent the Germans from successfully withdrawing three of their four divisions to the Italian mainland before Axis resistance on Sicily collapsed on August 17. The battle for Sicily involved 475,000 Allied soldiers, sailors, and airmen, of whom 22,000 were casualties. The Axis powers lost 275,000 men on Sicily, all but 25,000 of them Italian.

Even while the Sicilian campaign was underway, on July 24 the Fascist Grand Council in Rome, disillusioned with Mussolini's leadership, stripped him of his powers, and later the same day King Victor Emmanuel III ordered him placed under arrest. A new Italian government under Marshal Pietro Badoglio opened secret surrender negotiations with Eisenhower's headquarters in Algiers so as to remove Italy from the war before it became a battleground between German and Allied forces. As explained below, the Anglo-American high command had no plans to follow up the conquest of Sicily with an invasion of Italy, but the opportunity was too great to be missed. The invasion of Italy in September 1943, even as the Italian government was about to surrender, had great consequences for the further Allied prosecution of the war.

   B. The U-Boat War, the Allied Strategic Air Offensive, and Hitler's V-Weapons. In 1942, the German U-boat campaign established a record for the war by sinking 1,279,000 tons of Allied shipping in the North Atlantic and 5,605,000 tons worldwide. In addition, Admiral Dönitz added 190 submarines to his U-boat fleet, while losing only 92. But in 1943, German fortunes at sea began to decline. Though U-boats sank 1,147,000 tons in the North Atlantic, the worldwide figure dropped to 2,649,000 tons. And while Dönitz added 225 submarines, he lost 234. The advent in 1944 of the *Schnorkel,* a pipe with a float-valve that enabled submarines to recharge batteries underwater, reduced the time submarines had to remain on the surface, but in all of 1944 U-boats sank only 169,000 tons in the North Atlantic and 694,000 tons worldwide. A total of 175 U-boats had been added, but 235 had been lost. In the less than five months of 1945 before Germany surrendered, U-boats sank 271,000 tons in the North Atlantic and 404,000 tons worldwide, but 165 submarines were lost and only 70 were added. For the war as a whole, German U-boats sank 6,846,000 tons of Allied shipping in the North Atlantic and 14,316,000 tons worldwide. This record was accomplished by 1,170 submarines, all but 57 of them built after the outbreak of the war. Over the course of the war, a total of 784 U-boats and 49,000 submariners were lost.

   The failure of the German submarine *guerre de course* is explained by several factors, including Hitler's unwillingness to give priority to a major expansion of the submarine fleet until the war was well underway, but also by the determination of the Anglo-American navies to build a huge antisubmarine fleet, including long-range patrol planes, and one equipped with radar and sonar. By 1943, the threat of land-based planes from the American Atlantic and Gulf coasts had forced Dönitz to order his submarines to stay deeper inside the Atlantic and away from some of the most important sea lanes. And there were important Allied innovations. The "jeep carrier" was actually a small aircraft carrier dedicated to accompanying convoys of merchant ships, and whose planes could patrol the seas beyond the range of land-based aircraft of the time. Finally, a huge Anglo-American shipbuilding effort between 1939 and 1945 added 35,300,000 tons to the Allied merchant fleets, as against their loss to all causes of 33,600,000 tons.

The U.S. Eighth Air Force joined RAF Bomber Command in England in the summer of 1942, but at first the Americans had only a handful of bombers. The RAF Bomber Command carried out the first of the "Thousand Bomber Raids" on Germany against the city of Cologne in the Rhineland as early as May 1942, although this was a one-shot affair and it would be months before raids of similar size could be staged on a regular basis. In addition, British attacks were usually made at night to hold down aircraft losses; bombing inaccuracy in darkness forced a resort to mass-area raids. Professor Frederick Lindemann (later Lord Cherwell), Churchill's scientific advisor, and Air Marshal Sir Arthur Harris, eventually chief of Bomber Command, justified mass-area bombings on the grounds that they would lower German civilian morale, but theory aside, German civilian morale never broke and industrial production in the Reich continued to rise until September 1944. Perhaps the theory would have been more effective had the bomb tonnages delivered been larger earlier in the war; 80 percent of the tonnage dropped on Germany was delivered in the last ten months of the conflict.

The American air doctrine in 1942 differed from the British in assuming that heavy bombers could make precision raids in daylight, that "pin-point" bombing of sensitive industries directly related to the enemy's war effort was both possible and more effective than mass-area bombing, and that such raids could be carried out with acceptable losses. Though the American doctrine proved essentially sound, it overlooked difficulties in putting it into practice. Extensive cloud cover over northern Europe often interfered with the optics of the Norden bomb sight, and unescorted bombers proved much more vulnerable to enemy fighters than expected. On August 1, 177 four-engined American bombers based in North Africa tried a low-level attack on the German-controlled oil refineries at Ploesti in Rumania, only to lose 54 aircraft and 532 aircrewmen. On August 17, the Eighth Air Force in England launched 516 B-17 bombers against the Messerschmidt works at Regensburg and the ball-bearing industries at Schweinfurt, and lost 60 bombers and 540 aircrew. The heavy losses expe-

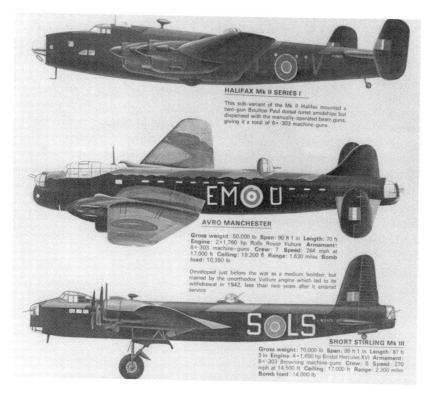

British long-range bombers of the World War II era:
Halifax, Manchester, and Stirling.

SOURCE: John Batchelor et al., *Air Power: A Modern Illustrated
Military History* (New York: Exeter Books, 1979, in association with
Phoebus Company/BPC Publishing, London).

rienced in attacking sensitive targets continued to mount until the "Black
Week" of the Eighth Air Force in October. On the last day, of 219 B-17s
attacking the ball-bearing plants at Schweinfurt, 60 were shot down and
138 returned to base seriously damaged. Taken as a whole, the week cost
the Eighth Air Force a quarter of its aircrews in England. German industry
recovered from the effects of the raids faster than the Eighth Air Force.

After the "Black Week," the Americans suspended daylight attacks on
Germany until February 1944. By then they had produced large numbers
of the new P-51 Mustang fighter, equipped with dropable fuel tanks so

that it could escort bombers all the way to their targets. General James Doolittle replaced General Ira Eaker as commander of the Eighth Air Force (Eaker assumed command of the Mediterranean Allied Air Forces), while General Carl Spaatz was appointed supreme commander of the American strategic air forces in the European Theater of Operations (ETO). In the so-called Big Week of February 22–25, 1944, U.S. air forces flew some 3,800 daylight sorties over Germany, while the British Bomber Command carried out 2,351 sorties, mostly at night. Though 226 U.S. and 157 RAF bombers were lost in these raids, German fighter losses were very heavy. As the round-the-clock pounding of Germany continued into March, the Americans concentrated especially on petroleum facilities, aircraft plants, and enemy airfields. By the end of March, the strength of the German Fighter Command had been reduced by 800 aircraft and many pilots. These losses and shortages of high-octane aviation gasoline reduced the German air forces in western France on June 6, 1944, to 125 operational aircraft.

Despite the Allied strategic bombing, 1944 as a whole was the best year of the war for German armament production, though shortages of fuel and damage to German transportation systems often made it impossible to deliver the armament to where it was needed. Of the 113,514 aircraft built by Germany during World War II, 40,593 were constructed in 1944. Of the 39,225 tanks and other armored fighting vehicles produced during the war, 19,050 were turned out in 1944. Hundreds of new jet-propelled fighters were also produced in 1944, planes that might have turned the tide of the air war over Germany had not fuel shortages kept most of them grounded. In retrospect, the strategic Allied air offensive might have been more quickly decisive had the proper targets—oil and transportation—been singled out earlier for concentrated Allied attention.

Hitler had no strategic air force with which to retaliate for the Allied bombing of Germany, but he put his hope in the new *Vergeltungswaffen* or "weapons of retaliation," the V-1 and V-2. The V-1 was a ground-launched cruise missile, about twenty-five feet in length, powered by a jet engine. Carrying a ton of high explosive, it flew as fast as 425 mph and had a range of about 200 miles. When its engine ran out of fuel, it crashed, exploded, and killed and destroyed indiscriminately. The Germans launched the first V-1s at England about two weeks after the Allied invasion of Normandy in June 1944. A total of 7,400 were launched from France and 800 from Holland against England before Allied ground advances put their bases out of range. Most of the launched missiles were destroyed in flight by British fighters and antiaircraft guns, but the ones that penetrated British defenses killed or injured 24,165 Britons. Another 7,800 V-1s were launched at Allied-occupied cities on the continent, especially against Antwerp, and inflicted a further 10,000 casualties.

The V-2 was a liquid-fuel, rocket-engine ballistic missile, carrying a ton of high explosive about 200 miles. Designed by Dr. Werner von Braun, the V-2 was fifty feet in length, five feet in diameter, and weighed twenty-four tons on lift-off. Nine tons of the total were fuel which was consumed in the sixty seconds in which the V-2 rose as high as sixty miles above the earth before plummeting toward its target as fast as 3,500 mph. Like the V-1, the V-2 had poor accuracy, but as a weapon of terror it was unrivaled. There was no defense against it once launched, and, traveling faster than the speed of sound, it struck without warning. A total of 1,500 V-2s were hurled across the Channel against England before the V-2 bases were neutralized either by bombing or capture. They killed or injured 9,235 Britons. Another 1,500 V-2s were lobbed at the cities on the continent occupied by the Allies (again, Antwerp was the chief target), and inflicted 10,000 casualties.

Though the V-weapons were introduced too late in the war to affect its outcome, next to the atomic bomb they were the most terrifying weapons to appear in World War II. Had they appeared five years earlier and been matched with atomic warheads, they might have altered the war's outcome. They heralded today's cruise and ballistic missiles, the most destructive systems invented to date, and opened a new pattern of war for the future.

C. From Sicily to the Liberation of France, August 1943–August 1944. The rearmament of the United States effectively began after the fall of France in June 1940. Congressional adoption of the draft in September was the first peacetime conscription act in American history. But the production of armaments was partially diverted to the aid of Britain, especially after the passage of the Lend-Lease Act in March 1941. Under the act, the President could "lend" U.S. arms and equipment to foreign powers whenever he judged that it served the national interest. Lend-Lease also provided an excuse for American naval operations in the fall of 1941 against German U-boats in a "Neutrality Zone" that Franklin D. Roosevelt finally extended more than halfway across the Atlantic. Meanwhile, American troops relieved British troops in the occupation of Iceland. By December 7, 1941, the strength of the Army of the United States had grown from 270,000 to 1,462,000 troops, but many of the new divisions were still untrained and without a full complement of arms and equipment.

Under these circumstances, it is remarkable that after the Joint Army-Navy Board was replaced by the wartime improvisation of the Joint Chiefs of Staff, General George C. Marshall, the Army Chief-of-Staff, believed that a cross-Channel invasion of France and a direct drive into Germany was possible in 1942. The Anglo-American allies had formed a Combined

Chiefs of Staff organization in early 1942 to facilitate joint planning, so Marshall's plan (Operation Sledgehammer) had to have the approval and support of the British. But General Dwight D. Eisenhower, Marshall's representative to the Combined Chiefs of Staff Committee in London, soon discovered that the British had no enthusiasm for Operation Sledgehammer. The British chiefs believed that a proper use of Anglo-American limited resources would be an invasion of Vichy French North Africa (Operation Torch) in order to threaten the rear of the Axis forces based in Libya. Reluctantly, first Eisenhower and then Marshall came around to the British point of view in July 1942.

Early in 1943, while the Tunisian campaign was underway, Roosevelt, Churchill, and their military advisors met at Casablanca to plan further moves. Marshall accepted the British arguments against a cross-Channel invasion in 1943 (Operation Roundup), but he was afraid that after operations in Tunisia were concluded another major Anglo-American operation in the Mediterranean would so tie up their forces that a cross-Channel invasion of France in 1944 would be either weakened or abandoned altogether. Churchill favored an attack on the "soft underbelly" of Europe, perhaps through the Balkans, and linking up with the Russians on the Eastern Front, in part to insure an Anglo-American presence in eastern Europe at the end of the war. To prevent any diversion from the cross-Channel operation, Marshall insisted that all future operations in the Mediterranean after Tunisia be limited in scope. The compromise finally reached was an invasion of Sicily (Operation Husky), which, if successful, would deal a heavy blow to Italian prestige and open the central Mediterranean to Allied shipping. Marshall did not intend that Sicily would also be a stepping-stone to Italy.

Operation Husky proved too successful. Before its conclusion, Mussolini had fallen from power and a new Italian government under Marshal Badoglio was offering to negotiate an Italian surrender. Even Marshall had to agree with General Sir Alan Brooke, chief of Britain's Imperial General Staff, that a chance to take Italy out of the war and to occupy the Italian peninsula quickly could not be ignored. From northern Italy, the Allied ground forces could threaten southern France, Austria, and the Balkans, and the Allied air forces would be much closer to their strategic targets in Germany. Accordingly, Eisenhower ordered General Alexander to form a new Fifteenth Army Group—composed of General Mark W. Clark's U.S. Fifth Army and Montgomery's Eighth Army—and as soon as practicable to invade the Italian mainland. Unfortunately for Allied plans, the Italian surrender negotiations, undertaken in secret, dragged on for so long that Hitler found time to send reinforcements to Kesselring, Commander-in-Chief, South, and to get General Heinrich von Vietinghoff's Tenth Army moved into southern Italy. Just as the Badoglio government

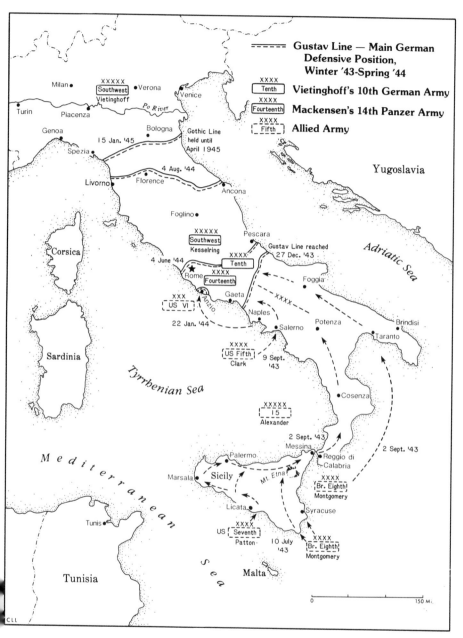

The Italian Campaign, July 1943–January 1945

signed an armistice with the Allies in early September, British and American forces crossed the straits of Messina and landed in southern Italy. A week later, forces of the Eighth Army invaded the "heel" of the Italian "boot" and Clark's Fifth Army landed at Salerno, south of Naples. As the Germans moved to occupy Rome, King Victor Emmanuel III, his prime minister, and his army chief-of-staff fled to the protection of British lines at Brindisi. About the middle of September, a daring German airborne raid freed Mussolini from captivity in his mountaintop prison and spirited him to northern Italy. He played out the rest of the war in Europe as head of a rump Fascist state totally dependent on German good will.

Allied hopes for a quick conquest of Italy went glimmering. Though the Fifth Army captured Naples, fierce German resistance reduced American progress west of the Appenines, and that of the Eighth Army east of the mountains, to a crawl. By winter the Allied advance had stalled before the German "Gustav Line," well south of Rome. At the Tehran Conference in November, Churchill urged postponement of the cross-Channel invasion, tentatively scheduled for the spring of 1944, in order to provide reinforcements for the Italian front. Marshall, his worst fears realized, found an unexpected ally in Joseph Stalin, who had been urging a major "Second Front" on the western Allies since 1942. A compromise was reached whereby it was agreed that more strength would be diverted to Italy, but in 1944 the extra forces would be used to invade southern France in Operation Anvil (later renamed Operation Dragoon) in conjunction with the cross-Channel invasion. Also at Tehran, President Roosevelt announced that Eisenhower had been chosen to command the cross-Channel invasion in 1944 (Operation Overlord). At the turn of the year, Eisenhower gave over his post as Allied Mediterranean Commander-in-Chief to British general Sir Henry Wilson and took up his new responsibilities at Supreme Headquarters, Allied Expeditionary Force (SHAEF), in London. Montgomery was transferred to serve as Eisenhower's commander of Allied ground forces in the initial phases of Operation Overlord. General Oliver Lease assumed Montgomery's old command of the British Eighth Army in Italy.

In January 1944 the U.S. Fifth Army tried to break through the "Gustav Line" in the Monte Cassino sector with the attack of a National Guard division, only to be bloodily repulsed on the banks of the Rapido. The episode was a smaller version of the British disaster in World War I on the Somme. An amphibious attack by the U.S. VI Corps at Anzio, just south of Rome, also in January, ended badly when its commander failed to take advantage of surprise. The VI Corps barely survived the counterattacks of General Eberhard von Mackensen's Fourteenth Panzer Army. Even after the VI Corps was reinforced, and despite strong air and naval support, the VI Corps was unable to break out of its beachhead. Not until May 1944 did the attacks of other Allied troops down the Liri valley finally bring about a link-up with the embattled troops at Anzio. German abandonment of the "Gustav Line" finally allowed Clark's Fifth Army to enter Rome on June 4, 1944, just two days before the beginning of Operation Overlord, but the delay in capturing Rome made it too late for Allied troops in the Mediterranean to invade southern France in conjunction with the Normandy invasion as originally planned. Operation Dragoon was postponed until August.

After D-Day in Normandy, the Italian theater became one of secondary importance. Upon the death of General Sir John Dill, Sir Henry Wilson was sent to Washington to represent Britain on the Combined Chiefs of Staff. Harold Alexander rose to become the Allied Mediterranean commander-in-chief. Clark succeeded Alexander as commander of the Fifteenth Army Group in Italy, and General Lucian Truscott replaced Clark as commander of the Fifth Army. On the opposing side, Kesselring was injured in a car accident in October 1944 and was replaced by Vietinghoff as the German Commander-in-Chief, South. With twenty under-strength divisions, the Germans defended northern Italy with such tenacity that the Fifteenth Army Group had only reached the valley of the Po River by April 1945. By that time Eisenhower's and Zhukov's armies were overrunning Germany. On April 29, Vietinghoff agreed to surrender his command to Clark. The day before, Mussolini and his mistress were shot after falling into the hands of partisans; the day after, Hitler committed suicide in his bunker in Berlin.

By June 1944 the war in Europe was approaching its climax. On the Eastern Front, the Red Army had reached a strength of 400 divisions (it mobilized 503 divisions at one time or another during World War II) and 6,500,000 men. The Eastern Front was then located approximately on the pre-war Russian frontiers in the west. Opposed to the Russians were 4,300,000 Axis troops in 198 divisions. They were not only outnumbered by the Russians, they were also inferior in arms and equipment. In 1944, Soviet industry produced 29,000 armored fighting vehicles, 56,000 pieces of artillery and antitank guns, and 32,300 aircraft. In all but one major category of armaments, Soviet production had outstripped the German. And, whereas German production had to be divided over several fronts, nearly all of the Russian production was concentrated on one front. In addition, partly by way of the Arctic route but mostly by way of the Persian Gulf and through Iran, the Anglo-American allies had sent Russia a total of 385,000 trucks, 22,000 aircraft, and 12,000 tanks.

In contrast to the Axis and Soviet behemoths on the Eastern Front, which were manpower-intensive and heavily dependent on railroad and horse-drawn supply transportation, the Allied forces assembled in England for Operation Overlord were smaller in numbers but much more

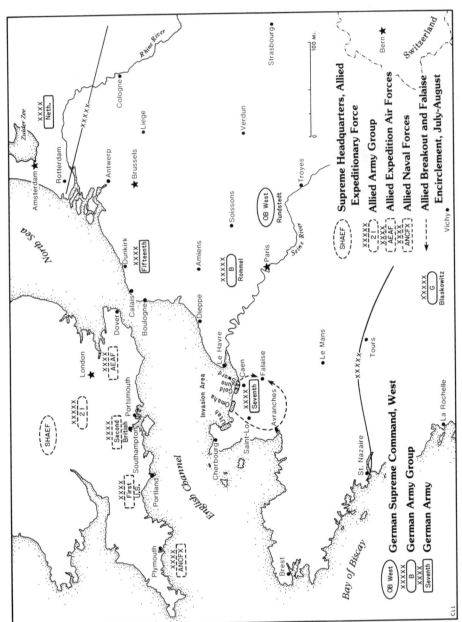

Allied and German Deployment in the West on Eve of June 6, 1944, and the

machine-intensive. On June 6, 1944, Eisenhower commanded 38 divisions (20 U.S., 14 British, 3 Canadian, and 1 Free French), all of them effectively motorized and many of them armored. His troops numbered 2,000,000, of which 1,627,000 were American. The ground forces were to be initially combined in the Twenty-First Army Group under Montgomery, the group to be composed of the U.S. First Army (Omar Bradley) and the Anglo-Canadian Second Army (Miles Dempsey). More forces and army head-quarters were to be introduced when there was a sufficient lodgment. The ground forces were supported by the mightiest air armada and fleet ever assembled for a single operation: 12,000 aircraft and 5,300 ships, including 1,000 warships. In addition, 36 U.S. divisions in the United States were preparing to go to the ETO. The "Mighty Endeavor," as President Roosevelt called the cross-Channel invasion of 1944, amounted to a powerful air-land-sea "fist" of men and machines aimed at northern France and eventually at Germany's solar plexus. Success would depend on an early lodgment on the French coast, to be followed by a rapid build-up of forces for a breakout from the beachhead. The spearhead of the attack amounted to 20,000 airborne and 70,000 amphibious troops, in all just 8 divisions, to be rapidly reinforced by two more, and upon whose performance everything else depended.

The German forces in Western Europe awaiting the invasion in June 1944 hardly compared with the forces which had so handily defeated the Anglo-French armies four years earlier. Field Marshal Rundstedt, Supreme Commander, West (OB West), had 58 divisions (including 10 panzer divisions) and 1,500,000 troops in France and in the Low Countries, but only a small number of the German divisions were entirely mobile. Thanks to Allied air operations and German shortages of oil, only 125 German aircraft in northern France were operational by June 6. Rommel, who commanded Army Group B (composed of the Seventh and Fifteenth armies), was responsible for defense of the coast between the Pas de Calais and Cherbourg. As it happened, the invasion would fall on the front of the Seventh Army. Given the Allied command of the air, Rommel placed his faith in a German defense near the beaches and German retention of vital ports without which, the Germans assumed, a sustained invasion would be impossible. Unknown to the Germans, the Allies had constructed secret artificial harbors ("Mulberries") which, once an initial lodgment was made on the French coast, would be towed from England and anchored off the invasion beaches. Protected by artificial breakwaters, the Mulberries would enable large ships to unload in deep water, and their cargoes would be moved from ship to shore by either landing craft or pontoon causeways. Probably no technological invention involved in the invasion surprised the Germans more, or did more to undermine their basic strategy, than the Mulberries.

The invasion, launched early on June 6, 1944—the most important D-Day in World War II—was led off by three airborne divisions (two American and one British) and five amphibious divisions on a forty-mile front between Caen and the base of the Normandy (or Cotentin) peninsula. Including supply troops, the initial force came to 174,320 troops and 20,081 vehicles. The fiercest German resistance was offered at Omaha Beach, a landing site of American troops, but lodgments were made there as well as on Utah (American), Juno, Sword, and Gold (Anglo-Canadian). About 10,000 Allied casualties were suffered in the first twenty-four hours. The period of Allied build-up and expansion of the beachhead continued until late in July, but as early as July 1 a million men and 150,000 vehicles had been funneled into the beachhead. By then it was clear that the Mulberries, and Allied air attacks on German reserves streaming to the beachhead, had confounded the German strategy of throwing the invasion back into the sea.

Under these circumstances, Rundstedt recommended to Hitler that the battle in western France be broken off and the German armies withdrawn to the defenses of the West Wall on the Reich's western frontiers. Instead, Hitler relieved Rundstedt on July 3 and appointed Field Marshal Günther von Kluge as OB West. But Kluge soon discovered the situation was as bad as Rundstedt had described, and, as July wore on, a series of disasters overtook the Germans. On July 17, Rommel's staff car overturned after being strafed by a British fighter, and the field marshal was badly injured. Kluge had to add the command of Army Group B to his other duties as OB West. Then on July 20 occurred the Bomb Plot against Hitler's life in his East Prussian headquarters, one hatched by a group of officers and civilians who believed that Hitler was leading Germany to certain defeat. Hitler survived the blast with only minor injuries, and took savage reprisals against Colonel Claus von Stauffenberg and others suspected of being in the plot. But the German high command was shaken by the episode. And in the Normandy beachhead twenty-five Allied divisions were poised for a breakout.

On July 25, the American First Army attacked from the western end of the beachhead, while the Anglo-Canadian Second Army pressed forward to pin down German forces on the eastern end near Caen. The Americans broke through at St. Lô and by July 31 were beyond Avranches. As their numbers were swelled by more reinforcements, the Allies reorganized their commands. By August 1, Montgomery's Twenty-First Army Group was composed of the First Canadian Army (Henry Crerar) and the Second British Army (Dempsey), and a new U.S. Twelfth Army Group (Bradley) was composed of the U.S. First Army (Courtney Hodges) and the U.S. Third Army (Patton). Threatened with encirclement of his Seventh Army, Kluge urged Hitler to allow him to order a retreat before it was too late.

Instead, Hitler insisted on mounting an armored counterattack. Warned by Ultra of German intentions, Bradley's army group redeployed to meet the threat, and beat back the last German assaults on the night of August 7. The Americans then began to hammer the Germans back toward the Anglo-Canadian anvil at Caen, and on August 18 Patton's Third Army captured the town of Falaise, severing the last line of retreat for the German Seventh Army. By the end of the Battle of the Falaise Pocket—an Anglo-American *Kesselschlacht*—perhaps as many as 300,000 German troops had been killed or captured.

Meanwhile, Operation Anvil-Dragoon took place on August 15 when the U.S. 7th Army (Alexander Patch), composed of an American corps and two French corps, began landing on France's Mediterranean shores against weak opposition. General Walther Model relieved Kluge as OB West, and Hitler finally sanctioned a general withdrawal of German forces from western and southern France. As the battered German forces withdrew into eastern France and the Low Countries, a Free French division led the Allied armies into Paris on August 25. By then the city was already partially liberated by the French Forces of the Interior (FFI), an umbrella organization of different Resistance groups totaling perhaps 200,000 men and women throughout France. After Paris was liberated, General Charles de Gaulle organized a provisional government and set about mobilizing more French forces to join the Allied war effort.

D. The Final Battles and the Defeat of Nazi Germany, September 1944–May 1945. Though in early September 1944 Hitler reinstated Rundstedt as OB West, the situation on the Western Front looked desperate for the German cause. The German armies which had tried to hold western and southern France had been decimated in the fighting since June 1944, and the Allied armies seemed on the point of over-running the Low Countries, eastern France, and sweeping into the Rhineland. But certain factors were working in favor of the German side. Hitler gave priority to the West in the allocation of his reserves and new armaments; the supply lines to his armies were shortening; the defenses of the West Wall and even of the old French frontier fortifications could be put to good use in helping to contain the Allied advance; and the Mulberries, the artificial harbors used by the Allies to reduce their need for ports since D-Day, had about reached their limits. Supply for Eisenhower's armies was lagging, especially fuel, and bypassed German garrisons at the Channel ports either fought on or, as had been the case with Cherbourg in June, surrendered only after destroying the docking facilities in a way that would take months to repair. Montgomery's army group managed to capture the inland port of Antwerp largely intact as it advanced into Belgium in September, but German troops still controlled the banks and islands of the river Schelde, Ant-

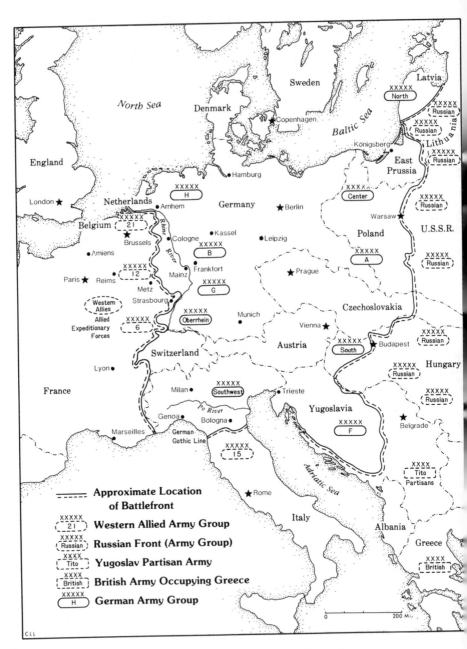

The European Battlefronts, December 15, 1944

werp's link to the sea. Thus, as German resistance began to stiffen in Holland and eastern France, the momentum of the Allied advance began to slow.

In late August, Montgomery convinced Eisenhower that his Twenty-First Army Group should receive temporary priority in fuel allocations so that it might complete the conquest of Belgium and the Netherlands, opening the possibility of an Allied thrust across the lower Rhine and thence into the north German plain. In mid-September, he launched Operation Market-Garden, an Anglo-American–Free Polish airborne effort to seize key bridges ahead of the British 30th Corps pushing overland across the watery eastern Netherlands. Though most of the airborne objectives were taken and held until the ground forces could link up with the airborne units, the British airborne effort at Arnhem miscarried. When 30th Corps could not reach Arnhem in time to prevent two panzer divisions from wiping out most of an airborne division, Montgomery's plan foundered. Eisenhower then rejected Montgomery's renewed proposal for a crossing of the lower Rhine and a "pencil-like thrust" across the north German plain to Berlin. He believed that he could not afford to restrict the fuel supplies of his other forces for what, after Arnhem, was a "long shot." Instead, and recognizing that Antwerp held the answer to the Allied supply problem, he ordered Montgomery's group to concentrate on protecting the northern flank of the Allied Expeditionary Force (AEF) and on opening the Schelde to the sea. Montgomery's forces finally cleared the length of the Schelde, but the first merchant ship bearing supplies for the Allied armies did not reach Antwerp until November 28. Even then, the port was the frequent target of V-1 and V-2 attacks.

The main burden of attacking the German frontier in October and November fell to the Allied Twelfth and Sixth Army groups, the latter created in part from the forces which had invaded southern France. Bradley's Twelfth Army Group—consisting of the U.S. Ninth, First, and Third armies from north to south—stretched from Aachen to a point south of Metz. General Jacob Devers's Sixth Army Group, consisting of the U.S. Seventh Army and the French First Army, carried the burden in southern Alsace-Lorraine as far as the neutral Swiss frontier. Though by November Eisenhower had 48 divisions on the continent, eight of them were stranded in western France for lack of transport. Accordingly, the front of Bradley's army group was stretched thin, particularly through the Ardennes, where only four U.S. divisions covered forty miles of front.

By December 1944 German intelligence had detected the American weakness in the Ardennes, and Hitler was eager to exploit it in what turned out to be his last major offensive of the war. Secretly the Germans massed 23 divisions and their last reserves of tanks and planes opposite the Ardennes in the first half of December. Though Ultra gave hints of a

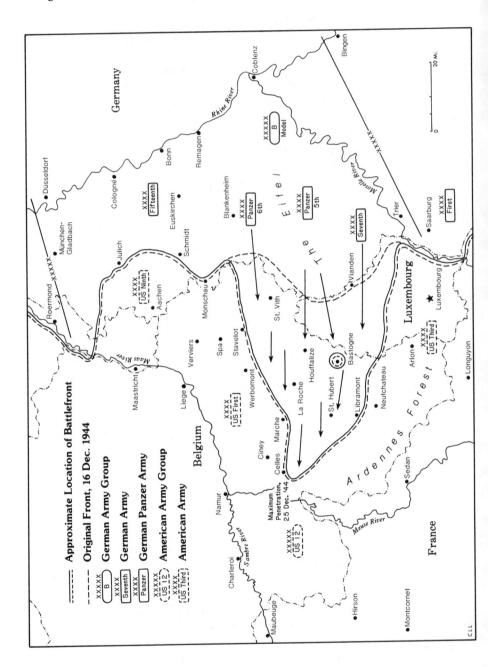

Approximate Location of Battlefront

Original Front, 16 Dec. 1944

German Army Group

German Army

German Panzer Army

American Army Group

American Army

possible German attack, Allied misreading of German intentions and the hindrance to aerial reconnaissance caused by bad weather allowed the German attack in the Ardennes to come as a surprise. Rundstedt launched his offensive on December 16 when ice, snow, and fog practically grounded the Allied air forces, and in short order the powerful German drive destroyed or drove back the four U.S. divisions. Eisenhower rushed two American airborne divisions by truck to occupy St. Vith and Bastogne—key road centers in the Ardennes—and those divisions, joined by elements of other divisions, kept both places out of enemy hands even after Bastogne was surrounded. The weather improved enough on December 23 that Allied air forces could go into action. After a fifty-mile advance, the German spearhead furthest west was stopped just short of Celle on the Meuse. The Allies then launched counterattacks on the "bulge" or salient in their lines, an Anglo-American effort from the north, and Patton's Third Army from the south. When the Second Battle of the Ardennes (or Battle of the Bulge) ended in late January 1945, Hitler had lost 300,000 troops, while Eisenhower's casualties came to perhaps 100,000 men.

Meanwhile, since D-Day in the West, the Red Army's operations in the East had removed Finland, Rumania, and Bulgaria from the war, and by early 1945 its forces had completed the occupation of Poland and were on the borders of the Reich. Hungary was under Russian attack by the time Roosevelt, Churchill, and Stalin held their last wartime conference in early February 1945, at Yalta in the Crimea. The Ardennes offensive, and the stubborn German defense even after its conclusion, had delayed the approach of the Western Allied armies to the Rhine. If the Germans could hold this formidable barrier for long against their attacks, the Red Army might well overrun most of Germany by war's end. Still, Stalin agreed at Yalta to a Western military presence in Berlin after the surrender, and to a Four-Power government (Britain, France, the United States, and the Soviet Union) over Germany after the war.

The unexpected American capture of the Ludendorff bridge intact at Remagen in early March 1945, compromised the German plan for an extended defense of the Rhine barrier, though it was late in the month before the Allied forces were across the river in great strength. A bare possibility then existed that the Anglo-American armies might share with the Russians the capture of Berlin. But Eisenhower was less concerned with Berlin than with a rumor that Hitler intended a final stand in a so-called National Redoubt prepared in the Bavarian Alps. (Actually, Hitler had no plans to leave Berlin, and there was no National Redoubt in Bavaria.) Eisenhower directed the Sixth and Twelfth army groups into central and southern Germany, while Montgomery's army group occupied the Ruhr and then wheeled north to pin the remaining German forces in the West in the peninsula of Jutland and against the North Sea. No Western forces were closer to Berlin than ninety miles before its fall.

On April 25, the U.S. First Army made contact with the Red Army at Torgau on the river Elbe, an event that severed Germany in half. By then Berlin was completely surrounded by Soviet forces, but the Soviet troops had to take the city in bitter fighting street-by-street. Hitler spent the final days of his life directing his capital's defense from his underground bunker behind the Reich Chancellery. Faced with defeat and capture, he committed suicide early on April 30. Before his death, his powers as Führer were transferred to Admiral Dönitz, Commander-in-Chief of the German navy since January 1943. From his headquarters on the Jutland peninsula, Dönitz served in his new post for only a week before he dispatched General Alfred Jodl, Chief of OKW Operations, to make an unconditional surrender at Eisenhower's headquarters at Rheims. Eisenhower accepted the surrender on behalf of the Allies early on May 8 (May 7 in the United States). At the time, he had under his command 4.5 million troops, 91 divisions (61 American), and 28,000 combat aircraft. A day later, Field Marshal Keitel ratified the surrender terms in occupied Berlin in the presence of Marshal Zhukov. Roosevelt having died of a cerebral hemorrhage on April 12, President Harry S Truman announced the coming of V-E Day from the White House.

III. The Pacific War, 1941–45

A. The Road to Pearl Harbor.   Tensions between Japan and the United States over the "China Incident" began to reach crisis proportions when France and the Netherlands fell before the German blitzkrieg in the spring of 1940 and Britain was forced to concentrate its forces at home and in the Middle East. The United States was left as the only major power that might check Japanese ambitions on British Burma and Malaya, French Indochina (Vietnam, Laos, and Cambodia), and the Dutch East Indies (Sumatra, Borneo, Java, and western New Guinea). This "Southern Resources Area," as the Japanese termed it, was rich in rice, rubber, tin, bauxite, and oil; in Japan's possession it could make the island-country self-sufficient in raw resources.

As early as May 1940, President Roosevelt ordered the United States Fleet (soon renamed the U.S. Pacific Fleet), then on maneuvers in waters off Hawaii, to remain indefinitely at its Pacific war station at Pearl Harbor instead of returning to its permanent base on the West Coast. But, despite the warning that the fleet's presence was intended to convey, in the summer of 1940 Japan sent troops into northern Indochina, and in September signed the Tripartite Treaty with Germany and Italy. Roosevelt countered

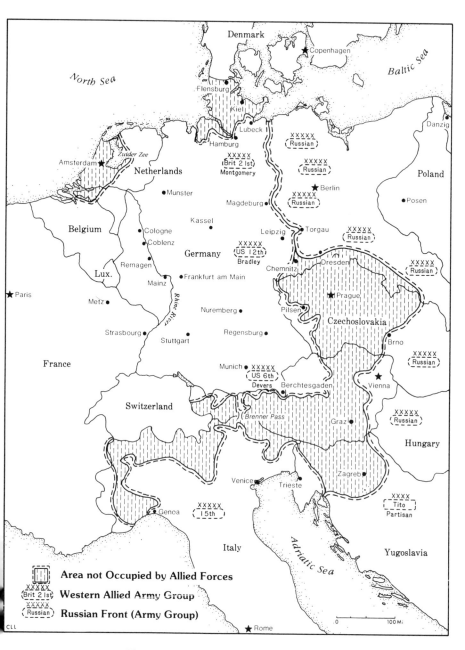

The European Battlefronts, May 7, 1945

by adding scrap iron and aviation gasoline to a growing list of forbidden exports to Japan, a measure which seemed to work when the Japanese made no further moves into Southeast Asia for the time being. Actually, Japan's councils were divided over what course to take. But in April 1941 Japan signed a nonaggression pact with Soviet Russia, securing Japan's rear in the event of war with the United States, and that summer Japanese forces occupied southern Indochina. (The French administration there was left intact as long as it cooperated with the Japanese, the only such Western colonial government to survive in Southeast Asia until nearly the end of the war in the Pacific.) Roosevelt retaliated by severing nearly all trade relations with Japan and imposing a total embargo on oil shipments. The oil embargo was especially damaging, for Japan normally imported 90 percent of its needs from the United States. When the British Middle Eastern and Dutch Far Eastern oil companies joined the embargo, Japan was left with an oil reserve that could last only eighteen months. The American price for resumption of oil shipments and other trade with Japan was stiff: total withdrawal of Japanese forces from Indochina and China.

While Japanese representatives in Washington tried to find a diplomatic compromise for the crisis in Japanese-American relations in the fall of 1941, Japan's cabinet, headed by General Hideki Tojo, made preparations for war. In a struggle that would hinge primarily on naval and air power, Japan would have the initial advantage. Admiral Isoroku Yamamoto's Combined Fleet numbered 10 battleships and battle cruisers, 6 large and 4 smaller carriers (basing a total of 750 planes), 36 cruisers, 113 destroyers, and 63 submarines. The U.S. Navy had 17 battleships and 6 aircraft carriers as major units, and it was undergoing further expansion, but about half of its battleships and carriers were with the Atlantic Fleet. The Pacific Fleet was assigned 9 old battleships and 3 aircraft carriers, but of these a battleship and a carrier were on the West Coast undergoing overhauls. The only other non-Japanese dreadnoughts in the Pacific were the British battleship *Prince of Wales* and the old battle cruiser *Repulse*, both at Singapore. The U.S. Navy had 24 cruisers, 80 destroyers, and 56 submarines in the Pacific, but the fleet at Pearl Harbor and Admiral Thomas Hart's Asiatic Fleet in the Philippines were separated by thousands of miles. A total of 11 cruisers, 20 destroyers, and 13 submarines of the British-Australian-Dutch navies were scattered about the Western and Southwestern Pacific.

The Naval Section of Imperial Headquarters originally planned to hold the main units of the Combined Fleet in reserve and to seize the Southern Resources Area, the American Philippines, Guam, and Wake Island with lesser naval forces. If the U.S. Pacific Fleet steamed into the Western Pacific in order to launch a counterattack, the Combined Fleet would sortie to destroy it. But this plan was based on the assumption that, at the outbreak of war, the fleet would be at its usual base near San Diego and beyond immediate striking range of the Japanese navy. When it became clear that the fleet was semi-permanently based at Pearl Harbor, 2,000 miles further west and within potential striking range, Admiral Yamamoto pressed for a change of contingency plans. In the event of a Pacific war, Yamamoto proposed to begin it with a surprise carrier-strike at Pearl Harbor. If the attack were successful, the U.S. Pacific Fleet would be destroyed or at least paralyzed for a long period, and Japanese forces would have little difficulty in overrunning the Western Pacific. When Yamamoto finally convinced the Naval Section that the attack on Pearl Harbor was both feasible and wise, Admiral Chuichi Nagumo's special carrier striking force, composed of 6 large carriers, 2 battleships, and several cruisers, destroyers and tankers, assembled at a secret base in the Kuriles and awaited orders to execute its mission.

On November 2, 1941, Tojo's cabinet received Emperor Hirohito's assent to war with the United States if the negotiations in Washington did not turn out successfully by the end of the month. Although the imperial decision was not mentioned in the radio cables sent to Japan's embassy in Washington, the tenor of those communications—read by the Americans through the code-breaking operation Magic—suggested that Japan would take military action against the United States before the end of the year. On November 24, General Marshall and Admiral Harold Stark, Chief of Naval Operations, sent their respective commands in the Pacific a war warning. Admiral Husband E. Kimmel, commander of the Pacific Fleet at Pearl Harbor, and General Walter Short, commander of U.S. Army forces in the Hawaiian Islands, believed that the initial Japanese attacks would fall on the Philippines, Guam, and Wake Island. Their measures of defense on Oahu, the island where Pearl Harbor is located, were restricted to preventing sabotage by the large Japanese resident population. When the Pacific Fleet returned from exercises at sea to Pearl Harbor on the first weekend of December, its battleships anchored together as usual in "Battleship Row" off Ford Island, without benefit of anti-torpedo nets, and many sailors were granted shore-leave. Air and sea patrols were carried out in the direction of the Japanese Marshalls and Carolines, but little attention was paid to the northern approaches to Oahu. The island's limited radar coverage was restricted to nighttime hours.

On November 26, Nagumo's carrier force left its base in the Kuriles under strict radio silence and set a course for Oahu by the unfrequented waters of the North Pacific. Just before dawn on December 7, 1941, after a voyage of 4,000 miles, Nagumo's force arrived at a point two hundred miles north of Oahu. Still undetected by the Americans, at first light the Japanese carriers—*Akagi, Kaga, Soryu, Hiryu, Shokaku,* and *Zuikaku*—

began launching the first of 360 planes in three waves. The first wave of planes arrived over Pearl Harbor about 8:00 a.m., and the last wave had completed its work and departed by 10:00 a.m. In just two hours, the raiders had sunk, beached, or capsized five American battleships and badly damaged three more. The attack also sank or damaged three cruisers, three destroyers, and lesser craft. Ashore, about two-thirds of the 300 Army and Navy planes on Oahu had been destroyed. A total of 3,500 American casualties had been suffered, two-thirds of them fatal. Nagumo's losses came to twenty-nine planes and fifty airmen, and, in addition, the Japanese lost a fleet submarine and five midget submarines sent on a separate sortie against Pearl Harbor.

As Yamomoto had hoped, the attack had so damaged the U.S. Pacific Fleet that it was unable to interfere seriously with the initial Japanese operations to seize the Southern Resources Area and the outlying Pacific territories necessary for Japanese defense. On the other hand, the Americans had been fortunate that none of the three carriers assigned to the U.S. Pacific Fleet were at Pearl Harbor on December 7. *Lexington* and *Enterprise* were still on their way to Pearl Harbor after ferrying planes to Midway and Wake Islands, and *Saratoga* was still on the West Coast. Indeed, Nagumo's uncertainty as to the whereabouts of the American carriers, once their absence from Pearl Harbor was reported, caused him to cancel plans for additional strikes at the fuel storage tanks and repair facilities at Pearl Harbor. Had the tanks and repair facilities been destroyed on December 7, the remains of the Pacific Fleet would have been withdrawn to the West Coast, and American communications to Australia and New Zealand might have been severed. Instead, the fleet remained based at Pearl Harbor, the base itself was repaired, and even the sunken battleships—save *Arizona*—were eventually raised, and, except *Oklahoma*, repaired and placed back in service.

B. *From Pearl Harbor to Midway, December 1941–June 1942.*   Pearl Harbor was not the only naval disaster to befall Japan's enemies in the first week of the Pacific War. On December 10, Japanese naval aircraft based on airfields around Saigon in Indochina attacked the British battleship *Prince of Wales* and the battle cruiser *Repulse* as they tried to break up Japanese landings in Malaya without benefit of air cover. Japanese bombs sent both ships to the bottom. Combined with the American losses at Pearl Harbor, Japanese air power had sunk or disabled more dreadnoughts in less than a week than had been lost to enemy action since the type first appeared early in the twentieth century. Clearly, a new pattern of naval war was emerging. The Imperial Navy also dealt swiftly with the remaining Allied naval power in the Far East. What was left by February 1942 was destroyed in the Battle of the Java Sea. In the same month, the Japanese captured Singapore—the most important Allied naval base west of Pearl Harbor. Though the Imperial Army committed only ten out of its fifty divisions to its Pacific and Southeast Asian drives, they seized Malaya, the Dutch East Indies, and Burma before the end of April. The great subcontinent of India was so seething with unrest in the wake of the Japanese victories that the British government hastily promised it post-war independence in order to gain Indian support against the Japanese.

Of the American possessions in the Far East and the Western Pacific, Guam fell almost at once, and the gallant Marine defense of Wake Island collapsed two days before Christmas, 1941. The only prolonged resistance encountered by the Japanese was in the Philippines. General Douglas MacArthur had been trying to make an "Asiatic Switzerland" out of the Philippines ever since his retirement from the U.S. Army in 1935 and subsequent appointment as Military Advisor to the Philippine Commonwealth in preparation for its independence in 1944. But in December 1941, his forces consisted of only 30,000 U.S. regular troops and the 100,000 half-trained and poorly armed troops of the Army of the Philippines. U.S. air strength in the Philippines consisted of 35 modern bombers and 107 fighters; half the bombers, caught on the ground, were destroyed on the first day of the war. After Japanese troops began to land on Luzon, the most northern and most important of the islands in the Philippines, MacArthur's forces began a fighting withdrawal to the peninsula of Bataan on the west side of Manila Bay. While they were still fighting there in March 1942, President Roosevelt ordered MacArthur to turn over his command to General Jonathan Wainwright and to proceed to Australia, where he assumed direction of the new Allied Southwest Pacific Command. Subsequently, the remains of Wainwright's command on Bataan retreated to the island of Corregidor for a final stand at the mouth of Manila Bay. Wainwright surrendered his forces on Corregidor and throughout the Philippines on May 7, 1942, six months to the day after Pearl Harbor.

Despite Japan's string of victories in the first months of the Pacific War, Imperial Headquarters had reason for concern. In April 1942, the American aircraft carriers *Enterprise* and *Hornet* made a daring sortie across the Pacific to within eight hundred miles of Japan's shores, *Enterprise* launching sixteen U.S. Army B-25 bombers under the command of Colonel James Doolittle against targets in Tokyo and other Japanese cities. Though the small force inflicted little damage, the episode raised Allied morale and was deeply embarrassing to Admiral Yamamoto.

A Japanese task force entered the Coral Sea in early May, intent on aiding in the capture of Port Moresby on New Guinea. It was surprised by the appearance of the U.S. carriers *Yorktown* and *Lexington,* sent to the Coral Sea after U.S. Navy code-breakers learned of Japanese intentions.

The Battle of the Coral Sea, on May 7–8, turned out to be the first sea battle ever carried out entirely through the air. American air strikes sank the small Japanese carrier *Shoho; Shokaku* was so damaged, and *Zuikaku* lost so many planes, that both large carriers were put of service for months. But Japanese air attacks so heavily damaged *Lexington* that it was finally abandoned and scuttled, and *Yorktown* suffered substantial damage. Still, the Japanese force withdrew from the Coral Sea, and, as the battered *Yorktown* limped back to Pearl Harbor for repairs, the Americans claimed their first significant—if qualified—naval victory of the war.

The carrier raid on the home islands in April and the outcome at Coral Sea confirmed Yamamoto in his belief that a decisive naval battle must be forced on the U.S. Pacific Fleet as soon as possible. His plan was to carry out a surprise occupation of the island of Midway, about a thousand miles from Pearl Harbor, then ambush the U.S. fleet when it rushed to launch a counterattack. The plan was sound in concept, but, unknown to Yamamoto, the same American code-breaking that had allowed Admiral Chester W. Nimitz, Kimmel's successor, to anticipate the Japanese sortie into the Coral Sea also forewarned him of the planned descent on Midway in early June. Accordingly, Nimitz ordered Admiral Raymond Spruance to prepare *Enterprise* and *Hornet* as the nucleus of one task force, and Admiral Frank Jack Fletcher to use the repaired *Yorktown* as the nucleus of a second, for a surprise of his own. These carrier forces would be located about three hundred miles north of Midway, where they might serve to ambush the approaching Japanese forces. Midway's garrison was also alerted and strengthened against the coming attack.

On June 4, Admiral Nagumo's carrier group, reduced to the carriers *Akagi, Kaga, Soryu,* and *Hiryu,* launched an air strike against Midway's defenses. While the recovered aircraft were being refueled and rearmed for a second attack against the island, a Japanese scout plane spotted the American carrier groups. Before the Japanese could rearm their planes with torpedoes and armor-piercing bombs, American planes swept down on the Japanese carriers. Japanese Zero fighters shot down Torpedo Squadron 8 to the last plane (only an ensign survived in the whole squadron), but American dive bombers soon turned *Akagi, Kaga,* and *Soryu* into flamming wrecks. An aerial strike from *Hiryu* severely damaged the already weakened *Yorktown,* and a Japanese submarine finished it off the next day, but more American air strikes sent *Hiryu* to the bottom. When the Americans withdrew their forces to the east to keep out of gun range of Yamamoto's battleships, the Battle of Midway was essentially over. On June 5, the Combined Fleet commenced a withdrawal to the Western Pacific, and the American fleet subsequently returned to Pearl Harbor. The Battle of Midway had cost the Japanese four large carriers, a cruiser, 322 planes, and 3,500 sailors and airmen. The Americans had lost a carrier, a destroyer, 150 planes, and 307 sailors and airmen. A few hundred American casualties had been suffered on Midway.

After the battles of the Coral Sea and Midway, the Japanese Combined Fleet did not risk another major action for two years. In the interval, it committed only detachments in support of the Japanese defense of key islands and in effect went over to the defensive in the Central Pacific. Still, in the South Pacific, the Japanese had hopes of capturing all of New Guinea and the Solomon Islands, stepping-stones to the New Hebrides and other island groups that might allow them to isolate Australia and New Zealand from American reinforcements. Accordingly, the safety of the British dominions in the South Pacific became the dominating factor in Allied strategy until 1943.

C. The Campaigns for Guadalcanal and Papua, August 1942– February 1943.   After the Japanese navy's reverse at the Battle of the Coral Sea, Japanese troops tried to cross the Owen Stanley Mountains in New Guinea to capture Port Moresby. Other Japanese forces moved to seize bases in the lower Solomons, with special attention given to building an airfield on Guadalcanal. But Anglo-American commanders in the South Pacific were taking their own measures. Admiral Robert L. Ghormley, then heading up a South Pacific Command to protect New Zealand, assembled General Alexander A. Vandegrift's First Marine Division in the New Hebrides and prepared to "cork up" the Solomons' "bottle" by an offensive into the islands. MacArthur's forces south of the Owen Stanley Mountains were preparing to hold their remaining position in Papua, the "tail" of bird-shaped New Guinea, at all costs. MacArthur had wanted to add the South Pacific Command to his Southwest Pacific Command, but on July 2, 1942, the Joint Chiefs in Washington decided that Ghormley and his command would remain subordinate to Admiral Nimitz, Commander-in-Chief, Pacific Fleet and the Pacific Ocean Area (the central and northern Pacific). Nimitz's headquarters remained at Pearl Harbor.

Operation Watchtower, the first American island-offensive of the war, began on August 7, 1942, when 20,000 U.S. Marines landed on Guadalcanal and the nearby island of Tulagi. Aside from construction workers, only 2,000 armed Japanese were on Guadalcanal, and they faded into the jungle. U.S. Naval Construction Battalions ("Seabees") set to work on the air strip, bringing it to completion on August 20. Named Henderson Field in honor of Major Lofton Henderson, a Marine aviator who had died at Midway, the air base soon hosted five Marine air squadrons. Admiral Fletcher covered the initial landings with the carriers *Saratoga, Wasp,* and *Enterprise,* but he soon left the scene to a force of American and Australian cruisers. On the night of August 9, a force of Japanese cruisers and destroyers from Rabaul—a base in the upper Solomons 600 miles from Guadalcanal—arrived under Admiral Gunichi Mikawa, surprising the Allied naval forces, and, in the Battle of Savo Island, sinking five of their cruisers and damaging the sixth. Mikawa's force might then have wrecked the Allied transports off Lunga Point, but it used the remaining hours of darkness to get beyond striking range of American planes and returned to Rabaul.

Mikawa's sortie from Rabaul down the "Slot"—the watery corridor between parallel strings of islands which formed the Solomons—was merely the first of many to come in the protracted Battle of Guadalcanal. The Japanese sorties aimed at damaging both Allied forces and landing reinforcements for the slowly growing Japanese garrison on the island. They came with such nighttime regularity that Marines referred to them collectively as the "Tokyo Express." As the naval fighting around the island intensified, Admiral William ("Bull") Halsey relieved the exhausted Ghormley of the South Pacific Command.

The Battle of Guadalcanal reached its climax in October–November, both ashore and afloat. On October 26, 29,000 Japanese troops launched an all-out effort to drive the Marines into the sea, and, after four terrible days of fighting, were defeated with difficulty. During November, the Marines were reinforced by 50,000 troops of the U.S. Army under General Alexander Patch, the only American general to command major forces in both the Pacific and European theaters of the war. At sea, Admiral Nobutake Kondo led the largest concentration of Japanese warships seen since Midway into the lower Solomons, but in a series of naval battles his force was compelled to retire to Rabaul at the end of November. By then the Naval Section of the Imperial Headquarters was ready to abandon Guadalcanal, but the Army Section—which had assembled 60,000 fresh troops at Rabaul—insisted that the effort go on. For another month, Japanese convoys continued to land troops on Guadalcanal at great cost. Finally, on January 4, 1943, Imperial Headquarters ordered the command at Rabaul to begin evacuating the forces left on the island. The last Japanese detachment left under cover of night on February 7, seven months to the day after U.S. Marines first landed at Lunga Point.

The battle for Guadalcanal cost both sides dearly. The Japanese army lost 23,000 of the 37,000 troops it committed to the island's defense, while the American forces suffered 5,800 casualties. The Japanese navy lost the small carrier *Ryujo*, the battleships *Hiei* and *Kirishima*, and numerous cruisers and destroyers. Both the small carrier *Zuiho* and the large carrier *Shokaku* were damaged. At sea, the Allies lost the American carriers *Wasp* and *Hornet*, while *Saratoga* and *Enterprise* were damaged. The new battleship *South Dakota* was damaged in one of the first battleship duels of the Pacific War, and the new battleship *North Carolina* was damaged by a tor-

USS *New Jersey*, 1943, firing broadside in World War II.
SOURCE: Peter Padfield, *The Battleship Era* (New York: David McKay, 1972).

pedo from a Japanese submarine. For a time, the new battleship *Washington* remained the only operational Allied dreadnought in the South Pacific. But Operation Watchtower had indeed "corked up" the "bottle" of the Solomons. In addition, even while the battle dragged on, American shipbuilding and aircrew and airplane replacement continued at a rate that the Japanese could not match. By 1943, the balance of power in the South Pacific had turned in favor of the Allies.

MacArthur's campaign for Papua in New Guinea was about as long and as grueling as the American campaign for Guadalcanal. American and Australian troops beat back the Japanese drive over the Owen Stanley Mountains, then seized the initiative to press the Japanese troops back on their base at Buna. But in his zeal to finish the enemy there, MacArthur ordered General Robert L. Eichelberger to use his 30,000 troops and three divisions to make a frontal attack against 12,000 Japanese troops in well-prepared positions. The Japanese fended off the attack while inflicting heavy losses. The Japanese navy also managed to evacuate all but 3,000 of their troops before their position at Buna became hopeless. Twice as many Allied troops died in the Papuan campaign as in the campaign for Guadalcanal, and the episode at Buna perhaps taught MacArthur the importance of bypassing enemy opposition wherever possible. In any case, he and other Allied commanders in the Pacific eventually raised the technique of "island-hopping" (i.e., leapfrogging strong enemy positions) to a fine art, and it established itself as a vital part of the pattern of the Pacific War.

   D. The Twin-Axis Strategy and the Drive to the Philippines to June 1944. Once the initiative in the South Pacific had passed to the Allies, MacArthur proposed to exploit it by a concentration of forces in his Southwest Pacific Command for a drive up the coast of northern New Guinea and then into the Philippines. If the Philippines could be seized, the Allies could sever Japan's lines of communication to the Southern Resources Area. Japan's economy, deprived of vital raw materials, would eventually collapse. MacArthur's plan relied heavily on Army troops and land-based aviation. In contrast, admirals Ernest J. King, since March 1942 Chief of Naval Operations, and Nimitz favored a strategy of severing Japan from the vital Southern Resources Area by means of a drive through the Central Pacific to either the Philippines or Taiwan, and relying primarily on operations by the U.S. Navy and Marine Corps. When the Joint Chiefs could not agree on which of the two plans to adopt, they passed the matter to President Roosevelt. Roosevelt finally decided that the United States had the resources to support both strategies simultaneously, though he made his decision more on grounds of preventing conflict among his top military and naval leaders than on strategic considerations. Still, the "Twin-Axis Strategy," as it came to be called, proved to be effective. It kept the Japanese guessing as to where the next American blow would fall, confusing their commanders and serving to keep their forces divided.

   But MacArthur was not mollified by Roosevelt's decision, and he was even less happy with the Joint Chiefs' decision that Admiral Halsey's South Pacific Command, established for a drive up the Solomons, would be kept separate from MacArthur's Southwest Pacific Command, poised for a parallel drive up the northern coast of New Guinea. Halsey remained subordinate to Admiral Nimitz at Pearl Harbor. In addition, Nimitz made it clear that when conflicts in timing and allocation of resources existed, he would give due weight to his belief that operations in the Central Pacific promised a more rapid advance toward Japan's lines of communications and were more likely to precipitate a decisive engagement with the Japanese Combined Fleet. Since Nimitz controlled the naval forces in the Pacific, he was in a good position to allocate or withhold naval and amphibious forces. Accordingly, "MacArthur's navy" (the Seventh Fleet and Seventh Amphibious Force under Admiral Thomas Kinkaid) was not entirely his to command, whereas Nimitz entrusted the Third Fleet and Third Amphibious Force to Admiral Halsey for operations in the Solomons, and gave Admiral Spruance command of

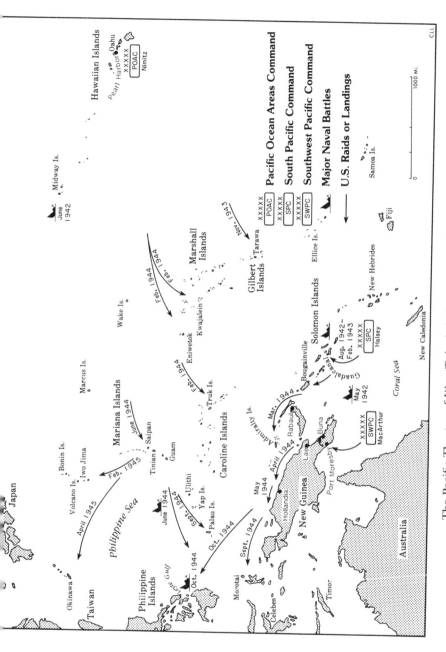

The Pacific Theater of War: Twin-Axis Strategy and Conversion on the Philippines

the Fifth Fleet and the Fifth Amphibious Force for the drive through the Central Pacific.

Despite MacArthur's problems with the Navy, by the spring of 1943 his forces were much stronger than during the Papuan campaign. In addition to support from the Seventh Fleet, his Southwest Pacific Command included four American and three Australian divisions, and two more American divisions were on the way. General George C. Kenney's Allied Air Force (formed around the U.S. Army Fifth Air Force) had a thousand land-based aircraft. Admiral Halsey's South Pacific Command had an initial strength of two Marine divisions, a New Zealand division, and several hundred Army-Navy aircraft. In addition, American carrier groups were assigned periodically to reinforce the South Pacific Command. In practice, and despite the fact that MacArthur's and Halsey's relationship was based on cooperation rather than command, their joint advance to isolate the main Japanese base at Rabaul was well coordinated. The Army's land-based airpower proved its worth when, in March 1943, Kenney's far-reaching aircraft surprised and sank a Japanese convoy in the Bismarck Sea on its way to land troops at Lae, New Guinea. An estimated 7,000 Japanese troops were drowned. Halsey's Air Command Solomons (Air-Sols) also proved its mettle after American code-breakers learned in April that Admiral Yamamoto was about to make an inspection tour of Japanese defenses on Bougainville. Army P-38 long-range fighters intercepted Yamamoto's plane over the island and shot it down. Neither Mineichi Koga, who succeeded Yamamoto as Commander-in-Chief of the Combined Fleet, nor any other Japanese admiral would prove to be as able as Yamamoto had been.

By the time Halsey's forces had "island-hopped" through the Solomons to reach Bougainville in November 1943, MacArthur's forces had parried a Japanese counteroffensive on New Guinea at Wau, outflanked Lae and Finschhafen, and placed themselves where they could invade New Britain, the location of Rabaul. Other landings by MacArthur's and Halsey's forces on Green, St. Matthias, and the Admiralty Islands in late 1943 and early in 1944 completed the encirclement of the Japanese naval base. Admiral Koga withdrew his fleet from Rabaul without a fight. The losing Japanese battle for the Solomons had cost 3,000 aircraft, while the battle on New Guinea had cost a thousand more. The Japanese army's aviation was becoming as decimated as that of the Japanese navy.

The American drive across the Central Pacific was delayed at its outset by the insistence of the Joint Chiefs of Staff that Attu and Kiska in the Aleutians, two of the islands in the chain extending southwest from Alaska, be recaptured from the Japanese, who had seized them in June 1942, as a diversion for the Midway operation. The Fifth Fleet's advance into the Central Pacific did not begin until November 1943, when American forces invaded the Gilbert Islands. Spruance's force boasted six large aircraft carriers, five light carriers, eight escort carriers, five new and seven old battleships, seventeen cruisers, fifty-six destroyers, twenty-nine troops transports, and hundreds of landing craft. The Fifth Amphibious Force, composed of both Marine and Army troops, was commanded by General Holland M. Smith, USMC. The Fleet Train, an innovation of the U.S. Navy, established a new pattern of naval warfare by accompanying the Fifth Fleet to serve as a mobile source of fuel, ammunition, and supply, and by setting up ship repair and maintenance facilities at advanced bases. Thanks to the Fleet Train, only the most seriously damaged American ships had to be sent back to Pearl Harbor or the West Coast.

In the American attack on the Gilberts, Spruance's forces met little opposition on the atolls of Makin and Abemama, but the story was very different when the Second Marine Division assaulted tiny Betio Island in Tarawa atoll. Some 3,000 Imperial Japanese marines manned positions well protected by concrete, log, and sand fortifications. The American sea and air bombardments of the island before the landing on November 20 had less effect than expected, and landing craft bearing 5,000 U.S. Marines became stuck on a coral reef a thousand yards from the beaches. When the Marines had to advance the rest of the way on foot through shallow water, hundreds of them were killed and wounded by the scathing Japanese fire. Two more bitter days of fighting were required to wipe out the Japanese resistance. All but a handful of the defenders either fought until killed or committed suicide rather than surrender. The U.S. Marines suffered 991 dead and 2,311 wounded.

Although Holland Smith called Tarawa a costly mistake, the lessons so painfully acquired there were usefully applied to the invasion of Kwajalein in the Marshall Islands on February 1, 1944. There the supporting fire was more carefully directed and the beaches were assaulted according to plan by 40,000 troops. In the outcome, only 372 Americans were killed and a few hundred more were wounded ashore, while nearly all Japanese casualties were fatalities, some 7,870 out of 8,675 defenders. The Fifth Fleet encountered such a weak Japanese air response that it was hardly touched. This American operation was rightly called an "almost perfect" amphibious assault; it demonstrated that proper doctrine and training could save lives as well as win battles.

In his fleet's movements through the Gilberts and the Marshalls, Admiral Spruance had hoped to provoke a decisive battle with the Combined Fleet. When in February 1944 the Combined Fleet was reported at Truk in the Carolines, Admiral Marc A. Mitscher's fast-carrier Task Force 58 struck in hopes of dealing a damaging blow to the major enemy fleet caught at anchor. Instead, the American pilots arrived to find that the Combined Fleet had retreated still further west in the Pacific, and they had to content themselves with sinking 200,000 tons of Japanese merchant shipping and two Japanese destroyers, and destroying 275 airplanes. But the Combined Fleet's retreat from Truk opened the way for the Americans to occupy Eniwetok, another stepping stone toward the Marianas and the Philippines beyond.

With the Japanese navy's abandonment of Rabaul and Truk, a new strategy debate ensued among American military and naval leaders over the issue of the final approach to the Philippines. President Roosevelt again settled the matter by approving a proposal by the Joint Chiefs that called for MacArthur's forces to continue up the northern coast of New Guinea, while Halsey's Third Fleet and amphibious forces in the Solomons would be shifted to the support of the Central Pacific drive. Henceforth, the Third and Fifth fleet headquarters would alternate in the planning and execution of operations with the same forces, still another innovation in the patterns of conduct of naval and amphibious operations.

The next goal of the Central Pacific drive was occupation of key islands in the Marianas, especially Saipan. When Spruance's Fifth Fleet moved against Saipan in mid-June 1944, it constituted the largest naval-amphibious force yet seen in the Pacific War: seven large carriers, eight light carriers, seven new battleships and seven old ones, twenty-nine cruisers, and sixty-nine destroyers. The carriers based a total of 956 aircraft. The entire force came to 535 ships of all kinds, the transports bearing 127,000 Marine and Army troops. Saipan, a mountainous island fourteen miles long and ten miles wide, was defended by 32,000 Japanese troops in well fortified positions. In addition, Admiral Soemu Toyoda, who had succeeded Koga as Commander-in-Chief of the Combined Fleet after the latter was lost at sea in March 1944, had adopted the A-Go Plan which provided for a novel use of Admiral Jisaburo Ozawa's Mobile Fleet (five battleships, three large carriers, six light carriers, and 460 planes).

The A-Go Plan called for Ozawa to keep his ships in the Philippine Sea beyond the reach of American carrier-based planes, while his planes would make attacks on Spruance's force, land on Saipan or Tinian for refueling, then fly back to the carriers for rearming and new strikes. But the plan was flawed in that Ozawa's flyers had only half as many flying hours on average as their American counterparts, and the Zero fighter was inferior to the new Navy F6F Hellcat. If caught in the air by American interceptors, the Japanese planes and pilots would be at a great disadvantage. Moreover, the American fleet boasted a vast array of antiaircraft batteries, the shells of some equipped with proximity or variable-time (V-T) fuses which multiplied the lethality of the antiaircraft gun. Those Japanese planes which penetrated the American fighter screen faced a veritable wall of flak.

The Battle of the Philippine Sea (June 19–20, 1944) commenced with a series of Japanese air attacks on Spruance's fleet off Saipan, but the Japanese naval strategy backfired. In the so-called Great Marianas Turkey Shoot, 315 Japanese planes were downed over an eight-hour period. At battle's end, the Japanese toll was 426 carrier planes and 445 naval airmen, plus the loss of another 50 land-based aircraft. Even worse for the Japanese, on June 19, Ozawa's carriers had blundered into a group of American submarines which promptly torpedoed and sank the new carrier *Taiho* and the veteran carrier *Shokaku*. On June 20, Spruance risked a long-range strike that resulted in the sinking of the carrier *Haiyo*, though 130 American planes had to ditch on the return flight when they ran out of fuel. Seventy-six of the pilots were rescued from the sea. Ozawa broke off action after the engagement on June 20 and retired his force from further fighting around Saipan. His Mobile Fleet still had carriers, but they were almost denuded of planes and pilots; in effect, the Battle of the Philippine Sea had about finished off Japan's naval aviation.

The land battle for Saipan was predictably bitter, the last Japanese resistance not being extinguished until July 10. Nearby Tinian and Guam, defended respectively by 9,000 and 18,000 troops, held out until nearly the end of July. Because of the large Japanese civilian population on Saipan, the final Japanese death toll reached 60,000. Many civilians, like the soldiers, preferred death to capture and committed suicide. The Japanese behavior reinforced the American belief that Japan would never come to terms until the home islands were either invaded or starved into submission. But the outcomes of the Battles of the Philippine Sea and Saipan finished Tojo as a war leader. His cabinet resigned on July 18, and the emperor appointed Admiral Mitsumasa Yonai as the new premier. Yonai received the doleful news that in addition to Japanese naval and military defeats, U.S. submarines were sinking Japanese merchant ships at such a rate that the supply of food and raw materials from overseas was dwindling. (During the war, U.S. submarines sank a total of 4 million tons of Japanese shipping.) But the Allied policy of "unconditional surrender" deterred Yonai from a direct approach to the American government. No cabinet could entertain a peace that threatened the safety of the semi-divine emperor.

E. The Philippines, Iwo Jima, and Okinawa, October 1944–June 1945. As the fighting for the Marianas was coming to a close in July 1944, admirals King and Nimitz proposed to the Joint Chiefs that the American forces bypass the Philippines, where there were very large Japanese forces, and seek to capture Taiwan instead. From Taiwan, American land, sea, and air forces could easily sever Japanese communications to the Southern Resources Area, and a Taiwan strategy would spare the Filipino people the ordeal of a long and bloody campaign of liberation. MacArthur fiercely opposed the proposal, arguing that he had made a personal pledge that American forces would return to the Philippines at the earliest possible moment, that American prisoners-of-war in the islands should be liberated as soon as possible, and that only in the Philippines would the Americans find indigenous support. When the Joint Chiefs referred the matter to Roosevelt, he decided in favor of MacArthur's arguments, and the Philippines once more became the focal point of the Pacific offensives.

In order to get forces into position for an invasion of the southern Philippines, MacArthur's command seized Morotai, an island just north of the "head" of the New Guinea "bird," in September 1944. Nimitz's forces invaded the Palaus and occupied Peleliu. While the capture of Morotai was relatively easy, the 10,000 Japanese troops on Peleliu put up ferocious resistance. A total of 2,000 Americans were killed and 10,000 were wounded, nearly 40 percent of the attacking force, and the highest combat casualty rate of any amphibious assault in American history. But the unopposed capture of nearby Ulithi provided the U.S. Navy an excellent anchorage, and every subsequent operation of the Central Pacific forces was launched in part from that base.

Meanwhile, American air strikes into the southern Philippines revealed that the southern islands were nearly empty of Japanese planes. MacArthur suggested, therefore, that his forces and those of the Central Pacific command should join in a daring landing on the island of Leyte in the east-central Philippines, making it a stepping stone to the key island of Luzon. When the Joint Chiefs accepted the proposal and advanced the date of the invasion of the Philippines by two months to October 20, 1944, the scene was set for the biggest amphibious assault of the Pacific War and the greatest naval battle in history.

The scale of the American operation against Leyte set new standards in the Pacific War. General Walter Krueger's Sixth Army numbered nearly 200,000 troops, 60,000 of whom were put ashore on the first day of the operation. They were supported by Admiral Kinkaid's Seventh Fleet, consisting of six old battleships under Admiral Jesse Oldendorff, and numerous light carriers, escort carriers, cruisers, destroyers, and patrol-torpedo (PT) boats. Admiral Halsey's Third Fleet assumed responsibility for maintaining general command of the air and sea should the Japanese Combined Fleet make an appearance. The most powerful component of the Third Fleet was Admiral Mitscher's Task Force 38 (TF-38), composed of eight large carriers, eight light carriers, seven new battleships, twelve cruisers, fifty-four destroyers, and over a thousand aircraft.

Within an hour of receiving the news that American forces had landed on Leyte, Imperial Headquarters ordered execution of the Sho-1 Plan. Ozawa's Mobile Fleet (four carriers but only ninety planes) was to serve as a decoy north of the Philippines in order to lure Halsey's forces away from the vicinity of Leyte. Admiral Takeo Kurita's First Striking Force (composed of the super battleships *Yamato* and *Musashi*, three other battleships, twelve cruisers, and fifteen destroyers) was to steam from Brunei Bay, Borneo, through the San Bernardino Strait in the Philippines, and finally descend from the north on the landing beaches at Leyte. Admiral Shoji Nishimura's Second Striking Force (two battleships, a cruiser, and four destroyers) would leave Brunei Bay and head for Surigao Strait in the Philippines, finally approaching the invasion beaches from the south. A third force, composed of three cruisers and four destroyers under Admiral Kiyohide Shima, based in the Pescadores near Taiwan, would follow.

The series of widely scattered naval actions between October 23 and October 26, 1944, are collectively known as the Battle of Leyte Gulf or the Second Battle of the Philippine Sea. The action commenced when, on October 23, American submarines spotted Kurita's force in the South China Sea, sank two Japanese cruisers with torpedoes, and so damaged a third that two destroyers were detailed to escort it back to Brunei Bay. Kurita and the rest of his force continued toward San Bernardino Strait. On October 24, American planes spotted Ozawa's Mobile Fleet north of the Philippines, and Nishimura's force was detected heading for Surigao Strait. Halsey's TF-38 launched air attacks on Kurita's force as it passed through San Bernardino Strait on the afternoon of October 24, the American planes sinking the super battleship *Musashi* with hits from nineteen torpedoes and many bombs. When Kurita's fleet reversed course and appeared to be withdrawing from the campaign, Halsey set a nighttime course to intercept Ozawa's carriers the next morning. Halsey was unaware that as his force traveled north, Kurita's force had reversed course again and was making a nighttime passage through San Bernardino Strait. Meanwhile, the naval forces protecting the landing beaches at Leyte were further denuded of support when Admiral Kinkaid sent Oldendorff's force of battleships and nearly all the rest of his heavy fighting units to intercept the Nishimura-Shima force at Surigao Strait.

October 25 proved to be the decisive day for the outcome at sea. Early that morning, Oldendorff's forces "crossed the T" of the Japanese force in Surigao Strait, and the fire from the battleships and waves of torpedoes from American destroyers and PT boats nearly tore the Japanese column apart. Of Nishimura's original force, only a destroyer survived. After a brush with the same American force, Shima's force turned back. But later that morning, Kurita's force completed its passage through San Bernardino Strait and rapidly approached the landing site at Leyte, the super battleship *Yamato* in the lead. As the huge collection of American shipping in Leyte Gulf frantically sought safety in flight, Kurita's force seemed on the verge of a great victory. Only a small force of escort carriers, destroyers, and destroyer-escorts fought heroically to delay the Japanese advance.

Then, at 9:00 a.m., when Kurita's force was still off the coast of Samar and twenty-eight miles from the landing site, it inexplicably reversed course and began a withdrawal to the north. It eventually negotiated the San Bernardino Strait, though Halsey's TF-38, racing south after destroying Ozawa's four carriers, got within air striking range of Kurita's force as it was crossing the Sibuyan Sea on October 26. Its planes sank two of Kurita's cruisers, but the climax of the battle had already passed.

The Battle of Leyte Gulf is the largest naval action in history to date, involving even more ships and tonnage than the Battle of Jutland. And, whereas Jutland was largely a tactical draw (though a strategic victory for the British), the outcome at Leyte Gulf was one of the most one-sided in naval annals. The Japanese navy lost three battleships (including one of the two largest in the world), four carriers, ten cruisers, and nine destroyers, for a total of 306,000 tons and 5,000 men. Numerous other vessels had been damaged. American naval losses came to one light carrier, two escort carriers, two destroyers, and a destroyer-escort, or 37,000 tons and 500 men. A number of other American vessels were damaged. The outcome of the battle finished the career of the Japanese Combined Fleet in World War II.

Even before the Battle of Leyte Gulf was over, the Japanese had resorted to new and unprecedented measures that promised heavy American losses. The first *Kamikaze* ("Divine Wind") attacks of the war fell on vessels in Leyte Gulf on October 24, and by the end of the day of October 25, additional raids had accounted for an escort carrier and damage to three additional escort carriers. The *Kamikaze* or Special Attack Corps was organized by Admiral Takijiro Onishi, commander of the First Air Fleet in the Philippines. The Corps sought volunteers willing to fly bomb-laden aircraft directly into American ships in order to insure hits. The *Kamikaze* craze soon spread to other Japanese commands, and became a standard air measure as the war went on. Yet the new tactic did not save Leyte. Though General Tomoyuki Yamashita managed to get 70,000 troops into Leyte during the fighting, the Americans declared the island secure on Christmas Day, 1944. The Japanese death count on Leyte came to 68,000 men, and another 10,000 troops were lost to drowning when their convoys trying to reach Leyte were bombed. American casualties on Leyte, ashore and afloat, came to 15,500 men.

It was Luzon's turn when Krueger's Sixth Army invaded the island in January 1945. While supporting the invasion, the Seventh Fleet was hit by waves of *Kamikazes*. Numerous American ships, most of them small, were sunk or damaged. On the night of January 9, Halsey's Third Fleet passed though Luzon Strait in order to ravage Japanese shipping on the South China Sea, and over subsequent days its carrier planes ranged as far south as Camranh Bay in French Indochina. Combined with U.S. submarine operations in the area, Halsey's foray completed the severing of the Japanese sea lanes between the home islands and the Southern Resources Area. In late January, Halsey's fleet returned to the anchorage at Ulithi, Halsey turned over command to Admiral Spruance, and the Third Fleet became the Fifth Fleet again.

On Luzon, the battle spread to Manila which was nearly demolished in a street-by-street battle until Japanese resistance collapsed in March. Yamashita and his remaining troops had already retired to the hills and mountains of northern Luzon, where they continued to resist until Japan surrendered in August 1945; only then did Yamashita order his remaining 40,000 men, out of the 170,000 troops he originally commanded, to lay down their arms. By July 1, when the U.S. Sixth Army handed over to Eichelberger's Eighth Army for the final mopping-up on Luzon, the Sixth had suffered 8,140 men killed and nearly 30,000 wounded or missing. Many thousands of Filipinos also died in the fighting on Luzon.

While the battle for the Philippines was in its early stages, the Americans completed work on a giant air base on Tinian in the Marianas, and other air bases were under construction on Saipan and Guam. From these bases the Army Air Forces (AAF) planned to launch a strategic bombing offensive against the Japanese home islands with the B-29 Superfortress, the largest four-engined bomber to be built in large numbers during World War II. The B-29's great range would enable it to reach many targets in Japan, about 1,700 miles from the Marianas, and return to base. The B-29s in the Marianas were concentrated in the Twenty-First Bomber Command, commanded by General Haywood S. Hansell, Jr. The first B-29 arrived in the Marianas on October 12, and the first B-29 raid from the Marianas over Japan—111 B-29s against Tokyo—was conducted on November 24. These raids, however, which used high explosive bombs dropped from a high level, proved to be less effective than expected, and in January 1945 General Curtis LeMay replaced Hansell as head of the Twenty-First Bomber Command.

By February 1945 LeMay's command boasted over three hundred B-29s, each capable of carrying eight tons of bombs or incendiaries as far as southern Japan. On March 9, 279 B-29s took off from airfields on Tinian and Saipan, and, in a low-level incendiary attack designed by LeMay, set off a firestorm in Tokyo that destroyed sixteen square miles of the city, including 267,000 buildings, while 83,000 people were dead and 41 injured. LeMay's raid was possibly the single most destructive air raid in World War II. Other B-29 low-level incendiary attacks that spring devastated Osaka, Kobe, and Nagoya. By summer, eight million Japanese had fled their cities, and the Japanese production of oil, aircraft, and shipping had plunged.

But the strategic bombing of Japan was at a price. Many damaged B-29s were failing to make the long return flight back to the Marianas, and early in 1945 the Joint Chiefs ordered a suitable island seized in the Volcano-Bonin group for an emergency landing strip and as a base for escort fighters. The choice fell on Iwo Jima. The U.S. Fifth Fleet and three Marine divisions set out for their objective in February, and, after the island had been heavily bombarded, the Marines landed on February 19. But instead of the quick, five-day operation expected, the seizure of Iwo required nearly a month, as 60,000 U.S. Marines battled 21,000 entrenched Japanese troops. In addition to bitter resistance on the island, waves of *Kamikaze* attacks from the Japanese home island imperiled the supporting American naval forces. When the battle finally ended, only 200 Japanese soldiers had been taken alive. Ashore and afloat, the Americans had suffered 24,891 casualties, 6,821 of them fatal. The carrier *Saratoga*, namesake of the original sunk earlier in the war, was so badly damaged that it had to be withdrawn from service for the duration of the war. Still, the airfield on Iwo eventually saved many American lives and planes; from March to August 1945, about 2,400 B-29s, bearing 25,000 aircrewmen, made emergency landings on the island.

Despite the bombing and blockade of Japan, American planners expected that a full-fledged invasion of the home islands would be necessary to end the war. For a staging base, they chose Okinawa, one of the Ryukyu Islands, sixty miles long and averaging eighteen miles in width. The island was defended by 97,000 Japanese troops under General Mitsuro Ushijima, and was within range of 2,000 Japanese planes in Japan and Taiwan. The mission of capturing Okinawa was given to General Simon Buckner's Tenth Army, composed of four Army and three Marine divisions, and totaling 285,000 troops. But in the softening-up attack by the Fifth Fleet between March 18 and March 21, 1945, Admiral Mitscher's TF-38 suffered heavy damage to the second *Wasp*, the second *Yorktown*, and the carrier *Franklin*. Fortunately for the Americans, the British Pacific Fleet (two battleships, four carriers, six cruisers, and fifteen destroyers) under Admiral Sir Bruce Fraser had arrived in time to take part. The main landings began on April 1, but resistance intensified inland beginning on April 4. Between April 6 and April 7, 700 Japanese aircraft, half of them *Kamikazes*, raided the Allied fleet off Okinawa. Thirty-four Allied naval craft were sunk, though none larger than a destroyer, and 368 other vessels were damaged. Among the more severely damaged ships were four American and three British large carriers, ten battleships, thirteen light and escort carriers, five cruisers, and sixty-seven destroyers. On April 7, 280 of Mitscher's planes sank the giant battleship *Yamato* when it sortied from Japan to help repel the invasion of Okinawa. Ashore, the battle for the island dragged on for three months. At its close only 7,400 of Ushijima's soldiers were taken alive, and at least 10,000 Japanese civilians on the island had died. The Allies suffered 49,000 casualties, 12,500 of them fatalities.

F. The Atomic Bomb, Russian Intervention, and the End of the Pacific War, August–September 1945. As the battle for Okinawa was ending, American staff planners were working on Operation Olympic (the invasion of Kyushu), a part of the larger plan for the invasion of the Japanese home islands (Operation Downfall). The planners came to some grim conclusions. Assuming the invasion of the home islands could be launched in the late summer or fall of 1945, they believed the battle might not be concluded before 1947 and might inflict a million American casualties. Without an invasion, the United States might starve or batter Japan into eventual submission through blockade or conventional bombing, but such measures would take some time to be effective. In contrast, and in fulfillment of Stalin's pledges made at the Yalta Conference in February, the Red Army was poised to enter the war against Japan, and was sure to overrun Manchuria and Korea. Once Manchuria and Korea were in Stalin's hands, the Anglo-American allies might be cheated of much say in the fate of Japan's empire on the mainland of northern Asia.

Unknown to the Americans planning for the invasion of Japan, the highly secret Manhattan Project, launched in early 1942, was about to reach fruition, and thereby offered the possibility of ending the war in the Pacific at a stroke. On July 16, 1945, a nuclear test-device (Trinity) was exploded in the deserts of New Mexico near Alamogordo. The news was flashed to President Truman, then attending the Potsdam Conference in Germany with Stalin and Churchill. While American scientists prepared two atomic bombs for use against Japan, on July 26 the Allies demanded again through the Potsdam Declaration that Japan surrender uncondi-tionally. Though the Japanese cabinet had been reshuffled several times since Tojo's resignation, no Japanese government could submit to such terms and survive. When Japan made no direct response to the Potsdam Declaration, Truman believed that he had no choice but to use atomic bombs in hopes of ending the war quickly and saving the lives of thou-sands of American servicemen. He was unaware that the Japanese govern-ment did not understand that the formula of unconditional surrender applied only to the Japanese armed forces.

The components for the two atomic bombs were sent to Tinian, partly by air and partly by sea, the latter components aboard the cruiser *Indian-apolis* (sunk by a Japanese submarine on its return voyage, with a great loss of life). The bombs were placed at the disposal of a specially trained squadron of B-29s commanded by Colonel Paul W. Tibbets, Jr. The city of Hiroshima was chosen as a target because it was both a military head-quarters and an industrial center. Tibbets himself piloted the B-29 *Enola*

Gay (named after his mother) when it took off from Tinian on August 6, 1945, and headed for Japan. The bomb, of a type called "Little Boy" and utilizing uranium, was dropped at 8:15 a.m., and detonated 2,000 feet above the city's center. The resulting blast—announced soon after as being the equivalent to that from 20,000 tons of TNT—and heat (temperatures hotter than the surface of the sun) killed an estimated 70,000 Japanese immediately and destroyed five square miles of the city. Injuries from flying debris, burns, and deadly radiation killed at least as many more over the next few weeks and months. Large numbers of survivors lived shortened lives from the bomb's effects.

Japan had hardly recovered from the shock of the news of the annihilation of Hiroshima when, on August 8, Soviet Russia declared war and troops of the Red Army began invading Manchuria, Korea, and southern Sakhalin Island. On August 9, a second atomic bomb, called "Fat Man" and utilizing plutonium, was exploded over Nagasaki. This weapon killed at least 45,000 people outright, and perhaps as many more perished from its effects eventually. Stunned by the mass slaughter from the air and by Soviet intervention, the Japanese cabinet received the emperor's assent to an armistice on almost any terms. The Japanese government was relieved to learn not only that the emperor's personal safety was assured, but that he might remain on his throne as a figurehead monarch. General MacArthur would head up the Supreme Command, Allied Powers (SCAP), which would rule Japan after the surrender. A general armistice was declared in the Pacific on August 14 (V-J Day), and, on September 2, a formal Japanese surrender to delegations from the Allied powers was conducted by MacArthur in Tokyo Bay on the decks of the U.S. battleship *Missouri*. Meanwhile, Washington and Moscow had agreed that Korea would be temporarily divided at the 38th parallel into Soviet and American zones of occupation. General Chiang Kai-shek's armies returned to northern China in the aftermath of the Japanese surrender, but the fate of Soviet-occupied Manchuria remained in doubt. Mao Tse-tung's Communist armies found there a new base for their war against Chiang.

The Pacific War cost the lives of 750,000 Japanese servicemen, to which number must be added 500,000 more Japanese troops who died on the Asian mainland after December 1941. Perhaps 750,000 Japanese civilians died in the home islands and on other islands in the Pacific. Approximately 350,000 American servicemen were casualties in the Pacific War and the war for East Asia, the latter fought in China and Southeast Asia between 1941 and 1945 (see next section). By any standard, the Pacific War had been an ordeal as terrible as the one in Europe.

G. The China-Burma-India Theater and the Close of the War for East Asia.   The China-Burma-India (CBI) theater was more closely connected with the Sino-Japanese War in East Asia than with the Pacific

War. Still, American policy-makers placed a high priority on assisting the British to hold India and on supporting Nationalist China in its war against Japan. In the spring of 1942, the Japanese invasion of Burma cut the Burma Road by which the British had sent supplies to the land-locked Nationalist government at Chungking, and until Burma could be recovered, the Americans undertook to fly the "Hump" of the Himalayas to keep the Chinese armies supplied. Chiang Kai-shek accepted U.S. General Joseph ("Vinegar Joe") Stilwell, an old "China Hand," as his chief-of-staff, and General Claire Chennault's American Volunteer Group (better known as the Flying Tigers) was expanded eventually into the Fourteenth Air Force.

Nationalist China proved to be a weak reed, primarily because of corruption in Chiang's bureaucracy. Stilwell, as tactless as he was honest, refused to turn a blind eye to Chiang's deficiencies. Under Wavell, the British in India were more interested in recovering their former colonies of Burma and Malaya than assisting Chiang. Often working at cross purposes, the Allies in the CBI had achieved little to the fall of 1943 except to train some Chinese and Indian divisions, and to carry out raids into Burma with Ord Wingate's Chindits (Long-Range Penetration Groups).

Matters began to improve in the CBI for the Allies in November 1943, when the Anglo-American Southeast Asia Command (SEAC) was formed under British admiral Louis Mountbatten, with Stilwell serving as his deputy. In India, the U.S. Tenth Air Force and RAF wings were combined into the Eastern Air Command (EAC) under U.S. General George E. Stratemeyer. Plans were laid to establish a Twentieth Bomber Command in China composed of B-29s, the command to begin a strategic bombing campaign against the Japanese home islands. In early 1944, Stilwell's Chinese armies and Mountbatten's Anglo-Indian armies began separate but coordinated offensives into Burma. The Chinese performance was disappointing, but, under the command of British general Sir William Slim, the Anglo-Indian armies inflicted heavy losses on the Japanese Fifteenth Army and recovered northwest Burma as far as Imphal. The major American achievement of 1944 in the CBI was a strike at Myitkyina by General Frank D. Merrill's 5307th Composite Unit ("Merrill's Marauders"). Once a pipeline was built from Ledo to Myitkyina, the air ferry into China could avoid the formidable "Hump." In China, however, the Japanese offensives in April–May 1944 took the airfields that the Americans were counting on to base their B-29s, and American interest in a strategic bombing campaign from China against Japan withered. Friction between Stilwell and Chiang reached the point in October 1944, that Roosevelt recalled Stilwell and replaced him with General Albert C. Wedemeyer. The old CBI theater was divided; thereafter Mountbatten's SEAC concentrated on operations in Burma.

Burma turned out to be the principal area of Allied success in Southeast

Asia in 1945. Much of the credit belongs to Slim, a great if under-celebrated commander in World War II. His Fourteenth Army outfought and outmaneuvered a tenacious Japanese enemy in some of the most difficult jungle terrain in the world. For weeks on end, Slim's troops had to depend almost entirely on supply from the air. After neutralizing the enemy's forces at Mandalay, Slim's forces entered Rangoon on May 3, effectively ending the campaign for southern Burma. In northern Burma, mixed American, British, and Chinese forces finally opened the Ledo Road to China, and the first truck convoy reached Kunming in February 1945. Mountbatten's plans for invading Malaya in the late summer of 1945 were superfluous after Japan's surrender in August.

IV. World War II and the Patterns of War

The patterns of war in a global conflict like World War II were necessarily diverse. The importance of machine warfare, mass production, and scientific development and application are so self-evident that they hardly require comment. Less obvious, but of as great importance to the trends of war, was the emergence of combined operations which increasingly erased the dividing lines among land, sea, and air forces. Especially among the Anglo-American forces, interservice doctrine and leadership became crucial to success. Combined operations implied close cooperation among Allied forces as well, and the Anglo-American Combined Chiefs-of-Staff was as unprecedented as it was necessary. The forthright debate within its councils over strategy and measures not only helped to point the way to final victory, it managed to do so with a remarkable economy of force, considering the scale of the challenge. And perhaps equally striking was the effectiveness of amphibious operations so soon after an earlier world war in which the very future of amphibious assault seemed in doubt.

Soviet Russia put an estimated 20 million people into uniform at one time or another during the war, and as many as 12,500,000 at one time near its end. Perhaps a peak strength of 11 million was reached in the Soviet ground forces. About 16 million American men and women served in uniform at various times during the war, with 12,100,000 being the American peak strength. Of this number, 6,100,000 were in the Army Ground Forces, 2,400,000 in the Army Air Forces, 3,000,000 in the Navy, and 600,000 in the Marine Corps. The British empire and its self-governing dominions mobilized 8,700,000, France 3,000,000, Germany 11,000,000, Japan 6,100,000, and Italy 3,000,000. Of all the major belligerents, Soviet Russia was hardest hit in terms of casualties, suffering an estimated 22,000,000 dead, of whom 7,500,000 were in the Soviet armed forces. China was the next hardest hit, with 13,500,000 military-civilian deaths. Britain suffered 485,000 military deaths and 100,000 civilian deaths, a total considerably under its losses in World War I. France, with 250,000 military fatalities and 360,000 civilian dead, suffered slightly more than half as many deaths as in the First World War. The United States suffered 850,000 casualties, 400,000 of them fatal, but relatively few of them civilian. Among the Axis Powers, Germany sustained 3,500,000 military deaths and 3,810,000 civilian deaths, far in excess of its fatalities in World War I. Japan suffered over a million military dead and 750,000 civilian deaths, while Italy had 330,000 military fatalities and 85,000 civilian dead. When the deaths in other countries are added, perhaps as many as 55 million people perished during World War II.

The outcome of World War II completely upset the traditional balance of power not only in Europe—long the focal point of world power—but all over the globe. While German, Japanese, and Italian power had been wholly eliminated, neither Britain nor France could recover their former importance. Soviet Russia emerged as the great Euro-Asian power, only offset for the foreseeable future by the power of the United States of America. The European empires in Asia, and ultimately in Africa, had been dealt a mortal blow from which they would never recover, as nationalism became rampant in their former colonies. And finally, the advent of nuclear weapons cast an ominous shadow over the peace achieved in 1945. Even in 1945 it was clear that the future world order would depend largely on the relationship between the United States and the Soviet Union, allies in World War II only by circumstance and with fundamentally different ideological and foreign policy goals.

7

The Patterns of the Cold War, 1945–89, and Their Aftermath

The patterns of war after World War II emerged against a background of several historic developments. The first was the continuing technological revolution in the twentieth century, especially as regards nuclear explosives, their carriers, precision-guided munitions of all kinds, and electronics. The second was four decades of Cold War between the United States of America and the Union of Soviet Socialist Republics, a rivalry compounded by the tendency of many countries to align themselves with one or the other of the two "superpowers" in opposing blocs. The third was the breakup of Western overseas empires in Asia and Africa, producing a myriad of successor states which oriented themselves to the West, the Communist bloc, or the so-called Third World of non-aligned countries. And finally, the United Nations, beset with Cold War rivalries and an explosion of national sovereignties across the globe, met with only limited success in its peace-keeping mission in the first decades of its existence. War became all too common in the turbulent world after 1945.

I. The Early Cold War, 1945–50

The Cold War began in Europe with quarrels between Soviet Russia and its former Western allies over a peace treaty with Germany and the Soviet imposition of Communist governments in countries overrun by the Red Army during the course of World War II. Britain, France, and the United States protested Joseph Stalin's arbitrary changes of the frontiers in Eastern Europe to Soviet advantage and without reference to the West. The Western powers were especially angered by Soviet treatment of Poland, for whose independence Britain and France had gone to war in 1939. Tensions were further heightened by the outbreak of a Communist-inspired civil war in Greece even before the end of World War II, followed by the internal Communist overthrow of the democratic government in Czechoslovakia in March 1948. When Stalin imposed a land blockade of the Western sectors of occupied Berlin in May 1948, the governments of Western Europe and North America concluded that Stalin was intent on dominating Europe and capable of using the Red Army—at the time, 175 mobilizable divisions and the largest military force in the world—as a tool of Soviet aggression.

While an Anglo-American Berlin Airlift supplied the garrisons and people of West Berlin for a year, and the Marshall Plan (announced in 1947) aided in Western Europe's economic recovery, the West European and North American governments began to take measures for their common defense. In April 1949, the representatives of twelve nations—the United States, Canada, Britain, France, Italy, Portugal, Belgium, the Netherlands, Luxembourg, Denmark, Norway, and Iceland—met in Washington, D.C., to sign the North Atlantic Treaty. The treaty created the North Atlantic Treaty Organization (NATO), a NATO Council, and a NATO Defense Committee. The members of the pact pledged that in time of peace they would undertake measures of collective defense, and in time of war they would treat an attack on any of their number as an attack upon all. After Stalin lifted the Berlin Blockade in May 1949, the United States, Britain, and France merged their occupation zones in Germany into the Federal Republic of (West) Germany, with a capital at Bonn in the German Rhineland. The FRG was placed under NATO protection. By the end of 1949, the Soviets had converted their zone in Germany to the German Democratic Republic (GDR) with a capital in East Berlin. West Berlin was left an enclave of West Germany 110 miles inside the territory of the GDR and, as such, a point of recurring friction between East and West for decades to come.

The remains of the Western empires and mandates in the Middle East were for the most part soon liquidated after World War II. But the decision of the United Nations to partition Palestine between Arabs and Jews in 1948 quickly led to war and an extension of the Cold War to the Middle East. When the Jewish community in Palestine proclaimed their territory as the state of Israel in May 1948, the Palestinian Arabs, who had opposed partition, took up arms against the new state. They were supported by the governments of Egypt, Jordan, Lebanon, Syria, and Iraq. The Israeli Defense Forces (IDF) were improvised from earlier Palestinian Jewish military institutions such as the Hagannah (militia) and the Palmach (striking companies), created before and during World War II for defense of the Jewish community against Arab attacks. Also, both arms and European

Jews had been smuggled into Palestine before 1948, and many of the officers who led the IDF had learned their craft while serving with the Allied forces.

Still, the world was surprised when the IDF threw back all Arab invasions in 1948 and went on to occupy all of Palestine except the Arab quarter of Jerusalem and the Gaza Strip adjacent to the Sinai Desert. The War of Liberation, as the Israelis called it, finally ended with a truce arranged by the United Nations in January 1949. By then, some 800,000 Palestinian Arabs had fled to other Arab countries, most of them to the Kingdom of Jordan. From the ranks of the exiled Palestinians were drawn, in time, recruits for various anti-Zionist movements, including the most important, the Palestinian Liberation Organization (PLO). In addition, after the 1948 war the more militant of the Arab governments exploited the willingness of the Soviet Union to supply the Arab armies with arms and military advisors. The more conservative Arab governments, such as the oil-rich Kingdom of Saudi Arabia, were caught between their suspicions of the USSR and their hatred of Israel.

The Far East was also an unstable region after World War II. Soviet forces withdrew from Manchuria in 1946, but not before turning over arms to Mao Tse-tung's armies, then on the point of resuming civil war with the government of Chiang Kai-shek. Despite American military supplies given to the Nationalists, Mao's forces finally drove the remnants of Chiang's forces to the island of Taiwan (Formosa) in October 1949. Mao proclaimed the People's Republic of China (PRC) on the mainland, and subsequently signed a mutual-aid pact with Stalin. The United States continued to recognize Chiang's government on Taiwan as the legitimate government of China. Soviet forces withdrew from Korea in 1948, but left behind a People's Republic under Communist Kim Il Sung. By the time American troops withdrew from southern Korea in 1949, President Syngman Rhee had established a Republic of Korea below the 38th parallel. Both Rhee's government in Seoul and Kim's government at Pyongyang claimed to be the sole legitimate government in Korea, and the danger of war between them was imminent by 1950.

Elsewhere in the Far East, the United States granted independence to the Philippines in 1946, but retained leased naval and air bases in the islands. In December 1946, after France refused to confer full independence on its colony of Indochina (composed of Vietnam, Laos, and Cambodia), Communist Ho Chi Minh, founder of the League for the Independence of Vietnam (Vietminh), launched a rebellion against French rule. Native opposition to the Dutch in the East Indies led to the creation of the Republic of Indonesia in 1949. Britain granted independence to India in 1947, and Muslim Pakistan promptly broke away from India to form a separate state. Britain granted independence to Burma in

1948, but in the same year a Communist rebellion broke out in Malaya. The British deferred their departure until they could hand over to a non-Communist government. The "Malayan Emergency" (also known as the "War of the Running Dogs") lasted twelve years before the successor Republic of Malaysia was secure. Thailand (Siam), never colonized by the West, retained its traditional independence.

In the period between 1946 and 1950, the United States gradually cobbled together a defense policy that reflected its expanded post-war responsibilities. The National Security Act of 1947 created the basic structure of post-war national defense by designating the armed forces as the National Military Establishment (NME) and dividing the NME into the departments of the Army, the Navy, and the Air Force. A civilian secretary presided over each department and was responsible to a Secretary of Defense. Statutory recognition was given to the Joint Chiefs of Staff, composed of the chiefs of staff of the Army and the Air Force and the Chief of Naval Operations. Assisted by a Joint Staff, the Joint Chiefs were to direct the interservice commands overseas and certain special branches such as the Air Force's Strategic Air Command (SAC). The 1947 Act also created the Central Intelligence Agency (CIA) and the National Security Council. In 1949, the Act was amended to transform the NME into the Department of Defense in order to broaden the powers of the Secretary of Defense and to create the post of the Chairman of the Joint Chiefs. (General Omar Bradley was first to hold the post.) In 1951, after the outbreak of the Korean War, the Commandant of the Marine Corps was added to the roster of the Joint Chiefs.

The administration of President Harry S Truman was the first to make air-atomic power the cornerstone of American defense. Even before the Army Air Forces became the United States Air Force in 1947, the Strategic Air Command was created in 1946 for the long-range delivery of nuclear weapons. After the creation of a separate Air Force, SAC remained the most important of its commands. The heavy reliance on air-atomic power reflected not only the great power of the atomic bomb, but also the unwillingness of the public to make either the personal or financial sacrifices necessary for the recreation of large conventional forces so soon after World War II. In addition, American monopoly of the atomic bomb was expected to last for many years, and during World War II the land-based American air forces had created a tradition of strategic bombing. Besides air-atomic power, the Truman Doctrine, announced in 1947, pledged arms and military advisors to any country threatened with indirect, as well as direct, totalitarian aggression, and was first applied against the internal insurgency in Greece. Subsequently, the royal Greek army was able to crush the leftist rebellion. Thus, through air-atomic deterrence, the NATO alliance, and aid under the Truman Doctrine, President Truman hoped to prevent either overt or covert Communist aggression without involving large numbers of Americans in combat.

In the early Cold War, SAC's principal types of bombers were the B-29, the B-50 (an improved version of the propeller-driven B-29), and the B-36 Peacemaker (an aircraft with six propeller engines and eventually four additional jet engines). All but the B-36 required overseas bases to be in range of targets in the Soviet Union. The huge B-36, the world's first intercontinental bomber, could make round-trip flights between bases in the continental United States and Russian targets 5,000 miles distant, carrying a five-ton nuclear bomb. Even after Russia began to produce large numbers of jet-engined interceptor fighters, such as the Mig-15, General Curtis LeMay, the head of SAC beginning in October 1948, believed that enough of his bombers could penetrate the Russian air defenses to inflict fatal blows on the Soviet population centers.

American confidence in the Truman defense policy was first shaken in August 1949, when Soviet Russia tested a nuclear fission bomb years ahead of American predictions. Though the Soviet Tu-4 "Bull" ("Bull" was a NATO designation), the most long-ranged bomber of the Soviet air fleet at the time, could not deliver an atomic bomb against a target in the continental United States and return to base, it could threaten cities in Europe and Asia. In addition, Soviet intercontinental bombers were under development. The CIA reported that the USSR was working on a thermonuclear (or hydrogen) bomb with many times the power of the nuclear fission bomb. On January 30, 1950, Truman signed an executive order for the development of an American H-bomb, and in April the National Security Council approved a policy of American limited conventional rearmament in a document known as NSC-68. But there was little time for the United States to promote rearmament of any kind before the outbreak of the Korean War.

II. The Korean War, 1950–53

On June 25, 1950, nine divisions and 135,000 troops of the North Korean People's Army (NKPA) crossed the 38th parallel in a general invasion of South Korea. When the resistance of the 100,000 troops of the Army of the Republic of Korea (ROK Army) proved of no avail, President Rhee's government in Seoul abandoned its capital and joined the retreat of its army deeper inside South Korea. North Korea's aggression challenged both the peace-keeping mission of the United Nations and the American policy of "containment" of Communist expansion in Europe and Asia.

Upon President Truman's initiative, the U.N. Security Council con-

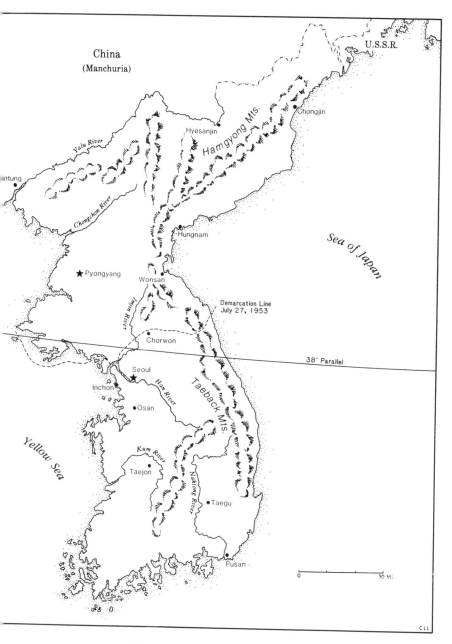

The Korean War Theater, 1950–53

vened on the Korean crisis. The Council took advantage of the absence of the Soviet delegate, who as a permanent member might have cast a veto that would have paralyzed action, and who was boycotting Security Council meetings over U.N. refusal to admit the People's Republic of China in the place of Nationalist China. The Council branded North Korea as an aggressor state, called on member-states of the U.N. to contribute forces to a United Nations Command for the defense of South Korea, and appointed the United States to serve as the executive agent for the U.N.'s intervention. The Council approved Truman's appointment of General Douglas MacArthur to serve as Commander-in-Chief, United Nations Command (CINCUNC), a duty MacArthur added to his existing posts of Supreme Commander, Allied Powers in Japan (SCAP), and Commander-in-Chief, U.S. Far Eastern Command (CINCFE).

Besides the remains of the ROK Army, initially the only ground forces MacArthur possessed to meet the aggression in Korea were elements of General Walton Walker's Eighth Army, four understrength U.S. Army divisions carrying out occupation duties in Japan. All the divisions were short of men and equipment, and three of them had to "cannibalize" the fourth in order to have enough arms and men to bring their formations up to strength. Even then their combat readiness left much to be desired. The U.S. Far Eastern Air Forces and the Seventh Fleet, based in the Philippines, were also not ready for the Korean emergency, and the Seventh Fleet, in addition to supporting the Eighth Army's operations in Korea, was given the task of "neutralizing" the Formosa Strait between mainland China and Taiwan. MacArthur rushed Task Force Smith, an improvised battalion-sized unit commanded by Lieutenant Colonel Charles Smith, U.S. Army, to Korea by air in order to slow the enemy's drive. Its ranks sustained the first American casualties of the war when it tried unsuccessfully to stem the tide of the enemy's advance near Osan on July 5. Its survivors soon joined the retreat of the ROK Army, the latter reduced by fighting and desertions to 40,000 men.

MacArthur's initial strategy pivoted on holding the port of Pusan in the extreme southeast corner of Korea, and on July 19 Walker established the headquarters of the Eighth Army at Taejon, established operational control over the ROK Army, and began to direct a withdrawal of U.S.-ROK forces to an arc of hastily improvised defenses known as the Pusan Perimeter. During August and into September, the NKPA made repeated efforts to break through the U.N. defenses, narrowly failing to make headway as Walker's command was reinforced by an Army division and a Marine brigade from the United States, miscellaneous U.S. units from Pacific posts, and a British brigade from Hong Kong. By mid-September, the strength of the U.N. forces inside the Pusan Perimeter had risen to 100,000 troops.

Meanwhile, the arrival of other American troops and supplies in Japan allowed the stripped U.S. Army division there to be refitted for combat. A Marine division also arrived from the United States. Instead of using these divisions to reinforce Walker's command in the Pusan Perimeter, MacArthur convinced the Joint Chiefs to allow him to form them into a Tenth Corps under General Edward Almond and to land the corps at the harbor of Inchon (Operation Chromite). Inchon was only a short distance from Seoul, the hub of road and rail communications in South Korea. In conjunction with an offensive by Walker's forces, the landing would eventually set the stage for a Korean-style *Kesselschlacht* in which the NKPA south of the 38th parallel would be encircled and destroyed. MacArthur was willing to risk the tricky tides at Inchon and a possible repulse on the coast in order to achieve that goal.

On September 15, the Tenth Corps went ashore at Inchon in the last major U.S. amphibious assault since World War II. Surprise was so complete that within two days the port was captured and the Tenth Corps could press on toward Seoul. On September 20, Walker's forces attacked the enemy's lines around Pusan and shattered them; within a week his forces had driven north to make contact with the Tenth Corps. Caught between the converging U.N. forces, the NKPA disintegrated, and only about 30,000 of its troops managed to escape death or capture by fleeing through mountainous eastern Korea and across the 38th parallel. On September 27, MacArthur flew from Tokyo to Korea in order to be present for President Rhee's triumphal return to his capital at Seoul.

As the return of the Soviet delegate to the Security Council made further action through that body impossible, the United States lobbied the U.N. General Assembly for expansion of war goals to include a unified Korea. While debate in the General Assembly continued, MacArthur, on his own authority, ordered ROK units to begin an invasion of North Korea on October 1. Other U.N. forces, including American units, followed on October 5. On October 9, the U.N. General Assembly passed a vaguely worded resolution favoring "the restoration of peace and security throughout Korea," which the Truman administration interpreted as approval of an invasion of North Korea. But the original goals of the U.N. intervention had changed and, as it turned out, with grave consequences for both the U.N. and the United States. Ten days after the U.N. resolution on Korea, and after the North Korean government had fled to Chinese protection at the Manchurian border, the American troops occupied Kim Il Sung's capital at Pyongyang. The Indian government, which had diplomatic relations with Beijing, passed along warnings that Mao Tsetung would not tolerate U.N. troops at the Yalu, the river which divides Manchuria from Korea over much of its length. On October 15, Truman met with MacArthur at Wake Island to discuss the danger of Chinese intervention, but MacArthur discounted the possibility and felt confident that he could deal with it should it occur. Truman authorized him to halt the U.N. advance at any point south of the Yalu if he believed that his command was in danger. He also ordered MacArthur to use only ROK troops at the Yalu in order not to antagonize Mao's government.

In the weeks following the Wake Island meeting, the Joint Chiefs expressed their concern about MacArthur's insistence on commanding the Tenth Corps and ROK troops west of the Hamgyong Mountains directly from his headquarters in Tokyo, a practice that created a split command in Korea and possible future confusion. MacArthur ignored the Joint Chiefs' concerns and Truman's restrictions, even to the point of downplaying the significance of the capture of Chinese prisoners and the fact that only a weak line of ROK troops connected the two wings of his forces. On November 24, MacArthur ordered a final closing to the Yalu on both fronts and predicted that the war would be over by Christmas.

MacArthur's prediction of an early victory was swept away on November 26 when an estimated 300,000 Chinese People's Volunteers (CPVs), actually veteran soldiers of the Chinese People's Liberation Army, launched a massive counteroffensive south of the Yalu. The main Chinese drive advanced down the mountain chain that divided the Tenth Corps from the rest of the Eighth Army and split the U.N. front. On November 28, MacArthur radioed Washington that he faced "an entirely new war," and requested permission to withdraw the Tenth Corps and attached ROK troops from North Korea by way of the ports of Hungnam and Wonsan. The Eighth Army west of the Hamgyong mountains reeled back from the blows of the Chinese and broke off action as best it could in order to conduct a retreat overland to South Korea. On December 23, matters worsened for the U.N. forces when Walker was killed in a jeep accident as the Eighth Army was crossing the 38th parallel. The Joint Chiefs immediately dispatched General Matthew Ridgway as his replacement. En route to Korea, Ridgway briefly conferred with MacArthur in Tokyo, where he insisted that all U.N. troops in Korea be placed under the headquarters of the Eighth Army. MacArthur agreed. On December 28, Ridgway took up his new duties at Taejon.

The longest unbroken retreat in American military history ended early in January 1951, when a U.N. line was formed across Korea which, at its nearest point, was about seventy miles south of Seoul. The Communist pressure on the U.N. Command began to slacken as Chinese and North Korean supply lines lengthened, and as fierce U.N. air attacks on those lines began to take their toll. But while the U.N. retreat was still underway in December, MacArthur bombarded the Joint Chiefs with demands to be allowed to take measures to broaden the war, claiming that otherwise the U.N. forces would be driven from Korea. MacArthur wanted permission to order air attacks on enemy bases in Manchuria and on bridges spanning the Yalu, and to accept Chiang Kai-shek's offer of Nationalist troops to serve in Korea. MacArthur also urged that the Seventh Fleet be ordered to permit Chiang's troops on Taiwan to attack the Chinese mainland.

Truman, the Joint Chiefs, and George C. Marshall, Secretary of Defense since September, were reluctant to comply with MacArthur's requests. On December 14, a new resolution of the U.N. General Assembly called for a ceasefire and a negotiated peace, not a broadening of the war. In addition, General Omar Bradley, Chairman of the Joint Chiefs, feared that a Soviet attack on Western Europe might be in the offing and was anxious to strengthen American forces assigned to NATO. The other members of the Joint Chiefs—General J. Lawton Collins of the Army, General Hoyt S. Vandenberg of the Air Force, and Admiral Forrest Sherman, Chief of Naval Operations—agreed with Bradley that the war in Korea should be broadened only if there were no other way to allow the U.N. Command to save South Korea from Communist occupation.

The matter of broadening the war was settled for the Joint Chiefs on January 15, 1951, when Ridgway briefed a delegation led by Collins and Vandenberg at his headquarters in Korea. Ridgway not only disagreed with MacArthur's allegation that the U.N. forces were about to be driven from Korea, he believed that with the arrival of reinforcements his command would be able to recover most of South Korea. When the Joint Chiefs reported Ridgway's optimism to President Truman, he agreed that the war would not be widened pending the success of Ridgway's predictions.

Ridgway proved to be as good as his word. Though his 365,000 troops faced an estimated half million Chinese and North Korean troops, his late winter and spring offensives in 1951 steadily drove the enemy back, and Seoul was recaptured on March 14. Truman was about to propose an armistice on the basis of the *status quo ante bellum* when MacArthur—perhaps chagrined by the rejection of his advice and Ridgway's success—broadcast a demand for the enemy to seek peace at his hands and implied more drastic military action if he did not. Truman canceled his plans for a more conciliatory speech and the United Nations was thrown into confusion over American policy and who was deciding it.

Truman's patience with MacArthur collapsed altogether when, on April 5, Joseph Martin, Republican leader in the House of Representatives, read a letter from MacArthur on the House floor in which the general agreed with Martin's critical views of Truman's conduct of the war. After consulting with Marshall and the Joint Chiefs, on April 11 Truman relieved MacArthur of all his commands. Ridgway succeeded MacArthur as CINCUNC, CINCFE, and SCAP, while General James Van Fleet replaced Ridgway as commander of the Eighth Army. MacArthur's abrupt relief and retirement stirred a wave of protest among his supporters in the United States, but it settled the question of limiting the war to Korea as long as the Truman administration was in power. A change on the Communist side occurred on June 23, 1951, when Jacob Malik, the Soviet representative to the U.N., announced a willingness on the part of the Communist high command in Korea to enter into armistice discussions. Talks began at Kaesong on July 8, and were moved later that summer to Panmunjom.

But no quick peace agreement was reached in Korea, and negotiations and the war dragged on for two more years. During those years, the battlefront came to resemble the Western Front in World War I. The Korean peninsula was bisected by two opposing lines of trenches, barbed-wire entanglements, bunkers, and mine fields. Battles were fought, sometimes repeatedly, for commanding ground such as Pork Chop Hill and Heartbreak Ridge, but no major breakthroughs were achieved by either side. The costly but indecisive fighting made the American electorate restless and frustrated. In 1952, General Dwight D. Eisenhower resigned his post as Supreme Allied Commander, Europe (SACEUR) in order to seek the Republican nomination for the presidential election, and in November he defeated Adlai Stevenson, the Democratic nominee, in part by promising that if elected, "I will go to Korea." Ridgway replaced Eisenhower as SACEUR, and General Mark W. Clark succeeded Ridgway as CINCUNC and CINCFE. (The position of SCAP was abolished after the signing of a peace treaty and a U.S.-Japanese mutual-defense pact in 1952.) General Maxwell Taylor replaced Van Fleet in command of the Eighth Army in January 1953.

While the Korean War dragged on, two lines of American nuclear research reached fruition. In November 1952, a thermonuclear device set off in the Pacific produced a blast equivalent to 10 million tons (10 megatons or 10 MT) of TNT set off at once. The device was five hundred times more powerful than the bomb that leveled Hiroshima. In January 1953, the U.S. Army opened the age of tactical atomic weapons when one of its 280-mm (11.2-inch) cannon test-fired an atomic shell. The shell released the force of about 2,000 tons of TNT (2 kilotons or 2KT), about a tenth of the blast produced by the Hiroshima bomb. Nuclear explosives could also be provided to small bombs and rockets. In the light of these developments, the Joint Chiefs recommended to Eisenhower on March 27, 1953, that the ban on the use of nuclear weapons in Korea be reconsidered. Eisenhower rejected the use of tactical atomic weapons in Korea, but they were to play a large role in his defense policy after the Korean War.

One reason for Eisenhower's decision not to resort to tactical nuclear weapons was the death of Joseph Stalin on March 5, 1953, and a perceptible change of attitude in the Kremlin under its new "collective leadership." Progress was at last made on the issue of the exchange of prisoners-of-war (POWs), long stalled because the U.N. Command was reluctant to force captured North Koreans and Chinese to return to their countries against their will. When President Rhee unilaterally ordered the release of all North Koreans held prisoner, and a compromise was reached in regard to other prisoners, the way was finally opened for an armistice to be signed at Panmunjom on July 27, 1953. The terms provided that a Demilitarized Zone (DMZ), approximating the position of the battlefront, would serve as the new frontier between North and South Korea. The DMZ zigzagged across the 38th parallel, but South Korea was left with its territory slightly expanded over that before the war.

The price for a relatively slight change of boundaries in Korea was high for both sides. An estimated 1,600,000 Korean civilians and 850,000 Korean soldiers (550,000 NKPA and 300,000 ROK) had been killed, wounded, or were missing. The Chinese may have suffered 900,000 casualties. American casualties came to 254,000 (54,000 dead). A total of 4,460 American POWs were returned, but 2,730 had died in POW camps and 7,800 were officially listed as missing in action (MIA). The American MIAs in Korea outnumbered those of the later Vietnam War by more than three to one. Though twenty-one "brain-washed" American POWs refused repatriation, 50,000 out of 120,000 NKPA prisoners, and 6,000 out of 20,000 Chinese prisoners, refused to return to their homelands. The U.N. Command charged the Communist side with brutality to POWs, while the Communists charged the U.N. Command with waging "germ warfare." Indeed, plagues swept Manchuria during the war, but they seem to have been the result of natural causes.

By the end of the war, sixty NKPA-CPV divisions manned the Korean battlefront, and thirty more divisions guarded the North Korean coasts against U.N. landings. These forces totaled perhaps 1.5 million men, and, for the most part, they were composed of hardy peasant-infantry armed with automatic small-arms and mortars. Though the USSR furnished much of their equipment and most of their arms, the Communist armies were relatively weak in armor, artillery, and air support. Nearly all the 4,000 aircraft furnished by the USSR were used to protect Communist lines of supply between the Chongchon River and the Yalu fifty miles further north. This fiercely contested airspace became famous as "Mig Alley." There, mostly U.S. F-86 Sabrejets tangled with Mig-15s, the Americans claiming to have downed 850 Migs for a loss of only 58 of their own aircraft between 1951 and 1953. The Mig-15 was an excellent fighter for its day, but most Communist pilots were inexperienced and usually no match for the more veteran American pilots, some of whom had been "aces" in World War II. Communist ground fire, not aerial combat, was the main source of U.N. air losses, and, as a type, the fighter-bomber was the most downed aircraft in the U.N. inventory. The United States lost 3,500 aircraft in Korea to all causes.

The equivalent of about twenty U.N. divisions were at the front toward the end of the Korean War, the best equipped being the British Commonwealth division and the eight American divisions. Among the American novelties introduced during the war was the 75-mm recoilless cannon, the plastic armored vest for torso protection, and the use of small helicopters for medical evacuations and liaison missions. The medevac helicopter enabled the rapid movement of wounded men from the front line and into the hands of surgeons in the mobile army surgical hospital (MASH) units in record time. In the first year of the war, the Truman administration relied primarily on regular army, federal reserves, and National Guard units (two National Guard divisions were eventually sent to Korea) to form the basis of the American mobilization, but later most of the American ground troops were draftees. A total of six army divisions, two National Guard divisions, and a marine division (reinforced) served in Korea, and a second marine division was kept in reserve in Japan. The 1951 Universal Military Training and Service Act envisioned the eventual recreation of a *Nation-in-Arms,* and, in theory, imposed liability to active and reserve service on all American males between certain ages.

The Korean War, and the associated demands of the Cold War, caused the American armed forces to grow almost exponentially by the close of the Korean War in 1953. The U.S. Army increased from 591,000 men and ten understrength divisions to 1,533,000 men and twenty full-strength divisions. The Marine Corps grew from 75,000 men and two understrength divisions to 245,000 men and three full-strength divisions. The Navy increased from 377,000 sailors and 600 warships to 765,000 men and almost 1,200 warships. (Most of the additional warships were recommissioned World War II vessels drawn from the Fleet Reserve, but new construction included the 72,000-ton *Forrestal,* the first of the supercarriers.) The Air Force expanded from 400,000 men and 7,500 airplanes to 800,000 men and 14,000 planes. The Navy-Marine air forces grew from 4,500 planes to 7,500 planes.

The U.N. effort in Korea involved the contributions of a sizable number of countries. The British Commonwealth Division (which included contingents from Britain, Canada, Australia, New Zealand, and South Africa) was the largest ground unit offered, aside from the American and the South Korean. Turkey sent an infantry brigade. The other countries which sent smaller combat forces were Belgium, Colombia, Ethiopia, France, Greece, the Netherlands, the Philippines, Thailand, and Luxembourg. The typical contribution was a battalion of infantry, though some countries also sent planes and ships, and little Luxembourg sent an infantry company. Aside from the American and South Korean troops, 44,000

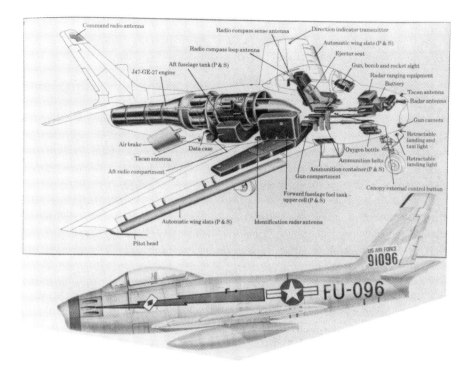

U.S. F-86 Sabre jet fighter, Korean War.

SOURCE: John Batchelor et al., *Air Power: A Modern Illustrated Military History* (New York: Exeter Books, 1979, in association with Phoebus Company/BPC Publishing, London).

U.N. troops served in Korea, of whom 17,260 were casualties by the end of the war. At peak strength, the U.N. Command had 793,000 soldiers, sailors, marines and airmen at its disposal.

III. The Eisenhower Years, 1953–60

In his first year as President of the United States, Eisenhower was preoccupied with bringing the Korean War to an end and with the early stages of demobilization of American forces in Korea (three, later two, Army divisions remained in South Korea, but main reliance for South Korea's future security was placed on the 550,000 troops of the ROK Army). Eisenhower began to place his own stamp on U.S. defense policy when, in 1954, Charles Wilson, Eisenhower's first Secretary of Defense, announced the so-called New Look. In essence, the New Look substituted nuclear firepower for manpower in the American armed forces. By a programmed transition to a heavy reliance on an atomic armory ranging from thermonuclear bombs to the smallest artillery shell that could be fitted with an atomic explosive, supposedly the United States would have "more bang for the buck" (in Wilson's words) and save on defense expenditures by reducing the numbers in uniform. In addition, John Foster Dulles, the new Secretary of State, announced that the United States was prepared to "retaliate massively" against local aggression as well as large. Supposedly, the American nuclear firepower would offset superior numbers of Soviet or Soviet-satellite conventional forces.

During Eisenhower's eight years in office the numbers of Americans in uniform declined in every service but the Air Force. By 1960, the U.S. Army had been reduced to 873,000 troops and fourteen divisions, and the Pentomic division, with which the Army was experimenting, was hardly capable of fighting in anything but a nuclear environment. The Navy had been reduced to 650,000 sailors and a thousand combat ships, but more super-carriers had been launched and the USS *Nautilus* (commissioned in 1955) was the world's first nuclear-powered warship and submarine. The Marine Corps had shrunk to 190,000 troops and three understrength divisions. In contrast, the Air Force had increased to 975,000 airmen and 137 wings, 54 of them assigned to SAC. During the 1950s, the six-engine B-47 Stratojet had replaced the B-29 and B-50 at overseas bases, while the B-52 Stratofortress, powered by eight jet engines, had replaced the B-36 as the nation's intercontinental bomber. Both the B-47 and B-52 could be refueled in air by a growing fleet of tanker aircraft. The B-47 had a maximum speed of 600 mph and carried a ten-ton bomb load. The B-52 could carry a thirty-ton bomb load as fast as 650 mph. At peak strength in manned aircraft in 1958, SAC boasted no fewer than 2,000 B-47 and B-52 bombers.

But Soviet military development was proceeding rapidly as well, and, in August 1953, Russia tested an H-bomb. During the rest of the 1950s and into the 1960s, the United States and the Soviet Union carried out frequent nuclear tests, 245 by the USA alone. The record for a single nuclear explosion was achieved in 1961 when the USSR detonated a device that supposedly produced a blast equivalent to 58 million tons of TNT (58 MT). Meanwhile, in 1954, two types of Soviet intercontinental bombers— the Mya-4 Bison and the Tu-95 Bear—went into production. In July 1955, Eisenhower offered the Open Skies Plan (OSP) at a Summit Conference at

Geneva with top Kremlin leaders, the plan calling for an exchange of strategic information, and overflights of each other's country to verify the data, in order to reduce the danger of surprise attack. Nikita S. Khrushchev, First Secretary of the Communist Party, USSR, then the dominant figure in the Kremlin, rejected the OSP on grounds that it was merely a blind for Western intelligence gathering. The next year Eisenhower authorized the beginning of a program of secret flights over the Soviet Union, using the new U-2 high altitude "spy plane" developed for the CIA. Until May 1960, when a Soviet surface-to-air missile brought down a U-2 piloted by Gary Powers near Sverdlovsk, the Soviets were helpless to prevent the flights over their territory. Among other things, the U-2's cameras revealed that the much-feared "Bomber Gap" was a figment of American imagination; no more than three hundred of the Bison and Bear aircraft had been produced, or about 15 percent as many aircraft as the USA had in B-47s and B-52s.

For a time in the 1950s, there seemed to be a more substantial "Missile Gap" in favor of the USSR. Though both the USA and the USSR had pressed the development of long-range cruise and ballistic missiles, the USSR had given greater attention to the latter. As early as April 1947, Stalin chaired the first session of Soviet rocket scientists on missiles in order to dramatize the importance he attached to ballistic missile development. Both the USA and USSR recruited scientists from the old German V-2 program, Werner van Braun working for the United States and other leading German scientists working for the Soviets. By 1955, Soviet research vehicles had delivered test-warheads over a range of a thousand miles, and that year the USSR went into mass production of the SS-3 Shyster, a medium-range ballistic missile (MRBM). Late in the decade, Russia put into production the SS-4 Sandal, a MRBM with a range of 1,500 miles. By mid-1957 the USA had a counterpart to the Shyster in the Thor and a counterpart to the Sandal in the Jupiter, both classified as intermediate-range ballistic missiles (IRBMs). Accordingly, American scientists assumed that the USSR was making about the same progress toward an intercontinental ballistic missile (ICBM) as the United States. Full-range tests of the U.S. Atlas and Titan, liquid-fuel ICBMs, were not scheduled until the end of the 1950s.

American complacency was rudely shaken in August 1957 when the USSR tested an ICBM—later identified as an SS-Sapwood—over a range of 5,000 miles and with a flight-time of just half an hour. In theory, such a weapon could be matched with a thermonuclear warhead to pose an appalling threat to American cities and SAC bases. Another blow to American confidence was struck in October 1957 when the rocket-engine of the Sapwood was used to loft into orbit Sputnik, the earth's first artificial satellite, opening the Space Age. The Eisenhower administration responded to the military implications of the Soviet rocket development with a crash program. Jupiter IRBMs were rushed to NATO bases in Europe as soon as they were ready for deployment, and many of SAC's bombers were placed on "Airborne Alert," ready to head for their assigned targets in Russia upon proper signal from the ground. Work on the ICBM program was accelerated, and in November 1958 the first full-range test of an Atlas was carried out. Over time, the Atlas and Titan would be replaced by the solid-fuel Minuteman, a type that could be fired from underground concrete silos less vulnerable to preemptive strike than the liquid-fuel, surface-launched ICBMs, and each of which carried a 1 MT warhead.

At sea the United States retained an important nuclear edge. The solid-fuel Polaris IRBM, which could be launched underwater from a new class of nuclear-powered, ballistic missile submarines (SSBNs), began to be deployed at the beginning of the 1960s. Each Polaris had a 1 MT warhead, but, with a range of only 2,800 miles, it was a substantially shorter-ranged weapon than the land-based Minuteman. Still, from European and Asian waters, the SSBN could threaten many parts of the USSR with the Polaris, and SSBNs were less vulnerable to preemptive strike than even the hardened Minuteman bases. In December 1960, as the Eisenhower administration was preparing to leave office, the USS *George Washington,* the first of the SSBNs, went on its first patrol from its base at Charleston, S.C. In the early 1960s, the administration of President John F. Kennedy planned for the building of forty-one SSBNs, each SSBN carrying sixteen Polaris missiles. Kennedy's program also called for the deployment of a thousand land-based Minuteman ICBMs.

American fears of a "Missile Gap" turned out to be as unfounded as the earlier fears of a "Bomber Gap." The Soviet SS-6 was more of a test-bed than a practical ICBM, and the more reliable SS-7 Saddler and SS-8 Sassin (each with a 5 MT warhead and a range of 7,000 miles) did not appear until the early 1960s. Even then, the accuracy of Soviet missiles was relatively poor, and Soviet production of new missiles did not compare with American ICBM production. By October 1962, the month of the Cuban Missile Crisis, SAC had eighty operational ICBMs to half as many for the USSR, while the U.S. Navy had nine SSBNs, bearing 144 Polaris missiles, to none in the Soviet fleet. Such diesel-powered, missile-armed submarines as the USSR possessed could not launch their weapons from underwater. Given SAC's great edge in bombers, any gap in thermonuclear power was clearly in favor of the United States.

Eisenhower was less successful in maintaining superiority over the Soviets in tactical nuclear weapons. By the late 1950s, such weapons were appearing among Soviet troops in Eastern Europe in large numbers, even while the Soviets continued to maintain their large superiority in numbers of conventional forces. Critics of the New Look argued that an exchange of tactical weapons would kill millions of civilians on either side of the "Iron Curtain" and might ignite a thermonuclear war between the superpowers as well. John Kennedy, the Democratic Party's nominee in the presidential election of 1960, claimed that the New Look left the United States and its allies with the unpalatable choice of "holocaust or humiliation." When Kennedy took office in January 1961, he was determined to bring about fundamental changes in many areas of American defense policy, especially in regard to the defense of Western Europe.

But the defense of Western Europe involved internal problems beyond the Soviet threat. At the Lisbon Conference of 1952, the NATO Council had approved plans for West European conventionally armed forces amounting to ninety-two divisions, half of them in reserve, and in the same year welcomed Greece and Turkey into NATO's ranks. But also in 1952, Britain tested an atomic bomb and opted to have its own national nuclear deterrent force independent of Supreme Headquarters, Allied Powers in Europe (SHAPE). In 1954, France rejected plans for integrated West European NATO forces (the so-called European Defense Community or EDC) in favor of a coalition of sovereign national forces. When in 1955 West Germany sought admission to NATO and the right to rearm, France and other NATO countries laid down as conditions that West Germany could produce no atomic weapons, nor secure them from other countries, while France went on to develop its own atomic bomb in 1960. Like Britain, France chose to have a national deterrent force not controlled by SHAPE. Meanwhile, the original plan for ninety-two NATO divisions had been watered down to twenty-seven active divisions and about as many divisions in reserve. Of the active divisions, five were American, and only they had direct access to American nuclear weapons. With such a variety of forces and obligations, the difficulty of coming up with a coherent plan for West European defense was apparent.

West Germany's admission to NATO in 1955 was the occasion for the Soviet organization of the Warsaw Pact the same year. Officially designated as a defensive alliance, the Warsaw Pact pledged a common defense against outside attack, and its original membership included the Soviet Union, East Germany, Poland, Czechoslovakia, Hungary, Rumania, Bulgaria, and Albania. Communist Yugoslavia, which, under Marshal Tito, had broken with Stalin in 1948, stood aloof and officially non-aligned. In practice, the Warsaw Pact served Soviet interests more than it promoted the defense of Eastern Europe. A Soviet marshal assumed command of the Warsaw Pact forces, and only Soviet forces in the Warsaw Pact armies had access to nuclear weapons. It was also soon demonstrated that membership in the Pact was not entirely voluntary. When a revolution in Hungary in 1956 threw up a Socialist government that desired to sever its ties

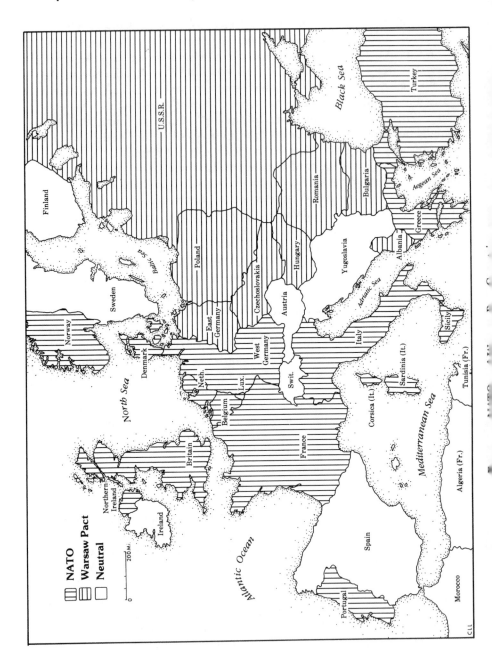

to the East Bloc, Khrushchev promptly dispatched Soviet tanks to Budapest, crushed the new government, and reinstalled the Communist government. Again in 1968, other Warsaw Pact armies joined the Soviet in overthrowing the reforming Czech Communist government of Alexander Dubček. (Albania, shielded by its borders with Yugoslavia, chose that moment to withdraw from the Warsaw Pact.) At the time of the crushing of the "Prague Spring," Leonid Brezhnev, who had succeeded Khrushchev as chief Kremlin leader in October 1964, announced the so-called Brezhnev Doctrine, namely the right and duty of the "Socialist Camp" to discipline any of its members which might err in domestic or foreign policy. Since the other members of the "Socialist Camp" could hardly "discipline" the Soviet Union, in practice the doctrine only served Soviet foreign policy.

Cold War problems extended far beyond Europe in the Eisenhower years. The rebellion of the Vietminh against French rule in Indochina reached its climax in the spring of 1954, when General Vo Nguyen Giap trapped 16,000 French Union forces in the fortress of Dienbienphu near the Lao border in northern Vietnam. By then the French colonial forces had suffered 150,000 casualties in eight years of fighting, and the French people were tired of the conflict. When the French high command appealed for help to the United States, already paying 80 percent of the costs of the war, the Eisenhower administration briefly considered armed intervention. But the American public showed little support for such a policy so soon after the Korean War, American's West European allies (save France) were also unenthusiastic, and on May 7 the surviving 8,000 French and allied troops at Dienbienphu surrendered. A peace conference at Geneva finally brought the war to a close in July. Under the terms of the Geneva Accords, the French left Indochina, Laos and Cambodia became independent and neutral states, and Vietnam was temporarily partitioned at the 17th parallel between Ho's Democratic Republic of Vietnam to the north and former emperor Bao Dai's State of Vietnam to the south. General elections in 1956 were supposed to determine the future of Vietnam.

John Foster Dulles, the U.S. Secretary of State, was determined that the partition of Vietnam would remain permanent and that South Vietnam would remain non-Communist. The United States offered military and economic aid to Ngo Dien Diem, Bao Dai's prime minister, who soon pushed Bao Dai aside in rigged elections and became President of the Republic of (South) Vietnam in 1955. An American Military Advisory and Assistance Group, Vietnam (MAAGV), set about training the Army of the Republic of Vietnam (ARVN). With Washington's encouragement, Diem ignored the mandate for general Vietnamese elections in 1956 set by the Geneva Accords, and the Demilitarized Zone (DMZ) at the 17th parallel became a political frontier between the two Vietnams. Meanwhile, in September 1954, the United States, Britain, France, the Philippines, Thailand, Pakistan, Australia, and New Zealand formed the Southeast Asia Treaty Organization (SEATO), with the avowed purpose of discouraging further Communist expansion in Southeast Asia. Under President Diem, South Vietnam became a signatory to the SEATO Pact.

In retrospect, American "adoption" of South Vietnam and Diem's violation of the Geneva Accords made war between the two Vietnams almost inevitable. Diem did not help matters when his policies alienated the majority of his citizens, who were mostly peasant and Buddhist, while he and his supporters were mostly Catholic and often associated with the better-off classes. In 1957 guerrilla warfare broke out in rural South Vietnam, and ARVN and internal security police proved unable to suppress it. By December 1960, an estimated 20,000 rebels were in the field when their leaders met in Hanoi to form the National Liberation Front (NLF). The fighting wing of the NLF was the People's Liberation Army (PLA). The NLF received support and encouragement from Ho's government, some supplies and men coming down the Ho Chi Minh Trail through Laos and eastern Cambodia. Diem referred to all supporters of the opposition as Viet Cong (Vietnamese Communists); the Americans would later call them the VC. In January 1961, just after John F. Kennedy took office, Diem made a special appeal to the new president for aid against the rising insurgency. Kennedy's response to that appeal would set the United States on the road to its most unfortunate foreign military involvement since the founding of the American republic, but the path that led to that point had already been embarked upon by the preceding Eisenhower administration.

French colonial troubles did not end with the withdrawal from Indochina. In September 1954, revolt against French rule broke out in Algeria and soon spread to neighboring Morocco and Tunisia. By 1956, France had abandoned Morocco and Tunisia, but Algeria was its oldest North African territory and technically a part of metropolitan France. The French colonial army and the *colons* threatened to revolt against any government in Paris that proposed peace negotiations with the Algerian rebels. Despite the commitment of 400,000 troops to Algeria, however, the war had reached a crisis point by May 1958, when the Fourth Republic abdicated its powers to General Charles de Gaulle. As President of the Fifth Republic, de Gaulle surprised the world by exercising a firm hand over the colonial army, bringing its terrorist Secret Army Organization (OAS) under control, and finally negotiating Algerian independence in 1962. French military-civilian casualties in the war came to 100,000, and perhaps twice that number of Algerians were killed or wounded.

The greatest crisis faced by the Eisenhower administration came in 1956 as the outcome of the Suez Crisis of that year. In 1952, a military coup had toppled the monarchy of King Farouk of Egypt and brought to power a militant Egyptian republic soon led by Colonel Gamal Abdel Nasser. Nasser dreamed of uniting the Arab peoples against Israel, and he tried to strengthen Egypt militarily by importing Soviet arms. The Suez Crisis began in July 1956 when Nasser nationalized the Suez Canal, thereby provoking the governments of Britain and France. As they began secret preparations for war, they found a natural ally in Israel, long barred from using the Suez Canal and often plagued by raids of Egyptian *fedayeen* from the Sinai Desert. The Second Arab-Israeli War erupted on October 29 when the Israeli Defense Forces (IDF) struck without warning into the Sinai, routed Nasser's forces there, and advanced toward the Suez Canal. Anglo-French planes raided Egyptian bases in the Nile valley, and an Anglo-French expeditionary force in the Mediterranean prepared for a landing at the northern end of the Canal. With Egypt on the brink of defeat, Khrushchev threatened Soviet military intervention, even to the point of raining down Soviet rockets on London and Paris.

In order to defuse a situation that might have led to world war, the Eisenhower administration moved in the United Nations for a resolution calling for a ceasefire and the withdrawal of all foreign troops from Egyptian soil. Without American support, Britain and France could not face down the Russians, nor could Israel carry on its war with Egypt. In early November, the Anglo-French invasion was halted and Israeli forces began to withdraw from the Sinai. U.N. peacekeeping forces temporarily occupied the Suez Canal and served as observers in the Sinai Desert. The crippled Canal was put back into operation in April 1957. The 1956 war seemed only to heighten Nasser's popularity among the Arabs and to increase Soviet influence in the Middle East. The outbreak of civil war between Christians and Muslims in Lebanon was only narrowly averted when Eisenhower sent U.S. Marines into the country briefly in 1958. By the time Eisenhower left office in January 1961, the Middle East was still another problem area without ready solutions.

The final problem of the Eisenhower years came close to home when on January 1, 1959, a long civil war in Cuba ended with the overthrow of right-wing military dictator General Fulgencio Batista and the installation of a revolutionary government under Fidel Castro. Within a few months, Castro moved to a Communist philosophy and thousands of Cubans fled to Florida. After Castro had appropriated American private property on the island (but left undisturbed the American base at Guantanamo), Eisenhower's administration was under great pressure to take action against the Castro regime. Eisenhower approved a CIA plan to train a Cuban exile brigade in Guatemala (where an American-inspired coup had overthrown a left-leaning government in 1954), but he left to his successor as president the decision as to how and when to use the force. Kennedy had pledged to take action against Castro in his 1960 campaign for the presidency, and the Cuban problem, like so many others, fell to his lot.

IV. The Vietnam War Era, 1961–75

A. The Strategic Race with the USSR in the 1960s.   After the Kennedy administration took office in January 1961, Robert S. McNamara, the new Secretary of Defense, announced a defense policy called Flexible Response. On the strategic level, the policy called for a Counter Force doctrine which would direct American strategic nuclear weapons selectively against Soviet military targets, including airfields and missile-launching sites, instead of Soviet cities, as long as the Soviets spared American cities from attack. The primary weapons of Counter Force were to be new solid-fuel missiles, the land-based ICBM Minuteman and the submarine-launched ballistic missile (SLBM) Polaris. McNamara foresaw no need for the strategic bomber over the long haul, hence he planned for the gradual elimination of the type and canceled plans for the development of the B-70 bomber.

After Kennedy's death in 1963 and Lyndon B. Johnson's accession to the presidency, another change in American strategic doctrine took place. The earlier American confidence that a strategic nuclear war could be both controlled and limited was waning, and by the time McNamara left office at the end of February 1968, a new doctrine of Mutual Assured Destruction (MAD) had replaced Counter Force. The MAD doctrine pre-supposed that the only value in American strategic weapons lay in their ability to deter a direct Soviet attack on the United States. It further presupposed that such an attack would never be considered by the leaders in the Kremlin if they believed that no possible "first strike" could destroy enough of the American strategic systems that a devastating American counterstrike could not be mounted. Thus, MAD implied that a finite number of strategic-weapons systems, suitably protected from a "first strike," would be sufficient. Since the USSR faced the same situation in regard to strategic nuclear weapons, it followed that the Soviet-American strategic arms race was reaching the point of diminishing returns. In that case, the security interests of both countries would be best served by a bilateral agreement to cap the race. The MAD doctrine and its assumptions led directly to the American interest in strategic arms limitation talks near the end of the decade.

The administration of President Lyndon B. Johnson not only completed the deployment of the strategic forces developed under the Eisenhower and Kennedy administrations, their destructive power was subsequently dramatically improved by exploiting new "MIRV" technology. The technology of MIRV (an acronym for "multiple, independently targetable vehicle") allowed multiple "smart" warheads to ride a single rocket-launcher into space, then separate to strike widely separated targets. The dramatic effects of "MIRVing" may be illustrated by the fact that when in 1968 the last of forty-one Polaris-armed submarines was commissioned, the single warhead on each of sixteen submarine-launched ballistic missiles (SLBMs) aboard each submarine brought the total of sea-based Polaris missiles to 656 (as a practical matter, 416 Polaris missiles were at sea at all times). But as the new MIRVed Poseidon gradually replaced the Polaris, the firepower of each SSBN was multiplied many times because each Poseidon could carry as many as fourteen MIRVs, each of the warheads with the equivalent explosive force of 40 KT. Similarly, MIRV technology multiplied the firepower of American land-based ICBMs. The Minuteman III was equipped with three MIRVs apiece, each MIRV with an explosive force of 170–350 KT, and eventually a total of 550 of the thousand Minuteman missiles were Mark IIIs. (In 1965 the last B-47 bomber was retired, leaving 650 B-52s in service. That year, for the first time, SAC's ICBMs outnumbered its manned bombers.) When Johnson left office in January 1969, the so-called Triad of American strategic forces— ICBMs, SLBMs, and B-52 bombers—could deliver a total of 4,500 nuclear warheads and bombs with a combined explosive force of 5,100 MT. In other words, the American strategic firepower was equal to perhaps millions of Hiroshima-sized atomic bombs. Such had been the pattern of development of American nuclear strategic forces in less than twenty-five years.

At the beginning of 1969, the USSR was lagging behind the USA in strategic nuclear forces. It possessed 850 ICBMs, all liquid-fuel, the most powerful types being the SS-9 Scarp and the SS-11 Sego, introduced in 1965 and 1966 respectively. Thanks to enormous rocket-engines, each type could hurl a 25 MT warhead, a reflection of the Soviet advantage in "throw-weight" as compared with American ICBMs, but also a compensation for poorer Soviet accuracy. The Soviet sea-based strategic nuclear forces were even further behind the American. In 1969, the Soviet navy had only a handful of nuclear-powered, ballistic-missile submarines, the whole of them mounting forty SLBMs of a design inferior to either the Polaris or the Poseidon. The first test of even a land-based Soviet MIRVed ballistic-missile did not occur until December 1974, and a sea-based weapon was not tested until still later. Only 155 of the old Soviet Bison-Bear bombers were still in service. The Soviet strategic forces were estimated to have 1,100 nuclear warheads and bombs, with a combined explosive force of 2,300 MT. On the other hand, the Soviets showed no signs of letting up in their deployment of new and better systems as they

U.S. Minuteman ICBM in its silo.
Source: Ray Bonds, ed., *The U.S. War Machine:*
An Illustrated History of American Military Equipment
and Strategy (New York: Crown Publishers, 1978).

became available unless some kind of strategic arms agreement could be reached with the United States.

The doctrine of Flexible Response also affected American preparations to deter or fight local and regional wars. Even before being elected president, John Kennedy was impressed by the arguments presented in B. H. Liddell Hart's book *Deterrent or Defence* (1960), in which the British defense expert made the case that a suitably armed but relatively modest conventional force made more sense for the defense of Western Europe than a force armed with nuclear weapons that might destroy Western

Europe in the process of defending it. Liddell Hart did not favor abandoning all nuclear weapons, but he believed that they should be weapons of last, not first, resort. Their real value lay in deterring the Warsaw Pact forces from resorting to their own nuclear weapons. In line with such thinking, Kennedy supported an expansion of American conventional ground forces, and, by the time of Kennedy's death in November 1963, the U.S. Army had reached a strength of 975,000 men and sixteen full-strength divisions, backed by a sizable Army Reserve and National Guard. About a third of the active divisions were serving in the U.S. Seventh Army in West Germany.

But the U.S. Army changed in more ways than just size. It abandoned its experiments with the Pentomic division in favor of a flexible organization for conventional warfare called ROAD (Reorganization Objectives, Army Division). ROAD was "sculpted" to perform a variety of missions, according to circumstances, by assigning to its three brigade headquarters any combination of specialized battalions (originally, motorized, mechanized, armored, and airborne). In addition, the U.S. Army pioneered the Airmobile Division, whose men and equipment could be moved almost entirely by helicopter, and developed Special Forces (Green Berets) which, as the American involvement in Vietnam deepened, concentrated on the techniques of counterinsurgency. Of all the American armed forces in the 1960s, the Army most perfectly conformed to the doctrine of Flexible Response and its emphasis on non-nuclear action.

During his 1960 campaign for the presidency, Kennedy had pledged to take action against Castro's government in Cuba. In April 1961, the Cuban exile brigade trained by the CIA in Guatemala was landed at the Bahia de Cochinos (Bay of Pigs), but no expected Cuban insurrection in support of the landings materialized. When Kennedy refused to send American forces to support the brigade, Castro's militia counterattacked and defeated it, a severe blow to the prestige of the Kennedy administration. Kennedy's prestige suffered another blow in August when the government of the German Democratic Republic solved the problem of skilled workers escaping from East Germany to the West by erecting the Berlin Wall. Though Kennedy denounced the action, it was obvious that his government could do nothing more than pledge never to abandon West Berlin.

But Kennedy's most serious challenge came in the fall of 1962. U-2 spy planes revealed that the Soviets were preparing launching sites for SS-4 and SS-5 missiles in Cuba. Once the missiles were in place, they would have been within range of targets in two-thirds of the continental United States, and would have about doubled the megatonnage that the Soviets could have launched against the USA in a nuclear war. By mid-October, when Kennedy resolved to take action, forty SS-4s were on the island, though not yet operational. In order to prevent further missiles from being introduced to Cuba, Kennedy imposed a "quarantine" by ordering the U.S. Navy to establish a line across the Atlantic which Soviet ships would pass at their peril. He then demanded that Moscow remove the missiles already in Cuba, and Soviet-made Il-28 jet bombers sent there earlier. After two tension-filled weeks in which the world seemed on the edge of nuclear war, the Khrushchev government agreed on October 28 to withdraw both the missiles and the bombers. In return, the Kennedy administration pledged not to threaten Castro's Cuba again, and, in an unannounced agreement, to withdraw the U.S. Jupiter missiles based in Turkey.

The near-brush with nuclear war sobered both Washington and Moscow, and made the American and Soviet leaders more amenable to the seeking of accommodation in some areas. In 1963, the so-called Washington-Moscow Hot Line was established, a direct teletype link for better "crisis management" in future. In the same year, the United States, the Soviet Union, and Great Britain signed a Partial Nuclear Test-Ban Treaty which obligated them not to conduct atomic explosions in the atmosphere or underwater. In 1968, the Nuclear Non-Proliferation Treaty committed all members of NATO and the Warsaw Pact, not already armed with nuclear weapons, to forego their manufacture and possession. Meanwhile, in 1966, President de Gaulle had withdrawn French forces from the NATO force structure, and required the removal of the NATO political and military headquarters from French soil to Belgium. (France continued to observe its pledge to come to the defense of Western Europe if threatened.) In 1968, the NATO Council approved negotiations with the Warsaw Pact for mutual and balanced force reductions, though nothing came of the idea until the 1970s.

B. The Vietnam War from 1961 to 1968.   The Cuban Missile Crisis aside, the most fateful events for the United States in the 1960s took place in the Far East. The critical turn in the American military involvement in Vietnam began just after Kennedy took office. He agreed to send President Diem of South Vietnam substantially more military aid to combat the rising strength of the insurgency in his country, and he subsequently sanctioned a CIA-directed secret bombing campaign against the Ho Chi Minh Trail in Laos in order to hamper the movement of reinforcements and supplies from North Vietnam to the insurgents. In February 1962, Kennedy sanctioned the creation of the new Military Assistance Command, Vietnam (MACV), which subsumed the old U.S. Military Assistance and Advisory Group, Vietnam (MAAGV), extant since 1954. MAAGV had never involved as many as a thousand uniformed Americans; at its peak in 1969, MACV commanded 543,000 American troops. During its existence until March 1973, MACV was variously commanded by generals Paul Harkins (1962–64), William Westmoreland (1964–68), Creighton Abrams (1968–72), and Frederick Weyand (1972–73).

By 1963, MACV had 11,300 advisory and technical personnel in South Vietnam, but the war was still not going well against the People's Liberation Army (PLA). The Army of the Republic of Vietnam (ARVN), created on the model of the U.S. Army, was well armed by Asian standards, but its methods seemed ineffectual against the PLA. Worse, Diem's policies alienated many non-Communists in South Vietnam, including the powerful Buddhist hierarchy and officers in the Joint General Staff. On November 1, 1963, with the collusion of the U.S. government, a military coup in Saigon overturned Diem's government. Diem surrendered on November 2 and was killed on orders of his own officers. Kennedy had scarcely begun to deal with the new government in Saigon when he fell victim to an assassin's bullets on November 22. The problem of Vietnam passed on to Lyndon Johnson.

Johnson believed that the key to solving the problem of the insurgency in South Vietnam lay in part in pressuring Ho Chi Minh's government in Hanoi to cease in aiding and assisting it. In 1964, he sanctioned a covert war under the Pentagon's Operations Plan 34A, which involved American assistance to South Vietnamese raids into North Vietnam, acts of sabotage north of the 17th parallel, and secret operations against the Ho Chi Minh Trail in Laos. Johnson also moved American naval forces into waters in the Gulf of Tonkin claimed by the Democratic Republic of Vietnam (DRV). After clashes between North Vietnamese patrol-torpedo boats and American destroyers early in August 1964 (the Gulf of Tonkin Incidents), Johnson ordered aircraft carriers to launch a retaliatory raid on Vinh on August 5, the first overt American act of war. At the call of the President, Congress on August 7 passed the so-called Gulf of Tonkin Resolution, which empowered Johnson to take whatever military measures he saw fit to protect South Vietnam and American servicemen in Southeast Asia.

In November 1964 Johnson handily defeated Republican challenger Barry Goldwater for the presidency, and, with another four years in office assured, he stepped up his war against North Vietnam. Using the machinery of the Southeast Asia Treaty Organization (SEATO), Johnson sent squadrons of fighter-bombers to bases in Thailand and increased U.S. naval strength in the Gulf of Tonkin. In February 1965 he shifted to a policy of overt war against North Vietnam, when, with the approval of General Nguyen Van Thieu, who had taken over the leadership of the Saigon junta (and was later elected as President of South Vietnam), Johnson launched a sustained bombing campaign against the DRV (Operation Rolling Thunder) on March 2. Before the month was out, Army and Marine combat units had arrived in South Vietnam, and by the end of 1965 MACV's strength had swelled to 185,000 troops with more on the way. What began as a civil war between the Saigon government and local insurgents aided by North Vietnam had become a conflict chiefly between the United States and the DRV.

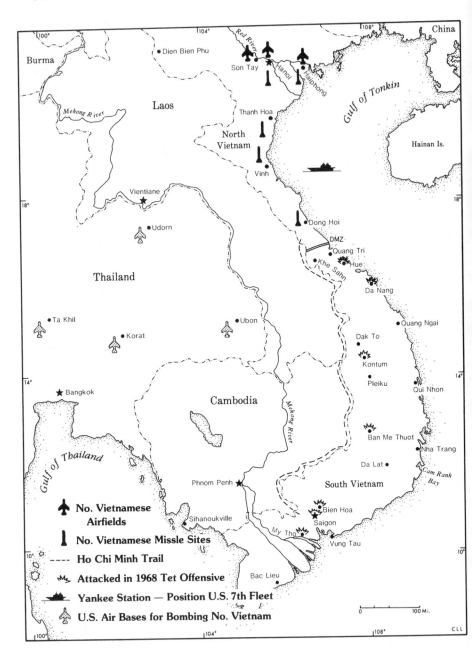

The Vietnam War: Southeast Asia

Operation Rolling Thunder's purpose was to injure North Vietnam to the point where Hanoi would call off the insurgency in the south rather than endure more, as well as interdicting lines of supply and reinforcement from north to south. From March 2, 1965, to October 31, 1968, U.S. Air Force and Navy planes flew 350,000 sorties over North Vietnam and delivered 3 million tons of ordnance against targets that ranged all the way from military training camps, supply depots, rail and road bridges, and transport vehicles to public utilities and the DRV's small factory system. Over a similar period of time in World War II, the Army Air Forces had dropped 1,554,463 tons of bombs on Germany and 502,781 tons of bombs on Japan. Yet, despite the greater tonnage sent against North Vietnam, the DRV, a nation of only 16 million people, maintained its morale and never lost the means to keep its economy working. Such phenomenal endurance raises interesting questions about the patterns of the air war in Vietnam, and the air weapons with which the war was waged.

The failure of Operation Rolling Thunder has been attributed to a number of factors, one being the gradualness with which Johnson permitted air power to be applied to North Vietnam. Both Johnson and McNamara, his Secretary of Defense to March 1968, apparently thought of Rolling Thunder as a kind of aerial tourniquet, gradually tightening until Hanoi accepted American demands. Hence, the early air attacks were restricted to the "panhandle" south of the 19th parallel, the least important part of North Vietnam economically. Even after the attacks were extended as far north as the Red River Delta, the heart of the DRV, the targets in Hanoi and the port of Haiphong were highly restricted. In consequence, the DRV was both able to endure the ordeal from the air and to import much economic and military aid from China and the USSR. The Johnson air strategy conflicted with the lessons of previous experience, especially those that suggested that air power is at its most effective when applied with the greatest possible intensity over the shortest possible time, and against the most vulnerable points in the enemy's socioeconomic structure. Ultimately, Johnson's strategy of attrition—that of wearing down Hanoi's will and material resources—proved to be a two-edged sword.

Another weakness of Rolling Thunder was the F-105 Thunderchief, the aircraft chiefly used by the U.S. Air Force in attacks on North Vietnam from 1965 to 1968. The F-105, an aircraft developed during the Eisenhower years with its penchant for tactical nuclear weapons, was never intended to fly at very low altitudes to deliver its ordnance, nor was it designed to be repeatedly exposed to conventional antiaircraft fire. Accordingly, it was not provided with armor protection for the pilot or vital parts of the aircraft, or equipped with redundant hydraulic systems and self-sealing fuel tanks. When F-105 squadrons based in Thailand were required to make repeated low-level raids against targets in the Red River Delta, a region defended by a formidable array of antiaircraft weapons, their losses were sometimes appalling. By 1968 no fewer than 8,000 antiaircraft guns, ranging from 20-mm to 100-mm in caliber (the larger ones radar controlled and with shells equipped with proximity fuses), made the skies over parts of North Vietnam the most flak-filled since World War II. Neither was the United States able to employ the B-52 freely against North Vietnam; in addition to antiaircraft guns, the Soviets supplied the DRV with batteries of SA-2 Guideline surface-to-air missiles (SAMs), designed for the attack of high-flying aircraft, and uncertainty about the effectiveness of the SAMs deterred any use of the B-52 very far into North Vietnam until nearly the end of the war.

By the time Rolling Thunder was abandoned at the end of October 1968, a total of 915 U.S. aircraft had been brought down over North Vietnam. These losses were mainly due to conventional antiaircraft guns and small arms fire, which accounted for no fewer than 750 (82%) of the American planes. Surface-to-air missiles (SAMs) destroyed 117 (13%), and Soviet-made Mig-17 and Mig-23 fighters accounted for 48 American aircraft (5%). In fact, there were relatively few air-to-air combats over North Vietnam compared to the war in Korea, though in the engagements over Vietnam the American fighters, most of them F-4 Phantoms, destroyed 111 North Vietnamese Migs. In the on-again-off-again U.S. air attacks on North Vietnam between 1969 and 1973, an additional 475 American planes were lost to all causes.

The Americans assumed primary responsibility for the ground war in South Vietnam about the time numerous regiments of the People's Army of Vietnam (PAVN), the North Vietnamese army, began coming down the Ho Chi Minh Trail. In the bloody battle of the Ia Drang Valley in the fall of 1965, MACV forces thwarted a PAVN attempt to cut South Vietnam in half across its narrow waist between the western highlands and the coast. By 1966, both PAVN and the PLA had returned to relatively small-scale guerrilla operations. In turn, General Westmoreland switched MACV tactics to "Search and Destroy," in an effort to uncover enemy bases in South Vietnam and to drive those enemy forces not destroyed into Laos and Cambodia. But a quick victory over an enemy practiced in the arts of protracted warfare was impossible, and Johnson was compelled to commit more and more forces. At the end of 1967, the strength of MACV stood at 480,000 troops. Meanwhile, the helicopter—both as a troop-carrier and a "gun ship"—proved invaluable against a fast-moving and elusive enemy.

As American numbers grew in Vietnam, so did American casualties. Between January 1, 1961, and March 1965, only 400 American servicemen had lost their lives in Southeast Asia. By the time Johnson left office in January 1969, the total of dead had reached 40,000, and about 250,000 men had been wounded. The fact that PAVN-PLA casualties were far higher than the American or the South Vietnamese was cold comfort to the American public, some of whom found measuring progress in the war in terms of enemy "body count" repulsive. Matters were made worse for the American war effort by Johnson's decision not to carry out a general mobilization of the Reserve and the National Guard, but to rely instead on a stepped-up draft. There was natural resentment when thousands of young men found themselves conscripted to fight when thousands of citizen-soldiers remained at home. In order to escape conscription, many fled to Canada and overseas, and still others simply became fugitives in their own country. By 1973, there were 570,000 apparent draft offenders, and, of the men who entered uniform between 1961 and 1973, 563,000 were given less-than-honorable discharges. About 2.7 million men served in Southeast Asia at one time or another during the war, 2.1 million of them in Vietnam.

The final blow to Johnson's war policy came early in 1968, when attention was focused on a PAVN siege of 5,000 U.S. Marines and a thousand allied troops in a fire-base (a fortified artillery camp) near Khe Sanh in the far north of South Vietnam. On January 30, and coinciding with the beginning of Tet, the Vietnamese lunar New Year holiday, the PLA, with PAVN support, launched a massive offensive throughout South Vietnam. The offensive finally affected 36 out of 44 provincial capitals, 5 out of 6 autonomous cities, 64 out of 242 district capitals, and 50 of the "strategic hamlets" or "new life" villages of the South Vietnamese rural pacification program. The city of Hue fell to the PLA, and much of it was destroyed in the bitter fighting involved in its recovery. By the time the fighting associated with Tet began to subside in March, Westmoreland estimated that 50,000 PLA troops had been killed, while 15,000 ARVN and fewer than 5,000 MACV personnel had been killed or wounded.

But the Communist losses in the Tet Offensive more than paid for themselves in the psychological effect that the offensive had on the American public. Led by Washington to believe before the offensive that the worst of the war was over, many American citizens, already war-weary and doubtful about the wisdom of the intervention in Vietnam, demanded an end to American participation. By March 31, 1968, Johnson had concluded that total victory in Vietnam was beyond America's grasp, and that night he went on national television to announce a new policy. He proposed negotiations with North Vietnam with a view to an armistice, he ordered the suspension of air attacks on North Vietnam above the 20th parallel in order to encourage negotiations, and he announced that he would not seek the nomination of his party for another term. Peace talks opened at Paris in May, but they turned out to last over twice as long as the lengthy negotiations that led to the armistice in the Korean War. Nor were they much affected by Ho Chi Minh's death from natural causes in September 1969. Premier Pham Van Dong and the Hanoi Politburo adhered to his policy of achieving a united Vietnam under Hanoi's rule at any cost.

   C. The Final Phase of the Vietnam War, 1969–75.   In his bid against the Democratic Party's nominee, Hubert Humphrey, Richard M. Nixon, the Republican standard-bearer, narrowly won the presidential election of November 1968. Nixon had campaigned under the slogan "Peace with Honor," and, early in 1969, Melvin Laird, the new Secretary of Defense, announced a new strategy called "Vietnamization," or the gradual turning over of the war to the South Vietnamese and the withdrawal of American combat forces from Vietnam. Nixon hoped that the last American combat troops could be withdrawn before the next presidential election in 1972, and that ARVN would be capable of waging the war successfully on its own with only American material aid and advice. Before "Vietnamization" went into effect, the American build-up in South Vietnam reached its peak, with 543,000 troops, eight Army divisions and two Marine divisions. While the four-year withdrawal was underway, another 20,000 Americans died and 115,000 were wounded.

   In March 1969, fearful that a reported PAVN-PLA build-up of forces in the Cambodian border sanctuaries would threaten his strategy, Nixon authorized a covert B-52 bombing campaign (Operation Menu). In March 1970, General Lon Nol led a military coup that toppled the Cambodian "neutralist" government of Prince Norodom Sihanouk. The new government in Cambodia successfully sought American recognition, a pledge of aid from the Nixon administration, and in April 1970 countenanced an ARVN-MACV invasion of the frontiers of Cambodia in order to seek out PAVN-PLA bases. But the "Cambodian Incursion," as Nixon called it, sparked angry protests on American college campuses, and on May 4 National Guardsmen fired on protesters at Kent State University in Ohio, killing and wounding several students. Public reaction to the incident, and to the Cambodian Incursion, was so hostile that Nixon announced that the American participation in the incursion would end by July 1. In June, reflecting the public mood against a widening of the war, Congress moved to revoke the Gulf of Tonkin Resolution and thereafter sought to limit the President's latitude in waging the war. (After American withdrawal from the Vietnam War, Congress passed a War Powers Act in November 1973, that limited the Presidential commitment of combat forces to ninety days without express Congressional consent.) Moreover, Lon Nol's coup had provoked civil war with Pol Pot's Khmer Rouge, the Cambodian Communist movement, a war that gradually turned against the government. Another ill omen for Nixon's strategy was an ARVN offensive into Laos in early 1971. The South Vietnamese effort to cut the

Ho Chi Minh Trail ended disastrously and threw doubt on the strategy of "Vietnamization."

The abortive ARVN offensive into Laos had further consequences. Daniel Ellsberg, a former official in the Department of Defense who had become disillusioned with the war, "leaked" to the *New York Times* a classified Pentagon history of American involvement to the end of Lyndon Johnson's administration. Beginning in June 1971, the *Times* serially published the so-called Pentagon Papers, and the public and most members of Congress learned for the first time of Kennedy's and Johnson's covert wars in Laos and against the DRV. Many people were especially outraged upon learning of how Johnson had manipulated overt American intervention in the war in Vietnam in 1964–65. Worried that "leaks" about his secret and illegal bombings in Cambodia might reach the public, Nixon ordered the creation of a White House Special Investigations Unit (nicknamed the "Plumbers") to prevent embarrassing revelations to the press from his staff. The Plumbers went on from their original assignment to a forced entry of the office of Ellsberg's psychiatrist and finally to the break-in at the Democratic Party's headquarters in the Watergate Office Complex in June 1972. The apprehension of the intruders eventually led to the Watergate Scandal and to Nixon's resignation in August 1974, though by that time direct American involvement in the war in Vietnam was over.

At Nixon's behest, in 1970 Congress overhauled the Selective Service System in order to make it more equitable and to reduce it as a factor in antiwar agitation. Under the reformed system, at age eighteen men were to be selected for military service by lottery, and those not chosen were free to go about their lives. The new system was better tolerated than the old system—which made men vulnerable to the draft from age eighteen to twenty-six—but the Vietnam War had struck a fatal blow to the principle of compulsory military service in the United States. When the draft law expired in 1972, neither the President nor Congress made any effort to revive it. Though in 1977 registration for the draft was reimposed under President Jimmy Carter, the draft was not resumed. At this writing military service in the United States remains voluntary. The end of the Cold War in 1989, and the success of American all-volunteer forces in the Gulf War with Iraq in 1991, have made a return to the draft in the United States unlikely for the foreseeable future.

At the beginning of 1972, only 70,000 American troops remained in South Vietnam, and Nixon's goal of getting them out before the November election seemed within reach. But in March a PAVN invasion of South Vietnam across the DMZ at the 17th parallel brought on a new crisis. The attack by fourteen PAVN divisions sent ARVN reeling back, and led to the overrunning of most of Quang Tri province. By May, even the city of Hue was in danger of capture. Nixon pulled out all stops in an air offensive against North Vietnam (Operation Linebacker I) and in naval operations, including the mining of North Vietnamese coasts, in order to hamstring the PAVN drive. The attack on the enemy's logistics, and renewed resistance by ARVN, finally brought PAVN's forward movement to a halt in July, and the war was at a stalemate. The focus then shifted to the peace negotiations at Paris, where Henry Kissinger, Special Assistant to the President for National Security Affairs, was orchestrating proposals from the American side. In late October, Kissinger announced that "peace is at hand," and in early November, Nixon won a landslide election victory over Democratic challenger George McGovern.

But the illusion that a peace had been achieved soon vanished. In December, the Communist delegation walked out of the negotiations, and Nixon retaliated by ordering Operation Linebacker II, a ten-day bombing campaign against the DRV that focused primarily on Hanoi and Haiphong with attacks by B-52 bombers. The so-called Christmas Bombing Campaign reportedly killed or injured 5,000 people (1,300 dead), and cost the United States fifteen of its B-52s, plus eleven other aircraft. Premier Pham Van Dong agreed to resume negotiations after the raids on December 29, and talks commenced again at Paris on January 4, 1973. Finally, on January 23, the signing of the Paris Peace Accords effectively brought an end to the longest war in American history.

The Paris Peace Accords provided for the complete withdrawal of uniformed Americans from South Vietnam except for Marine embassy guards at Saigon and a fifty-man military mission to the Saigon government. All Americans held as prisoners-of-war were to be returned, and a good faith effort was to be made by the Communist side to account for those reported missing-in-action (MIA). A prohibition was placed on the reinforcement of the 150,000 PAVN troops believed to be in South Vietnam, as well as limits on the replenishment of arms and equipment consumed by both sides. Once a general armistice was in effect, a national council, representing all Vietnamese parties, was supposed to work out the final fate of Vietnam through peaceful means. A total of 595 American POWs had been returned by March 29 when MACV cased its colors and the last of its troops left Vietnam. At that time some 2,300 Americans remained officially listed as missing-in-action. Most if not all of these MIAs are believed dead; and, since the American withdrawal, only one person listed as MIA in 1973 has returned alive.

If the MIAs are counted as among the dead, the war cost the United States over 60,000 fatalities and over 300,000 wounded. Material losses included 3,700 fixed-wing aircraft, more fixed-wing aircraft than in the Korean War, and over 4,000 helicopters. Enormous quantities of arms and equipment were used up by the ground forces. The direct costs of the war to the United States in 1973 dollars was placed at $109 billion, though direct and indirect costs may have amounted to half a trillion in equivalent 1993 dollars. Nor had the United States received much support from its SEATO allies during the war. Some forces were sent by Australia, New Zealand, the Philippines, and Thailand, but the only large "Third Country" contribution was two army divisions from South Korea. Worst of all, the American sacrifices in the Vietnam War proved in vain. The armistice in South Vietnam soon collapsed, and Communist offensives in Laos, Cambodia, and South Vietnam in 1975 rolled forward to victory. In the wake of Saigon's surrender on April 30, 1975, the name of the city was changed to Ho Chi Minh City, a final American humiliation in a long and unhappy ordeal.

D. The U.S.-Sino-Soviet Détente, *1972.*   Even as the Vietnam War was entering its final throes for the United States in 1972, relations between the USA on the one hand and Soviet Russia and the People's Republic of China on the other underwent the most drastic change since World War II to that time. Part of the change resulted from tensions between Moscow and Beijing, as the result of conflicts over ideology and territorial boundaries. In 1969, Soviet forces and troops of the PRC even fought a relatively large-scale battle along the Manchurian border. Accordingly, both Moscow and Beijing had reason to seek better relations with the United States.

Early in 1972, Nixon flew to Beijing to confer *de facto* diplomatic recognition of Mao Tse-tung's government and to join Mao in a declaration opposing Soviet hegemony in the Far East. In May, Nixon joined Brezhnev in Moscow to sign the long-sought Strategic Arms Limitation Treaty (SALT I), the most significant arms-control measure since the Washington Naval Treaty of 1922. A five-year Interim Agreement under SALT I imposed an upper limit of 1,618 ICBMs and 950 SLBMs on the USSR and 1,054 ICBMs and 710 SLBMs on the United States. (The larger numbers allowed the USSR reflected the American advantage in MIRVed missiles.) Parity was granted in the new class of Anti-Ballistic Missiles (ABMs), each side being allowed two hundred ABM launchers with single warheads and restricted to two launch-sites. The ABM Agreement was of indefinite duration. Provision was made for the negotiation of a second Interim Agreement on offensive weapons before the first expired in 1977. The signing of SALT I was widely hailed as the beginning of a new era of *détente* between the United States and the Soviet Union.

E. The Arab-Israeli Six-Day War and the Yom Kippur War, 1967 and 1973.   The final events of the Vietnam War Era of importance to the patterns of war were the Six-Day War between Israelis and Arabs in 1967, and another round between Israelis and Arabs in the so-called Yom Kippur War of 1973.

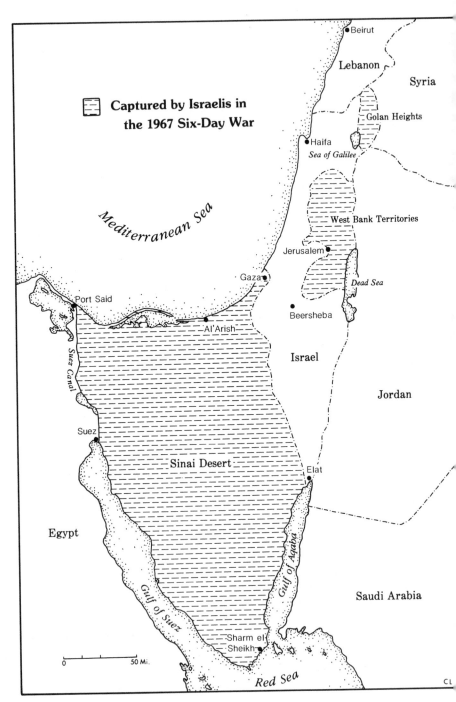

The Arab-Israeli Theater of War, 1948–73

By 1967 the Israeli Defense Forces (IDF) had perfected their *Nation-in-Arms*, one of the most thorough-going in history. As friction between Israel and its Arab neighbors moved toward the breaking point, 75,000 troops were on active duty (3,000 of them professional soldiers), backed by 250,000 reservists. In a nation that then numbered only 2 million Jews, both mobilization and the conduct of the war had to be carried out with great speed so as not to place too great a strain on the economy and national morale. The IDF possessed 800 tanks, 350 modern jet fighters and ground-attack aircraft, and 31 mobilizable brigades. In contrast, Nasser's Egypt, Israel's primary enemy, had an army of 275,000 troops, 900 tanks, and 385 jet aircraft. Most of the Egyptian arms were of Soviet manufacture. Syria, likewise armed by the Soviets and then linked with Egypt through the United Arab Republic, had an army of 65,000 troops, 350 tanks, and 76 jet aircraft. The Kingdom of Jordan, joined with Egypt through a military alliance signed just before the war, had 55,000 troops, 300 tanks, and 21 jet aircraft.

Under the circumstances, and if war with its Arab neighbors were inevitable, Israel's best chance lay in mobilizing rapidly for a sudden strike at its most powerful enemy—Egypt—and then dealing with Syria and Jordan as circumstances developed. Moshe Dayan, Minister of War and former IDF chief-of-staff in the 1956 War, ordered mobilization on June 2, and by the night of June 4 the Israeli forces were ready for action. Early on June 5, Israeli planes circumvented Egyptian radar by flying out over the Mediterranean and then approaching the coast from an unexpected direction. Most of Nasser's planes were destroyed on the ground by noon. The morning air blitz was accompanied by a rapid drive of Israeli forces into the Sinai Desert and the adjacent Gaza Strip. Only two out of seven Egyptian army divisions were deployed for battle, and all of them were rapidly beaten. A total of 50,000 Egyptian troops were killed or captured, and the IDF destroyed or captured 300 tanks, 500 pieces of artillery, and 10,000 trucks. Within six hours, troops of the IDF had crossed the whole of the Sinai to the east bank of the Suez Canal. The IDF losses came to 275 men killed and 800 wounded.

Elsewhere, and within three days of the start of the war, the IDF defeated 55,000 Jordanian and Palestinian troops in Jordan's West Bank territories and occupied the Arab quarter of Jerusalem. On the fourth day of the campaign, 20,000 Israeli troops and 250 tanks stormed the Golan Heights on Syria's frontier, and, within two days, defeated 40,000 Syrian troops supported by 300 tanks. When the Israeli government decided to heed the U.N. call for a ceasefire on the Syrian front, its forces were halfway to Damascus, the Syrian capital. Syrian losses came to 10,000 men killed or captured, while IDF casualties on the Jordanian-Syrian fronts came to 200 killed and 400 wounded. In its economy and effectiveness, the Israeli performance in the Six-Day War was almost a perfect application of the blitzkrieg doctrine. Israel's opponents were so thoroughly beaten that a major Arab threat to the Jewish state was not mounted again until the fall of 1973.

The Yom Kippur War had its origins in Egypt's defeat in 1967 and Israeli occupation of the Sinai Desert, including the east bank of the Suez Canal. The Israeli occupation of the east bank made the Canal useless to Egypt, a major blow to the Egyptian economy which depended heavily on its tolls. After Nasser died in 1970, he was succeeded by Anwar Sadat. The new President of Egypt set out to regain enough of the Sinai that the Canal could be repaired and placed again into operation for Egypt's benefit. He accepted Soviet armaments for his project, and he coordinated his plans with President Hafez al-Assad of Syria, who was also rearming his country in hopes of regaining the Golan Heights. By the fall of 1973, Egypt's army consisted of 285,000 troops, 2,000 tanks, 500 jet aircraft, and hundreds of antitank weapons and antiaircraft guns and missiles. Syria's forces consisted of 125,000 troops, 800 tanks, 300 jet aircraft, and also many antitank and antiaircraft weapons.

The Israeli government was not unaware of the Egyptian-Syrian rearmament, and by 1973 had raised the strength of the Israeli Defense Forces to 270,000 troops, 1,175 tanks, and 400 jet aircraft. At the beginning of October 1973, about 100,000 IDF troops were on active duty and the IDF reserves could be mobilized in two days. But whereas reservists in Jewish communities close to the Syrian and Jordanian frontiers could join the active forces quickly, the nearest Israeli communities to the Suez Canal were 250 miles away. In order to contain an Egyptian attack until reservists could arrive on the Southern front, the IDF General Staff caused the building of the Bar Lev Line on the east bank of the Canal, one that consisted of bunkers and strongpoints manned by an Israeli infantry brigade, backed by artillery and an Israeli armored brigade. But a successful defense of the Bar Lev Line could only be assured if the IDF General Staff had enough warning to mobilize and deploy reservists before an Egyptian attack.

Sadat's military planning between 1970 and 1973 accomplished two important goals. By secret arrangements with Syria, the first goal was achieved by the preparation of a joint Egyptian-Syrian attack that would catch the Israelis by surprise, and, on the Southern front, allow the Egyptian army an opportunity to breach the Bar Lev Line too quickly for the Israeli reserves to arrive in time to defend it. The second goal was to prepare an effective defense against an Israeli counterattack to regain the Line and the East Bank of the Canal. Even if the Syrian attack on the Golan Heights was unsuccessful, it would divert Israeli forces from the Southern Front and improve the chances of success for Sadat's plan.

The Syrian-Egyptian attacks were timed to take place simultaneously on Yom Kippur, the Jewish Day of Atonement, which fell on October 6 that year, when the Israelis presumably would be at a low level of readiness. The Egyptian attack was even timed for 2 o'clock in the afternoon, an unusual hour for the commencement of an offensive, further adding to the surprise element. Both the timing and manner of the Egyptian attack marked a new level of competence in Egypt's military leadership.

Israeli intelligence had just begun to sense that something was amiss when Egyptian planes suddenly descended on Israeli artillery positions behind the Bar Lev Line on the afternoon of October 6 and quickly put the guns out of action. Then special Egyptian assault troops, using pneumatic boats and supported by high-pressure hoses that quickly bored holes through the sandy escarpment on the opposite bank, crossed the Canal and penetrated the Bar Lev Line in several places. With its Israeli defenders trapped in pockets within the Line, the Egyptians deployed more troops beyond it to meet the expected Israeli armored counterattack. Their antitank weapons made short work of the Israeli armored brigade, and, as the Israeli air forces belatedly tried to redress the balance in the Sinai, Egyptian antiaircraft guns and missiles on both sides of the Canal inflicted heavy losses on them. As still more Egyptian troops poured over pontoon bridges thrown over the Canal, they occupied a bridgehead eventually some ten miles in depth. Meanwhile, the Syrian attack on the Golan Heights further distracted the Israeli forces.

On the first day of the war, as the IDF hastily mobilized its reserves, its General Staff decided to give priority to the defense of the Golan Heights where a Syrian breakthrough would jeopardize the Jewish communities immediately adjacent. In fierce fighting lasting three days, the Syrian attack was contained. But in the south, IDF reserves, arriving late and thrown into the battle piecemeal, were unable to penetrate the Egyptian-occupied territory inside the Sinai, and suffered the destruction of two Israeli armored brigades. Meanwhile, IDF air strikes against the pontoon bridges across the Canal that fed Egyptian reinforcements and supplies into the occupied zone were rebuffed by antiaircraft guns and surface-to-air missiles. The IDF General Staff finally ordered its Southern Command to suspend his offensive operations temporarily and to review its tactics before launching further attacks. It also appealed to the United States to rush aircraft and tanks to Israel in order to offset the heavy losses in materiel.

The lull in the fighting in the south was put to good purposes by the IDF. With the arrival of American-supplied armor and planes, and a careful analysis of the situation, the Southern Command was able to work out new tactics and strategy for a renewed counteroffensive. On October 15, the artillery of three IDF divisions mounted such a well-directed fire that most of the Egyptian antitank units in the Sinai were destroyed. Then infantry and armored brigades went forward in mutual support, penetrating the enemy's front between the Egyptian Second Army and Third Army all the way to the Canal. Israeli pontoon bridges thrown over the Canal enabled IDF armored and motorized forces to pass to the Egyptian side, some of the forces wheeling north in order to destroy the network of antiaircraft defenses that had so hindered IDF air attacks on the Egyptian pontoon bridges, other units wheeling south to cut the communications of the Egyptian Third Army and to set up the situation for a *Kesselschlacht*. When Israeli troops reached the city of Suez at the southern end of the Canal within days, the Egyptian army teetered on the brink of a catastrophe. But the battle never came to its natural conclusion. Repeated efforts by the United Nations to halt the fighting finally succeeded on October 25. Both Israel and its enemies agreed to an armistice.

Under subsequent arrangements, the IDF withdrew its units back into the Sinai and to a line about ten miles from the Canal, thus enabling Egypt to begin revival of the waterway. Later in the 1970s, and with the help of American mediation under President Jimmy Carter, Sadat further changed the equation by recognizing Israel's right to exist in return for a staged withdrawal of IDF forces from the rest of the Sinai, a process completed in 1982. But, in the face of unremitting Syrian hostility, the IDF retained its positions on the Golan Heights.

The long-term effect of the Yom Kippur War for Israel was a significant shift in its security concerns. Egypt, which adhered ever more closely to the United States during the 1980s, was no longer a primary threat (and this despite the assassination of Sadat in 1981, and the succession of Hosni Mubarak as Egypt's president). Syria, Lebanon, and the occupied Gaza Strip and the West Bank territories of Jordan posed most of Israel's security problems. Beyond these areas, a more distant threat was posed by Saddam Hussein, who had gained a monopoly on power in Iraq in 1979. The IDF aerial bombing of the Iraqi Osirak nuclear reactor, one allegedly capable of producing weapons-grade plutonium, in June 1981 demonstrated how far Israel was prepared to go in its search for national security.

For the study of the patterns of war in the era of the Vietnam War, the Yom Kippur War was significant in at least two respects. One was the striking effectiveness of antitank and antiaircraft weapons, an effectiveness which in turn was in part responsible for the second significant aspect, namely the very high consumption of armor and aircraft on both sides. The IDF lost a quarter of its pre-war armor, and a fifth of its pre-war air force, in fighting that lasted less than three weeks. The 3,000 Israelis killed and wounded in 1973 exceeded the combined Israeli human losses in the 1956 and 1967 wars. The Egyptians may have sustained the loss of 15,000 troops killed or wounded, and 8,301 troops were taken prisoner, while Syrian forces suffered 10,000 casualties. Like Israel, both Egypt and Syria sustained heavy losses in tanks and planes. These facts gave students of desert warfare much to ponder.

V. The Cold War and Other Wars, 1975–89

A. The Continuing Arab-Israeli Problem. Beginning in 1975, Lebanon was torn by civil war between Christians and Muslims as Palestinian guerrilla groups shifted their bases of operations against Israel from Jordan to southern Lebanon. Israel launched a "Lebanese Incursion" in 1982 that went all the way to Beirut, but the occupation proved costly and the Israelis were finally content to withdraw their forces to a buffer zone in southern Lebanon and to follow a policy of supporting friendly Christian militia in the area against their Muslim enemies. Lebanese Muslim movements believed connected to Syria and Iran took American and other Westerners in Lebanon as hostages, and Muslim terrorists turned to assassination of Westerners and their Middle Eastern sympathizers. They also hijacked and bombed Western civilian airliners within and beyond the Middle East. American peace-keeping interventions in Lebanon under Republican President Ronald Reagan in the 1980s turned out badly, some three hundred U.S. Marines losing their lives, and the American forces were finally withdrawn. As of this writing in the early 1990s, Syrian and Israeli forces remain in a divided Lebanon, the civil war in Lebanon continues intermittently, and, although Arab-Israeli peace talks are underway, the Palestinian Arab problem remains unresolved.

B. Intensification of the Cold War. Tensions rose between the United States and the Soviet Union during the decade between 1975 and 1985. Among other causes, the United States considered Soviet meddling in the Middle East and Africa to be unwarranted. In Africa, the United States objected to Soviet use of Cuban surrogate troops to influence the outcome of civil war in Angola, and also to the Soviets' aiding clients in wars in Ethiopia and Somalia. Events in the Middle East redounded to Soviet advantage when a fundamentalist Muslim revolution in Iran toppled the pro-American Shah of Iran in January 1979, and an anti-American government under the Ayatollah Ruhollah Khomeini came to power. While the Soviets had played no part in Khomeini's rise to power, the revolution in Iran seemed more to their advantage than to that of the United States. Still, in June 1979, President Carter and Chairman Brezhnev signed a second Interim Agreement (so-called SALT II) on strategic arms. It turned out to be the last gesture of *détente* in the decade.

The SALT II agreement allowed each side a maximum of 2,400 offensive strategic weapon-systems, to be reduced to 2,250 systems by January 1981, with a subcategory of limitations on land-based ICBMs, SLBMs, cruise missiles, and strategic aircraft. But as of the time of the signing of SALT II, the Soviet strategic forces had come a long way since the ratification of SALT I seven years earlier. The USSR had 1,400 ICBM launchers, 880 SLBMs, 140 Bison-Bear bombers, and a giant SS-18 ICBM under deployment; together, these forces were capable of delivering 5,600 nuclear bombs and warheads, worth 5,500 MT of nuclear explosive. In June 1979, the United States possessed 1,054 land-based ICBMs, 656 SLBMs, and 385 B-52 bombers, but it no longer had a monopoly on MIRVs. The 9,800 American strategic nuclear bombs and warheads could deliver a combined yield of 4,000 MT, or slightly less than in 1972.

Though conservative factions in the U.S. Senate strongly opposed SALT II, the Senate Foreign Relations Committee reported the treaty favorably to the Senate floor in November 1979. But in the same month militant Iranians seized the grounds and staff of the American embassy in Tehran and held the staff members hostage for the return of the former Shah, then undergoing medical treatment in the United States. The events in Tehran caused a wave of xenophobia to sweep over the United States, one unfavorable to ratification of SALT II. Any remaining chance of ratification was swept away on December 24 when Soviet forces intervened in the civil war in Afghanistan on the side of the Communist government in Kabul. In January 1980, President Carter withdrew the SALT II treaty from further consideration by the Senate and vowed not to resubmit it until the Soviet forces were withdrawn from Afghanistan. However, an executive agreement implementing the terms of SALT II remained in effect.

In the final months of the Carter presidency, important changes in American defense policy took place. Carter approved the development of both a new heavy MX ICBM and a new Trident II SLBM for deployment in the 1980s, though he rejected development of a B-1 bomber to replace the B-52. He began moving the country toward a greater reliance on nuclear weapons in July 1980 when he approved Presidential Directive 59 (PD-59). PD-59 was the foundation of a new Pentagon doctrine called Nuclear Utilization Target Selection (NUTS), and envisioned a controlled nuclear response to Soviet aggression against Western Europe. In addition, Carter approved a NATO Council recommendation to take effect in December 1983, calling for the deployment of a so-called "Two Track Missile System" of Pershing II ballistic missiles and Tomahawk cruise missiles in Western Europe. The planned deployment was in response to Soviet deployment of MIRVed SS-20 ballistic missiles aimed at Western Europe.

The failure of Delta Force—an American military rescue mission in 1980—to liberate the embassy hostages in Tehran, along with raging inflation in the American domestic economy, contributed to Carter's defeat at the polls at the hands of Ronald Reagan, the Republican nominee, in November. On the day Reagan took office in January 1981, the hostages in Tehran were released, but thereafter, and unknown to the public and the Congress, the Reagan administration tried to get Tehran's help in freeing the American hostages in Lebanon by providing arms to Iran, at war with Iraq since September 1980. The illegal diversion of monies from Iranian arms deals to aid the Contras in their fight against the Communist Sandinista government in Nicaragua led to the Iran-Contra Scandal in Reagan's second term.

Reagan, a long-time critic of both the SALT process and *détente* with the Soviet Union, embraced Carter's belated "hard line" on defense with a vengeance. He reaffirmed Carter's decisions on the MX ICBM and the Trident II, and went beyond them by resurrecting the B-1 bomber project. (When finally produced and deployed, the B-1 proved to be a disappointment; the B-52 remained the most numerous effective strategic bomber in the American armory into the early 1990s.) Reagan also approved the exploration of "Stealth" technology to develop radar-resistant aircraft, research that would later produce the secret F-117 and B-2 designs before the end of the decade. His program included expansion of American conventional forces, including the goal of a navy of six hundred warships. In addition, Reagan approved the NATO plan for Two-Track Missile deployment in Western Europe. The purest Reagan stamp on American defense policy was his proposal for the Strategic Defense Initiative (SDI), a revival of the strategic antiballistic missile program, one largely abandoned since the 1960s. Reagan believed that new technology such as lasers, particle-beam weapons, and kinetic energy weapons could make the continental United States immune to Soviet ballistic missile attack. The SDI would become one of the most controversial parts of his defense program.

Reagan's actions in his first term in office, combined with fierce verbal denunciations of the Soviet Union, brought on a renewed intensification of the Cold War, but his approach did not go unresisted. Much of his opponents' criticism was directed against Reagan's sending of military aid and advisors to the republic of El Salvador, caught up in a revolt by left-leaning guerrillas. But most opposition was focused on the planned deployment of the Two-Track Missile System to Europe, which, its critics alleged, would merely accelerate the Cold War. Bowing in part to this pressure, Reagan agreed to negotiations with the Soviets on Intermediate-Range Nuclear Forces (INF) in the fall of 1981, and also to negotiations toward a Strategic Arms Reduction Treaty (START), beginning in June

1982. Little progress was made in either set of negotiations down to November 1983. Then, ahead of schedule, Reagan ordered the first batteries of the Pershing II ballistic missile to West Germany and the first of the land-based Tomahawk cruise missiles to Britain. Brezhnev, who had died in November 1982, was succeeded by Soviet leader Yuri Andropov, and Andropov promptly broke off INF talks and suspended the START negotiations indefinitely. Even the Mutual and Balanced (Conventional) Force Reduction negotiations in Vienna were suspended. For the first time in fourteen years, no nuclear or conventional arms negotiations of any sort were underway between the United States and the Soviet Union. The slide into deeper Cold War did not halt until the deaths of Andropov and his successor, Konstantin Chernenko, and the rise to power in the Kremlin of Mikhail Gorbachev in March 1985.

C. The Wars of the Late 1970s and 1980s.   Numerous wars wracked the globe in the late 1970s and 1980s, many of them in the shadow of the Cold War. One of the bloodiest, and one lasting almost the entire length of the decade of the 1980s, was fought between Iran and Iraq, and inflicted perhaps a million military and civilian casualties. Its origins lay in Saddam Hussein's long-standing quarrel with Iran over his eastern border with Iran. In September 1980, Iraqi forces invaded Iranian territory adjacent to the Shatt-al-Arab, the estuary of the Tigris and Euphrates rivers at the head of the Persian Gulf, in an effort to take advantage of the revolutionary upheaval in Iran and of Iraqi technical superiority. Saddam expected that those advantages would offset the fact that the population of Iraq was only 17 million while that of Iran was 40 million.

The Iranians remained technically inferior to the Iraqis throughout the war, in part because they were hampered by lack of enough spare parts for their mostly American-made armaments, one of the reasons for their secret negotiations for "weapons for hostages" with the United States. Still, the Iranians managed to contain the Iraqi advance a short distance inside their territory and to commence a long war of attrition. The Khomeini government exploited Shi'ite religious fundamentalism to enlist many thousands of Iranian infantry to hurl themselves against Iraqi firepower. For their part, the Iraqis, in addition to relying on great numbers of artillery and tanks of Soviet origin, resorted to poison gas and occasional bombardments of Tehran with medium-range ballistic missiles. Intermittently the Iranian air force managed to strike back at Baghdad. The war eventually degenerated into a stalemate not unlike that on the Western Front through much of World War I, each side incapable of inflicting decisive damage on the other. In 1988, the Khomeini government in Tehran finally accepted the marginal territorial gains of the Iraqis

Soviet SAM-2 Guideline, surface-to-air missile.
SOURCE: Ray Bonds, ed., *The Illustrated Encyclopedia of the Strategy, Tactics and Weapons of Russian Military Power* (New York: Bonanza, 1982).

in order to have peace, and the Iraqi armed forces emerged from the war with an exaggerated reputation for martial effectiveness.

The only significant naval war of the 1980s was the Anglo-Argentinian war over the Falklands and the dependency of South Georgia in 1982, a war primarily decided by conventional but sophisticated air-naval weapons. After diplomacy failed to settle conflicting claims, Argentine forces occupied the Falklands and South Georgia early in April 1982. Great Britain responded by dispatching to the South Atlantic the largest task force sent out from the home islands since World War II. The task force, commanded by Admiral John Woodward, was composed of two aircraft carriers basing thirty-six Hunter Harrier VERTOLs (vertical takeoff and landing aircraft, or "jump jets"), twenty-three modern destroyers and frigates, four nuclear-powered attack submarines, eight large amphibious warfare vessels, and some thirty transports, tankers, and auxiliary vessels. It also transported about 9,000 army troops and marines, together with their arms and equipment.

The British drew first blood in late April when a naval helicopter disabled a surfaced Argentine submarine off South Georgia with an air-to-surface missile. The island was then reoccupied against minimal Argentine resistance. On May 2, a British submarine torpedoed and sank the old Argentine cruiser *General Belgrano* on the edge of the war zone the British had proclaimed around the Falklands, and 370 Argentine sailors lost their lives. Thereafter, the largely obsolescent Argentine navy remained outside the war zone and near Argentina's coasts.

As Woodward's force entered the waters of the Falklands, the Argentines carried the fight to the British fleet with 250 jet aircraft based on the mainland. The first Argentine air success occurred on May 4 when a French-made Exocet missile, launched from an Argentine plane twenty miles from the target, struck the new British frigate *Sheffield* and sent it to the bottom. Later, another air-launched Argentine Exocet sank the cargo vessel *Atlantic Conveyor.* The air attacks on Woodward's fleet reached their peak after British landing operations commenced against East Falkland on May 21; within a few days an assault ship, two frigates, and a destroyer had been sunk, and ten other British warships had been damaged. But all of these losses were inflicted by conventional bombs; a lack of vital components kept the remaining Argentine Exocet missiles out of action. Nine British Harriers were also lost to all causes, but air-to-air missiles launched from Harriers, British surface-to-air missiles (both sea and land based), and antiaircraft guns claimed 109 of the attacking Argentine planes. Fighting ashore on East Falkland ended in early June with the surrender of the Argentine garrison of 13,000 troops. British losses in the campaign came to 255 killed and 777 wounded. Argentine casualties were placed at 1,500 men killed, wounded, or missing-in-action.

The Soviet intervention in the civil war in Afghanistan at the end of 1979 turned into an unexpectedly long war for the Soviet Union. After replacing the Communist leader in Kabul with one more to their liking, the Soviets believed that 115,000 Soviet troops and the Afghan army could take the measure of the Afghan rebels. Though the rebels were relatively primitive tribesmen divided among at least a dozen resistance groups, the *mujahidin* resistance proved unexpectedly tenacious and persevered despite heavy losses from the fire of Soviet tanks, airplanes, and helicop-

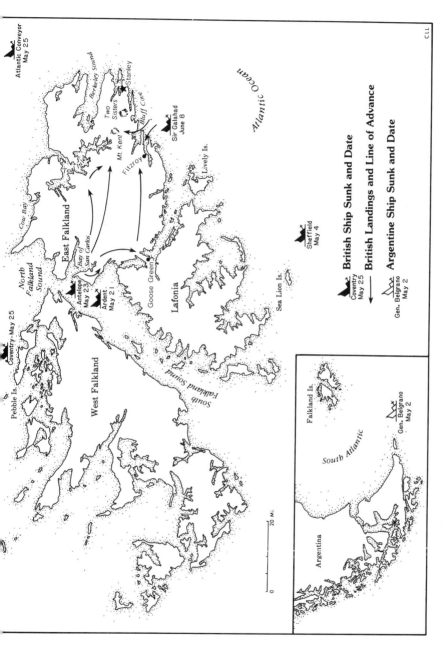

The Anglo-Argentine War in the Falklands: Operations May 21–June 8, 1982

ters. In addition, the People's Republic of China, still at odds with the USSR, sent material aid across its common border with Afghanistan to the rebels, while Pakistan became a conduit for covert American military assistance. Especially important in the growing Afghan ability to deal with Soviet air superiority was the American-supplied, shoulder-fired "Stinger" surface-to-air missile. By February 1988, when the USSR withdrew the last of its forces from Afghanistan, the Soviets admitted to the loss of 35,000 dead and several times that number wounded. After another change in leadership in Kabul, and with Soviet aid in military materiel, the Communist government continued to survive for a time, but it was eventually toppled in May 1992. Perhaps as many as a million Afghans were casualties of the war.

VI. The Close of the Cold War

The process of ending the Cold War commenced soon after the arrival of Mikhail Gorbachev to leadership in the Kremlin in March 1985. Gorbachev's adoption of policies of *glasnost* (openness) and *perestroika* (political and economic restructuring) within the Soviet Union aimed at internal political and economic liberalization in order to deal with a general Soviet economic and political malaise under Marxist policies. But Gorbachev's policies also encompassed the beginning of a profound change in Soviet foreign policy; within a few years of his arrival to power, the causes of the Cold War had been dismantled.

The log-jam in negotiations on intermediate-range nuclear forces of the two superpowers was broken when Gorbachev proposed complete abolition of all American and Soviet land-based missiles with a range between approximately 300 and 3,000 miles, both ballistic and cruise. Gorbachev also accepted President Reagan's insistence on on-site verification of the scheduled destruction of existing weapons in these categories and the monitoring of facilities where they could be manufactured. In December 1987, Gorbachev and Reagan signed the Intermediate-Range Nuclear Forces Treaty (INF Treaty), which, for the first time in the Cold War, provided for the complete abolition of a category of nuclear weapons in the U.S.-Soviet arms race.

Less progress was made at the time of the signing of the INF Treaty in the Strategic Arms Reduction Talks (START) and in the negotiations on conventional forces in Europe, but other events soon overtook U.S.-Soviet arms negotiations in importance. After the Gorbachev government abandoned the Brezhnev Doctrine—the claimed right of the Soviet Union to intervene in the internal affairs of the Communist states of Eastern Europe—there occurred in 1989 one of the seminal events of the twentieth century. Taking place appropriately in the bicentennial of the French Revolution, the populations in the East European satellite countries rebelled and either drove the Communist regimes from power or forced them to remodel themselves into more democratic governments. The opening of the Berlin Wall and the other barriers that divided East and West Germany on November 9, 1989, marked the beginning of the end for the German Democratic Republic (GDR). The bloodiest of the overthrows of the Communist regimes occurred in Rumania where, in December 1989, the Rumanian army, with the support of most of the population, defeated the country's internal security forces and executed its Communist dictator.

In 1990, Moscow acquiesced to German reunification by agreeing to the merger of the provinces of the GDR with West Germany, and to the continued membership of the enlarged Federal Republic in NATO. The formal political unification of East and West Germany took place through democratic processes late in 1990. The new Germany was bound to respect its eastern borders set by the Soviets after World War II, and to maintain an active military force of no more than 370,000 troops (in 1992 reduced to 345,000 troops). In return, Soviet troops in former East Germany were to be gradually withdrawn from German soil, the last by 1994. Early in 1991, Moscow abrogated the Warsaw Pact and pledged early withdrawal of Soviet forces from the soil of all of its former Warsaw Pact allies.

The only major area of disagreement between the USSR and the USA by the summer of 1991 concerned the stalled START negotiations. George Bush, Reagan's Republican successor as President, finally got over the last hurdles at a meeting with Gorbachev at Moscow on July 31, 1991. They signed a treaty which for the first time reduced rather than capped the numbers of strategic nuclear weapons of the two superpowers. The approximately 12,000 strategic nuclear bombs and warheads of the United States would be reduced to about 9,000, and those of the USSR from 9,000 to about 7,000. In September, Bush ordered cancellation of the alert status of bombers of the Strategic Air Command. It was the first time that some of SAC's aircraft had not been continuously armed and manned for immediate action since 1957. A similar stand-down was ordered for some of the U.S. land-based ICBMs, and a planned reduction in older U.S. ballistic missile submarines was accelerated.

Again, political developments outraced developments in arms control. Unintentionally, Gorbachev's internal reforms had unleashed a rash of ethnic and national upheavals within Soviet borders. The Baltic states (Latvia, Estonia, and Lithuania), annexed to the USSR by Stalin early in World War II, declared their independence, and other Soviet republics— such as Georgia, Armenia, and Moldavia (renamed Moldova)—also demanded independence or at least autonomy. When Boris Yeltsin became head of the Russian Soviet Federated Republic, the largest of the fifteen republics composing the USSR, he not only proposed abolition of Marxism as the chief tenet of state, but also called for a decentralized commonwealth of former Soviet states. The political and economic upheaval within the USSR reached its turning point in August 1991, when eight members of Gorbachev's cabinet—including the minister of defense, the minister of the interior, and the head of the KGB—mounted a coup to topple Gorbachev and to reverse the direction of reform. The heroic stance of Yeltsin at the parliament of the Russian Federated Republic, mass popular support for reform, and division in the Soviet armed forces all contributed to the failure of the coup within three days. Gorbachev was released from house arrest in the Crimea to return to his duties as President of the USSR, but Yeltsin emerged as the dominant personality of the reform movement. A subsequent purge of Soviet hard-liners from the government and the armed forces and the virtual outlaw-ing of the Communist party in many functions of state heralded a massive acceleration of the process of reform.

In December 1991 the presidents of the republics of Russia, Belarus (Bylorussia), and Ukraine met independently of Gorbachev and agreed to form a Commonwealth of Independent States (CIS), one open to membership by any of the other former Soviet republics. Gorbachev's earlier offer of a union treaty, creating a USSR with democratic but federated powers, was brushed aside. Even the capital of the new political unit was to be not Moscow, nor even Leningrad (renamed St. Petersburg on October 31), but Minsk in Belarus. When eight of the other republics also joined the CIS on December 21, it left only the three Baltic states and Georgia (the latter torn by civil war) of the original fifteen republics of the USSR that were not members. As 1992 began, Russia and the other constituent parts of the former Soviet Union were officially under non-Communist governments for the first time since the era of the Bolshevik Revolution.

The implication of the dissolution of the Soviet Union for the former Soviet armed forces is not fully certain at this writing, but each constituent republic of the CIS seems likely in future to have its own conventional military forces. The republics have agreed to a single interim minister of defense and some form of centralized control over all strategic nuclear forces. The Ukrainian republic has laid claims to at least part of the former Soviet Black Sea fleet. Yeltsin has pledged that all tactical nuclear weapons of the former Soviet armed forces will be withdrawn to the territory of the Russian republic and destroyed, and the Russian republic, the largest of the CIS, is reportedly planning on a military establishment of 1.4 million personnel, or a force about a third of the size of the former Soviet armed forces.

The end of the Cold War was also reflected in American military reorganization. Despite the delay imposed by the 1990–91 crisis in the Persian Gulf (see below), the Pentagon began the process of not only reducing the size of the American armed forces, but reforming them for a post–Cold War future. In 1989, the U.S. Army had an active-duty strength of 775,000 troops and eighteen divisions; in 1992, Pentagon plans called for a reduction to 535,000 troops and ten divisions by 1995. The Navy was to be reduced to about four hundred warships, and the Air Force and Marines were also to undergo substantial reductions. But perhaps nothing in the restructuring of the American armed forces was more symbolic of the end of the era of the Cold War than the abolition of the Strategic Air Command (SAC) on June 1, 1992.

In the same month that SAC was formally abolished, Bush and Yeltsin signed a new codicil to the START treaty which pledged a reduction of strategic nuclear warheads to 3,500 on each side, abolition of the Soviet "heavy" SS-18 ICBMs, the limiting of land-based ICBMs on both sides to one warhead apiece, and a reduction in the number of MIRVs aboard ballistic missile submarines. In January 1993 the two heads of state formally signed a START II treaty embodying these features with the proviso that the U.S. might retain 3,500 strategic nuclear warheads and the Russian republic 3,000, all former Soviet strategic systems to be returned to the soil of the Russian republic from Belarus, Ukraine, and Kazhakistan. If the treaty is ratified, the reductions are to be completed by the year 2003. Though the American armed forces would retain a reduced nuclear capability for the indefinite future, the end of the Cold War and other developments suggest that they are likely to move in the direction of becoming smaller, conventionally armed, and more rapidly deployable forces.

VII. Desert Storm: The U.N.'s War with Iraq, 1991

The first major international crisis in the post–Cold War period commenced on August 2, 1990, when Iraqi forces invaded the tiny but oil-rich Arab state of Kuwait. Formal resistance in Kuwait, a country of fewer than 2 million people, was overcome within a few hours. The invasion was brought about in part by President Saddam Hussein's attempt to solve the problem of Iraq's massive debt created by the long war with Iran in the 1980s. With Kuwait's oil supplies combined with those of Iraq, Saddam would control about 20 percent of the world's known supply. In addition, Saddam's forces would be well positioned for further aggression against Saudi Arabia, a country of only 5 million people but the greatest oil producer in the Persian Gulf.

The end of the Cold War allowed the permanent members of the United

Nations Security Council—the United States, Britain, France, the Soviet Union, and the People's Republic of China—to act in rare concert. They voted without dissent to impose economic sanctions on Iraq, and, in late November, except for the PRC which abstained from voting but did not cast a veto, they approved the use of "all necessary measures" to expel Iraqi forces from Kuwait unless they were withdrawn voluntarily by January 15, 1991. By the time of the vote, the buildup of American and allied forces for the defense of Saudi Arabia (Operation Desert Shield) was well advanced. These forces served as the core of the U.N. forces assembled for the liberation of Kuwait, the whole placed under the command of General H. Norman Schwarzkopf, U.S. Army, and dubbed the U.N. Coalition Forces (UNCF).

President Bush obtained Congressional approval for the mobilization of 228,000 American reservists and National Guard troops, and by January 15, 1991, 105,000 reservists and National Guard soldiers were among the 540,000 uniformed Americans in the theater of operations. Of the American troops, 35,000 were women. The rest of the mobilized reserves and Guard were either assigned to help meet American commitments elsewhere or still undergoing further training when the war ended. In about six months, the United States assembled in the Gulf region the equivalent of eight Army and two Marine divisions, a ground force as large as the United States had committed to the war in Vietnam at its peak, plus impressive air and naval forces. Besides U.S. forces, the equivalent of one or more ground divisions were provided by Britain (1), France (1), Egypt (2), Saudi Arabia (1), and Syria (1), as well as lesser units. Additional, air, land, or sea forces were sent by Canada, Italy, Bahrain, Oman, the United Arab Emirates, Qatar, and Bangladesh. Volunteers from the Kuwaiti population in exile also formed a contingent, and even a token force of Afghan "freedom fighters" joined the UNCF. Altogether, more than two dozen countries offered military, financial, or other aid. By mid-January 1991 over 800,000 soldiers, sailors, airmen, and marines had been committed to the UNCF, slightly more than in the U.N. command at the peak of the Korean War.

Though a country of fewer than 20 million people, Iraq was heavily armed. Its army could mobilize 900,000 troops and many of them had been tested by the long war with Iran. By mid-January 1991, Saddam had concentrated 300,000 troops, 4,200 tanks, 2,800 armored personnel carriers, and 3,100 pieces of artillery in Kuwait and southern Iraq. Iraq also possessed Soviet-designed anti-tank missiles, Chinese anti-ship missiles, and the ubiquitous French Exocet missile. The Scud ballistic missile, an improved version of an earlier Soviet design, was the "strategic" weapon in Saddam's armory. With the Scud, Iraq could strike urban areas in much of Saudi Arabia and even Israel. Saddam was also believed to possess large quantities of poison gas, and perhaps biological weapons as well, but probably not nuclear weapons.

The UNCF's greatest edge over the Iraqi forces was in the air and on the sea. With over 2,000 fixed-wing aircraft, the UNCF air forces outnumbered their Iraqi counterparts by a ratio of at least four to one, not to mention the technical and training superiority of especially the American, British, French, Canadian, and Italian air units. Whereas the UNCF had hundreds of helicopters—including U.S. attack helicopters such as the Apache (AH-1S1)—the helicopter capability of the Iraqis was minor. Before the war the Iraqi air force had purchased some excellent fixed-wing aircraft from other countries (e.g., the Mig-29 Fulcrum from the USSR and the French Mirage F-1), but its standards of training and maintenance did not compare with those of the UNCF air forces. The Iraqi navy hardly existed, but the U.S. Navy stationed 37 warships in the Persian Gulf, including two battleships (*Wisconsin* and *Missouri*) and two aircraft carriers (*Midway* and *Ranger*), plus supporting cruisers, destroyers, frigates, and submarines. There were 32 American warships in the North Arabian Sea and the Gulf of Oman, and 26 U.S. warships in the Red Sea, including four aircraft carriers (*America, Roosevelt, Saratoga,* and *Kennedy*). There were also some 50 allied war vessels in the UNCF armada.

With the passing of the deadline on January 15, 1991, Schwarzkopf's headquarters was free to initiate hostilities. The aerial phase of Operation Desert Storm commenced at 2:45 a.m., January 17, Persian Gulf time (6:45 p.m., January 16, EST in the United States), General Charles Horner, USAF, directing the air offensive. The air doctrine practiced by the UNCF reflected the lessons of past wars: air defenses must be destroyed or neutralized, not merely penetrated, before effective air attacks may be made on other targets. Accordingly, among the first targets were communications centers, especially those that linked the Iraqi air defense forces and their central command, Iraq's electric grid, and the antiaircraft missile and gun sites. For this purpose, the UNCF were especially well equipped, having the radar-resistant U.S. F-117 Stealth fighter-bomber, the U.S. F-4 Wild Weasel (whose missiles homed on centers emitting radar transmissions), and aircraft employing laser-guided bombs, such as the Paveway, first employed late in the Vietnam War. In addition to aircraft, ship-launched Tomahawk missiles used sophisticated map-matching electronics to monitor the terrain below and thus guide the missiles to their intended targets. Schwarzkopf achieved a public relations coup by releasing televised motion pictures of the most spectacular successes with precision-guided munitions (PGMs), though no more than 9 percent of the aerial ordnance used against the Iraqis was of the "smart bomb" variety.

The Iraqi air force hardly made an effort to prevent the bombardment. Those few aircraft which rose to intercept the waves of attacking aircraft

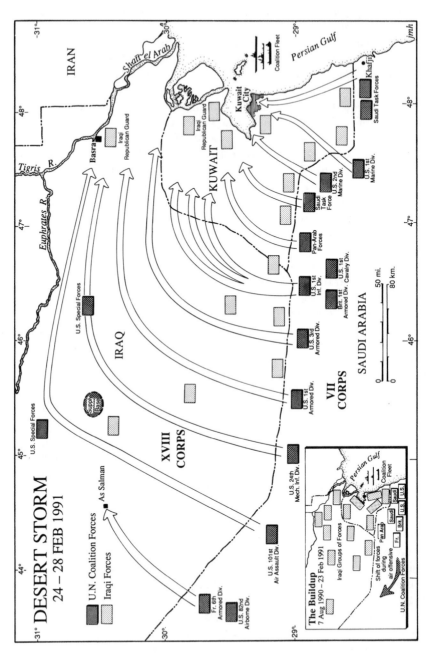

Desert Storm: February 24–28, 1991

were speedily destroyed, and the rest remained in hardened shelters where, in many cases, PGMs destroyed or neutralized them. Some Iraqi aircraft later escaped to air bases in Iran where they were interned for the duration of the war. The absence of radar control largely rendered the Iraqi antiaircraft artillery (AAA) ineffective at night in defense of Baghdad; although Iraqi AAA fired an enormous amount of ammunition, only 29 UNCF aircraft were officially lost to enemy action during the whole campaign.

As the UNCF air attack gradually shifted from strategic targets to interdiction of enemy supply lines and tactical attacks on enemy forward positions in Kuwait, aircraft such as the A-10 Thunderbolt II (better known as the Warthog for its inelegant appearance) proved important. Though only 150 A-10s were in operation, they were credited with destroying about 1,000 Iraqi armored, fighting vehicles (AFVs), 25 percent of all those destroyed during the campaign. Part of the reason for the A-10's success was that it was well armored and damage resistant. The venerable B-52s also put on an impressive show by carpet-bombing Iraqi troop positions. But most of the news media's attention was showered on high performance aircraft such as the U.S. F-14 Tomcat, F-15 Eagle, F-16 Falcon, F/A-118 Hornet, and the British Tornado. They, other aircraft such as helicopters, and the ground forces accounted for the rest of the 4,000 Iraqi AFVs destroyed during Operation Desert Storm.

Despite the outstanding performance of the UNCF's air forces, had not Schwarzkopf's headquarters also employed a skillful ground strategy, the well dug in Iraqi forces in Kuwait might have inflicted heavy losses on the UNCF ground forces and prolonged the war. In order to thwart that outcome, Schwarzkopf carried out a massive and undetected shift of troops to the west. There, the reinforced U.S. 18th Airborne Corps (composed in part of the U.S. 101st Air Assault Division, the U.S. 82nd Airborne Division, the French Sixth Light Armored Division, and French Legionnaires), and the reinforced U.S. 7th Corps (composed *inter alia* of the U.S. First and Third Armored divisions and the British Second Armoured Division), would attempt an envelopment of the enemy's forces in Kuwait from an unexpected direction. The logistics involved in the undetected shift of so many divisions was a triumph of planning and execution.

But while Schwarzkopf was preparing his ground offensive, Saddam Hussein ordered his Scud ballistic missiles into action. Batteries of these weapons appeared from secret shelters to begin an indiscriminate bombardment of population centers in both Israel and Saudi Arabia. Though such weapons could not affect the outcome on the battlefield, unresisted they could have demoralized the urban populations of both Israel and Saudi Arabia. The UNCF command was especially concerned that the attacks might provoke Israel to enter the war and thereby rupture the unity of the U.N. effort. Batteries of the U.S. Army's Patriot anti-ballistic missiles were rushed to Israel in return for the Israeli promise to withhold countermeasures against Iraq if the Patriot proved an effective defense. Patriots were already deployed to protect Saudi Arabian centers of population. In the event, Patriots downed a number of Scuds before they could reach their targets in either Israel or Saudi Arabia, and Israel remained out of the war. (However, one failure at Patriot interception resulted in a Scud striking a barracks in Dhahran, killing twenty-eight American men and women soldiers, the largest number of American troops killed in any one place during the war.) The UNCF air forces stepped up their search-and-destroy missions against Scud bases and suspected hiding places, and many Scuds were destroyed before they could be launched.

At 4:00 a.m. on February 28, the general UNCF ground offensive commenced. Accompanied by part of a U.S. Army armored division, elements of the U.S. First and Second Marine divisions struck north into eastern Kuwait, and a group of Arab forces followed suit. In the Gulf, as they had been doing for days, UNCF warships bombarded enemy coastal positions to suggest that an amphibious assault was imminent, and managed to tie down nine Iraqi divisions. But the main UNCF blow fell far inland. The 18th Airborne Corps, moved largely by helicopters, advanced toward Alfaman airfield, which was to be used as a staging base for a continuation of the drive to the Euphrates. Once the river was reached, the 18th Corps would be in a position to block further Iraqi reinforcements from reaching Kuwait and southern Iraq. Further east, the 7th Corps broke through the sand berm barriers erected by the Iraqis and pressed forward on the inner wheel of the envelopment. Many of the frontline Iraqi troops proved to have no fight left in them and surrendered in large numbers, but where Iraqi armor put up a fight, the greater range of the UNCF tank guns, and their superior night fighting capabilities, resulted in massive destruction of Iraqi forces. Especially the American Abrams M1-A1 tank proved in every respect superior to the Soviet T-72, the best of the Iraqi tanks.

As it became clear that they were about to be enveloped, Iraqi units in Kuwait City and its environs began a flight toward Basra. (An exception was a determined resistance by Iraqi units at the Kuwait City airport, overcome by U.S. Marines.) But as they fled up the road toward Basra, the Iraqi troops were not only threatened with being cut off on the ground, they made perfect targets for air attack. On the "highway of death," as some commentators called it, thousands of Iraqi troops were slaughtered as their convoys of tanks, trucks, and buses were shattered by bombs, rockets, and strafing. A *Kesselschlacht,* or battle of encirclement and annihilation, of the Iranian forces in Kuwait, was in the offing when, at the passing of the hundredth hour of the ground offensive, President Bush ordered Schwarzkopf to halt offensive operations and to allow the mangled enemy to withdraw from Kuwait. By then, part of the 18th Corps was at Nasiriya on the Euphrates, and other elements of the corps were engaging Saddam's elite Republican Guard south of Basra. A formal armistice between the UNCF and Iraq was reached on March 4.

The UNCF liberation of Kuwait was accomplished with a maximum of destruction of the Iraqi enemy and minimal casualties among the UNCF forces. Estimates of Iraqi dead and wounded vary greatly, but probably at least 25,000 Iraqi soldiers were killed or fatally wounded, and perhaps three times that number survived wounds or illness. Some 15,000 Iraqi civilians were the unintended victims of bombing and missile attacks. Even with "smart bombs" it proved impossible not to inflict some "collateral casualties," a case in point being the death of three hundred Iraqi men, women, and children in a bomb shelter in Baghdad thought by Schwarzkopf's headquarters to be a command center. UNCF casualties were fewer than a thousand, of which 147 were American dead and 467 American wounded. Few campaigns in history have been as one-sided in their outcome as Desert Storm.

Still, the operation was not an unadulterated success. Target identification proved difficult in the fast-moving ground battle, and, as a consequence, thirty-seven of the American fatalities were due to "friendly fire." An additional seventy-two Americans were wounded by accident. Some allied casualties were also inflicted by mistake. Another mixed performance was the American mobilization of reserves and National Guard. One American mechanized infantry division found its "round-out" National Guard brigade unfit for combat, and had to borrow a brigade stationed in Germany. Army National Guard units performed best in supporting roles in Desert Storm, but Air National Guard units, as well as the Air Force Reserve units, performed outstandingly well in both combat and support missions.

For the patterns of war, Desert Storm revealed again the importance of electronics to modern warfare, especially in the attack of, and the defense against, aircraft and missiles, and, to a lesser extent, to the successful engagement of ground forces, a trend of long standing. But the ultramodern nature of the UNCF's weaponry tended to conceal the importance of the training of the troops and the operational skill of the UNCF's high command to the outcome. The Iraqi army, which had proved such a stubborn enemy of the Iranians in the 1980s, had collapsed like a house of cards in the face of such opposition. Soldiers were left to ponder what a future desert war might be like between equally well-equipped, well-commanded, and well-motivated forces. As has ever been the case, every war has its own distinctive pattern, and the ultimate significance of Desert Storm to the conduct of war in general awaits the longer judgment of history.

Epilogue

According to one authority, the number of armed conflicts around the globe dropped from about forty in the early 1980s to the low twenties in the early 1990s. Nearly all of these current wars are internal struggles, the most serious perhaps being the civil war in Yugoslavia, the first prolonged armed conflict in Europe since 1945. Though both Croatia and Slovenia made good their breakaway efforts from Yugoslavia, the Serbs have bitterly contested the secession of Bosnia-Herzegovina. To this writing, the most bitter fighting has occurred around Sarajevo, the city where the assassination of the Austrian archduke in 1914 set in train the events that led to the outbreak of the First World War. This conflict in the Balkans has been accompanied by so-called Serbian "ethnic cleansing" of Croats and Muslims from Bosnia-Herzegovina through atrocities and concentration camps—measures all too reminiscent of the Nazi "racial purification" efforts in the Second World War.

Elsewhere, ethnic and religious differences have led to civil war in some former Soviet territories such as Georgia, Armenia, and Azerbaijan, and still other armed conflicts continue in Africa and Asia. The war in African Angola has ended, perhaps momentarily, with a shaky peace following sixteen years of war and perhaps a million deaths. In Somalia, several years of civil war degenerated into such chaos that more people were dying of starvation than from the fighting. An estimated 300,000 Somalis have died as of this writing. Beginning in December 1992, a U.N.-sanctioned armed intervention by U.S. and other national forces took place in Somalia on humanitarian grounds for the purpose of restoring a measure of order. In Asia, the U.N. presides over an uneasy truce in war-torn Cambodia, where a transitional government under Prince Norodom Sihanouk has been put in place. The Middle East is once more threatened by war as the result of Saddam Hussein's continued violations of the

U.N.-imposed sanctions after the Gulf War in 1991. And the aforementioned conflicts are only a few of the trouble spots around the world.

Still, with the passing of the Cold War, the danger of war has been chiefly associated with lesser states rather than with great powers, their motives stemming from ultranationalism, ethnocentrism, conflicts of religion and culture, and the search for economic and military security. Thus, while the world continues to seek peaceful resolutions to the conditions that breed war, new patterns of war unfortunately continue to evolve. Perhaps it is reasonable to predict that in the near future armed conflicts will be regional, fought among and within lesser states, and with occasional U.N.-sanctioned interventions or interventions by regional organizations. While there has been discussion of a standing military force under control of the United Nations for repelling aggression and enforcing peace, for the foreseeable future international military interventions under U.N. auspices will probably be conducted by *ad hoc* collections of military forces, such as that which liberated Kuwait from Iraq in 1991. And the national interests of the intervening powers will doubtless influence their willingness to participate. It has been suggested by some that the intervention on Kuwait's behalf by Western powers was as much due to their concern for the Middle East's sources of oil as to a wish to uphold international order.

The United Nations and regional organizations will probably continue to rely chiefly on the United States of America for major military interventions as long as it has the will and the means to serve in that capacity. On the other hand, acquisition by lesser powers of nuclear weapons will enhance their ability to intimidate stronger powers from intervening in any wars they care to launch—a disquieting circumstance for the future of international peacekeeping.

Perhaps the most encouraging pattern that seems to be emerging in the post–Cold War era is a willingness of the great powers to seek accommodation with each other and even work together, at least on occasion, to repel international aggression and promote the peaceful settlement of quarrels among lesser states or factions. Thus, as troubling as the present situation in former Yugoslavia is, there is little chance that a conflict in the Balkans could suddenly kindle war among the major powers as it did in 1914, and a negotiated end to Yugoslavia's civil war is not outside the realm of possibility. Nor, at this writing, does there seem to be any point around the globe where fighting might erupt between major states. Even the worldwide economic recession of the early 1990s has not promoted war and conquest by major powers, as was the case in the 1930s with Nazi Germany, Fascist Italy, and Imperial Japan. In at least that sense of the term, militarism seems on the decline. And since the greatest danger of war at present is armed conflict among lesser powers, if some peaceful method can be found for resolving differences among and within those states, perhaps new patterns of peace will replace the old search for new patterns of war. If so, it would be a fitting development for the post–Cold War era and for the beginning of a new millennium.

Selected Bibliography

Addington, Larry H. *The Blitzkrieg Era and the German General Staff, 1865–1941.* New Brunswick, N.J.: Rutgers University Press, 1971.
——. *The Patterns of War through the Eighteenth Century.* Bloomington: Indiana University Press, 1990.

Albion, R. G. *Forests and Sea Power: The Timber Problem of the Royal Navy, 1652–1862.* Hamden, Conn.: Archon Press, 1965.

Alden, John Richard. *The American Revolution, 1775–1783.* New York: Harper and Row, 1954.

Ambler, John S. *The French Army in Politics, 1945–1962.* Columbus: Ohio State University Press, 1966.

Ambrose, Stephen E. *Eisenhower: A Life.* New York: Simon and Schuster, 1983.
——. *Eisenhower and Berlin, 1945: The Decision to Halt at the Elbe.* New York: W. W. Norton, 1967.
——. *The Supreme Commander: The War Years of General Dwight D. Eisenhower.* Garden City, N.Y.: Doubleday, 1969.

Amrine, Michael. *The Great Decision: The Secret History of the Atomic Bomb.* New York: Charles Scribner's Sons, 1959.

Anderson, Bern. *By Sea and by River: The Naval History of the Civil War.* New York: Alfred A. Knopf, 1963.

Anderson, Nancy Scott, and Dwight Anderson. *The Generals: Ulysses S. Grant and Robert E. Lee.* New York: Alfred A. Knopf, 1988.

Anderson, Romola, and R. C. Anderson. *The Sailing Ship.* New York: W. W. Norton, 1963.

Andreski, Stanislav. *Military Organization and Society.* Rev. ed. Berkeley: University of California Press, 1968.

Asprey, Robert B. *The First Battle of the Marne.* Philadelphia and New York: J. B. Lippincott, 1962.
——. *War in the Shadows: The Guerrilla in History.* 2 vols. Garden City, N.Y.: Doubleday, 1975.

Ballard, Colin R. *The Military Genius of Abraham Lincoln.* Cleveland and New York: World, 1952.

Barber, Noel. *A Sinister Twilight: The Fall of Singapore, 1942.* Boston: Houghton Mifflin, 1968.
——. *The War of the Running Dogs: The Malayan Emergency, 1948–1960.* New York: Weybright and Talley, 1971.

Baritz, Loren. *Backfire: A History of How American Culture Led Us into Vietnam and Made Us Fight the Way We Did.* New York: William Morrow, 1985.

Barker, Arthur J. *Arab-Israeli Wars.* New York: Hippocrene Books, 1980.
——. *The War against Russia, 1854–1856.* New York: Holt, Rinehart and Winston, 1970.

Barker, Ralph. *The Thousand Plane Raid.* New York: Ballantine Books, 1965.

Barnaby, Frank. *The Automated Battlefield.* New York: Free Press, 1986.

Barnett, Correlli. *Britain and Her Army, 1509–1970: A Military, Political and Social Survey.* New York: William Morrow, 1970.

———. *The Desert Generals.* New York: Viking, 1961.

———. *Engage the Enemy More Closely: The Royal Navy in the Second World War.* New York: W. W. Norton, 1991.

———. *The Sword-Bearers: Supreme Command in the First World War.* New York: William Morrow, 1963.

Barrett, John G. *Sherman's March Through the Carolinas.* Chapel Hill: University of North Carolina Press, 1956.

Barthorp, Michael. *The Zulu War: A Pictorial History.* Poole, Dorset: Blandford Press, 1980.

Bartlett, C. J. *Great Britain and Sea Power, 1815–1853.* Oxford: Clarendon Press, 1963.

Bartov, Omer. *Hitler's Army: Soldiers, Nazis, and War in the Third Reich.* New York: Oxford University Press, 1991.

Baskir, Lawrence M., and William A. Strauss. *Chance and Circumstance: The Draft, the War and the Vietnam Generation.* New York: Alfred A. Knopf, 1978.

Bauer, K. Jack. *The Mexican War, 1846–1848.* (Macmillan Wars of the United States, Louis Morton, ed.) New York and London: Macmillan, 1974.

———, ed. *Soldiering: The Civil War Diary of Rice C. Bull.* New York: Berkley Books, 1988.

Baxter, J. P. *The Introduction of the Ironclad Warship.* Hamden, Conn.: Shoe String Press, 1968.

Beatie, R. H. *Road to Manassas: The Growth of the Union Command in the Eastern Theater from the Fall of Fort Sumter to the First Battle of Bull Run.* New York: Cooper Square, 1964.

Beckwith, Charlie, and Donald Knox. *Delta Force.* San Diego: Harcourt Brace Jovanovich, 1983.

Bekker, C. D. *Defeat at Sea: The Struggle and Eventual Destruction of the German Navy, 1933–1945.* New York: Henry Holt, 1955.

Bennett, Geoffrey. *Nelson the Commander.* New York: Charles Scribner's Sons, 1972.

Benoist-Méchin, Jacques. *Sixty Days That Shook the West: The Fall of France, 1940.* Trans. by Peter Wiles. New York: Charles Putnam's Sons, 1963.

Berger, Carl. *The Korean Knot: A Military-Political History.* Rev. ed. Philadelphia: University of Pennsylvania Press, 1964.

Berghahn, V. R. *Germany and the Approach of War in 1914.* New York: St. Martin's Press, 1973.

Berman, Larry. *Planning a Tragedy: The Americanization of the War in Vietnam.* New York and London: W. W. Norton, 1982.

Bernardo, C. J., and Eugene H. Bacon, *American Military Policy: Its Development since 1775.* Harrisburg, Pa.: Stackpole, 1961 [1955].

Bernstein, Iver. *The New York City Draft Riots: The Significance for American Society and Politics in the Age of the Civil War.* New York and Oxford: Oxford University Press, 1990.

Billias, George A., ed. *George Washington's Generals.* New York: William Morrow, 1964.

———. *George Washington's Opponents: Generals and Admirals in the American Revolution.* New York: William Morrow, 1969.

Billington, James H. *Fire in the Minds of Men: Origins of the Revolutionary Faith.* New York: Basic Books, 1980.

Black, Robert C. *The Railroads of the Confederacy.* Chapel Hill: University of North Carolina Press, 1952.

Blair, Clay, Jr. *MacArthur.* Garden City, N.Y.: Doubleday, 1977.

———. *Silent Victory: The U.S. Submarine War Against Japan.* New York: J. B. Lippincott, 1975.

Bliven, Bruce, Jr. *Battle for Manhattan.* Baltimore: Pelican Books, 1955.

Blumenson, Martin. *Patton: The Man behind the Legend, 1885–1945.* New York: William Morrow, 1985.

———. *The Patton Papers.* 2 vols. Boston: Houghton Mifflin, 1974.

Blumenson, Martin, and James L. Stokesbury. *Masters of the Art of Command.* Boston: Houghton Mifflin, 1975.

Boettcher, Thomas D. *Vietnam: The Valor and the Sorrow.* Boston and Toronto: Little, Brown, 1985.

Bonds, Ray, ed. *The Illustrated Encyclopedia of the Strategy, Tactics and Weapons of Russian Military Power.* New York: Bonanza Books, 1982.

———. *The U.S. War Machine: An Illustrated Encyclopedia of American Military Equipment and Strategy.* New York: Crown, 1978.

Bowman, John S., ed. *The Civil War, Day by Day.* Greenwich, Conn.: Dorset Press, 1989.

Bowyer, Chaz. *The Encyclopedia of British Military Aircraft.* London: Bison Books, 1982.

Bradford, Ned, ed. *Battles and Leaders of the Civil War.* Abridged. New York: Fairfax Press, 1988 [1887–1888].

Bradley, Omar N., and Clay Blair. *A General's Life.* New York: Simon and Schuster, 1983.

Brenner, Eliot, and William Harwood, *Desert Storm: The Weapons of War.* New York: Orion Books, 1991.

Brodie, Bernard. *A Guide to Naval Strategy.* Rev. ed. New York, Washington and London: Praeger, 1965.

———. *Strategic Air Power in World War II.* Santa Monica, Calif.: Rand Corporation, 1957.

———. *Strategy in the Missile Age.* Princeton: Princeton University Press, 1959.

Brodie, Bernard, and Fawn Brodie. *From Crossbow to H-Bomb.* Rev. ed. Bloomington: Indiana University Press, 1973.

Broughton, Jack. *Thud Ridge.* New York: Popular Library, 1969.

Browne, Courtney. *Tojo: The Last Banzai.* New York: Holt, Rinehart and Winston, 1967.

Brownlow, Donald G. *Panzer Baron: The Military Exploits of General Hasso von Manteuffel.* North Quincy, Mass.: Christopher, 1975.

Bryant, Arthur. *Triumph in the West: A History of the War Years based on the Diaries of Field Marshal Lord Alanbrooke.* . . . Garden City, N.Y.: Doubleday, 1959.

———. *The Turn of the Tide: A History of the War Years Based on the Diaries of Field Marshal Lord Alanbrooke.* . . . Garden City, N.Y.: Doubleday, 1957.

Bucholz, Arden. *Hans Delbruck and the German Military Establishment: War Images in Conflict.* Iowa City: University of Iowa Press, 1985.

Bunting, Josiah. *The Lionheads.* New York: Popular Library, 1972.

Butler, David. *The Fall of Saigon: Scenes from the Sudden End of a Long War.* New York: Simon and Schuster, 1985.

Caidin, Martin. *Black Thursday: The Schweinfurt Raid, October 14, 1943.* New York: Bantam Books, 1981 [1960].

———. *Flying Forts: The B-17 in World War II.* New York: Ballantine Books, 1968.

———. *The Tigers Are Burning.* New York: Hawthorne Books, 1974.

Callahan, Raymond. *The Worst Disaster: The Fall of Singapore.* London and Newark: Association of University Presses and University of Delaware Press, 1977.

Calvocoressi, Peter, and Guy Wint. *Total War: Causes and Courses of the Second World War.* London: Penguin Books, 1979.

Carver, Michael, ed. *The War Lords: Military Commanders of the Twentieth Century.* Boston and Toronto: Little, Brown, 1976.

Cate, Curtis. *The War of the Two Emperors: The Duel between Napoleon and Alexander, Russia, 1812.* New York: Random House, 1985.

Catton, Bruce. *Glory Road: The Bloody Route from Fredericksburg to Gettysburg.* Garden City, N.Y.: Doubleday, 1956.

_____. *This Hallowed Ground: The Story of the Union Side of the Civil War.* Garden City, N.Y.: Doubleday, 1956.

Chaissin, Lionel M. *The Communist Conquest of China: A History of the Civil War, 1945–1949.* Trans. from the French by Timothy Osato and Louis Gelas. Cambridge: Harvard University Press, 1965.

Challener, Richard, D. *The French Theory of the Nation in Arms, 1866–1939.* New York: Russell Press, 1955.

Chambers, John W. *To Raise an Army: The Draft Comes to Modern America.* New York and London: Free Press, 1987.

Chandler, David G. *Atlas of Military Strategy.* New York: Free Press, 1980.

_____. *The Campaigns of Napoleon.* New York: Macmillan, 1966.

_____. *Dictionary of the Napoleonic Wars.* New York: Macmillan, 1979.

Chapman, Guy. *Why France Fell: The Defeat of the French Army in 1940.* New York: Holt, Rinehart and Winston, 1968.

Chomsky, Noam. *At War with Asia: Essays on Indochina.* New York: Vintage Books, 1969.

Chuikov, Vasili I. *The Battle for Stalingrad.* Trans. by MacGibbon and Kee, Ltd. New York: Holt, Rinehart and Winston, 1964.

_____. *The Fall of Berlin.* New York: Holt, Rinehart and Winston, 1968.

Clark, Alan. *Barbarossa: The Russian-German Conflict, 1941–1945.* New York: William Morrow, 1965.

_____. *The Donkeys.* New York: William Morrow, 1961.

Clausewitz, Carl von. *On War.* Ed. and trans. by Michael Howard and Peter Paret. Princeton: Princeton University Press, 1976 [1832].

_____. *War, Politics, and Power: Selections from On War and I Believe and I Profess.* Ed. and trans. by Edward M. Collins. Chicago: Henry Regnery, 1962.

Clendenen, Clarence C. *Blood on the Border: The United States Army and Mexican Irregulars.* (Macmillan Wars of the United States, Louis Morton, ed.) London: Macmillan, 1969.

Coates, James, and Michael Kilian. *Heavy Losses: The Dangerous Decline of American Defense.* New York: Viking Penguin, 1985.

Coffman, Edward M. *The War to End All Wars: The American Experience in World War I.* Madison: University of Wisconsin Press, 1986 [1969].

Coggins, Jack. *Arms and Equipment of the Civil War.* Garden City, N.Y.: Doubleday, 1962.

_____. *The Campaign for North Africa.* Garden City, N.Y.: Doubleday, 1980.

Cohen, Stephen P. *The Indian Army: Its Contribution to the Development of a Nation.* Berkeley: University of California Press, 1971.

Cohen, Steven. *Vietnam: Anthology and Guide to a Television History.* New York: Alfred A. Knopf, 1983.

Cole, Garold D. *Civil War Eyewitnesses: An Annotated Bibliography of Books and Articles, 1955–1986.* Columbia: University of South Carolina Press, 1988.

Coles, Harry L. *The War of 1812*. Chicago and London: University of Chicago Press, 1965.

Collier, Basil. *A History of Air Power*. New York: Macmillan, 1974.

———. *The Lion and the Eagle: British and Anglo-American Strategy, 1900–1950*. New York: Capricorn Books, 1982.

Committee of Concerned Asian Scholars. *The Indochina Story*. New York: Bantam Books, 1968.

Connell, Evan S. *Son of the Morning Star: Custer and the Little Bighorn*. New York: Harper and Row, 1984.

Cook, Chris, and Stevenson, John. *The Atlas of Modern Warfare*. New York: G. P. Putnam's Sons, 1978.

Cooling, Benjamin Franklin. *Forts Henry and Donelson: The Key to the Confederate Heartland*. Knoxville: University of Tennessee Press, 1987.

Cooper, Matthew. *The German Army, 1933–1945: Its Political and Military Failure*. New York: Stein and Day, 1978.

Cornish, Dudley Taylor. *The Sable Arm: Black Troops in the Union Army, 1861–1865*. Lawrence: University Press of Kansas, 1987 [1956].

Corum, James S. *The Roots of Blitzkrieg: Hans von Seeckt and German Military Reform*. Lawrence: University Press of Kansas, 1992.

Corvisier, André. *Armies and Societies in Europe, 1494–1789*. Bloomington and London: Indiana University Press, 1979.

Cox, Arthur M. *Russian Roulette: The Superpower Game*. New York: Times Books, 1982.

Craig, Gordon. *The Battle of Königgrätz: Prussia's Victory over Austria, 1866*. Philadelphia and New York: J. B. Lippincott, 1964.

———. *The Politics of the Prussian Army, 1640–1945*. New York: Oxford University Press, 1964.

Cross, Robin. *The Bombers: The Illustrated History of Offensive Strategy and Tactics in the Twentieth Century*. New York: Macmillan, 1987.

———, ed. *Warfare: A Chronological History*. Secaucus, N.J.: Wellfleet Press, 1991.

Cunliffe, Marcus. *Soldiers and Civilians: The Martial Spirit in America, 1775–1865*. Boston: Little, Brown, 1968.

Curtiss, John S. *The Russian Army under Nicholas I, 1825–1855*. Durham, N.C.: Duke University Press, 1965.

Dallin, Alexander. *German Rule in Russia, 1941–1945: A Study of Occupation Policies*. New York: St. Martin's Press, 1957.

Davis, Burke. *The Campaign That Won America: The Story of Yorktown*. New York: Dial Press, 1970.

———. *The Cowpens-Guilford Courthouse Campaign*. (Great Battles of History, Hanson W. Balwin, ed.) Philadelphia and New York: J. B. Lippincott, 1962.

———. *Gray Fox: Robert E. Lee and the Civil War*. New York and Toronto: Rinehart, 1956.

Davis, William C. *Battle at Bull Run: A History of the First Major Campaign of The Civil War*. Garden City, N.Y.: Doubleday, 1977.

Dawidowicz, Lucy. *The War Against the Jews, 1933–1945*. New York: Holt, Rinehart and Winston, 1975.

Deichmann, Paul. *German Air Force Operations in Support of the Army*. New York: Arno Press, 1962.

Demeter, Karl. *The German Officer Corps in Society and State, 1650–1945*. Trans. by Angus Malcolm. New York and Washington: Praeger, 1965.

Deutsch, Harold C. *The Conspiracy against Hitler in the Twilight War*. Minneapolis: University of Minnesota Press, 1968.

Dew, Charles B. *Joseph R. Anderson: Ironmaker to the Confederacy.* New Haven and London: Yale University Press, 1966.

Divine, Robert A., ed. *The Cuban Missile Crisis.* Chicago: Quadrangle Press, 1971.

Dower, John W. *War without Mercy: Race and Power in the Pacific War.* New York: Pantheon Books, 1986.

Downey, Fairfax. *The Guns at Gettysburg.* New York: Collier Books, 1962.

Doyle, Edward, and Samuel Lipsman. *The Vietnam Experience.* 3 vols. Boston: Boston Publishing Co., 1981.

Duffy, Christopher. *The Army of Frederick the Great.* New York: Hippocrene Books, 1974.

_____. *The Army of Maria Theresa.* London: Newton Abbot, 1977.

_____. *Fire and Stone: The Science of Fortress Warfare, 1668–1860.* London and Vancouver: David and Charles, 1975.

_____. *Red Storm on the Reich: The Soviet March on Germany, 1945.* New York: Atheneum, 1991.

_____. *Russia's Military Way to the West: Origins and Nature of Russian Military Power.* London, Boston, and Henley: Routledge and Kegan Paul, 1981.

Dunlop, J. K. *The Development of the British Army, 1899–1940.* London: Methuen, 1968.

Dunnigan, James F. *How to Make War: A Comprehensive Guide to Modern Warfare.* New York: William Morrow, 1982.

Dupuy, R. Ernest, and Trevor N. Dupuy. *Encyclopedia of Military History from 3500 B.C. to the Present.* New York: Harper and Row, 1970.

Dupuy, T. N. *A Genius for War: The German Army and General Staff, 1807–1945.* London: Macdonald and Jane's, 1977.

_____. *The Evolution of Weapons and Warfare.* Indianapolis and New York: Bobbs-Merrill, 1980.

Dyson, Freeman. *Weapons and Hope.* New York: Harper and Row, 1984.

Earle, Edward M., ed. *Makers of Modern Strategy: Military Thought from Machiavelli to Hitler.* Princeton: Princeton University Press, 1943.

Edelman, Bernard, ed. *Dear America: Letters Home from Vietnam.* New York and London: W. W. Norton, 1985.

Eggenberger, David. *An Encyclopedia of Battles: Accounts of Over 1,560 Battles from 1479 B.C. to the Present.* New York: Dover, 1985 [1967].

Eisenhower, John. *The Bitter Woods: . . . Hitler's Surprise Ardennes Offensive.* New York: G. P. Putnam and Sons, 1969.

Ellis, John. *Cassino, The Hollow Victory.* New York: McGraw-Hill, 1984.

_____. *The Social History of the Machine Gun.* New York: Pantheon Books, 1975.

Ellis, Joseph, and Robert Moore. *School for Soldiers: West Point and the Profession of Arms.* New York: Oxford University Press, 1974.

Ellsberg, Daniel. *Papers on the War.* New York: Simon and Schuster, 1972.

Emme, Eugene M., ed. *The Impact of Air Power: National Security and World Politics.* Princeton: D. Van Nostrand, 1959.

Erickson, John. *The Soviet High Command.* New York: St. Martin's Press, 1962.

Esposito, Vincent J., ed. *The West Point Atlas of American Wars, 1869–1953.* 2 vols. New York: Praeger, 1959.

Esposito, Vincent J., and John Robert Elting. *A Military History and Atlas of the Napoleonic Wars.* New York: Praeger, 1964.

Falk, Richard A., Gabriel Kolko, and Robert Jay Lifton. *Crimes of War: A Legal, Political-Documentary and Psychological Inquiry into . . . Criminal Acts in War.* New York: Vintage Books, 1971.

Fall, Bernard B. *Hell in a Very Small Place: The Siege of Dien Bien Phu.* New York: Vintage Books, 1968.

————. *The Two Viet-Nams: A Political and Military Analysis.* Rev. ed. New York and London: Praeger, 1964.

Falls, Cyril. *The Art of War from the Age of Napoleon to the Present Day.* New York: Oxford University Press, 1961.

————. *The Great War, 1914–1918.* New York: Capricorn Books, 1959.

————. *A Hundred Years of War, 1850–1950.* New York: Collier Books, 1953.

Farago, Ladislas. *Patton: Ordeal and Triumph.* New York: Dell, 1963.

Farrar, L. L., Jr. *The Short-War Illusion: German Policy, Strategy and Domestic Affairs, August-December 1914.* Santa Barbara and Oxford: ABC Clio, 1973.

————, ed. *War: A Historical, Political and Social Study.* (Studies in International and Comparative Politics, No. 9, Peter H. Merkl, series ed.) Santa Barbara and Oxford: ABC Clio, 1978.

Farwell, Byron. *Queen Victoria's Little Wars.* New York and London: Harper and Row, 1972.

Fay, Sidney. *The Origins of the World War.* 2 vols. London and New York: Free Press, 1966 [1928–1930].

Fehrenbach, T. R. *This Kind of War: A Study in Unpreparedness.* New York: Macmillan, 1963.

Feis, Herbert. *Japan Subdued: The Atomic Bomb and the End of the War in the Pacific.* Princeton: Princeton University Press, 1961.

Ferro, Marc. *The Great War, 1914–1918.* Trans. by N. Stone. London: Routledge and Kegan Paul, 1973.

Fitzgerald, Frances. *Fire in the Lake: The Vietnamese and the Americans in Vietnam.* New York: Vintage Books, 1973.

Foote, Shelby. *The Civil War: A Narrative.* 3 vols. New York: Vintage Books, 1958–1974.

Forester, C. S. *Rifleman Dodd.* New York: Bantam Books, 1952 [1932].

Forty, John. *Desert Rats at War: North Africa and Europe.* London and New York: Ian Allen, Ltd., and Ottenheimer, 1980 [1975, 1977].

Frankland, Noble, ed. *The Encyclopedia of Twentieth Century Warfare.* New York: Crown, 1989.

Fredette, R. H. *The Sky on Fire: The First Battle of Britain, 1917–1918, and the Birth of the Royal Air Force.* New York: Holt, Rinehart and Winston, 1966.

Freedman, Lawrence. *The Evolution of Nuclear Strategy.* New York: St. Martin's Press, 1981.

Friedrich, Otto, ed. *Desert Storm: The War in the Persian Gulf.* Boston: Little, Brown, 1991.

Fuller, J. F. C. *A Military History of the Western World.* 3 vols. New York: Funk and Wagnalls, 1954–1956.

————. *The Conduct of War, 1789–1961.* New Brunswick, N.J.: Rutgers University Press, 1961.

Fussell, Paul. *The Great War and Modern Memory.* New York: Oxford University Press, 1975.

————. *Wartime: Understanding and Behavior in the Second World War.* New York and Oxford: Oxford University Press, 1989.

Gallagher, Matthew P. *The Soviet History of World War II: Myth, Memories, and Realities.* New York and London: Praeger, 1963.

Galland, Adolf. *The First and the Last: The Rise and Fall of the German Fighter Forces, 1938–1945.* Trans. by Mervyn Savill. New York: Henry Holt, 1954.

Garthoff, R. L. *Soviet Military Doctrine.* Glencoe, Ill.: Free Press, 1953.

_____. *Soviet Strategy in the Nuclear Age.* New York: Praeger, 1958.

Gates, John M. *Schoolbooks and Krags: The United States Army in the Philippines, 1898–1902.* Westport, Conn., and London: Greenwood Press, 1973.

Gettleman, Marvin, et al., eds. *Conflict in Indochina: A Reader.* . . . New York: Vintage Books, 1970.

Giap, Vo Nguyen. *The Military Art of People's War: Selected Writings of General Vo Nguyen Giap.* Ed. by Russell Stetler. New York and London: Modern Reader, 1970.

Gibbons, Tony. *Warships and Naval Battles of the Civil War.* New York: Gallery Books, 1989.

Gibbs, Peter. *The Battle of the Alma.* (Great Battles of History, Hanson W. Baldwin, ed.) Philadelphia and New York: J. B. Lippincott, 1963.

Gibson, James N. *The History of the U.S. Nuclear Arsenal.* Greenwich, Conn.: Brompton Books, 1989.

Glatthaar, Joseph T. *Forged in Battle: The Civil War Alliance of Black Soldiers and White Officers.* New York and London: Free Press, 1990.

_____. *The March to the Sea and Beyond: Sherman's Troops in the Savannah and Carolinas Campaigns.* New York and London: New York University Press, 1985.

Glover, Michael. *Wellington as Military Commander.* London: B. T. Batsford; Princeton: D. Van Nostrand, 1968.

Goldberg, Alfred, ed. *A History of the United States Air Force, 1907–1957.* Princeton, New York, Toronto, and London: D. Van Nostrand, 1957.

Goodspeed, D. J. *The German Wars, 1914–1945.* Boston: Houghton Mifflin, 1977.

_____. *Ludendorff: Genius of World War I.* Toronto: Macmillan, 1966.

Gordon, Harold J. *The Reichswehr and the German Republic, 1919–1926.* Princeton: Princeton University Press, 1957.

Gordon, John W. *The Other Desert War: British Special Forces in North Africa, 1940–1943.* (Contributions in Military Studies, Number 56.) New York: Greenwood Press, 1987.

Görlitz, Walter. *History of the German General Staff, 1657–1945.* Trans. by Brian Battershaw. New York and London: Praeger, 1953.

Gosnell, H. Allen. *Guns on the Western Waters: The Story of River Gunboats in the Civil War.* Baton Rouge: Louisiana State University Press, 1949.

Goulden, Joseph C. *Korea: The Untold Story of the War.* New York: Times Books, 1982.

_____. *Truth Is the First Casualty: The Gulf of Tonkin Affair—Illusion and Reality.* Chicago: James B. Adler, 1969.

Goutard, A. *The Battle of France, 1940.* Trans. by A. R. P. Burgess. New York: Ives Washburn, 1959.

Graham, Gerald S. *The Politics of Naval Supremacy: Studies in British Maritime Ascendancy.* New York: Cambridge University Press, 1965.

Grant, U. S. *Memoirs and Selected Letters.* New York: Viking, 1990.

Graves, Robert. *Sergeant Lamb's America.* New York: Vintage Books, 1962. [1940.]

Gray, Edwyn A. *The Killing Time: The German U-Boat War, 1914–1918.* New York: Charles Scribner's Sons, 1972.

Greene, Jack. *War at Sea: Pearl Harbor to Midway.* New York: Gallery Books, 1988.

Greenfield, Kent R., ed. *Command Decisions.* New York: Harcourt, Brace, 1959.

Gregory, Barry, and John Batchelor. *Airborne Warfare, 1918–1945.* New York: Exeter Books, 1979.

Grenfel, Russell. *The Bismarck Episode.* New York: Macmillan, 1962.

Griffith, Samuel B., ed. and trans. *Mao Tse-tung on Guerrilla Warfare.* New York and Washington: Praeger, 1961.

Gunston, Bill. *The Illustrated Encyclopedia of Combat Aircraft of World War II.* London: Salamander Books, 1978.

Hackett, John Winthrop. *The Profession of Arms.* New York: Macmillan, 1983.

Hagerman, Edward. *The American Civil War and the Origins of Modern Warfare.* Bloomington and Indianapolis: Indiana University Press, 1988.

Halberstam, David. *The Best and the Brightest.* New York: Random House, 1969.

Hamilton, Nigel. *Monty the Field Marshal, 1944–1976.* London: Hamish Hamilton, 1986.

Hammer, Ellen J. *A Death in November: America in Vietnam, 1963.* New York and Oxford: Oxford University Press, 1987.

Hammond, Thomas T. *Red Flag over Afghanistan: The Communist Coup, the Soviet Invasion, and the Consequences.* Boulder, Colo.: Westview Press, 1984.

Handel, Michael I., ed. *Clausewitz and Modern Strategy.* Totowa, N.J.: Frank Cass, 1986.

Harries, Meirion, and Susan Harries. *Soldiers of the Sun: The Rise and Fall of the Imperial Japanese Army.* New York: Random House, 1991.

Haskell, Frank A. *The Battle of Gettysburg.* Ed. by Bruce Caton. Boston: Houghton Mifflin, 1958.

Hassler, Warren B., Jr. *General George B. McClellan: Shield of the Union.* Baton Rouge: Louisiana State University Press, 1957.

Hastings, Max. *The Korean War.* New York: Simon and Schuster, 1987.

———. *Overlord: D-Day and the Battle for Normandy.* New York: Simon and Schuster, 1984.

Hastings, Max, and Simon Jenkins. *The Battle for the Falklands.* New York and London: W. W. Norton, 1983.

Heckman, Wolf. *Rommel's War in Africa.* Trans. by Stephen Seago. Garden City, N.Y.: Doubleday, 1981.

Herken, Gregg. *Counsels of War.* New York: Alfred A. Knopf, 1985.

———. *The Winning Weapon: The Atomic Bomb in the Cold War, 1945–1950.* New York: Alfred A. Knopf, 1980.

Herold, J. Christopher. *Bonaparte in Egypt.* New York, Evanston and London: Harper and Row, 1962.

Herring, George C. *America's Longest War: The United States and Vietnam, 1950–1975.* 2nd ed. New York: Alfred A. Knopf, 1986.

———. *Cold Blood: LBJ's Conduct of Limited War in Vietnam.* (Harmon Memorial Lectures, No. 33.) Colorado Springs, Colo.: U.S. Air Force Academy, 1990.

Herrington, Stuart A. *Peace with Honor? An American Reports on Vietnam, 1973–75.* Novato, Calif.: Presidio Press, 1983.

Hersh, Seymour, M. *My Lai 4: A Report on the Massacre and Its Aftermath.* New York: Vintage Books, 1970.

Herwig, Holger H. *The German Naval Officer Corps: A Social and Political History, 1890–1918.* Oxford: Clarendon Press, 1973.

Hezlet, Arthur. *Aircraft and Sea Power.* New York: Stein and Day, 1970.

Hibbert, Christopher. *The Destruction of Lord Raglan: A Tragedy of the Crimean War, 1854–55.* Boston and Toronto: Little, Brown, 1961.

———. *The Great Mutiny: India, 1857.* New York: Viking, 1978.

———. *Waterloo: Napoleon's Last Campaign.* New York, Toronto, and London: New American Library, 1967.

Higgins, Hugh. *Vietnam.* 2nd ed. (Studies in Modern History.) London and Exeter: Heinemann Educational Books, 1982 [1975].

Higginbotham, Don R. *The War of American Independence: Military Attitudes, Policies and Practice, 1763–1789.* New York: Macmillan, 1971.

Higgins, Trumbull. *Soft Underbelly: The Anglo-American Controversy over the Italian Campaign, 1939–1945.* New York: Macmillan; London: Collier-Macmillan, 1968.

Higham, Robin. *Air Power: A Concise History.* New York: St. Martin's Press, 1972.

_____. *Armed Forces in Peacetime: Britain, 1918–1940.* London: Foulis, 1963.

_____. *The Military Intellectuals in Britain, 1918–1939.* New Brunswick, N.J.: Rutgers University Press, 1966.

Hilton, Richard. *The Indian Mutiny: A Centenary History.* London: Hollis and Carter, 1957.

Hittle, James D. *The Military Staff: Its History and Development.* Westport, Conn.: Greenwood Press, 1975 [1961].

Hogg, Ian V. *Artillery.* New York: Ballantine Books, 1972.

_____. *Fortress: A History of Military Defense.* New York: St. Martin's Press, 1975.

Holley, I. B., Jr. *General John M. Palmer, Citizen Soldiers, and the Army of a Democracy.* Westport, Conn., and London: Greenwood Press, 1982.

_____. *Ideas and Weapons: Exploitation of the Aerial Weapon by the United States during World War I. . . .* New Haven: Yale University Press, 1953.

Holloway, David. *The Soviet Union and the Arms Race.* New Haven and London: Yale University Press, 1983.

Hosmer, Stephen T., Konrad Kellen, and Brian M. Jenkins, eds. *The Fall of South Vietnam: Statements by Vietnamese Military and Civilian Leaders.* New York: Crane Russak, 1980.

Horne, Alistair. *The Fall of Paris: The Siege and the Commune, 1870–1871.* New York: St. Martin's Press, 1965.

_____. *The Price of Glory: Verdun, 1916.* New York: St. Martin's Press, 1963.

_____. *A Savage War of Peace: Algeria, 1954–1962.* New York: Viking, 1977.

_____. *To Lose a Battle: France, 1940.* Boston and Toronto: Little, Brown, 1969.

Hough, Richard, and Denis Richards. *The Battle of Britain: The Greatest Air Battle of World War II.* New York and London: W. W. Norton, 1989.

Howard, Michael. *Clausewitz.* (Past Masters, Keith Thomas, ed.) Oxford and New York: Oxford University Press, 1983.

_____. *The Franco-Prussian War: The German Invasion of France, 1870–1871.* New York: Macmillan, 1962.

_____. *Restraints on War.* Oxford: Oxford University Press, 1979.

_____. *War in European History.* Oxford: Oxford University Press, 1976.

_____, ed. *The Theory and Practice of War.* Bloomington: Indiana University Press, 1975.

Howarth, David. *Trafalgar: The Nelson Touch.* New York: Atheneum, 1969.

_____. *Waterloo: Day of Battle.* New York: Atheneum, 1968.

Howarth, Stephen. *To Shining Sea: A History of the United States Navy, 1775–1991.* New York: Random House, 1991.

Hoyle, Martha Byrd. *A World in Flames: The History of World War II.* New York: Atheneum, 1970.

Hoyt, Edwin. *The Last Kamikaze: The Story of Admiral Matome Ugaki.* Westport, Conn.: Praeger, 1993.

Huntington, Samuel P. *The Soldier and the State: The Theory and Politics of Civil-Military Relations.* Cambridge and London: Belknap Press of Harvard University Press, 1957.

Irving, David. *Hitler's War.* 2 vols. New York: Viking, 1977.

_____. *The Trail of the Fox.* New York: E. P. Dutton, 1977.

Isaacs, Arnold R. *Without Honor: Defeat in Vietnam and Cambodia.* Baltimore and London: Johns Hopkins University Press, 1983.

Jackson, Gabriel. *A Concise History of the Spanish Civil War.* New York: John Day, 1974.

James, D. Clayton. *The Years of MacArthur.* 2 vols. Boston: Houghton Mifflin, 1975.

Janowitz, Morris. *The Professional Soldier.* New York: Free Press, 1960.

Jastrow, Robert. *How to Make Nuclear Weapons Obsolete.* Boston and Toronto: Little, Brown, 1983.

Jeffords, Susan. *The Remasculinization of America: Gender and the Vietnam War.* Bloomington and Indianapolis: Indiana University Press, 1989.

Johnson, R. W. *Shootdown: Flight 007 and the American Connection.* New York: Viking, 1986.

Jomini, Baron de. *The Art of War.* Trans. by G. H. Mendell and W. P. Craighill. Westport, Conn.: Greenwood Press, 1974 [1862].

Jones, Archer. *The Art of War in the Western World.* Urbana and Chicago: University of Illinois Press, 1987.

————. *Civil War Command and Strategy: The Process of Victory and Defeat.* New York: Free Press, 1992.

————. *Confederate Strategy from Shiloh to Vicksburg.* Baton Rouge: Louisiana State University Press, 1961.

Jones, R. V. *Most Secret War: British Scientific Intelligence, 1939–1945.* London: Hamish Hamilton, 1978.

Kahn, David. *The Code-Breakers.* New York: Signet, 1973 [1967].

Kahn, Herman. *On Thermonuclear War.* Princeton: Princeton University Press, 1960.

————. *Thinking About the Unthinkable.* New York: Horizon Books, 1962.

Kaplan, Fred. *The Wizards of Armageddon.* New York: Simon and Schuster, 1983.

Karnow, Stanley. *Vietnam: A History.* New York: Viking, 1983.

Karsten, Peter, ed. *The Military in America: From the Colonial Era to the Present.* New York: Free Press, 1980.

Kaufman, William W. *The McNamara Strategy.* New York: Harper and Row, 1964.

Keegan, John. *The Face of Battle: A Study of Agincourt, Waterloo, and the Somme.* New York: Vintage Books, 1977.

————. *The Mask of Command.* New York: Viking Penguin, 1987.

————. *The Price of Admiralty: The Evolution of Naval Warfare.* New York: Viking Penguin, 1989.

————. *The Second World War.* New York and London: Viking Penguin, 1990.

————. *Six Armies in Normandy: From D-Day to the Liberation of Paris, June 6th–August 25th, 1944.* New York: Viking, 1982.

Keegan, John, and Richard Holmes. *Soldiers: A History of Men in Battle.* New York: Viking Penguin, 1986.

Keegan, John, and Andrew Wheatcroft. *Zones of Conflict: An Atlas of Future Wars.* New York: Simon and Schuster, 1986.

Kemp, Peter. *The History of Ships.* Stamford, Conn.: Longmeadow Press, 1988.

Kemp, P. K. *Key to Victory: The Triumph of British Sea Power in World War II.* Boston and Toronto: Little, Brown, 1957.

Kemble, C. Robert. *The Image of the Army Officer in America: Background for Current Views.* (Contributions in Military History, Number 5.) Westport, Conn., and London: Greenwood Press, 1973.

Kennan, George F. *The Fateful Alliance: France, Russia, and the Coming of the First World War.* New York: Pantheon Books, 1984.

_____. *The Nuclear Delusion: Soviet-American Relations in the Atomic Age.* New York: Pantheon Books, 1982.

Kennedy, John. *The Business of War.* New York: William Morrow, 1958.

Kennedy, Paul. *The Rise and Fall of the Great Powers: Economic Change and Military Conflict from 1500 to 2000.* New York: Random House, 1987.

Kennedy, William V., et al. *Intelligence Warfare: Penetrating the Secret World of Today's Advanced Technology Conflict.* New York: Crescent Books, 1987.

Kennett, Lee. *The First Air War, 1914–1918.* New York: Free Press, 1991.

_____. *The French Armies in the Seven Years' War: A Study of Military Organization and Administration.* Durham, N.C.: Duke University Press, 1967.

Kerr, E. Bartlett, *Flames Over Tokyo: The U.S. Army Air Forces' Incendiary Campaign against Japan, 1944–1945.* New York: Donald I. Fine, 1991.

Ketchum, Richard M., ed. *The American Heritage Picture History of the Civil War.* 2 vols. New York: American Heritage Magazine, 1960.

Kimball, Jeffrey P., ed. *To Reason Why: The Debate about the Causes of U.S. Involvement in the Vietnam War.* New York: McGraw-Hill, 1990.

Kimche, Jon. *The Unfought Battle.* New York: Stein and Day, 1968.

King, Jere Clemens. *Generals and Politicians.* Berkeley and Los Angeles: University of California Press, 1951.

Kitchen, Martin. *The German Officer Corps, 1890–1914.* Oxford: Clarendon Press, 1968.

_____. *A Military History of Germany from the Eighteenth Century to the Present Day.* Bloomington and London: Indiana University Press, 1975.

Koch, H. W. *The Rise of Modern Warfare, 1618–1815.* Greenwich, Conn.: Bison Books, 1981.

Kohn, Richard H. *Eagle and Sword: The Federalists and the Creation of the Military Establishment in America, 1783–1802.* New York and London: Free Press, 1975.

Kolko, Gabriel. *Anatomy of a War: Vietnam, the United States, and the Modern Historical Experience.* New York: Pantheon Books, 1985.

Korb, Lawrence J. *The Joint Chiefs of Staff: The First Twenty-Five Years.* Bloomington and London: Indiana University Press, 1976.

Krepinevich, Andrew F., Jr. *The Army and Vietnam.* Baltimore and London: Johns Hopkins University Press, 1986.

Lamb, Richard. *Montgomery in Europe, 1943–45.* London: Franklin Watts, 1984.

Laffin, John. *Fight for the Falklands!* New York: St. Martin's Press, 1982.

Lafore, Laurence. *The Long Fuse: An Interpretation of the Origins of World War I.* 2nd ed. (Critical Periods of History.) Philadelphia and New York: J. B. Lippincott, 1971 [1965].

Larrabee, Harold A. *Decision at the Chesapeake.* London: William Kimber, 1965.

Layton, Edwin T., Roger Pineau, and John Costello. *And I Was There: Pearl Harbor and Midway—Breaking the Secrets.* New York: William Morrow, 1985.

Leckie, Robert. *Conflict: The History of the Korean War, 1950–1953.* New York: Charles Putnam's Sons, 1962.

_____. *The Wars of America.* Rev. ed. New York: Harper and Row, 1981.

Lefebvre, Georges. *Napoleon.* 2 vols. Trans. by Henry F. Stockhold. New York: Columbia University Press, 1969.

Leonard, Roger A. *A Short Guide to Clausewitz on War.* New York: Capricorn Books, 1967.

Lewin, Ronald. *The Life and Death of the Afrika Korps.* New York: Quadrangle Books, 1977.

_____. *Rommel as Military Commander.* New York: D. Van Nostrand, 1970.

————. *Ultra Goes to War: The First Account of World War II's Greatest Secret Based on Official Documents.* New York: McGraw-Hill, 1978.

Lewis, Emanuel Raymond. *Seacoast Fortifications of the United States: An Introductory History.* Washington: Smithsonian Institution, 1970.

Lewis, Michael. *The History of the British Navy.* Harmondsworth: Penguin Books, 1957.

Liddell Hart, B. H. *Defence of the West.* New York: William Morrow, 1950.

————. *Deterrent or Defense: A Fresh Look at the West's Military Position.* New York: Praeger, 1960.

————. *History of the Second World War.* New York: G. P. Putnam's Sons, 1970.

————. *The Real War, 1914–1918.* Boston and Toronto: Little, Brown, 1964 [1930].

————. *Strategy: The Indirect Approach.* New York: Praeger, 1954.

————. *The Tanks.* 2 vols. London: Cassell, 1959.

Lifton, Robert Jay. *Home from the War: Vietnam Veterans, Neither Victims nor Executioners.* New York: Simon and Schuster, 1973.

Lincoln, W. Bruce. *Passage Through Armageddon: The Russians in War and Revolution, 1914–1918.* New York: Simon and Schuster, 1986.

Livermore, T. L. *Numbers and Losses in the Civil War in America, 1861–65.* New York: Kraus, 1968.

Long, Franklin A., and George W. Rathjens, eds. *Arms, Defense Policy, and Arms Control.* New York: W. W. Norton, 1975.

Long, Franklin A., et al., eds. *Weapons in Space.* New York: W. W. Norton, 1986.

Longford, Elizabeth. *Wellington: The Years of the Sword.* New York and Evanston: Harper and Row, 1969.

Lucas, James. *Kommando: German Special Forces of World War Two.* New York: St. Martin's Press, 1985.

Lundin, C. L. *Finland in the Second World War.* Bloomington: Indiana University Press, 1957.

Luttwak, Edward N. *On the Meaning of Victory: Essays on Strategy.* New York: Simon and Schuster, 1986.

————. *The Pentagon and the Art of War: The Question of Military Reform.* New York: Simon and Schuster, 1985.

Luttwak, Edward N., and Dan Horowitz. *The Israeli Army.* New York: Harper and Row, 1975.

Luvaas, Jay. *The Education of an Army: British Military Thought, 1815–1940.* Chicago: University of Chicago Press, 1964.

————. *The Military Legacy of the Civil War: The European Inheritance.* Chicago: University of Chicago Press, 1959.

Lyall, Gavin, ed. *The War in the Air: The Royal Air Force in World War II.* New York: William Morrow, 1968.

Lynn, John A. *The Bayonets of the Republic: Motivation and Tactics in the Army of Revolutionary France, 1791–94.* Urbana and Chicago: University of Illinois Press, 1984.

————, ed. *Tools of War: Instruments, Ideas, and Institutions of Warfare, 1445–1871.* Urbana and Chicago: University of Illinois Press, 1990.

Macdonald, John. *Great Battlefields of the World.* New York: Macmillan, 1984.

Macdonald, Peter. *Giap, the Victor in Vietnam.* New York: W. W. Norton, 1993.

Mackesy, Piers. *The War for America, 1775–1783.* Cambridge, Mass.: Harvard University Press, 1964.

Mackintosh, Malcolm. *Juggernaut: A History of the Soviet Armed Forces.* New York: Macmillan, 1967.

Macintyre, Donald. *Aircraft Carrier: The Majestic Weapon.* New York: Ballantine Books, 1968.

Macksey, Kenneth. *Afrika Korps.* New York: Ballantine Books, 1968.

_____. *Guderian: Creator of the Blitzkrieg.* New York: Stein and Day, 1976.

_____. *Panzer Division: The Mailed Fist.* New York: Ballantine Books, 1968.

Macksey, Kenneth, and John H. Batchelor. *Tanks: A History of the Armoured Fighting Vehicle.* New York: Scribner's, 1970.

Maclear, Michael. *The Ten Thousand Day War: Vietnam, 1945–1975.* New York: St. Martin's Press, 1981.

Mahan, Alfred T. *The Influence of Sea Power upon History, 1660–1783.* New York: Sycamore, 1957 [1890].

Mahon, John K. *The War of 1812.* Gainesville: University Presses of Florida, 1972.

Manchester, William. *The Arms of Krupp, 1587–1968.* Boston and Toronto: Little, Brown, 1964.

Marcus, G. J. *A Naval History of England: The Formative Centuries.* Boston and Toronto: Little, Brown, 1961.

_____. *The Age of Nelson.* New York: Viking, 1971.

Marder, Arthur. *From the Dreadnought to Scapa Flow: The Royal Navy in the Fisher Era, 1904–1919.* 5 vols. New York: Oxford University Press, 1961–1971.

Markham, Felix. *Napoleon.* New York: Mentor, 1966.

Marshall, S. L. A. *Battle at Best.* New York: Pocket Books, 1964.

_____. *Crimsoned Prairie: The Wars between the United States and the Plains Indians.* . . . New York: Scribner's, 1972.

_____. *The Fields of Bamboo: . . . Three Battles Just Beyond the China Sea.* New York: Dial Press, 1971.

_____. *The River and the Gauntlet.* New York: Warner Books, 1952.

_____. *The Soldier's Load and the Mobility of a Nation.* Quantico, Va.: U.S. Marine Corps Association, 1980 [1950].

Martienssen, A. K. *Hitler and His Admirals.* London: Secker and Warburg, 1948.

Marwick, Arthur J. *War and Social Change in the Twentieth Century: A Comparative Study of Britain, France, Germany, Russia and the United States.* New York: St. Martin's, 1975.

Mason, Herbert Molloy, Jr. *The United States Air Force: A Turbulent History.* New York: Mason/Charter, 1976.

Massie, Robert K. *Dreadnought: Britain, Germany, and the Coming of the Great War.* New York: Random House, 1991.

Matter, William D. *If It Takes All Summer: The Battle of Spottsylvania.* Chapel Hill and London: University of North Carolina Press, 1988.

Maurer, Harry. *Strange Ground: Americans in Vietnam, 1945–1975, An Oral History.* New York: Henry Holt, 1989.

Maxwell, Neville. *India's China War.* Garden City, N.Y.: Doubleday, 1978.

McAlister, John T., Jr. *Vietnam: The Origins of Revolution.* Garden City, N.Y.: Doubleday, 1971.

McDonough, James L., and James P. Jones. *War So Terrible: Sherman and Atlanta.* New York and London: W. W. Norton, 1987.

McElwee, William. *The Art of War: Waterloo to Mons.* Bloomington and London: Indiana University Press, 1974.

McFeely, William. *Grant: A Biography.* New York and London: W. W. Norton, 1981.

McKee, Alexander. *Last Round Against Rommel: Battle of the Normandy Beachhead.* New York: Signet, 1966.

McMahon, William E. *Dreadnought Battleships and Battle Cruisers.* Washington, D.C.: University Press of America, 1978.

McNeill, William H. *The Pursuit of Power: Technology, Armed Force, and Society since* A.D. 1000. Chicago: University of Chicago Press, 1982.

McNamara, Robert S. *The Essence of Security: Reflections in Office.* New York: Harper and Row, 1968.

McPherson, James M. *Battle Cry of Freedom: The Civil War Era.* (Oxford History of the United States, C. Van Woodward, ed., Vol. VI.) Oxford: Oxford University Press, 1988.

McWhiney, Grady, and Perry D. Jamieson. *Attack and Die: Civil War Military Tactics and the Southern Heritage.* Auburn: University of Alabama Press, 1982.

Mellenthin, F. W. *Panzer Battles: A Study of the Employment of Armor in the Second World War.* Trans. by H. Betzler, ed. by L. C. F. Turner. New York: Ballantine, 1971 [1956].

Melman, Seymour. *The Permanent War Economy: American Capitalism in Decline.* Rev. ed. New York: Simon and Schuster, 1985 [1974].

Meredith, Roy. *Storm Over Sumter.* New York: Simon and Schuster, 1957.

Merrill, James M. *The Rebel Shore: The Story of Union Sea Power in the Civil War.* Boston: Little, Brown, 1957.

Mersky, Peter B., and Norman Polmar. *The Naval Air War in Vietnam.* Annapolis: Nautical and Aviation Publication Company of America, 1981.

Middlebrook, Martin. *The First Day on the Somme: 1 July 1916.* New York: W. W. Norton, 1972.

Miers, Earl Schenk. *The Web of Victory: Grant at Vicksburg.* New York: Harper, 1952.

Miles, Jim. *Fields of Glory: A History and a Tour Guide of the Atlanta Campaign.* Nashville: Rutledge Hill Press, 1989.

―――. *To the Sea: A History and Tour Guide of Sherman's March.* Nashville: Rutledge Hill Press, 1989.

Miller, David, and Christopher F. Foss. *Modern Land Combat.* London: Salamander Books, 1987.

Millett, Allan R., and Peter Maslowski. *For the Common Defense: A Military History of the United States of America.* New York: Free Press, 1984.

Millis, Walter. *Arms and Men: A Study of American Military Policy.* New York: Mentor, 1956.

Mitchell, Joseph B. *Military Leaders in the Civil War.* New York: G. P. Putnam's Sons, 1972.

Mitchum, Samuel W. *Hitler's Legions: The German Army Order of Battle, World War II.* New York: Stein and Day, 1985.

―――. *Rommel's Last Battle: The Desert Fox and the Normandy Campaign.* New York: Stein and Day, 1983.

―――. *Triumphant Fox: Erwin Rommel and the Rise of the Afrika Korps.* New York: Stein and Day, 1984.

Montgomery, Bernard L. *A History of Warfare.* Cleveland: World, 1968.

―――. *The Memoirs of Field-Marshal Montgomery.* Cleveland and New York: World, 1968.

Moorehead, Alan. *Gallipoli.* New York: Harper, 1956.

―――. *The Russian Revolution.* New York: Harper and Row, 1958.

Morgan, J. H. *Assize of Arms: The Disarmament of Germany and Her Rearmament, 1919–1939.* New York: Oxford University Press, 1946.

Morison, Samuel Eliot. *History of United States Naval Operations in World War II.* 15 vols. Boston: Little, Brown, 1947–1962.

―――. *John Paul Jones: A Sailor's Biography.* Boston and Toronto: Little, Brown, 1959.

Morris, M. E. H. *Norman Schwarzkopf: Road to Triumph.* New York: St. Martin's Press, 1991.

Morrison, Wilbur H. *Fortress without a Roof: The Allied Bombing of the Third Reich.* New York: St. Martin's Press, 1982.

Murray, Williamson. *Luftwaffe.* Baltimore: Nautical and Aviation Publishing Company of America, 1985.

Myatt, Frederick. *Modern Small Arms: An Illustrated History . . . from 1873 to the Present Day.* London: Salamander Books, 1978.

Natkiel, Richard, and John Pimlott. *Atlas of Warfare.* New York: Gallery Books, 1988.

Newell, Nancy, and Richard S. Newell. *The Struggle for Afghanistan.* Ithaca: Cornell University Press, 1981.

Nickerson, Hoffman. *The Armed Horde, 1793–1939: A Study of the Rise, Survival and Decline of the Mass Army.* New York: G. P. Putnam's Sons, 1940.

Ogorkiewicz, Richard M. *Armor: A History of Mechanized Forces.* New York: Praeger, 1960.

Oman, Carola. *Nelson.* Mystic, Conn.: Verry, 1967.

———. *Sir John Moore.* Mystic, Conn.: Verry, 1953.

Osgood, Robert E. *Limited War: The Challenge to American Strategy.* Chicago: University of Chicago Press, 1957.

Overy, R. J. *The Air War, 1939–1945.* New York: Stein and Day, 1981.

Padfield, Peter. *The Battleship Era.* New York: David McKay, 1972.

Pakenham, Thomas. *The Boer War.* New York: Random House, 1979.

———. *The Scramble for Africa, 1876–1912.* Random House, 1991.

Paret, Peter. *Clausewitz and the State.* New York: Oxford University Press, 1976.

———. *Yorck and the Era of Prussian Reform, 1807–1815.* Princeton: Princeton University Press, 1966.

———, ed. *Makers of Modern Strategy: From Machiavelli to the Nuclear Age.* Princeton: Princeton University Press, 1986.

Park, S. J., and G. F. Nafziger. *The British Military: Its System and Organization, 1803–1815.* Cambridge, Ontario: Rafm, 1983.

Parkes, Oscar. *British Battleships: Warrior 1860 to Vanguard 1950: A History of Design, Construction and Armament.* London: Seeley, 1958.

Parkinson, Roger. *Clausewitz: A Biography.* New York: Stein and Day, 1970.

Parish, Peter J. *The American Civil War.* New York: Holmes and Meier, 1974.

Peckham, Howard H. *The Toll of Independence: Engagements and Battle Casualties of the American Revolution.* Chicago: University of Chicago Press, 1974.

———. *The War for Independence: A Military History.* Chicago: University of Chicago Press, 1958.

Perret, Geoffrey. *A Country Made by War: From the Revolution to Vietnam—the Story of America's Rise to Power.* New York: Random House, 1989.

Perrett, Bryan. *A History of the Blitzkrieg.* New York: Stein and Day, 1983.

Pimlott, John, ed. *Vietnam: The History and the Tactics.* New York: Crescent Books, 1982.

Pisor, Robert. *The End of the Line: The Siege of Khe Sanh.* New York and London: W. W. Norton, 1982.

Piston, William G. *Lee's Tarnished Lieutenant: James Longstreet and His Place in Southern History.* Athens and London: University of Georgia Press, 1987.

Plocher, Hermann. *The German Air Force versus Russia, 1941.* New York: Arno Press, 1965.

Pogue, Forrest C. *George C. Marshall.* 3 vols. New York: Viking, 1963–1975.

Porch, Douglas. *The Conquest of Morocco.* New York: Alfred A. Knopf, 1983.

———. *The French Foreign Legion: A Complete History of the Legendary Fighting Force.* New York: Harper/Collins, 1991.

———. *The March to the Marne: The French Army, 1871–1914.* Cambridge: Cambridge University Press, 1981.

Potter, E. B., and Chester W. Nimitz, eds. *Sea Power: A Naval History.* Englewood Cliffs: Prentice-Hall, 1960.

Prados, John. *The Soviet Estimate: U.S. Intelligence Analysis and Russian Military Strength.* New York: Dial Press, 1982.

Prange, Gordon W. *At Dawn We Slept: The Untold Story of Pearl Harbor.* New York: McGraw-Hill, 1981.

———. *Miracle at Midway.* New York: Penguin Books, 1982.

Preston, Richard A. *Canada and "Imperial Defence": A Study of the Origins of the British Commonwealth's Defense Organization, 1867–1919.* Durham, N.C.: Duke University Press, 1967.

Preston, Richard A., et al. *Men in Arms: A History of Warfare and Its Interrelationships with Western Society.* 5th ed. San Diego: Harcourt, Brace, Jovanovich, 1991 [1956].

Quick, John, ed. *Dictionary of Weapons and Military Terms.* New York: McGraw-Hill, 1973.

Quimby, Robert S. *The Background of Napoleonic Warfare.* New York: AMS Press, 1968 [1957].

Reed, Rowena. *Combined Operations in the Civil War.* Annapolis: Naval Institute Press, 1978.

Rees, David. *Korea: The Limited War.* New York: St. Martin's Press, 1973.

Reynolds, Clark G. *Command of the Sea: The History and Strategy of Maritime Empires.* New York: William Morrow, 1974.

———. *The Fast Carriers: The Forging of an Air Navy.* New York: McGraw-Hill, 1968.

Rhodes, Richard. *The Making of the Atomic Bomb.* New York: Simon and Schuster, 1988.

Ridgway, Matthew B. *The Korean War.* New York: Popular Library, 1967.

Ritter, E. A. *Shaka Zulu: The Rise of the Zulu Empire.* New York: Longmans Green, 1964.

Ritter, Gerhard. *The Schlieffen Plan: Critique of a Myth.* Trans. by Andrew and Eva Wilson. New York: Praeger, 1958.

———. *The Sword and the Scepter: The Problem of Militarism in Germany.* Trans. by H. Norden. 3 vols. Coral Gables: Miami, 1970–1974.

Robertson, James I., Jr. *General A. P. Hill: The Story of a Confederate Warrior.* New York: Random House, 1987.

———. *Soldiers Blue and Gray.* Columbia: University of South Carolina Press, 1988.

Robinson, Anthony, ed. *Weapons of the Vietnam War.* Greenwich, Conn.: Bison Books, 1983.

Robinson, D. H. *The Zeppelin in Combat.* Rev. ed. London: Foulis, 1966.

Ropp, Theodore. *History and War.* Augusta, Ga.: Hamburg Press, 1984.

———. *War in the Modern World.* 2nd ed. New York: Collier Books, 1962 [1959].

Roskill, Stephen W. *The Strategy of Sea Power: Its Development and Application.* London: Collins, 1962.

Ross, Steven. *From Flintlock to Rifle: Infantry Tactics from Flintlock to Rifle, 1740–1866.* Cranbury, N.J.: Associated University Presses, 1979.

Rosser-Owen, David. *Vietnam Weapons Handbook.* Wellingborough: Patrick Stephens, 1986.

Rostow, W. W. *Pre-Invasion Bombing Strategy: General Eisenhower's Decision of March 25, 1944.* (Ideas and Action Series, No. 1.) Austin: University of Texas Press, 1981.

Rothenberg, Gunther E. *The Army of Francis Joseph.* West Lafayette, Ind.: Purdue University Press, 1976.

———. *The Art of Warfare in the Age of Napoleon.* Bloomington: Indiana University Press, 1978.

Ryan, Cornelius. *The Last Battle.* New York: Simon and Schuster, 1966.

———. *The Longest Day.* New York: Simon and Schuster, 1959.

Ruge, Friedrich. *Der Seekrieg: The German Navy's Story, 1939–1945.* Annapolis: U.S. Naval Institute, 1957.

———. *Scapa Flow, 1919: The End of the German Fleet.* Trans. by Derek Masters, ed. by A. J. Watts. London: Ian Allan, 1973.

Salisbury, Harrison E. *The 900 Days: The Siege of Leningrad.* New York: Harper & Row, 1969.

Savory, Reginald. *His Britannic Majesty's Army in Germany during the Seven Years' War.* New York: Oxford University Press, 1966.

Schandler, Herbert Y. *Lyndon Johnson and Vietnam: The Unmaking of a President.* Princeton: Princeton University Press, 1977.

Scheer, George F., and Hugh F. Rankin. *Rebels and Redcoats.* New York: Mentor, 1957.

Scheliha, Von. *A Treatise on Coast Defense: Based on the Experience gained by . . . the Army of the Confederate States . . . from 1861 to 1865.* Westport, Conn.: Greenwood Press, 1971 [1868].

Schell, Jonathan. *The Village of Ben Suc.* New York: Vintage Books, 1968.

Schurman, D. M. *The Education of a Navy: The Development of British Naval Strategic Thought, 1867–1914.* Malabar: Robert E. Krieger, 1984 [1965].

Schwarzkopf, H. Norman, and Peter Petre. *It Doesn't Take a Hero: The Autobiography.* New York: Linda Grey/Bantam Books, 1992.

Seaton, Albert. *The Russo-German War, 1941–1945.* New York: Praeger, 1970.

Segur, Philippe-Paul de. *Napoleon's Russian Campaign.* Trans. by J. David Townsend. Boston: Houghton Mifflin, 1958.

Seymour, William. *Yours to Reason Why: Decision in Battle.* New York: St. Martin's Press, 1982.

Shawcross, William. *The Quality of Mercy: Cambodia, Holocaust and Modern Conscience.* New York: Simon and Schuster, 1985.

———. *Sideshow: Kissinger, Nixon and the Destruction of Cambodia.* New York: Simon and Schuster, 1979.

Sheehan, Neil. *A Bright Shining Lie: John Paul Vann and America in Vietnam.* New York: Random House, 1988.

Sheehan, Neil, et al. *The Pentagon Papers as Published in the New York Times.* New York: Bantam Books, 1971.

Sherman, W. T. *Memoirs of General W. T. Sherman.* New York: Library of America, 1990 [1875].

Shirer, William L. *The Rise and Fall of the Third Reich: A History of Nazi Germany.* New York: Simon and Schuster, 1960.

Showalter, Dennis E. *Railroads and Rifles: Soldiers, Technology, and the Unification of Germany.* Hamden, Conn.: Shoe String Press, 1975.

Shulman, Milton. *Defeat in the West.* Rev. ed. New York: Ballantine Books, 1968.

Shy, John. *Toward Lexington: The Role of the British Army in the Coming of the American Revolution.* Princeton: Princeton University Press, 1965.

Sick, Gary. *All Fall Down: America's Tragic Encounter with Iran.* New York: Random House, 1985.

Simmons, Edwin H. *The United States Marines: The First Two Hundred Years, 1775–1975.* New York: Viking, 1976.

Simpson, Colin. *The Lusitania.* Boston and Toronto: Little, Brown, 1972.

Singletary, Otis A. *The Mexican War.* Chicago and London: University of Chicago Press, 1960.

Slim, William. *Defeat into Victory.* New York: David McKay, 1956.

Smith, S. E., ed. *The United States Navy in World War II.* New York: William Morrow, 1966.

Sokolovsky, Vasilii D., ed. *Military Strategy: Soviet Doctrine and Concepts.* New York: Praeger, 1963.

Sommers, Richard J. *Richmond Redeemed: The Siege at Petersburg.* Garden City, N.Y.: Doubleday, 1981.

Spanier, J. W. *The Truman-MacArthur Controversy and the Korean War.* Cambridge, Mass.: Harvard University Press, 1959.

Speer, Albert. *Infiltration.* Trans. by Joachim Neugroschel. New York: Macmillan, 1981.

Stacy, C. P. *Canada and the British Army: A Study in Responsible Government.* Rev. ed. Toronto: University of Toronto Press, 1963.

Stallings, Laurence. *The Doughboys: The Story of the AEF, 1917–1918.* New York: Harper and Row, 1963.

Stanton, Shelby L. *The Rise and Fall of an American Army: Ground Forces in Vietnam, 1965–1973.* Novato, Calif.: Presidio Press, 1985.

Stein, George H. *The Waffen SS: Hitler's Elite Guard at War, 1939–1945.* Ithaca: Cornell University Press, 1966.

Sternberg, Fritz. *The Military and Industrial Revolution of Our Time.* New York: Praeger, 1959.

Stokesbury, James L. *A Short History of World War I.* New York: William Morrow, 1981.

──────. *A Short History of World War II.* New York: William Morrow, 1980.

Strachan, Hew. *European Armies and the Conduct of War.* London: George Allen and Unwin, 1983.

Strawson, John. *The Battle for North Africa.* New York: Charles Scribner's Sons, 1969.

Suchenwirth, Richard. *The Development of the German Air Force, 1919–1939.* New York: Arno Press, 1968.

Sueter, M. F. *The Evolution of the Tank.* London: Hutchison, 1937.

Summers, Harry G. *On Strategy: A Critical Analysis of the Vietnam War.* Novato, Calif.: Presidio Press, 1982.

──────. *Vietnam War Alamanac.* New York: Facts on File, 1985.

Sunday Times of London Insight Team. *War in the Falklands: The Full Story.* New York: Harper and Row, 1982.

──────. *The Yom Kippur War.* New York: Doubleday, 1974.

Suvorov, Viktor. *Inside the Soviet Army.* New York: Macmillan, 1982.

Taylor, A. J. P. *A History of the First World War.* New York: Berkeley Medallion, 1966.

Taylor, Telford. *The Breaking Wave: The Second World War in the Summer of 1940.* New York: Simon and Schuster, 1967.

──────. *The March of Conquest: The German Victories in Western Europe, 1940.* New York: Simon and Schuster, 1958.

_____. *Sword and Swastika: Generals and Nazis in the Third Reich.* New York: Simon and Schuster, 1952.

Tedder, Arthur. *With Prejudice.* London: Cassell, 1966.

Terraine, John. *A Time for Courage: The Royal Air Force in the European War, 1939–1945.* New York: Macmillan, 1985.

Thayer, Theodore. *Yorktown: Campaign of Strategic Options.* (American Alternative Series, ed. by Harold M. Hyman.) Philadelphia: J. B. Lippincott, 1975.

Thomas, Hugh. *The Spanish Civil War.* New York: Harper and Row, 1961.

Thompson, W. Scott, and Donaldson D. Frizzelle, eds. *The Lessons of Vietnam.* New York: Crane, Russak, 1977.

Tilford, Earl H., Jr. *Setup: What the Air Force Did in Vietnam and Why.* Montgomery, Ala.: Air University Press, 1991.

Toland, John. *Battle: The Story of the Bulge.* New York: Random House, 1959.

_____. *But Not in Shame: The Six Months after Pearl Harbor.* New York: Random House, 1961.

_____. *Infamy: Pearl Harbor and Its Aftermath.* Garden City, N.Y.: Doubleday, 1982.

_____. *The Last 100 Days.* New York: Random House, 1965.

_____. *The Rising Sun: The Decline and Fall of the Japanese Empire, 1936–1945.* 2 vols. New York: Random House, 1970.

Trevor-Roper, H. R., ed. *Hitler's War Directives, 1939–1945.* London: Sidgwick and Jackson, 1964.

Tuchman, Barbara W. *The First Salute: A View of the American Revolution.* New York: Alfred A. Knopf, 1988.

_____. *The Guns of August.* New York: Macmillan, 1962.

_____. *Stilwell and the American Experience in China, 1911–1945.* New York: Macmillan, 1970.

Turner, George E. *Victory Rode the Rails: The Strategic Place of the Railroads in the Civil War.* Indianapolis: Bobbs-Merrill, 1953.

Turner, Gordon B., and Richard D. Challener. *National Security in the Nuclear Age: Basic Facts and Fallacies.* New York: Praeger, 1960.

Tute, Warren. *The Deadly Stroke.* New York: Coward, McCann and Geoghegan, 1973.

Upton, Emory. *The Military Policy of the United States.* New York: Greenwood Press, 1968 [1904].

U.S. News Staff, *Triumph without Victory: The Unreported History of the Gulf War.* New York: U.S. News and World Report, 1991.

Vagts, Alfred. *A History of Militarism: Romance and Realities of a Profession.* 2nd ed. New York: Free Press, 1967.

Van Creveld, Martin. *Command in War.* Cambridge: Harvard University Press, 1985.

_____. *Supplying War: Logistics from Wallenstein to Patton.* London, New York, and Melbourne: Cambridge University Press, 1977.

Vandiver, Frank E. *Black Jack: The Life and Times of John J. Pershing.* College Station and London: Texas A&M University Press, 1977.

_____. *Rebel Brass: The Confederate Command System.* Baton Rouge: Louisiana State University, 1956.

Van Dyke, Jon M. *North Vietnam's Strategy for Survival.* Palo Alto: Pacific Books, 1972.

Van der Vat, Dan. *The Pacific Campaign: World War II, the U.S.-Japanese Naval War, 1941–1945.* New York: Simon and Schuster,1991.

Von der Porton, Edward P. *The German Navy in World War II.* New York: Thomas Y. Crowell, 1969.

Wallace, Willard M. *Appeal to Arms: A Military History of the American Revolution.* Chicago: Quadrangle Books, 1951.

Wallach, Jehuda L. *The Dogma of the Battle of Annihilation: The Theories of Clausewitz and Schlieffen and Their Impact on the German Conduct of Two World Wars.* Westport, Conn.: Greenwood Press, 1986.

Ward, Christopher. *The War of the Revolution.* Ed. by John Richard Alden. 2 vols. New York: Macmillan, 1952.

Warlimont, Walter. *Inside Hitler's Headquarters, 1939–1945.* Trans. by R. H. Barry. New York and Washington: Praeger, 1964.

Warner, Dennis, and Peggy Warner. *The Tide at Sunrise: A History of the Russo-Japanese War, 1904–1905.* New York: Charterhouse, 1974.

Webster, Sir Charles, and Noble Frankland. *The Strategic Air Offensive against Germany, 1939–1945.* 4 vols. London: HMSO, 1961.

Weigley, Russell F. *The American Way of War: A History of United States Military Strategy and Policy.* New York: Macmillan, 1973.

———. *History of the United States Army.* New York: Macmillan, 1967.

Weller, Jac. *Wellington in the Peninsula, 1808–1814.* London: N. Vane, 1962.

Werth, Alexander. *Russia at War, 1941–1945.* New York: E. P. Dutton, 1964.

Wheeler-Bennett, J. W. *The Nemesis of Power: The German Army in Politics, 1918–1945.* New York: Compass, 1964.

Whiting, Charles. *Hunters from the Sky: The German Parachute Corps, 1940–1945.* London: Leo Cooper, 1974.

Whitton, Frederick E. *Moltke.* London: Constable, 1921.

Wiley, Bell I. *The Common Soldier in the Civil War.* New York: Grosset and Dunlap, 1952.

Wiley, Bell I., and Hirst D. Milhollen. *They Who Fought Here.* New York: Bonanza Books, 1959.

Williams, Kenneth P. *Lincoln Finds a General: A Military Study of the Civil War.* 5 vols. New York: Macmillan, 1950–1959.

Williams, T. Harry. *The History of American Wars: From Colonial Times to World War I.* New York: Alfred A. Knopf, 1981.

———. *Lincoln and His Generals.* New York: Alfred A. Knopf, 1952.

Wilson, Dale E. *Treat 'em Rough: The Birth of American Armor, 1917–1920.* Novato, Calif.: Presidio Press, 1989.

Winter, Denis. *Death's Men: Soldiers of the Great War.* Penguin Books, 1979 [1978].

Winterbotham, F. W. *The Ultra Secret.* New York: Harper and Row, 1974.

Winton, Harold R. *To Change an Army: General Sir John Burnett-Stuart and British Armored Doctrine, 1927–1938.* Lawrence: University Press of Kansas, 1988.

Wintringham, Tom. *Weapons and Tactics.* Updated by J. N. Blashford-Snell. Harmondsworth: Penguin Books, 1974. [1952].

Wise, Stephen R. *Lifeline of the Confederacy: Blockade Running During the Civil War.* Columbia: University of South Carolina Press, 1988.

Wolf, Eric. *Peasant Wars of the Twentieth Century.* New York: Harper and Row, 1970.

Wolff, Leon. *In Flanders Fields: The 1917 Campaign.* New York: Viking, 1958.

Wood, Derek, and Derek Dempster. *The Narrow Margin: The Battle of Britain and the Rise of Air Power, 1930–1940.* New York: McGraw-Hill, 1961.

Woodham-Smith, Cecil. *The Charge of the Light Brigade.* New York: McGraw-Hill, 1954.

Woodrooffe, Thomas. *The Enterprise of England: An Account of Her Emergence as an Oceanic Power.* London: Faber and Faber, 1958.

Woodward, Bob. *The Commanders.* New York: Simon and Schuster, 1991.

Woodward, E. L. *Great Britain and the German Navy.* London: E. L. Cass, 1964.

Wright, Robert K., Jr. *The Continental Army.* (Army Lineage Series.) Washington, D.C.: Center of Military History, U.S. Army, 1986.

Wright, Robin. *Sacred Rage: The Wrath of Militant Islam.* New York: Simon and Schuster, 1986.

Wright, Quincy. *A Study of War.* 2nd ed., abridged. Chicago: University of Chicago Press, 1965.

Wyden, Peter. *Bay of Pigs: The Untold Story.* New York: Simon and Schuster, 1979.

———. *Day One: Before Hiroshima and After.* New York: Simon and Schuster, 1984.

———. *The Passionate War: The Narrative History of the Spanish Civil War.* New York: Simon and Schuster, 1983.

Wynn, G. C. *If Germany Attacks: The Battle in Depth in the West.* London: Faber and Faber, 1940.

Yardley, Herbert O. *The American Black Chamber.* New York: Ballantine, 1981 [1931].

Young, Desmond. *Rommel the Desert Fox.* New York: Harper and Row, 1950.

Young, Peter, and J. P. Lawford. *History of the British Army.* London: Arthur Barker, 1970.

Zhukov, Georgi K. *Marshal Zhukov's Greatest Battles.* Trans. by Theodore Shabad. New York and Evanston: Harper and Row, 1969.

Zook, David H., Jr., and Robin Higham. *A Short History of Warfare.* New York: Twayne, 1966.

Index

Abrams, Creighton, 292
Afghanistan: civil war in, 308, 312, 314
Afghan Wars (1880s), 122
aircraft carriers: development of between 1919 and 1939, 181–82; in World War I, 155
Air Force (U.S.): establishment of, 186; in World War II, 224–26
air forces: development of between 1919 and 1939, 185–89; rise of in World War I, 152–55
Albania: and Cold War, 285
Aleutians: in World War II, 252
Alexander, Harold, 231
Algeria: war of independence from France, 286; in World War II, 221
Allenby, Sir Edmund, 164, 170
Alabama (CSS), 58
Alexander I (Tsar), 29, 38–39
Alexander II (Tsar), 64, 65
Alexander, Sir Harold, 221, 222
Alger, Russell, 127
Almond, Edward, 273
American Revolution (1775–83), 12–19
Andropov, Yuri, 310
Anglo-American War of 1812, 34–35
Anglo-German Naval Treaty (1935), 175
Anglo-Japanese Treaty (1902), 116, 130
Angola: civil war in, 324
Antietam, Battle of (1862), 76, 81, 84
Argentina: and Falklands War, 311–12
Armenia: civil war in, 324; independence of, 315
armies: between 1919 and 1939, 176–80; and dynastic warfare, 1–7; German system prior to 1914, 102–105. *See also* specific countries; specific wars
armored fighting vehicles (AFV). See tanks
army divisions, 21–22
Arnim, Hans-Jürgen von, 222
Arnold, Benedict, 14, 17
Arnold, Henry H., 186

artillery: development in period between 1871 and 1914, 103–104; technological change in nineteenth century, 49
Ashanti Wars (1870s), 122
al-Assad, Hafez, 304
Aube, Théophile, 113, 114
Auchinleck, Sir Claude, 218, 220, 221
Austerlitz, Battle of (1804), 29
Australia: in World War I, 146, 149; in World War II, 249
Austria: and Franco-Austrian War, 67–68; and French Revolution, 22, 24; and Napoleonic wars, 25, 27, 28–29, 35; in Wars of German Unification, 94, 96–97; in World War II, 176. *See also* Austro-Hungarian Empire
Austro-Hungarian Empire: alliance systems and contingency war plans prior to 1914, 105–12; army prior to 1914, 103; assassination of Archduke Francis-Ferdinand, 134; involvement in the Balkans, 120–21, 132–33, 134; in World War I, 144, 170
Austro-Prussian War (1866), 50
Azerbaijan: civil war in, 324

Badoglio, Pietro, 223, 228–29
Baker, Newton D., 160
Balbo, Italo, 188
Balkan Wars of 1912–13, 104, 132–33
Barton, Clara, 65
Batista, Fulgencio, 287
battalions, 3
battle cruisers, 118–19
battleships, 55, 117–18, 119
Bay of Pigs (Cuba, 1961), 291
Bazaine, François, 99, 100
Beatty, David, 151–52
Beauregard, P. G. T., 83, 88
Beck, Ludwig, 195–96
Belarus: and Commonwealth of Independent States (CIS), 316

Pope, John, 83–84
Porter, David, 77–78
Portugal: and Napoleonic wars, 31
Potsdam Declaration (1945), 261
Powers, Gary, 281
Précis de l'Art de la Guerre (Summary of the Art of War) (Jomini, 1836), 44–45
Price, Sterling, 89
Princeton (USS), 54
prisoners of war (POWs): Korean War, 277; Vietnam War, 300
privateers: in American Revolution, 15; and dynastic warfare, 9; international outlawing of practice, 58
Prussia: and dynastic warfare, 2, 3, 6; and French Revolution, 22, 24; General Staff, Nation-in-Arms, and Kesselschlacht doctrine, 50, 52–54; and Napoleonic wars, 29, 38, 39–40; in Wars of German Unification, 94–101
Prussian War College, 45, 46
Purchase System, 2

Queen Elizabeth (HMS), 119
Quisling, Vidkun, 202

radar: World War II and electronic warfare, 189–90
radio: development of between world wars, 190–91
Raeder, Erich, 183, 201, 210
Raglan, Lord, 62, 64
railroads: and American Civil War, 70; and Prussian military organization, 53; technological revolution in land warfare, 48
Reagan, Ronald, 307, 309–10, 314
Red Cross, 67
Reign of the Hundred Days (1815), 41
Rennenkampf, Pavel von, 142, 144
Reserve Officer Training Corps (ROTC): World War I and establishment of, 161
Reynaud, Paul, 201, 207, 208
Rhee, Syngman, 268, 270, 273, 277
Ridgway, Matthew, 274, 275
Roberts, Frederick, 122, 124
Robespierre, Maximilien de, 24
Rochambeau, Comte de, 18
Rommel, Erwin, 211, 213, 218, 220–21, 222, 233, 234
Roon, Albrecht von, 52–53
Roosevelt, Franklin D., 186, 227, 230, 233, 239, 240, 240, 242, 245, 250, 254, 256, 263
Roosevelt, Theodore, 117, 126, 128
Root, Elihu, 112
Rosecrans, William S., 90, 91
Royal Air Force (RAF): in World War I, 152, 154–55; in World War II, 209, 224–26

Rozhdestvenski, Zinovi, 131–32
Rumania: overthrow of Communist regime in, 315; in World War I, 151; in World War II, 215, 239
Rundstedt, Gerd von, 199, 204, 206, 215–16, 233, 234, 235, 239
Russell, William Howard, 65
Russia: air forces between 1919 and 1939, 187, 188; alliance systems and contingency war plans prior to 1914, 105–12; armies between 1919 and 1939, 178; army prior to 1914, 103; Civil War of 1918–19, 191–92; Crimean War, 62–65; dissolution of Soviet Union, 315–16; dynastic warfare, 2; German invasion of Poland, 199, 200; invasion of Baltic states and Finland, 200; Japanese invasion of China, 193; Korean War, 276–77; Napoleonic wars, 25, 27, 29, 34, 38–40; navy between 1919 and 1939, 183; Nazi-Soviet Pact, 176; nonaggression pact with Japan in 1941, 242; Russo-Japanese War, 128, 129–32; Russo-Turkish War, 120–21; World War I, 134–35, 142–44, 162; World War II, 191, 213–18, 219–20, 231, 239, 240, 261, 262. *See also* Cold War
Russian Civil War (1918–19), 191–92
Russian Revolution (1917), 162
Russo-Japanese War (1904–5), 117, 128, 129–32
Russo-Turkish War (1877–78), 120–21

Sadat, Anwar, 304, 306
Saddam Hussein, 306, 310, 317, 318–19, 321, 324–25
Saint-Arnaud, Armand, 62
Sampson, William T., 126
Sampsonov, Alexander, 142, 144
Sanders, Liman von, 146
Santa Anna, Antonio Lopez, 59
Saratoga, Battle of (1777), 17
Saudi Arabia: and Cold War, 268; in Persian Gulf War, 318, 321, 322
Scharnhorst, Gerhard Johann David von, 38, 40
Scheer, Reinhardt von, 151–52
Scheidemann, Philip, 170
Schley, Winfield S., 127, 128
Schlieffen, Alfred von, 106, 109
Schwarzenberg, Prince Felix von, 40
Schwarzkopf, H. Norman, 318, 319, 321, 323
Scott, Winfield, 34, 61, 81
Sedan, Battle of (1870), 53–54
Seeckt, Hans von, 179
Selassie, Haile, 193
Selective Service Act (1917), 160
Selective Service Act (1970), 299

LARRY ADDINGTON is Professor of History at the Citadel and has taught military history for more than twenty-five years. His previous books include *The Blitzkrieg Era and the German General Staff* and *The Patterns of War through the Eighteenth Century.*